Child Survivors of the Holocaust in Israel

"Finding Their Voice"

T0327042

Child Survivors of the Holocaust in Israel

"Finding Their Voice"

Social Dynamics and Post-War Experiences

SHARON KANGISSER COHEN

sussex
ACADEMIC
PRESS

BRIGHTON • PORTLAND

2 4 6 8 10 9 7 5 3 1

First published 2005 in Great Britain by
SUSSEX ACADEMIC PRESS
Box 2950
Brighton BN2 5SP

and in the United States of America by
SUSSEX ACADEMIC PRESS
920 NE 58th Ave   Suite 300
Portland, Oregon 97213-3786

British Library Cataloguing in Publication Data
A CIP catalogue record for this book is available from the British Library.

Library of Congress Cataloging-in-Publication Data
Cohen, Sharon Kangisser.
   Child survivors of the Holocaust in Israel : social dynamics
   and post-war experiences : finding their voice / Sharon
   Kangisser Cohen.
   p. cm.
   Includes bibliographical references and index.
   ISBN 1-84519-088-2 (p/b : alk. paper)
   1. Jewish children in the Holocaust--Interviews.
   2. Holocaust, Jewish (1939–1945)—Psychological aspects.
   3. Holocaust survivors—Israel—Interviews. I. Title.
D804.48.C64 2005
940.53'18'092'25694—dc22

                                    2005009808

This book was published with the aid of the Alexander D. Dushkin Fund from the Avraham Harman Institute of Contemporary Jewry at The Hebrew University of Jerusalem.

Typeset & Designed by G&G Editorial, Brighton & Eastbourne
Printed by TJ International, Padstow, Cornwall
This book is printed on acid-free paper.

Contents

Contents

Contents

Foreword by Dalia Ofer

My personal acquaintance with survivors' life stories goes back to my early childhood, when a number of relatives immigrated to Israel and stayed with us for a while. These relatives were from Eastern Europe – Poland or Latvia. When they arrived, they shared their experiences with my parents, telling them what had happened to friends, relatives and acquaintances. Since they spoke in Yiddish, my understanding was somewhat limited. Also, being only six years old at the time, I connected their stories with the fairy tales I was familiar with. My relatives spoke of escapes, hiding, and living in forests, which reminded me of all the tales in which children got lost in the forest or met up with wild animals, but always came to a happy ending. I had never seen a forest nor experienced an Eastern European white winter. Thus, the horrors my relatives recounted to my parents during the hours they sat drinking tea in the kitchen went unnoticed by me. To my ears, their stories sounded like heroic legends of courage, adventure, and victory.

One day a family of cousins from the area near Krakow arrived: a mother, father and three children. I soon learned that two of the children were their own and that the third, a girl, was a niece whose parents were murdered. My cousins never told their stories, and I never thought to ask – we were too busy playing. It was only years later, after we were all adults and I had become a historian of the Holocaust, that their silence struck me, and we started to talk. I learned that, although the family had come together to Israel, they had not always been together in Europe. They had gone through different experiences and had different recollections of the war. And yet the children rarely told their own stories. Most often their voices were woven into the adult narrative.

Reading the manuscript of *Finding Their Voices: The Life Stories of Child Survivors of the Holocaust in Israel* was an enlightening experience. In this work, Sharon Kangisser Cohen reveals the hidden voices of child survivors of the Holocaust. Beyond that, however, she also examines just why it was that these children so often found themselves unable to share their experiences or their complex feelings of anxiety, anger, fear, shame, and remorse.

When and why did a survivor maintain silence or, alternatively, become ready to speak of past experiences? And how was the story then told in terms of content and manner? In a work that combines theoretical and empirical research, Kangisser Cohen establishes the connection between the personal and the communal – specifically, the tension between individual and collective memory in the emerging Israeli society. In this way she is able to identify the social and political factors that worked to suppress or to enable child survivors' stories to be told, listened to, and rendered meaningful.

Finding Their Voices is based in part on interviews, conducted by the author with men and women born in a variety of European countries who were children (up to age 16) during the war years. These interviews were conducted in Israel in the late 1990s, when most of the child survivors were already grandparents. Kangisser Cohen's expertise in two different disciplines, psychology and history, gives these interviews an added dimension. As a psychologist, she employs a personal approach, using narrative analysis alongside psychological theory in order to elicit a deep and meaningful account. As a historian, she is especially alert to the factual framework. She places her subjects' life stories in historical context, addressing, for instance, the relations between Jews and non-Jews in the different European societies and how these relations affected the children's chances of being rescued. Beyond this, Kangisser Cohen also addresses each individual's place in Israeli society – an important consideration, since some child survivors essentially grew up as Israelis, whereas others arrived only as adults.

The survivor subjects have been grouped into a number of meaningful categories, which will be a boon to other researchers in this field. Each narrative in this collection nonetheless retains its individuality. *Finding Their Voices* is compelling and convincing, and represents a breakthrough in the analysis of the life stories of Holocaust survivors.

Dalia Ofer
The Hebrew University of Jerusalem

Acknowledgments

This book began as a doctoral dissertation at The Hebrew University in Jerusalem. I would like to thank my doctoral supervisors Dalia Ofer and Ruthellen Josselson, who have not only been my mentors, but also became close friends. Without their support, faith in my abilities, and in me, I do not know if I could have completed this work nor enjoyed it as much as I have. Thank you both for your time, care and for opening my mind.

To all the teachers and staff at the Avraham Harman Institute of Contemporary Jewry, my home away from home, I owe much appreciation.

A special acknowledgment also goes to Zeev Mankowitz who has also guided me over the last few years. His insight has been invaluable. Appreciation also goes to the Melton Center for Jewish Education in the Diaspora and the Cherrick Center for the Study of Zionism, the Yishuv and the State of Israel at The Hebrew University, which also supported my doctoral studies.

My ideas were nourished by my mentors, my soul by my family and friends. Thank you to Udi, who has brought love and strength into my life, and who has traveled this journey with me every step of the way. To all my close friends and colleagues in Jerusalem, thank you for the friendship.

This work could not have been done without my interviewees. Thank you for your courage and for trusting me with your memories.

I would also like to acknowledge the invaluable assistance of Anita Grahame at Sussex Academic Press in preparing this book for publication. As a child survivor in Poland throughout the war, she has been deeply understanding of the narratives presented here.

Finally, I want to thank my mother, Myrna, whose love and generosity know no bounds.

1

Introduction – Inhabiting Three Separate Worlds

Child survivors of the Holocaust inhabit three separate worlds. The first is the world into which they were born. The second is the destruction of that world. The third is their struggle to to rebuild their lives after the war. Most child survivors were born into a safe and secure world, which ended abruptly with the arrival of the Nazis. From the Nazi perspective, Jewish children were useless as slave labor, yet dangerous as they represented Jewish continuity. They were therefore to be murdered automatically. Yet, miraculously, with the help of adults, some children managed to survive. They survived in hiding, in camps, ghettos, and forests. Many child survivors were orphaned as a result of the war. In other cases, either one or both parents, or other members of the child's immediate or extended family, survived and came to reclaim them from the people who had sheltered them during the hostilities. In some instances, the children had come to know and believe that these caretakers were in fact their parents, making the separation very difficult. Those who survived with their parents and went on to build new lives together, carried with them the baggage and terror of their immediate pasts.

At liberation, most child survivors were still too young to be independent. They were reliant on adults to take care of them. The 'horror' of the war ended and they re-entered the 'free world' once again. There, they were confronted with the difficult task of rebuilding normal lives after a narrow escape from certain death and devastating loss. This book tells the story of those child survivors and their attempts to navigate their lives after the war – they now had to learn to survive the survival.

Who Are Child Survivors?

A child survivor is defined as any Jewish child who survived in Nazi-occupied Europe by whatever means, whether in hiding, as a partisan, in the ghettos or in the camps. To be considered a child survivor, the individual must have been no older than sixteen at the end of the war. Their ages at the time from which their 'survival' was endangered depended largely upon the timing of the Nazi domination in the lands in which they lived. Given the different cognitive and emotional levels of children at different ages, when trying to understand the experiences of the child survivors, it is important to relate to them according to their different ages at the time of occupation.

In 1998, I participated as an observer in a course for Holocaust survivors at Yad Vashem, the Holocaust Martyrs' and Heroes' Remembrance Authority, in Israel. The intention of the course was to equip survivors with public-speaking skills, so that they would be able to speak confidently and effectively to large audiences about their experiences during the war. I was introduced to a special group of survivors who were called 'child survivors'. For many of these individuals, the course was the first time they had spoken publicly about their past. Thus, to do so now, and in front of an audience was no easy task. These 'child survivors' were more hesitant to share their stories than other survivors, yet once encouraged by the facilitators and other members of the group, they told very powerful and moving tales.

Throughout the four-day course I became acutely aware of the unique experience of child survivors of the Holocaust. They were a group of individuals who had recently begun to feel the need to speak about their pasts and identify themselves publicly as survivors of the Holocaust. Why they had been silent for more than fifty years and were only now beginning to speak was unclear to me. How had the relationship between the survivor and his/her past changed and developed over time, and in what ways? These are the questions that this book sets out to explore.

Child Survivors in Israel

At the end of the war, many child survivors of the Holocaust made their way to Palestine. Some arrived with their parents, others alone or as part of a group. There they were confronted with a society that was struggling with its own quest for survival and in coming to terms with the devastating events of the Holocaust. Due to its ideological foundations and imperatives, Israel provided a specific context for telling about and relating to the Holocaust. Yet, the meaning of the Holocaust in Israeli society has not been static. Collective memory of the Holocaust in Israel has changed and developed over time, usually in response to a particular event which forced Israel to examine anew its relationship to the Holocaust. Hanna Yablonka has identified three main phases which characterize this dynamic relationship between the State of Israel, the Holocaust, and the survivors: 1944–52, 1955–72, and 1973–97.[1] Thus, public discourse on the *Shoah* has been present throughout the history of the State, albeit in sometimes louder and softer tones. Consequently, child survivors who found their new homes in Israel grew up within this socio-cultural context, and absorbed the messages and meanings that were created and projected by Israeli society. Inevitably they experienced and inherited a legacy which influenced the way they perceived themselves and their pasts.

The First Phase, 1944–52

Public image of survivors   The ideology of the Zionists and many others in the years immediately preceding the World War II held that the ultimate commemoration of the *Shoah* must be a sovereign Jewish state in the land of Israel. After the catastrophe of the Holocaust, Zionism then seemed to be the only path open to the rehabilitation of Jewish existence, whether on a personal or on a collective level. Thus, memory of the Holocaust was central to Israeli collective memory; it became one of the sources of legitimacy for the state. "The instruments of the state were used to promote the myth of the Holocaust and the myth of Redemption as the two poles of Jewish experience in the twentieth century."[2] This concept of *Shoah u'Tekumah*[3] became a central part of the legacy of Israeli society, the core of a commemorative view that evolved and was shaped by the experience of a nation active in absorbing and rehabilitating survivors of the Holocaust and in the foundation of the state.

Zionism, even its pre-World War II stage, saw in the exilic situation not only an absence of sovereignty but equally, and perhaps cardinally, an expression of national-social illness. "The idea of *galutiyut* – the exilic condition – in the Zionist myth is not a political concept but a description of a mental state manifesting itself mainly in the lack of self respect *vis-à-vis* the gentile ... Immediately after the Holocaust, this reproachful attitude produced the accusatory and shameful view of the victims who had allowed the murderers to lead them to the killing fields and to the gas chambers 'like sheep to the slaughter'."[4] Zionism represented the antithesis of passivity, and thus in its relationship to the Holocaust, it

3

glorified resistance and heroism. This deep-seated negative attitude towards all the Jews of the Diaspora prejudiced the Israelis' attitude towards the survivors of the European Holocaust too. Hanna Yablonka notes that "The myth of heroism which they subsequently faced on their arrival to Israel put to shame their actual experiences and the way that they had behaved during the Holocaust years."[5] According to Anita Shapira, the disdainful attitude towards the survivors, especially the accusation of Jewish passivity during the Holocaust, were prevalent amongst the Israeli-born youth. This resulted in the "demand of 'assimilation' of the young child survivors among 'healthy' youth in Palestine."[6]

One of the main institutions which concerned itself with the "assimilation" of the young survivors into the 'healthy' youth in Palestine was Youth Aliya. Between the years 1945–52, 29,447 child survivors made *aliya* as part of the Youth Aliya movement.[7] Thus, a substantial number of child survivors who made their way to Israel after the war passed through this institution, and it was within this framework that many child survivors first encountered Israeli society and began their interaction with Israelis. For most of them, it was the beginning of a life-long relationship which influenced their identity as child survivors and as new Israelis.

Recha Freier of Berlin laid the foundation of Youth Aliya between the years 1932–3, in the hope of helping young Jews escape German persecution, and training them in the building of the *Yishuv*. By contacting *kibbutzim* and other institutions on behalf of the Jewish youth in Germany, Freier promoted the transfer of thousands of Jewish youth to Palestine. The first group of young boys arrived in Palestine in October 1932. Under the direction of Henrietta Szold, the organization grew into a unique, educational and rescue operation. Youth Aliya continued to operate during the war, yet its activities were severely restricted in Europe.

After the war, "scores of *shlichim* (emissaries) and instructors embarked on their errand of mercy to seek out Jewish children surviving in the concentration camps, in the forests, in the convents and on the roads of devastated Europe . . . To provide temporary asylum in liberated Poland, children's homes were established with the aid of the Youth Aliya representatives and instructors."[8] Moshe Kol,[9] a member of the first delegation dispatched by the Jewish Agency to establish contacts with the survivors, recalls seeing these children for the first time. "At the railway stations we saw the children who had returned from war-torn Soviet Union – filthy, diseased and hungry. Youth Aliya collected them, placed them in children's homes, washed them, fed them, and clothed them. For a short time they remained to convalesce under loving care, before they left in organized groups on their journey to permanent homes in Eretz Israel."[10] According to Shlomo Bar-Gil the initiative to direct child survivors to Palestine came from the survivors themselves. Immediately after the war survivors who were members of youth movements started collecting and organizing Jewish child survivors. According to Bar-Gil it was only in the second half of 1945 that emissaries were sent from Palestine to Europe.[11]

After a period of time, Youth Aliya extended its activities beyond rescue and developed into a major educational enterprise, "imbued with a unique spirit of pioneering and attachment to the soil."[12] For the children, their Zionist education began whilst still in Europe. In their temporary homes, which were the first stations *en route* to Israel, "they were taught the elements of Hebrew and were told about *Eretz Yisrael*, their future home and the part they must play in it."[13] Once in Israel, most of the children were absorbed into *kibbutzim*, while a few were settled in boarding schools and agricultural settlements.[14] The educational objective of Youth Aliya was to train the children for a life on the land, "for it is on the land that the young people are transformed socially and culturally, strike deep roots in the country and achieve a new spiritual balance."[15] Thus, the institution of Youth Aliya saw itself as providing a "remedy for the wounded souls." According to Haim Schatzker, children who accepted the norms and ideological imperatives of the movement 'adapted', while those who didn't were labelled as 'deviant', 'regressive', 'ungrateful', "the product of inner turmoil caused by the convulsions of the Holocaust."[16] Thus the image of child survivors as 'damaged' was associated with their unwillingness to adapt to the norms and ideological values of the institution, and their refusal to rebuild their lives in accordance with the dominant social values. Those dominant social values included looking towards the future and forgetting the past. The image of the adult survivor was hardly complimentary.

Anita Shapira cautions that not everyone shared this attitude towards European Jewry, yet it was quite widespread amongst Jews in Palestine, "as a kind of emotional and psychological basis (not always fully conscious)"[17] and influenced their attitude towards the survivors. This attempt on behalf of the veteran Israeli population to distance itself from the survivors manifested itself in jokes deriding the victims and in using mocking names which dubbed the survivors 'sabon' (soap), referring to the myth that the Nazis used the bodies of murdered Jews to make soap. Many survivors thus chose not to speak about their pasts because they were already condemned.[18] Nevertheless, as Yisrael Gutman explains, despite the disdainful attitude towards the survivors, it was clear that it was the *Yishuv's* duty, and part of their political plans, to absorb them.

"Yet doubts persisted about whether the *Yishuv* could build itself from this human material: they had not undergone the requisite training, were not basically a pioneer orientated group, were not even an ordinary group of emigrants lacking in motivation, they seemed a motley rabble, 'human dust' with no redeeming qualities."[19]

The attitudes of Israeli society towards the survivors must be understood in light of the historical and cultural processes taking place during this dramatic time. The War of Independence (1948) was a critical event, which played an important role in the construction of the image of the survivor and the attitudes of the fledgling state towards them. Hanna Yablonka explains, "that the largest wave of immigration from Europe arrived in Israel during the War of Independence, at a time of national crisis, which required the recruitment of all available and potential manpower. Here, the survivors were judged by their ability to fulfil these needs – both on a personal and a national level. Their image was based on the impressions sent home by the emissaries as well as other considerations . . . the survivors were seen as people who had lost faith in humanity, a fact which made them hard to approach and to persuade to join the struggle for rehabilitating their lives. They were labelled as people who had no confidence in society and in human ideals and were therefore a problem."[20] Zahava Solomon argues that within this context of a national struggle for survival, those who were engaged in the struggle needed inspiration and role models. "Holocaust survivors who had suffered terrible indignities would not do; nor would soldiers who broke down in battle."[21] Furthermore, for many of the 'listeners' the tales of the survivors were particularly difficult to hear and contain because, for many of the new Israelis, the stories told of the fate of their own families whom they had left behind when immigrating to Palestine. The survivors' audience in Israel was also mourning the loss of their families and their former homes.

Despite the tendency to view survivors as a 'shameful remnant', the *Yishuv* also made attempts to overlook the fact that the newcomers were survivors. They were simply to be welcomed as equal citizens sharing in the common struggle of the state for survival and building of the new state. Furthermore, "in matters pertaining to physical care and sustenance, 'veteran' Israelis received the refugees with open arms and remarkable generosity. Many veteran Israelis made considerable material sacrifices for the Holocaust survivors."[22] It must be noted that the survivors were also seen in mythological terms. On a visit to the DP camps in Germany in 1945, Ben-Gurion could not conceal his amazement at the Zionist passion that he found amongst the survivors, and what seemed to him to be a great spiritual strength.

In his semi-autobiographical work *Michvat HaOr* [Searing Light],

Aaron Appelfeld, a child survivor, explains that once in Israel, survivors were either perceived by the veteran population as heroes or as demons for having survived the Nazi hell. One of the questions that circulated was, 'What kind of people are these survivors, who had managed to survive such horrors?' "The consensus was that a selection had taken place within the Jewish nation, and the question remained, 'Which sector of the community had been annihilated: the superior one or the inferior one?'"[23] Dina Porat explains that there was a suspicion that those who had survived had done so because they had not wanted to sacrifice themselves fighting against the Nazis. In 1949, in a closed Mapai Central meeting, Ben-Gurion expressed the idea that, among the camp survivors were "people who would not have been alive were that not what they were – hard, mean, and selfish – and what they have been through erased every remaining good quality from them."[24] Thus, Holocaust survivors were blamed for surviving and not surviving. "They were accused of passivity, going like sheep to the slaughter, and staying alive by ignominiously complying with Nazi decrees."[25]

This simplified and often stigmatized image of the Holocaust survivor only exacerbated the already existing gap that separated those who had been 'there' and had personal experience of the trauma, and those who had no way of sensing, internalizing or relating to what had happened in the Holocaust. It was particularly difficult for those who had not been 'there' to understand the survivors' relationship to their pasts, to death, to material possessions, to the enormity of their personal losses, and to their reliving of memories of the past and their struggle to fit themselves into a new reality. Thus, during the first period of memory building many "survivors discovered that people did not always want to listen to them, or could not."[26] Yet it is important to remember that the perception of the survivors in Israeli society was a dynamic one, beginning with overwhelming pride and emotion, giving way to "emotional detachment, lack of recognition and at times blaming of the victim in early stages and social acceptance and empathy later on."[27]

Survivors' view of themselves It is clear that Holocaust survivors in the first years of the state not only suffered from a "lack of recognition" but also from "*mis*recognition." In his work on multiculturalism Charles Taylor writes that the individual's "identity is partly shaped by recognition or its absence, often by the *mis*recognition of others."[28] According to this theory, societal attitudes towards survivors of the Holocaust and their representation in public memory, invariably affected survivors' own view of themselves. Misrecognition may result in the individuals adopting a deprecating image of themselves and internalizing a picture of their own inferiority. It must be noted that in many cases these accusations, which were made externally, sometimes matched and reflected the survivor's internal struggles, which made these agonizing feelings of guilt and shame even more painful. In relation to "survivor guilt," or as Primo Levi describes it, "are you ashamed because you are alive in the place of another?" He explains, "it's a supposition, but it gnaws at us; it has nestled deeply like a wormwood; it is not seen from the outside but it gnaws and rasps."[29]

Yisrael Gutman notes that after the war "the community of survivors also did not see itself in a positive or optimistic light and was just as uncertain about whether it could integrate itself into a productive human society and overcome the wounds of the past."[30] In questioning their 'humanity', 'normality', or ability to rejoin the 'normal' world after experiencing such an agonizing past, survivors of the Holocaust became victims once again. Yet now they were victims of their own past. Many survivors felt that although they had survived the war physically, they remained dead emotionally; they saw themselves as walking corpses.

Thus, for many survivors of the Holocaust, the memory wounds of the past, which would remain with them for much of their lives and could erupt without any warning, were silenced. Survivors began to focus on rebuilding their lives and "Memories from 'there' seemed more of a hurdle than a bridge to 'Israeliness'."[31] Anita Shapira ascribes this silence to the cultural norms of the *Yishuv* at the time, as well as to the pervasive political reality: "The ethic of bereavement accepted at the time was one of controlled, inhibited behaviour." Mourning the soldiers who had fallen in the War of Independence was also restrained. Reconstruction was viewed as the "proper remedy for pain and loss."[32]

Having survived the Holocaust, many survivors believed they had two basic responsibilities, which were in turn reinforced by Israeli society. "The first was expressed explicitly as an obligatory act: to remember, to preserve and transmit the knowledge of this terrible experience from one generation to the next. The second was to overcome what had happened and to serve as living evidence that the Nazi attempt at annihilation had ultimately failed. These were usually carried out through actions: returning to 'normal life', marrying, having children, actively building a continuation of pre-war life."[33] Thus, some survivors welcomed the "conspiracy of silence."[34] They decided on their own to forget their Holocaust experiences for fear that the memories would corrode their present lives. They believed that silence would protect their children from pain and ensure that they were healthy, 'normal' children. For many survivors, it was difficult to carry out both of these obligations, as it seemed that the one contradicted the other.

For other survivors, remembering was essential for rebuilding: they needed to communicate their experiences in order to attest that the Holocaust had really happened. The first acts of collecting testimony and documents on the Jews during the Holocaust had been initiated and conducted by the Jews themselves under the Nazi occupation. "From 1944 on, the survivors in the liberated countries continued this tradition . . . They set up historical committees, which established networks of workers to cover the European countries and the large number of survivors."[35] Groups of survivors formed remembering communities amongst themselves, where the memory of their experiences was discussed and retold.

During this period in Israel, the voices and experiences of survivors were barely audible on a public level, yet they were not completely silent. Survivors who had not sealed off their pasts tended to share their experiences with fellow survivors. Painful discussions of the past, of their murdered loved ones and of their traumatic experiences, were usually held with other survivors or on memorial days and commemorative occasions. Associations of ghetto fighters, war veterans and partisans, and concentration camp survivors were established, bespeaking the need for formal recognition and identification. Thus, the imperative to tell persisted amongst the survivors, but was still primarily expressed within their own homes and their own survivor communities. They became involved in public commemoration where they felt obligated to build memorials to commemorate their lost loved ones and communities. "They initiated the erection of the first commemorative sites, shipped the ashes of Jews murdered in Poland and buried them in cemeteries in Israel, and published *Yizkor* books for different communities." [36] Survivors also wrote their memoirs.

Historians have found that the survivor communities who were the most vocal in the years following the World War II were those who had been involved in resistance movements during the war. In public commemoration, the resistors were usually called upon to speak, whilst the other survivors participated as part of the audience. Thus, the daily dilemmas of everyday life under Nazi occupation was hardly heard. When war experiences were discussed, the protagonists seemed to fall into two major categories. There were the fragile, helpless, martyred *victims*, present more often in the homes of camp survivors, and the superhumanly strong, capable, heroic *fighters*, generally found in homes of former partisans and resistance fighters. What is crucial here is that this dynamic reveals that one of the reasons for the stigmatization of the survivors in Israeli society – the distinction between the 'fighters' and those who 'went like sheep to the slaughter' – was related to the survivors themselves. Hanna Yablonka explains that the first, "in fact virtually the only, representatives of the Holocaust survivors' community (until the large wave during the War of Independence), to arrive in Israel were those Jews who had taken part in the Ghetto uprisings, and not people who had survived the concentration camps. It was easy for them to convince the local population that theirs had been the right way, since, of course, resistance and uprising, not surrender, were in perfect accordance with the *Yishuv*'s ethics and values at the time. It was a simple matter, then, to push the Holocaust as a whole the way the vast majority had experienced it – out of sight – and to place disproportionate emphasis on the significance of armed resistance, as compared with the enormity of the Holocaust itself."[37]

Yehiam Weitz writes that "the 'filter of memory' in the 1950s was perfectly compatible with the inner world, value system and self-image of Israeli society at the time. Above all, though, it reflected a basic sense of insecurity that made it impossible for contemporary Israeli society to come to grips with horror, fear and weakness."[38] Interestingly, the "filter of memory" also reflected the inner world of many survivors who questioned the nature of their own survival and behavior during the war. Perhaps most significantly, the very existence of a Jewish State and the rebuilding of a new life in the land of Israel were interpreted as an answer to the last wish of the murdered Jews to be remembered and avenged. In spite of the mass murder of one-third of the Jewish people, the State of Israel was a living proof of the failure of Nazism. Therefore, Israel had to prove its existence and display strength and force; it needed to show that the weakness and helplessness that characterized Jewish life during the period of the Holocaust had disappeared.[39]

The Second Phase, 1955–72

Public memory The second period of memory building identified by Hanna Yablonka was perhaps the most formative in the way that Israel related to and perceived the Holocaust. The Reparations Agreement in 1951, the trial of Rudolph Kastner in Jerusalem in 1954, and the Eichmann Trial in 1961 necessitated a public and political confrontation with the Holocaust.

The Eichmann Trial, held in Jerusalem in 1961, was a major turning point. In the period between Eichmann's arrival in Israel and his execution, Israeli society began to look at the past with more "humility"[40] and sensitivity than they had before. At the trial, forty-six witnesses took the stand. They were carefully selected and were mostly Israelis from all walks of life, representing a broad sweep of the Jewish communities that had suffered under Nazi occupation. Their testimonies reflected their deep pain and loss, and told the stories of average people who had endured all aspects of the Holocaust experience. The testimonies of the survivors showed the complexity of the Jewish condition under the Nazis and how "sensitive and open-minded" [41] one needed to be in order to grasp the tragic events. Gidon Hausner, the state prosecutor, was to challenge the collective memory of the Holocaust which had been formed in the early years of the state, one that valued heroism and resistance, and looked upon those victims and survivors who had not been involved in physical, armed resistance questioningly and critically. His aim was that the testimony of 'ordinary' survivors should have such a compelling impact on the audience and the public that they would be able to identify with and understand the impossible situation that the Jews faced under the Nazis. Because of the trial, attitudes towards survivors in Israel began to change. A new kind of wonder began to form around the survivors and veteran Israelis began to marvel at the very fact of their tenacity and survival.

However, coupled with this wonder of the survivors, the Eichmann trial also "planted the seeds for distancing oneself from the Holocaust."[42] The Holocaust was so inconceivable that one could give up any attempt to comprehend. The survivor and writer (*alias*) Ka-Tzetnik argued at the trial that only those who had been there could really understand the Holocaust and judge the behavior of the victims. The idea of resistance still dominated Israeli discourse, yet it was now defined on a much broader level, which was formulated after the survivors gave their testimony. Yet this process as Dalia Ofer points out, while legitimizing and empathizing with other forms of resistance and behavior, boosted the idea of armed resistance.

From the testimonies of the survivors at the Eichmann Trial, Israeli society became more appreciative of their traumatic past and their rehabilitation after the war. Survivors' rehabilitation represented the meaning of Jewish rebirth. Thus, the Holocaust became even more mystifying and the survivors even further removed from 'normal' society. Holocaust survivors became 'living memorials'. With their new status, survivors became increasingly involved in shaping Holocaust commemoration and education. They were asked to tell their stories to students and soldiers, and education became a central element of Holocaust memory and commemoration.

After Israel's victory in the 1967 war, the stabilization of the Israeli economy and Israel's increased recognition as a member of the community of nations, Israeli society became more confident and began to look at the Holocaust more openly and honestly. Literature and history of the period began to be written with greater intensity. The experience of the Jewish victim started to become a topic for historical inquiry. One example is Yehuda Bauer's work *Bricha* (Escape), in which the contribution of the survivors to the establishment of the State was recognized.

On a political level, after the Six-Day War, the universal and moral implications of the Holocaust were frequently raised in public discussions and in intellectual deliberations, when the repercussions of ruling almost two million Palestinians became apparent. The Six-Day War also led to the 'politicization' of the Holocaust, and both the right and left in the Israeli political spectrum used the Holocaust in their political rhetoric. The Holocaust came to be used in various contexts, demonstrating is centrality in Israeli collective memory.

During the first phase (1944–52) and the second phase (1955–72) Israeli society was preoccupied with the behavior of the victims during the *Shoah*, and seemed less interested in the behavior of the perpetrators or bystanders. Blaming the victims as in some way responsible for Holocaust events (for not getting out earlier, or escaping or resisting) was a defense mechanism against a fear that 'it could happen to us'.

During the 1970s, Israeli society began to change socially and politically, exemplified by the decline in the political power of the Labor movement in Israel. The elite was defeated and voices on the periphery began to be heard. With the defeat of the Labor party in 1977, Labor culture that had shaped the country's identity and formulated the legitimate images of 'Israeliness' was challenged. The new political reality ushered in a new cultural reality in which different kinds of Israeliness became legitimate. It also facilitated a new awareness of the Holocaust and the survivors. Furthermore, Shapira points out that the increasing influence of Western society on Israeli society during the 1960s and 1970s, in which symbols and messages of individualism replaced collective messages, was the time when "private memories of the Holocaust began seeping through."[43]

Private memory As a result of the Eichmann Trial in 1961, many survivors who before the trial had been hesitant to share their experiences with non-survivors now came to feel a responsibility to do so. The trial had legitimized the public telling of personal memory and signified the willingness of people to listen. This process has continued to develop up to the present time, where survivor testimony has become the most central element of Holocaust memory, commemoration, and education. Henry Greenspan, reflecting on this phenomenon in the United States in his recent work, writes: "Few could have imagined, during these earlier years, that those who survived the destruction would eventually be greeted as celebrants of life, redeemers of the human spirit, and voices of heroic affirmation."[44]

Despite the fact that survivors' voices began to be heard, the *Shoah* was still related to in 'major' terms: six million Jews, Auschwitz, Majdanek, Treblinka. As a result, the dominant voices were of those survivors who had been incarcerated in these 'major' camps. A possible explanation for this phenomenon is connected to the nature of historical writing taking place during this time. The focus of historical writing during this period was on the perpetrators, a seminal work being Raul Hilberg's *The Destruction of European Jewry*, first published in 1961, which focused on a description of the killing apparatus of the Third Reich in which the Death Camps occupied center stage. Thus, the experiences of the survivors of the death camps were most audible, which in turn affected public memory, as "whoever expresses his memories in the public space leaves a deeper impact than those who keep (or who are kept) silent."[45] The experience of other survivors, for example those who had survived the war in hiding, under false identities, or had fled to the USSR, were less audible. As a result public memory continued to contain certain types of experience and ignore the experience of others. By the 1970s those survivors who had been part of the armed resistance or had been imprisoned in and miraculously survived camps like Auschwitz, Majdanek or Treblinka, could be viewed as the 'elite'. They were the ones who had the power to impact the construction of public and collective memory. Those who remained silent, whose experiences did not seep into public consciousness, remained on the periphery of collective memory.

The Third Phase, 1973–97

The third period of Holocaust remembrance that Hanna Yablonka describes reflected the sense of vulnerability and self-doubt which pervaded Israel from the 1970s onwards. The Holocaust was related to in a more personal, sensitive way and usually on an individual level. The near disaster of the Yom Kippur War in 1973, the Lebanon War of 1982, and the *Intifada*, in 1987, led to a de-mythologization of the Israeli hero and of Israel's invincibility. Included in the process of demystification of the image of the *sabra* was the de-mystification of Zionism. The meaning of the Holocaust was broadened to include a broader Jewish perspective in which the Zionist message was presented as one of the options open to Jews. The universal implications of the specific Jewish experience – the Holocaust – began to be stressed. As Israeli society developed, as its needs, socio-political reality and self-perception changed, its understanding and perception of the Holocaust also changed. Anita Shapira points to the Six-Day War and the Yom Kippur War as turning points, when private memory became more legitimate. After these events a trend developed criticizing Israel's policies and methods of integration during the 1950s, and "its historical narrative in general."[46]

13

Criticism of Israeli society in its treatment of the survivors emerged as part of the "post-Zionist" historical debate, which used the Holocaust as one of its central themes. This issue was catapulted into social consciousness with the publication of Tom Segev's *The Seventh Million*.[47] Israel was accused of manipulating those who had survived the horrors, not responding to their misery, and of attempting to reinforce its own position in world opinion by exploiting their suffering. They claimed that it was the Zionists who wanted the survivors to come to Palestine and not the survivors themselves. The survivors had been forced; they had no choice as no other country was willing to take them in. Upon arrival in Palestine, the survivors were sent directly from the ships and into battle, where many lost their lives. The critics argue that, whilst the *Yishuv* failed to address the need of the survivors when they first arrived in Palestine, they created another problem by "dispossessing the local Arab population of its own homeland. So one injustice caused another."[48]

This debate pushed to the fore many issues concerning the immigration and absorption of immigrants to the fledgling state, including the immigration from North Africa. Survivors were able to openly explore their experiences in their post-war environment, and began to articulate the pain and misery which had been involved in their integration into Israeli society. Anita Shapira has argued that integration in Israel for the survivors for the most part meant giving up the culture, way of life, values and norms that they had known in their parents' home, for a new struggle to understand the language, and to come to [terms] with new social norms that they were expected to adopt. They also had to cope with insults (real or imagined) that they experienced and felt powerless to respond to. Dina Porat explains that it was only once they had fully integrated into Israeli society – socially and culturally – that they now demanded that their private memory be integrated into the collective memory. A crucial point is made by Anita Shapira who cautions to recognize the difference between the post-Zionist debate and the demands made by survivors: post-Zionism tries to undermine the very legitimacy of the state, whilst survivors made no attempt to challenge the "myth of the state; rather they demanded their right to be recognized as part of it."[49]

During this period, survivors had already begun to organize themselves in groups and associations, different from the survivor groups established immediately after the war. After the war, survivors organized themselves into groups according to their countries of origin. The main objective of these groups was to remember and record the histories of their own destroyed communities. However, the First International Gathering of Holocaust Survivors, which took place in

1981 in Jerusalem, was different. The focus of this gathering was to commemorate the *Shoah* and to publicly recognize and validate the experiences of Holocaust survivors during and after the war. Eva Fogelman and Helene Bass-Wichelhauss argue that except for the Eichmann Trial in 1961, in Israel, "the Holocaust survivors' ordeals were not validated for almost two generations of silence following the destruction of European Jewry. Twenty years after the Eichmann Trial, at the World Gathering of Holocaust Survivors in Jerusalem, in 1981 the survivors' dignity as human beings was restored."[50] The conference brought together survivors and their families from all over the world, facilitating the reunification of families and friends; it publicly validated the survivors' experience, and honored their survival. These gatherings and conferences seemed to strengthen the survivor's sense of belonging and identity. It indicated survivors' willingness to be seen and heard publicly. In recent years a large number of memoirs have been published and survivors have been involved in giving testimony. In institutions such as Yad Vashem, videotaping oral history has become a major venture. Video testimony has become a public record of personal experience and pain, which can be accessed long after the witness has passed away. Thus through oral and video testimony Holocaust memory has broadened. It comprises thousands of memories and experiences that differed according to gender, age, environmental, political, cultural and social background, and existential reality. Different experiences were legitimized and replaced the critical stance common towards the survivors in the early years. Today oral and video testimonies relate the entire experience of individuals, their pain in remembering, and their difficulty in retelling. Through oral and video testimony, the Holocaust has developed a human face. The survivor in his/her retelling, speaks in lower tones, touching stories of pain and exposing weakness, "the things that they had been ashamed of talking about before."[51] One of the commemorative traditions instituted in Israel on *Yom Hashoah ve Hagevurah* is the reading of the names of victims who died in the *Shoah*. Dalia Ofer remarks that this ceremony demonstrates a change in how Holocaust Remembrance Day is observed as public and private commemorations have now merged, signifying that the Holocaust is remembered publicly as an individual as well as a national trauma.

Over the past thirty years, psychological research has focused on the trans-generational affects of the *Shoah*. Research into the children of Holocaust survivors which attempts to evaluate the impact of the parent's experiences during the war on the personality and behavior of their children, with special emphasis on the nature of the relationship between the survivor and his/her offspring, has become part of the collective discourse around the *Shoah*. In the late 1970s in the United States, the second generation, gained national visibility as a distinct entity in the Jewish community. At the World gathering of Holocaust Survivors in Jerusalem, 1981, Menachem Rosensaft founded the International Network of Jewish Children of Holocaust Survivors, and chapters started worldwide.[52] Whilst mental health professionals in the United States began dealing with this issue in the 1970s, Eva Fogelman claims that only after the Lebanon War began in 1982, did children of survivors in Israel begin to acknowledge their special identity as descendants of the few Jews who survived the *Shoah*.[53]

Survivor Testimony Today

The social role of survivors has changed radically in the last decade. Survivor testimony is no longer solely used for historical and scientific inquiry, or education. Furthermore, during the last ten to fifteen years, the new use of survivors testimony has personally affected those child survivors who have begun to identify themselves openly as survivors. The 1990s cast survivors as educators and symbols of moral and ideological imperatives. Today, survivors accompany Israeli and Diaspora youth on educational trips to Eastern Europe and Poland, serving as living testimonials to the historical narrative being told at the sites of destruction. Thus, the narrative of the Holocaust continues to be constructed in individualistic terms.

One of the most impressive projects dedicated to collecting the stories of the survivors is Steven Spielberg's Survivors of the Shoah Visual History Foundation. Spielberg has embarked on a massive video testimony project which seeks out all living Holocaust survivors in an attempt to document on film their stories, voices and faces. This project has arguably placed survivor testimony and the voice of the individual survivor at the forefront of collective memory. Annette Wieviorka claims, "Today . . . the purpose of testimony is no longer to obtain knowledge . . . The mission that has devolved to testimony is no longer to bear witness to inadequately known events, but rather to keep them before our eyes. Testimony is to be a means of transmission to future generations."[54] Society's present upsurge of interest in looking again at the Holocaust after decades of avoidance, as well as the renewed manifestations of neo-Nazism that have emerged, encourage many survivors to reveal details of their past.

Some may argue that this 'new role' for the survivors continues to distance them from the rest of Israeli society. Seeing them as symbolic figures is another way of not engaging seriously with the real pain and loss that the survivors feel on an everyday basis. Yet others maintain that testimony has brought the Holocaust as an event closer to Israelis. Anita Shapira explains that an important step in the integration of the Holocaust into Israeli consciousness is the recognition that the Holocaust was not something that happened to other people, somewhere else, but is directly part of Israeli collective identity and the Israeli experience. However, there does exist considerable debate within Israeli society around this new level of integration and engagement. Voices can be heard today which criticize the centrality of the Holocaust in contemporary Jewish identity, education, and self-perception.

In addition, as can be gleaned from current events in Israel, the Holocaust continues to be remembered and used in 'giant terms', and for political gain. Shlomo Breznitz argues that "this centrality of the Holocaust SOM (State of Mind) makes it a tempting political instrument, and Holocaust-related imagery and language enter the political discourse. The protagonists on both side of the national debate often use the so-called lessons learned by the Holocaust to advance their arguments."[55] The rhetoric is used for either the legitimization or de-legitimization of the State of Israel, or policy relating to the Arab–Israeli conflict. Politicians have begun to evoke images of the Holocaust in order to demonize their political opponents.

In terms of 'heroism', Holocaust Memorial Day continues to be referred to as *Yom Hashoah ve Hagevurah* (Holocaust and Heroism Remembrance Day). Yet, the meaning of resistance has expanded over the years. 'Resistance' today refers to not only "those who rebelled in the camps and the ghettos, who fought in the woods, in the underground with the Allied forces, or those who braved their way to *Eretz Yisrael* and those who died sanctifying the name of God."[56] Resistance is now defined as "any group action consciously taken in opposition to known or surmised laws, actions or intentions directed against the Jews by the Nazis or their supporters."[57] Despite the extension of the definition, heroic behavior as a supreme value remains unchallenged. The idea of Jewish activity, resistance and response, is still a cardinal part of collective memory of the *Shoah*.

One of the most sensitive issues that has emerged over the past few years is the validity of survivor testimony as an accurate representation of the past and a reliable historical source. This issue came to the fore especially after the Demjanjuk trial (1987),[58] in which additional hearsay evidence submitted in Demjanjuk's appeal contradicted the eyewitness testimony of survivors. Contradictory evidence led to confusion over the identity of the defendant, engineering his subsequent acquittal. For many, the contradictory evidence challenged the credibility of eyewitness testimony, which may lead to the prevention of further war crimes trials. Efraim Zuroff, director of the Simon Wiesenthal Center in

Jerusalem, argues, "war crimes defense lawyers [are] likely to claim that their client, like Demjanjuk, might just be the 'wrong man', that aging survivors can no longer be relied upon, that the mind plays tricks and memories fade."[59] More recently the publication of the book *Fragments* by Benjamin Wilkomirski[60] has brought the issue to the fore. Considerable debate broke out over the book after an investigation was launched that questioned the authenticity of the account and the identity of the author. As a result, the question of fact and truth in survivor testimony has become a sensitive issue, especially as Holocaust Denial continues to grow and become more pervasive. One of the most recent incidents is the controversy over the accuracy of the testimony of a Holocaust survivor living in the United States, Deli Strummer.[61] Deli Strummer was removed from a list of recommended speakers for the Baltimore Jewish community, after Holocaust scholars exposed inaccuracies in her accounts. The experts who reviewed her story and relevant historical records say she probably was a captive of the Nazis, but some details in her account are impossible or highly unlikely. Deli Strummer acknowledged making 'innocent errors' and getting dates wrong, but remained adamant concerning the truthfulness of her accounts.[62]

With the recent growing suspicion of survivor testimony as an accurate historical source, survivors may find themselves stripped of their 'celebrity role'. This issue threatens to become one of the central concerns relating to survivors and their testimony in the coming years. It is a painful issue, especially for the survivors themselves, who now not only have to try to live with the memory of their experiences, but also have to prove the validity of those experiences. Suspicion of survivors testimony is more pervasive in the United States than in Israel, probably due to the prevalence of Holocaust Denial.

The periods outlined above facilitated a certain discourse about Holocaust survivors, one that seemed to be determined by the needs of society at that time and not necessarily by the needs of the survivors themselves. Private memories were blanketed under public memory. Henry Greenspan argues against this handling of Holocaust survivors. "Two distinct ways of imagining survivors have evolved since the late 1970s – a ceremonial rhetoric in which we honor survivors as celebrants and heroes and a psychiatric rhetoric in which the same survivors are depicted as ghosts and wrecks. Between the two sets of images, both the ongoing life and the ongoing death that survivors know *are* represented. But, the problem, as I have suggested, is that each of these ways of representing survivors has evolved into a separate and self-sufficient discourse . . . that they are increasingly detached – not only from each other – but from remembering the Holocaust itself . . . Indeed so much have we come to celebrate the *act* of testimony – congratulating survivors for giving it and, perhaps, ourselves for getting it – that the specific content of that testimony is left as mostly background. That is, survivors' speech tends to be esteemed in the abstract – as the *idea* of testimony rather than the reality. At times, it seems specifically to be acclaimed instead of being listened to."[63]

Dalia Ofer, in her work on collective memory and the Holocaust in Israel, comments that whilst the dialogue with the Holocaust is inter-woven with political reality, "in spite of its vulgarization," [64] one cannot only view it through the political prism. Survivors must have had some power in fashioning their memories of the past, their identities as survivors, and their decision to re-tell. Thus when tracing the experience of survivors in Israel, one needs to look at the survivors' role in the construction of collective memory, as well as their personal motivations and inhibitions in relating to and communicating their past.

The Role of the Life Cycle and Life Stages in Determining Survivors' Relationship to their Past

According to psychologists, survivors reacted to their past in different ways at different stages of their lives. The life cycle, with its cognitive and emotional phases of development, is instrumental in individuals' ability to deal with and articulate their past. According to develop-mental psychologists, life stages are crucial in the development of the individual and each life stage brings with it opportunities and obstacles in the individuals' ability to cope with their present reality and their past. The nature and timing of these forces vary from person to person, yet certain patterns can be ascertained.

The Post-War Period

The mental health world *has* conducted quite extensive research with child survivors over the last two decades. Dan Bar-On[65] argues that the primary wish of most survivors was to achieve normalization after the Holocaust as quickly as possible. Researchers have noted that in their immediate post-war worlds, child survivors coped psychologically by focusing on the future, repressing memories and feelings, and relating to remnant memories as belonging to an irrelevant past.[66] They gener-ally re-socialized reasonably quickly into peacetime mores. Child survivors focused on everyday issues, such as learning new languages, adjusting to new places, and academic performance. It is doubtful whether children forgot their war-time experiences as a consequence of the social silence around them; rather, an element of repression was

probably necessary as a way of avoiding being continually haunted by
by memories whilst growing up.

Building and Rebuilding Lives

This period of 'not remembering' continued to be the survivors' key
means of coping with their pain and trauma. Psychological defences –
negation, denial, repression, and half knowing – helped. Personal
potential was directed towards achievement in this phase. Child
survivors during this period were consumed with rebuilding their lives.
Paul Valent, psychiatrist, researcher and child survivor, observes, "The
most potent creative force in child survivors was creating life. Children
overcame genocide; they were a triumph over Hitler. They were an
unsullied, innocent future which blossomed out of a painful past."[67]
Most established themselves financially, married, and became devoted
parents. Despite the silence, child survivors continued to carry their
painful memories with them. For child survivors who have survived
with their parents, the experiences of the war were seldom spoken about
between parents and children. Even among siblings and with fellow
child survivors, who were unwittingly drawn to each other, relationships were built without any reference to the past. Thus the 'conspiracy
of silence' continued between the generations. Bergmann and Jucovy
found that child survivors began to share in many ways the same reality
as those of second generation descendants.[68]

Aging Child Survivors

Today, years after the Holocaust, many survivors who had been children, adolescents or young adults during the war are expressing both
a willingness and a need to talk about their past – to return to and even
to attempt a belated working through of their Holocaust experiences.
Past means of coping such as looking forward and silencing memories
and feelings "no longer have survival value, and negate developmental drives to make sense and generate wisdom."[69] Dr Henry Krystal, a
psychiatrist who has contributed to the understanding of the long-
term effects of the Nazi Holocaust on its survivors, affirmed that the
major task for an aging person is integration. Krystal's work, based on
Erik Erikson's theory of the "critical conflict of ego integrity versus
despair in aging,"[70] argues that "old age, with its losses, imposes the
inescapable necessity to face one's past."[71] Krystal sees this as a consequence of the shift "from doing to thinking, from planning to
reminiscing, from pre-occupation with everyday events and long-
range planning to reviewing and rethinking one's life."[72] In facing the

past, "one either accepts one's self and one's past or continues to reject it angrily."[73]

Integration implies looking back and finding a continuum between one's war experiences and one's present life, the 'survivor experience'. For child survivors, this is a complicated process as one of the characteristics of child survivors is their lack of memory: repressed memory or lost memory. Thus, integration becomes even more difficult for child survivors. Integration is prefaced by a search for memory. The search for memory constitutes one of the most central challenges of child survivors today. According to Robert Krell, retrieval of one's memories entails a reversal of the psyche and the negation of past messages that child survivors 'could not' or 'should not' remember. Therefore, claiming one's memories requires assertiveness over such admonitions. But remembering also entails an "unleashing of the demons of remembrance to haunt the already haunted."[74]

Shamai Davidson provides a theory that encompasses both theoretical models: the socio-historical and the psychological interpretations. He writes, "Of central importance are the personality resources of the survivor and a nurturing and supportive dyadic relationship. Each phase of the life cycle presented new opportunities for working through the war experiences and losses and possibilities for releasing delayed mourning."[75] Breaking the silence is therefore dependent upon the individual's need to tell, together with the audience's ability and willingness to listen. According to this theory, the openness of contemporary Israeli society and the life-stage at which child survivors find themselves today, provide a unique opportunity for child survivors to articulate their experiences.

The above notwithstanding, the return of memory may also occur completely independently of the need or will of the survivor and of the social context in which they may find themselves. Rather, extrinsic factors, for example the death of a spouse, political unrest, etc.; may force the traumatic memory to the fore of experience. "Under specific conditions, and occasionally long after the initial set of 'traumatic events', these extrinsic contexts can produce overwhelming recall. At this point the memory crowds out everything else; it is potentially paralytic."[76]

The Research Method

This work is not a historical examination of the period of the Holocaust itself but rather an exploration of the survivor's memory and interpretation of it. In it, I am not seeking to validate the "truth" in the survivor's life story, but rather as Jerome Bruner points out, to explore the "meaning of experience."[77] I use the narrative method in order to explore the experience of being a child survivor subsequently living in Israel. Thus, my research material consists of a collection of life stories given to me in interviews with survivors, in which I encouraged them to speak about their pre-war, war and post-war experiences, in order to reveal the 'narratives' that they have built around the major events in their lives. It must be noted, however, that a life story that is provided in an interview is but one instance of *the* life story; it is a hypothetical construct that develops and changes through time and is affected by the context in which it is told. The reconstruction of my research can therefore also be seen as a story of a story. As each participant had their own model for retelling their own story, "so too have I drawn from various models in translating our conversations into a text and becoming myself, a certain kind of storyteller."[78]

Exploring the Meaning of the Experience

Personal narratives are an important source of data for the historian, as they tell of the individual's experience *in* history. This is often referred to as 'social history'. Social history provides us with a rich and unique tool for understanding the workings and effect of a specific socio-historical context on the lives of individuals. Within their personal narratives, child survivors re-member their experiences, not only as new immigrants and survivors in the fledgling state of Israel, but also as citizens throughout its entire history. These child survivors have in fact 'grown up' with the State of Israel, and their maturation takes place parallel to the development of Israeli society. Their narratives provide social historians with insight into the experiences of young survivors, in adapting and acclimatizing to their new socio-cultural environment, and as adults who see themselves as equal members of society. Their narratives also inform researchers of their perceptions of Israeli society, their experience of it as an absorbing community, and of the treatment they received as new *olim* generally, and as Holocaust survivors specifically. Nevertheless, these narratives alone do not provide a complete picture of Israeli society and its attitudes towards, and treatment of, Holocaust survivors. Without a better sense of how the absorbing community – those *sabras* who received the survivors – remember and make meaning of the period, it will not be possible to construct a more exhaustive social history of the period.

Personal narratives are also important to social scientists and medical health professionals in their attempt to understand how individuals cope with massive trauma, and to learn about the kinds of tools and coping skills they used in readapting their lives after the war, in surviving the survival. As Judith Herman points out, "Insight into the recovery process may also be gained by drawing upon the wisdom of the majority of trauma survivors worldwide, who never get formal treatment of any kind. To the extent that they recover, most survivors must invent their own methods, drawing on their individual strengths and the supportive relationships naturally available to them in their own communities. Systematic studies of resilience in untreated survivors hold great promise for developing more effective and widely adaptable methods for therapeutic intervention."[79]

Therefore, for both historians and mental health professionals, these individual life stories provide us with windows into larger historical and psychological processes. Furthermore, personal narratives also reflect existential issues over which individuals contemplate. As Ruthellen Josselson writes, "People's personal narratives are efforts to grapple with the confusion and complexity of the human condition."[80] Yet, she cautions against making generalizations, for whereas the "Narrative approaches allow us to witness the individual in her or his complexity and recognize that although some phenomena will be common to all, some will remain unique."[81]

This study reflects diversity and difference: it comprises twenty-one voices, spanning eight countries of origin, multiple experiences during the war and diverse family backgrounds. Additional layers of complexity include: different age groups, socio-economic levels (before and after the war), and levels of education. Each narrative represents the thread of an individual's unique life. Yet together they weave a tapestry of the experiences of child survivors: of what life was like in a number of different socio-historical contexts as victims, survivors, and Israeli citizens. Alongside the diversity there are general patterns that emerge from the narratives, as each of life story tells of a life-long struggle to deal with their past. Throughout their lives, these child survivors have had to negotiate their identities as survivors of the Holocaust, their relationship to their pasts, and their decision to talk about their personal histories or to remain silent. However, if having decided to speak, each individual alone has then to choose what to say, and how to say it.

Personal Narrative: The Individual's Experience in History

Using the dynamics of silence and retelling as markers of difference among the survivors, this work describes child survivors as falling into **four groups**. The **first group** comprises most of the interviewees, child survivors who chose to remain silent after the war. However, in the last few years, most of them have 'found their voices' and have started to tell their stories publicly. This group is mainly composed of what I call '*hidden child survivors*'. The **second group** consists of individuals I have termed 'resistant speakers'. These individuals also chose not to speak about their pasts after the war, and continue to feel a strong resistance to retelling and identifying publicly as survivors. The **third group** comprises those individuals who, since liberation, have 'always spoken' publicly about their past. This group consists of two individuals, both survivors of Auschwitz–Birkenau. The **fourth group** includes those who 'retreated away from speech'. This group is represented by child survivors who were initially silent about their pasts, they found their voices at a later stage in their lives and began to retell their stories publicly, yet now feel the need to retreat away from speaking.

The chapters that follow demonstrate that when forging their relationship to their past and identity, child survivors have not only responded to their own internal, individual needs and inhibitions, but more significantly to external pressures. These include the nature of their experiences during the war, and most notably the social-cultural context in which they lived after the war (i.e. Israeli society and the commanding collective memory constructed around the events of the *Shoah*), a context that powerfully defined and evaluated their personal trauma. This work demonstrates that collective memory has been instrumental in determining which stories are to *be* told, and what *is* told during the telling. Both determinants affected the individuals' relationship to their past and their identity as survivors, as well shaping the writing of history.

Thus, the narratives of child survivors can be understood as more than simply memories, 'facts', or the life story of an individual. In essence this work explores how child survivors have been able to manage and make sense of the three worlds they inhabit: the world of their birth, the world of their personal and collective destruction, and the world of their revival. Their narratives are also mirrors of larger social-cultural concerns.

2

The Protagonists

The total experience of the *Shoah* remains essentially an untold tale as "only the dead know the full bitterness of their victimhood, and they are silent – except for a few voices, like that of Anne Frank, miraculously preserved in all its eagerness and bright promise; a single voice which forces recognition of the incalculable cost to us all of those years of systematic Nazi killings."[1] Of those few who survived, fewer still have chosen to record what they endured. Thus, what follows is limited in that it speaks only of the small minority of children who miraculously survived the Nazis. Furthermore, not only did the Nazis murder most of the Jewish children, of those who survived, only a handful are willing and able to tell their stories. Those child survivors who are unable or unwilling to share their past, are therefore not presented here. Humbly I need to accept the limitations of my research, which points to the quintessential nature of the tragedy.

Kalman, a child survivor, heightened my awareness to this issue, and in his interview gave me invaluable insight. He taught me that my research was exploring and describing the experiences of a minority, and that I would never be able to make broad inferences as I was actually studying a historical error – those few Jewish children who had lived owing to 'mistakes' or oversights of the Nazis. Kalman is one of those 'mistakes': a child survivor, who had been incarcerated in Auschwitz–Birkenau as a Mengele twin. He was fourteen years old when he was deported from his home-town in Hungary. In this part of our interview, he is trying to explain the role that silence has played in the telling of the *Shoah*.

"I am comparatively normal and, most important, I am ready to talk. The average 'Ka-tzetnik'[2] doesn't want to talk . . . cannot, will not or a combination of both . . . I will explain my sister's problem in this area. Devorah refuses to talk to this day. She didn't talk to her husband, she didn't talk to her children, her grandchildren . . . she doesn't talk to me! I mention this because she constitutes the opposite of her twin brother. 'Are you ready to talk?' I can express myself, because amongst our brethren there are some who can talk and will talk but they cannot express themselves in any language . . . Communicative skills are not given to everyone . . . both verbal and written . . . so those who left the camps are a minority in any case and of the minority there is another minority who is ready to talk! And of that minority of the minority, only a small minority can talk, let alone write."

Kalman made me aware of my privileged position: I was a researcher who had found child survivors and were willing to talk about their experiences. In fact, I had found a sufficient number of them, enough to make a detailed, qualitative study of their life stories.

Locating the Participants

When I began my search for participants, I chose them randomly. My initial source was Yad Vashem where, in 1998, as mentioned previously, I had participated as an observer in a course for Holocaust survivors. For many of these child survivors, the course was the first time they had spoken publicly about their past, let alone in front of an audience. Many struggled to find the words to express their feelings and some only had fragments of memory. One woman admitted that she was 'embarrassed by her lack of memory'. There were other child survivors who attended the course in order to assert their identity as survivors, and were committed to claiming their right to tell their stories publicly. The survivors were still seen as 'children' in the group, which made me acutely aware of the dynamics that operate amongst groups of survivors. Individuals are defined and related to according to where they were during the war and their age at the time of their persecution. The course lasted four days, during which I was able to meet all the participants, yet I only managed to form a relationship with a few individuals. By the end of the course, most survivors expressed an interest and willingness to help me with my research. However, it took some time and a large amount of reading for me to formulate ideas for a book and only once this was done did I contact the child survivors whom I had met at the course to ask them if they were willing to be interviewed. All of them agreed and were eager to help me. They were motivated to tell their life stories for their own personal gain, and perhaps more significantly, out of social necessity, to help *me* with *my* research. This encounter strengthened my assumption that telling is dependent upon the construction of an empathic relationship between interviewer and interviewee.

Yad Vashem was also able to provide me with a list of child survivors who had participated in previous courses, giving me a rich source of possible interviewees. However, after interviewing a number of them, I realized that most of those who had participated in the course had already reached that point where they were willing and able to speak about their experiences. Realizing the limitations that this conferred in terms of my own research, I began to look for child survivors who had not spoken publicly about their experiences. Fortunately, I was able to find a few such individuals who had related their experiences to a group of significant others, but had refrained from speaking openly and publicly about their pasts. They had chosen to keep their past closed to the 'public', which included giving testimony to Yad Vashem and other research projects. I refer to this group of survivors as the 'resistant speakers'. I usually found the resistant speakers through referrals made by other survivors I had previously interviewed. Yehiel, for example, referred me to his younger sister Ruth, and Ruth, in turn, gave me the name of her close friend Kalman. Shalom, who works extensively with a survivor organization, gave me the names of a few of its members. He cautioned me that they might not agree to talk, but suggested that I try anyway as he saw my research as a good opportunity for people who rarely spoke about their past to begin speaking. Not all of the people that Shalom suggested agreed to be interviewed. Some of them who did found it difficult to communicate their pasts. Once relatives, friends, and fellow students became aware that I was interviewing child survivors, many gave me the names of their family members and friends so that I was never short of potential interviewees. One aunt urged me to interview her husband, Shlomo. She explained that he never speaks about the *Shoah*, and she felt it was important that his story be recorded. Interviewing Shlomo was a difficult experience, not only because of the nature of his experiences, but also because of our relationship. Today, whenever I meet Shlomo at a family events, he takes me into a corner and tells me another part of his story, or about another incident that he had witnessed in Auschwitz–Birkenau. Shlomo relates to me as 'the listener' in the family, yet, interestingly, he does not recall ever being interviewed by me.

A friend of mine gave me the names of a few members of her *kibbutz* who she 'was pretty sure' were child survivors. One of them refused to be interviewed. Two others agreed. Leah, a woman with whom I studied at university, gave me Yaacov's name. She had personally interviewed him a few years before, and this was the only interview Yaacov had ever given. She urged me to contact him, explaining that besides herself no one really knew his fascinating story. When I contacted Yaacov, he agreed to be interviewed because, he explained, 'he loved and trusted Leah'. I also managed to meet child survivors with the help of my supervisor, Professor Dalia Ofer, who met child survivors through her own research and work. These child survivors were usually more vocal about their pasts, as they usually identified openly as survivors, had participated in conferences and previous research, and were interested in the academic discourse around the subject.

Thus, my data collection took on a 'snowball effect', which provided me with a richness and diversity of experience. Fortunately, finding participants was not a difficult task; rather it proved to be an enlightening one. The 'data collection' process taught me how present the *Shoah* in Israeli society and how integrated child survivors are within Israeli society. It also revealed that the child survivors who were reaching the later part of their adult lives, were now more willing to share their pasts. Yet, the question that remained unanswered, and which became more and more compelling was: 'why talk now?'

Interviewing these individuals was a deeply rewarding and moving experience. I was surprised at the openness of my interviewees in revealing themselves, and in their search for understanding and meaning. Moreover, many expressed their appreciation that 'such a nice young girl' was interested in them, in their life stories, and in the Holocaust in general. In fact, this was probably one of the most interesting dynamics in the interviewing process; the way they responded to me as an interviewer. For some of the interviewees, I represented a granddaughter figure. As I looked particularly young to them, they saw me as representative of 'the younger generation', to whom they were transmitting their 'historical legacy'. Henry Greenspan explains, "While some writers suggest that survivors recount in order to 'integrate' their memories, or to create form and meaning for their own sakes, the essential truth is that survivors recount in order to be heard. Indeed, without at least a remnant of that hope, survivors do not recount at all."[3]

Some interviewees expressed their concern that they were burdening me with their stories of pain and suffering, and they felt the need to protect me from their painful memories. One of the child survivors whom I interviewed was concerned about the effect that studying the *Shoah* would have on me. She urged me not to lose an optimistic outlook on life and to prevent the *Shoah* from clouding my vision of the world. I felt that I was receiving 'grandmotherly' advice. Thus, I felt that my age was beneficial to the interviewing process, as most survivors wanted to share their experiences and 'teach me' about the past. However, sometimes my age was not always to my advantage. As mentioned before, some of the survivors wanted to protect me from the Holocaust whilst others felt that I couldn't possibly understand their experiences because I was too young. Each interview became a process of knowing and being known. As I listened attentively to their stories, many came to feel increasingly comfortable with me, and certain of my willingness and ability to hear their stories. The question of whether I would be able to understand their stories is another issue.

Introducing the Characters

Countries of Origin

Because Nazi policy against the Jews differed according to the countries of occupation, the survivor's country of origin is crucial to understanding the nature of their experiences during the war. Holocaust historian Michael Marrus writes that, "However devastating, the Holocaust in Eastern and Central Europe was of an entirely different character from that in the East. Although the impact was catastrophic, the Nazis operated outside Russia and Poland with a certain restraint. Much of the destruction process was hidden from the surrounding populations and even from the Jews themselves . . . " In Eastern Europe, the level of terror and cruelty was higher than in Western Europe. Marrus argues that "the racial composition of the eastern territories justified to the Nazis the most brutal and cruel policies. In a subhuman environment, Nazis told themselves that scruples were both unnecessary and dangerous."[4]

Marrus explains that an important factor in determining Nazi policy was the number of Jews in the areas. "In Poland and in the Soviet Union the great density of the Jewish population precluded the removal of those destined to be killed. There were simply too many Jews to be sent on long journeys to their massacre . . . "[5] Thus, Jews in the USSR from 1941 onwards were mainly killed on the spot, in their own villages or surrounding areas, by special mobile killing units – *Einsatzgruppen*. In Poland, during the first years of Nazi occupation in 1939, Jews were ghettoized in the most appalling conditions for a number of years, before being deported to concentration and death camps. Thus, children born in Poland and in some areas of the Baltic States endured a period of ghettoization before deportation to concentration and death camps. The Jews also perceived the ghetto as a method of 'natural killing'.

There was no centralized policy of ghettoization in Western Europe. Therefore, Western European Jews were not usually ghettoized before being deported to camps in the east. However, some may have been sent to ghettos in Poland en-route to their deaths in the east. Jews living in occupied Western European countries – France, Belgium, Holland, Denmark, Norway and Italy – were subject to anti-Jewish legislation and property confiscation between the years 1940–2. Jews in Austria were also subject to these policies since 1938, and Jews in Germany since 1933. In 1942, deportation of Western European Jewry to the East began. Jews in the West were relatively fewer in number and could therefore be transported directly from their homes to the killing centers in the East.

In January 1942 forced labor camps were set up in Holland, and the Jews were concentrated into the downtown area of Amsterdam in an 'open' ghetto. Deportations from Holland began in July 1942, and ended in effect in September 1943. Of the 103,000 Jews deported from Holland, 5,540 returned. Most were deported to Auschwitz or Sobibor. On August 4, 1942, the first transport of Belgian Jews began. The destination was unknown; however, many Jews refused to obey the 'invitation' and went into hiding because of warnings issued by the Jewish underground. Nevertheless, out of the 25,437 Belgian Jews were who deported, 1,276 returned after the war. Deportation of French Jews, from the northern zone, began in March 1942 and continued until July 1944. In August 1942, Jews from the southern zone of Vichy were deported. The Nazis murdered a total of 77,320 French Jews,[6] most of whom were sent from transit camps in France, to Auschwitz.

Another factor that determined Nazi policy in specific regions was the nature of the occupation. The German forces were never as strong in the West as they were in the East. Consequently, in the West they needed the more or less willing collaboration of local authorities. In some countries, the local authorities were more resistant to anti-Jewish measures, especially deportations, which facilitated the rescue and hiding of Jews. Two countries that stand out in this regard are Denmark and Italy. In both countries, Jews were rescued by the local population. In Belgium, more than half the Jewish population survived the war, largely with the help of the gentile population and the activities of various Jewish underground groups. The number of Jewish victims in France would have been much greater if Catholics and Protestants had not aided the Jews. In both zones in France, after July 1942, the security of children whose parents had been deported became a concern. Eventually the security of all Jewish children became a major problem. Jewish organizations, with the help of non-Jews, managed to smuggle Jewish children into hiding, saving many lives as a consequence. The number of Jewish children who managed to escape extermination in France is estimated to be 72,400. And among them 62,000 remained with their parents or were placed in non-Jewish families or institutions. The number of children saved by Jewish organizations is estimated at between 8,000 and 10,000. Jewish organizations also assisted children who remained with their parents, by giving them false identity papers and various other sorts of assistance.[7] In Holland, with the help of their neighbors, 24,000 Jews went into hiding, of whom about two-thirds survived. Those who were hidden unsuccessfully were usually found out by the Dutch Nazis, who formed almost 10 percent of the population; despite all rescue efforts, approximately 100,000 out of the 140,000[8] Jews living in the Netherlands before the war were killed.

The experience of Jews in Germany's satellite states – Slovakia, Croatia, Hungry, and Bulgaria – was closer to the experience of Western European Jewry. German demands on the satellite countries for participation in the Final Solution varied. Both Slovakia and Croatia owed their existence to Nazi Germany, and the Germans set up very aggressive, extreme right-wing leaders in these countries. Hungary and Romania had far more independence, and both gained from their alliances with Hitler. At some point between 1939 and 1941, all five satellite states moved against the Jews on their own accord, issuing anti-Jewish legislation and confiscating Jewish property. At various times, the Germans pressured all of the satellites for Jewish deportees, usually as a request for forced labor. Persecution of the Jews in Bulgaria, which began in 1941, was far milder than elsewhere and included many exemptions. Furthermore Bulgaria resisted deporting Jews from what was considered 'Old' Bulgaria. However it did agree to deport Jews from 'New' Bulgaria, that is Yugoslav and Greek territories occupied by Bulgaria. In March 1943, 11,343 Jews were deported to their deaths from Thrace and Macedonia.[9] Historians argue that Slovakia eagerly deported its 98,000 Jews. Romania distinguished between the acculturated Jews of Old Romania in the heart of the country, and the unassimilated, non-Romanian Jews of Bukovina and Besserabia, areas that Romania had been forced to surrender to the Russians in 1940. In 1941 as the Germans invaded Russia with the aid of the Romanian army, Besserabia and Bukovia were re-conquered. In these re-conquered provinces Romanian troops and *Einsatzgruppen D* murdered the Jews. Between July and August 1941, approximately 100,000 Jews were killed in mass shootings, aimless and endless marches of men, women and children, and by drowning in the Dniester river.[10] Romania then moved relentlessly against these provinces and some 185,000 Jews were deported from the re-conquered provinces and from the region of Dorohoi in Old Romania, and sent to Transnistria. In Transnistria some people were packed into ghettos, whilst most were 'housed' in pigsties and village stables or slave labor camps on the shores of the Bug river. The mortality rate in these areas was enormous. In 1942 the Nazis demanded the deportation of all Romanian Jews to Poland, yet Antonescu[11] refused to comply with these demands. In the end, most of the Romanian Jews were not deported. "Of the 380,000 Romanian Jews who died, 60,000 were killed in Besserabia, Bukovia and Transnistria and 120,000 in northern Transylvania, which had come under Hungarian rule in 1940. Most of the Jews of old Romania survived."[12] The story of Hungary is particularly dramatic. In 1941, there were 825,000 Jews in Hungry, some of whom were refugees who had found a safe haven there. Between 1941 and 1944, Hungarian Jews lived a tenuous existence, persecuted at home but protected from repeated German requests for deportation. However, on March 19, 1944, the Germans invaded Hungary, fearing that the Hungarians might make a separate peace with the allies. In their eagerness to implement the 'Final Solution', in May 1944, convoys of Jews began to be sent to Auschwitz, totaling 437,000. Others were murdered on the spot or sent elsewhere on transports or forced marches. The total mortality rate was over 600,000.

The child survivors whom I interviewed represent diversity in terms of their countries of origin. Twelve were born in Eastern Europe and nine in Western Europe. The relationship between the nature of the victims' experience during the war and their country of origin is clearly reflected in the narrative of each child survivor. Yet, most went into hiding at some stage in the war which perhaps is not surprising as it was generally the only way that Jewish children were able to survive the Nazis. Marion Kaplan writes that children who survived the war in hiding are considered to be 'success stories', yet "'success' is only in comparison with those whom the Nazis found and murdered. Although their physical lives were saved, they experienced irretrievable loss and immeasurable grief. Their previous lives and health had been ravaged. Moreover, they faced the agonizing disclosures of the genocide; each had lost parents and siblings, as well as nearly their entire extended family and many friends. The Nazis had destroyed their homes, desecrated their synagogues . . . "[13] and robbed them of their childhood.

The Nature of the Experience During the War

Through my research, I have attempted to answer the following questions: have child survivors spoken about their past, and, if so to whom? When? And why? Judith Kestenberg, after years of research with child survivors of the Holocaust, argues the nature of the war experience is crucial to understanding the child survivors' relationship to their past. Furthermore, Shamai Davidson writes, "We have to be aware that the different vicissitudes of individual experience in ghetto, hiding, forced labor, concentration camp, or extermination camp demanded specific personality defenses that revealed themselves during and after the end of persecution."[14]

It is necessary to investigate a wide range of experiences in order to understand the post-war adaptation of child survivors living in Israel. I have attempted to give the reader a glimpse of what these individuals endured during the war, which will shed some light on their post-war adaptation and their identities as child survivors. I have not included the entire narrative of their experiences during the war; rather only those sections that not only summarize their experiences, but also relate some of what they consider to be the most 'significant' moments. In analyzing the narratives of survivors, Brian Schiff argues that "instances where death is encountered, such as through the loss of a loved one and where death is narrowly escaped, are structurally central in these life-histories . . . these moments of crisis normally stand out, apart from the rest of the interview as 'stories' within the life-history."[15] Whilst confirming Brian Schiff's findings, I have also found that stories of loving kindness, caring and companionship also feature as central elements around which life-stories of survivors are constructed. Sarah Moskowitz and Robert Krell's work corroborates my findings. They write, "In almost every child survivor's life story there are moments recalled that, compared with the years of terror, may have only been a few seconds – moments recalled in which some small act of kindness was done by a stranger; a peasant offering food, a Nazi guard turning away. Most often it is a recollection of being given food. The intensity of feeling with which the incident is told reveals the extent of hope given in a moment when the constant grind of desperation, despair and hurt is relieved by a flash of hope that goodness exists."[16]

In writing a synopsis of their experiences during the war, I have tried to remain as close to the narrative texts as possible. Yet, my writing is an interpretation of their experiences, especially as most of the interviews were translated from Hebrew into English. My writing thus constitutes a third voice as I have constructed a narrative out of their narratives.

In Hiding   "Indeed, first and foremost the children were saved by their parents. The act of giving up one's child, of surrendering one's own daughter or son, of recognizing that one no longer could protect and shelter that small person to whom one had given life, was the first and most radical step in the chain of rescue. It was a paradox: to save one's child one had to accept that one was unable to protect and defend the child."[17]

Ariala
Ariala was born in Paris in 1934, and was six years old when the war broke out. Her parents were immigrants from Poland who, fleeing the rising anti-Semitic climate of Eastern Europe, came to France in search

of freedom and security. Ariala was one of four children; she had an older brother, and two younger siblings. When France was occupied in 1940, Ariala does not recall having been affected by the invasion. She recalls her home during that period as being full of life and warmth. Yet, one night her life changed dramatically; she was woken up in the middle of the night by her father and told to get dressed. When she entered the living room, she saw that her younger siblings, Claude and Nicole, were already there, dressed and waiting. Asking where her mother was, Ariala's father explained that, "she had taken ill and had been taken to the hospital during the night . . . and once she got better, they would all be able to come home." Ariala and her siblings were led into a car which was driven by two strange women, and taken to a children's home in Paris.

Upon reaching the institution, she was separated from Claude and Nicole and taken to sleep in a very large dormitory. The next morning, when she asked the nurse where she was and what was happening to her, the nurse told her that she was "in a home for unwanted children . . . that my father and mother have abandoned me and they don't want me anymore. I didn't believe it. So I said: 'Where are Claude and Nicole?' And they said that my siblings are too small. Nicole is with the babies and Claude is with the boys. I would not be seeing them again. Not father, not mother, not my brother, not my sister. I was shocked."

Ariala is unsure as to how long she spent in the institution. She only remembers the routine of eating, sleeping, and walking around aimlessly. One night a nurse told her that she would be leaving and she secretly hoped that her parents had arrived to collect her to take her home. But this was not the case, and she was taken by bus, together with some other children, to the train station. Because she was one of the oldest children, she was instructed to take care of the younger ones and in so doing she recognized her brother and her sister. Ariala became hysterical, and her frenzy heightened when the women supervisors argued that she was mistaken. Eventually they admitted that these were indeed her siblings, and they were allowed to travel together on the train to their next destination, yet, their reunion was short-lived as, at some point in the journey, the siblings were separated once again, and sent to different villages to live with different families. Ariala lived with a French Catholic family for three and a half years, all the while hoping that everything was a mistake and that one day soon she would be reunited with her family.

Ariala's reunion with her family took place sometime after the war. One day, she was called out of class by the principal of the school, and found her father waiting for her in the corridor. After some time searching, he had managed to find her and had come to take her home.

When Ariala arrived home, she found that 'nothing had changed' physically about her home, but that everyone and everything in it had disappeared. Her entire family had been murdered during the *Shoah*, except for her father and siblings.

After the war, Ariala tried desperately to put her life back together, and it took some time before her younger siblings were found and brought home. But life was never the same, Ariala explains, as her family had grown distant as a result of their individual experiences. Ariala decided to "bury the past" and assimilate as quickly as she could into French society. She married another child survivor, and together they decided to forget the past and identify only minimally as Jews. However, during the Six-Day War, Ariala was drawn to Israel and experienced a very strong need to rejoin Jewish destiny. She vowed that one day she would leave France and make her home in Israel. Ariala and her family set sail for Israel in January 1970. My interview with Ariala reminded me of Ruth Behar's fascinating work, in which she reflects on the personality of her protagonist, Esperanza. She says that Esperanza "did not simply tell me her *historias*, she performed them, telling virtually the entire story in dialogue form, changing voices like a spirit or medium or a one-woman theatre of voices to impersonate all the characters of her narratives. I did not have to 'elicit' her account; rather, it was necessary for me to hear how to listen to her storytelling and performance."[18]

Avivit

Avivit was born to an academic family in Kovno,[19] Lithuania, on March 25, 1936. Her sister was a few years older than she. When the Nazis invaded in 1941, Avivit was five years old. Once the Nazis entered the town they wasted no time passing anti-Jewish legislation. Avivit explains, "When the Nazis entered Kovno, they rounded up all the children and put them into a ghetto. Soon afterwards, there was an *Aktion*, and most of my family was taken away in the first *Aktion* – aunts, uncles, and cousins." Avivit insists that she remembers everything from the ghetto clearly and in detail, yet would not give a detailed account of her experiences. What she did say was that during the war she lost her childhood and her family. Avivit spent three years with her nuclear family in the ghetto, during which she neither attended school, nor worked. Rather, her main task was to survive by hiding from the Nazis. Towards the end of the ghetto's existence, the Nazis carried out a *kinderaktion*.[20] They entered the ghetto during the day, whilst the parents were at work, and took the children away. Most parents, on returning home in the evening, found that their children had been taken away. Avivit recalls that, "When the *kinderaktion* began, I was seven years old. My mother decided to smuggle me out of the ghetto and hide me with non-Jews in order to save my life." Avivit recalls that her mother was also involved in smuggling other children out of the ghetto, and placing them in hiding with non-Jews in the area.

Avivit's rescuers were acquaintances who "were not from the village and were not the sort that hid me for payment. They were members of the Lithuanian aristocracy. Another memory that I have is that one day the ghetto was liquidated and then burnt to the ground, and the remaining inhabitants were sent to concentration camps. So when the ghetto was burning, my rescuers took me onto the balcony and said: 'look, you don't have a mother or father anymore. The whole family is burnt. Now you will be our child and we will adopt you'. They were very nice to me. I was seven years old then. I didn't come from a religious home. However, I said to them: 'No way. You are Catholics and I am a Jew. I want to remain Jewish' . . . I remained with this family for a year. In the meantime [whilst she went into hiding], my parents remained in the ghetto and were later deported to concentration camps. My sister was part of the underground. She had also been smuggled out of the ghetto." After the war, Avivit's sister made her way back to Kovno in search of Avivit, and once they were reunited they joined the *Bricha* movement. Avivit, who was more inclined to speak about her life after the war, explains that "we fled Lithuania with Abba Kovner's *Bricha*. We wandered around Europe for a while. We crossed Byelorussia, Poland, Hungary, and Romania. After the war, we found ourselves in the Russian zone. We had hoped to make our way from Romania to Constantinople and then to Israel, but the Russians would not permit us to leave. Therefore, we fled once again and made it over to the English zone. The English imprisoned us, as they thought we were Russian spies. Eventually we made it to Italy with the help of the Jewish Brigade. I spent four years in Italy, in an institution run by *Aliyat Hanoar*."

Fortunately, Avivit's mother also survived the war and was reunited with her daughters in Italy. Their father, however, did not survive. In November 1948 Avivit, together with her mother, set sail for Israel. Upon arrival, Avivit became active in Israeli society, and became very involved in the Scouts youth movement. She married a *sabra*, who came from a well-known and established Jerusalem family. Together they have two daughters and a grandchild. One of Avivit's passions is travel. Her home is decorated with art she has collected from all over the world and she hinted during her interview that she thinks this passion for travel is connected to her experiences as a child during the *Shoah*.

Naomi

Naomi was born on May 11, 1935 in Biala Rawska, Poland. Biala Rawska is a small village 40 kilometers from Warsaw. Naomi recalls, "My mother was a tailor, a special tailor. She had studied a special sewing technique in Warsaw. My father was a fur merchant. I thought that life was wonderful. I was an only child, and my mother's family, whom I was very close to, lived around the corner from the market . . . what could be better? A river, vineyard, friends . . . usually all my friends were girls. My parents gave me the feeling that anything was possible, that when I grew up I could be anything that I wanted to be, because I was pretty, and nice and clever."

When war broke out in Poland in 1939 her father was conscripted and Naomi and her mother were left alone to fend for themselves. Not long after the invasion, Naomi's mother made the decision to leave Biala Rawska. Naomi explains, "I don't know why mother decided to flee with her Polish friends, to get away from the advancing Germans. When we got to a forest, bombs started exploding around us . . . I didn't know what was happening . . . and we ran . . . in the middle I stopped and I said to my mother: 'I have sand in my shoes'. I was a spoilt child who could not walk with sand in her shoes. Until today, I have difficulties with beach sand in my shoes. I can't stand sand. We stopped and it was good that we stopped. My mother was very angry with me, she wanted to pull me to walk on, and I said: 'I am not moving. I have sand in my shoes'. It was good that we stopped because the people who were running ahead were killed."

Realizing the futility of escape, Naomi and her mother returned to Biala Rawska where they were reunited with her father, and life continued 'pretty normally' until 1941, when the Nazis ordered the Jews of Biala Rawska to move into a ghetto. Yet, Naomi's family was exempt from ghettoization as her mother was a highly acclaimed seamstress, and was employed to sew dresses for German women. These women did not want to go inside the ghetto to have their dresses made, so Naomi's family was permitted to remain in their own home, which was outside the ghetto. Naomi's mother decided that she would use her privileged position to help those less-fortunate Jews in the ghetto. Everyday she made a huge pot of soup and would go to the ghetto to distribute it to its inhabitants. Naomi remembers that her mother made the soup out of the best ingredients she could find. She explains that through this her mother had taught her a very important lesson: "I will remember this for the rest of my life. That when you give you need to give with your whole heart. If not, it's not giving, so don't give."

Slowly the ghetto was emptied of its inhabitants. Those who were deported were transported to Treblinka where almost all were killed on arrival. Naomi and her immediate family managed to avoid deportation for quite some time, although her extended family did not. She recalls: "My mother ran after the wagons, throwing pieces of bread to my grandmother . . . the wagons got further away. I was sitting on the floor and I saw those big wooden wheels, with the brown horses . . . with hair on their legs, I saw it all from underneath."

Naomi's parents soon realized that their lives were in danger and they decided to hide. Naomi was hidden with a Polish woman for a few days, during which she refused to eat, drink, or speak. Eventually Naomi's mother came back for her and they hid together, in the forest, in a hole, which they had dug underground. Naomi is unsure as to how much time they spent in their hiding place, but she recalls the time fondly because she was with both her parents. This hiding place eventually became unsafe too, as the Nazis began patrolling the forest regularly. The family made its way back to Biala Rawska, where Naomi and her mother managed to obtain false identification papers and were told of a place where they could hide in Warsaw. Naomi's father was unable to obtain false identification papers, and he decided to join the partisans. The family arranged to meet one another after the war in Biala Rawska, but her father did not survive.

Naomi and her mother made their way to Warsaw and into hiding. They hid with a Polish family for a period of two years. During those two years, they never left the apartment, yet they were well cared for and loved by the Polish family who were concealing them. Naomi recalls that one night she was woken by the sounds of explosions. Running to the window, they saw the Warsaw ghetto in flames, in response to the revolt of the ghetto inhabitants against the Nazis. After a few days, the Polish woman with whom they were hiding informed them that the ghetto was burned completely and that no Jews remained alive.

After the Polish uprising broke out in 1944, the Nazis began to round up Poles living in Warsaw, and sent them to concentration camps in Germany. Naomi, her mother and the Polish family with whom they were hiding, were also sent. They were incarcerated for some time in a German concentration camp. In March 1945, the Russians liberated the camp. Naomi remembers that the liberation was very difficult as the Russians frequently abused the women in the camp. Seeing the cruelty of their liberators, Naomi's mother, together with this Polish family, decided to escape and began making their way back to Poland on foot. Naomi and her mother walked 350 kilometers to Poland, a very difficult journey. The roads were blocked and the dead lay on the roadside. Naomi recalls her mother saying, "Close your eyes, close your eyes."

Naomi and her mother arrived in Biala Rawska on May 10, 1945, where they were greeted with the question from their Polish neighbors: "What, did you and your daughter survive?" After realizing that Naomi's father was dead, Naomi's mother sold their house, and the two of them left Biala Rawska forever. Naomi and her mother eventually settled in Lodz, where Naomi's mother remarried and started a new family. In 1949, in response to rising anti-Semitism in Poland, Naomi and her mother and her new family decided to make *aliya* to Israel. They left on the ship *Independence* and Naomi remembers that when she saw the Carmel for the first time, she felt that she had arrived home. She recalls thinking, when she was thirteen years old, that the past was over, and that she would 'start a new page'. Today Naomi lives in Tel Aviv. She is married, and has one son and two grandchildren. Now retired, she used to work as a nurse. A few years ago Yad Vashem published Naomi's story as a children's book, which is used to teach children about the *Shoah*.

Ehud

Ehud was born in 1934, in the town of Buhl in the district of Baden in Germany. He recalls: "I remember the town well. It was a small town, very picturesque, in a wonderful location in south-west Germany. It was world-renowned for its famous plums. I remember the streets, the houses, the yards, the small river, and the church. The train station that looked very big. And of course, the house of my grandparents, where we lived until we were expelled in 1940."

On the October 22, 1940, the Jewish community of Buhl was deported to the Gurs concentration camp, which was situated in southern France. He recalls that, "The journey took three days from the October 22, 1940 . . . there were 6,538 Jews on the transport. A lot of old people, elderly, who were above 100 years of age, sick people. Two-thirds of the transport was women." After a few months in the camp, Ehud explains that "in February or March 1941, I had left Gurs. I never returned, and I never saw my mother again." Ehud was smuggled out of the camps by an organization that engineered the removal of children under the age of twelve from the camp. Thereafter, Ehud was at first placed in a children's home and then hidden by several Christian families. He was moved from one family to another regularly, as it was too dangerous to leave Jewish children hidden for a lengthy period in the same place.

Ehud reflects that, "The words that encapsulate the entire period are: isolation and loneliness. Even with all that's around you, the children, the teachers and the *madrichim*, you are alone, totally alone. Even more when you leave the children's home and are absorbed into a Christian environment, with people who want to save you, and do save you, but it is another world. A world of prohibitions. You cannot walk, you cannot play, you can't go out, you can't speak, and you are alone. You are not with Jews, not with children, with no one. You are conscious of the danger. They taught you about the danger. The danger can come at any moment, in another day, another week. And you live alone, you have no support. I think that it's the hardest thing. Not only the loss of your parents, the loss of your home, but knowing that you are alone, you have nowhere to go. You have to do what you are told, and hope that the bitter moment will not arrive, not tomorrow and not the day after."

Ehud remained with a Christian family until 1946 when distant relatives managed to locate him. They adopted him and he was taken to Geneva, Switzerland, to live with them. Yet Ehud never felt completely at home in Europe and after completing his studies he decided to move to Israel in the 1960s. Ehud married a *sabra* and raised a family. He furthered his studies and became a Professor at the Hebrew University of Jerusalem. In 1993, Ehud became one of the original members of a narrative group for child survivors of the Holocaust, run by AMCHA. In the past few years, Ehud has become one of the more dominant voices in the child survivor community, where he struggles for the validation of child survivors' experiences during the war.

Eliezer

Eliezer was born in 1932, in Strasbourg, France, to an Orthodox family. When the war broke out in 1939, Eliezer and his family began to move south-east, together with the general population of the area. Soon his father began to have difficulties supporting the family. Thus, the children were sent away to various institutions in France to be cared for. Eliezer remarks, "That's how I found myself, until 1940, in the most beautiful places in France, like the Alps, the Pyrenees which bordered Spain." Towards the end of 1942, Eliezer and his younger brother were sent to an institution for Jewish children which was run by the Joint Distribution Committee. However, one night the orphanage was evacuated and Eliezer was separated from his younger brother. He was given a new name and a new identity and sent off to a boarding school in the town of Issoudun with five other Jewish children. He explains that, "I understood quickly that I had entered a world of lies, as I had to lie all the time. Thus, I developed a dualism – internally I knew what my truth was and, on the other hand, I was conscious that in order for me to survive I had to lie." Unfamiliar with Christian theology and ritual, Eliezer approached one of the priests and asked him for assistance. He remarks that, "within two weeks the priest had explained and taught me how to look like a good Catholic."

After the war, Eliezer's mother had a strong feeling that Eliezer had survived, and she pressured his older sister, who had been active in the anti-fascist underground, to find him. Eliezer's sister traveled around the countryside for six months looking for him. He explains that, "one day I was called and they said to me that a woman wanted to see me. I came and I recognized my sister immediately. It was the first time in many years that I cried real tears." Yet, coming home was traumatic for Eliezer. He had been adopted by a non-Jewish family and had begun to build a new life for himself in a French non-Jewish, environment. His father had died during the war and he felt estranged from his mother culturally and emotionally. In 1947, together with his mother and sister, Eliezer left France and made *aliya* to Israel. Upon arrival he was absorbed into the Youth Aliya movement and almost immediately enlisted into the *Haganah* at the age of fifteen, where he fought in the defense of Safed in 1947. For many years, Eliezer fought for the right to study at university, and finally was accepted to study economics at the university when he was twenty-eight years old. Eliezer married Miriam, who also considers herself a child survivor of the Holocaust. Together they have two children and grandchildren. When I met Eliezer, I found him to be an intriguing individual. He is both an intellectual and an artist, creative and passionate about his views. This was reflected throughout his narrative, in which he expressed strong anti-religious and anti-establishment views. He refuses to be defined by anything or anyone, and he refuses to be a 'slave to the past'. He insists on living in the present.

Noah

Noah was born in France in 1939 to an immigrant Eastern European family. They had left Eastern Europe during the 1930s, in the hope of seeking out better economic opportunities and in order to escape the escalating anti-Semitism. Once the deportation of French Jews to Auschwitz began in 1942, Noah and his older sister were separated from their parents and hidden with a French family in the countryside in a village near the city of Blans. Noah infers, although does not directly state, that his parents were deported to Auschwitz during those deportations, where they were murdered. Noah and his sister were hidden by a French family, who were also members of the French underground, from 1942 until 1945. During the day, they were hidden in a pig-sty or in a hole underground. Despite this deprivation, Noah does not recall suffering during those years in hiding as he explains, "We ate fresh food: fruit and vegetables. There was no shortage of food there like there was in Paris at the time." In our interview Noah does not relate much about his past because, as he explains, he has very few memories of his time in hiding.

After the war, Noah's uncle, who was living in Palestine, began to look for surviving relatives. With the help of a Jewish organization whose function was to locate surviving Jewish children, Noah's uncle managed to locate Noah and his sister. Noah remembers vaguely that letters began to arrive in 1947–8 from this uncle in Palestine. In 1950, Noah and his sister were taken away from their rescuers and placed in a Jewish boarding school that was run by the *Oeuvre de Secours aux enfants*. Felix Goldschmidt, who is remembered fondly by Noah, ran the boarding school for these refugee children. The boarding school was a religious Zionist Institute where, according to Noah, "my religious life began. Before that I knew nothing about Judaism, I was far away from Judaism." Noah and his sister lived and studied there until 1953, when they were taken to Israel on *aliya*. Noah explains that "it's difficult for me to say that I was a Zionist then," for the decision to make *aliya* was not his own. Upon arrival in Israel, Noah was taken to an Orthodox *kibbutz*, where he has remained a member to this day.

Rivka

Rivka was four years old when the war broke out in Holland. Realizing the danger ahead, Rivka's parents handed two of their four children over to the Dutch underground to be hidden. One of the few memories that Rivka has of the period is being taken away from her family on the back of a bicycle. During the war, Rivka was placed with five different families. She explains: "I stayed with the fifth family until the end of the war. I was there for nearly two and a half years. I remained in contact with them. They are no longer alive, but I remained in contact with them. I don't know who the other families were, and I want to thank them too, but I don't know who to thank."

Rivka has mixed memories from the war. She remembers being safe and protected whilst under the care of her rescuers, but at the same time she remembers moments of tension and panic. A particularly strong memory she has is being forbidden to walk around the house freely, as Germans were patrolling the area. Realizing the danger, her rescuer cut a hole into the floor of the house and sent Rivka underground for some time along with another Jewish girl they were hiding. Rivka explains, "We were there for a day, sometimes two days, sometimes a week. The two of us, two girls alone. We were scared to be alone down there, so he would come down with us and his wife would remain upstairs." For most of her time in hiding, Rivka was not allowed to leave the house and had to watch the world outside from her bedroom window.

Rivka remained with this couple until the end of the war when her mother, who had survived, managed to find and reclaim her. Rivka remembers: "The first time she came, I was sleeping. The second time she came, I saw her, but I didn't want her. There is a phenomenon . . . that when one is very, very hungry, or due to starvation, everything is swollen and one looks terrible. I did not recognize her and I didn't want her . . . the third time my mother came with my brother. He was five years older than me and I recognized him."

Eventually, Rivka left her beloved rescuers and returned to live in Amsterdam with her mother and her siblings. Unfortunately, her father, who survived the war, had died some time after liberation. The dynamic between Rivka and her mother was very tense; she felt distant from her and missed her rescuers a great deal. Life for the family after the war was difficult; there was no money and Rivka's mother had to work hard to support her children. Because Rivka's grandparents were living in Israel, her mother decided to relocate the family to Israel in order to join them. Sending the children first, it took some time before the family could be fully reunited. Rivka effectively grew up in Israel and became very involved in Ultra Orthodox Judaism. She believed that her mission in life was to 'replace' her family, who had been killed during the Holocaust. She explains that "seventy members of my family were killed in the *Shoah*. When my family reached seventy people again, which included my children, my grandchildren, and me I said to my children: I have done what I have needed to do."

Shalom

Shalom was born in Kovno, Lithuania, in 1933. His mother was a nurse and a poet; his father, a teacher and a writer. With the Nazi invasion of Lithuania in 1941, Shalom and his family were forced to move into the ghetto. Surviving the numerous *Aktionen* on his mother's initiative, Shalom was eventually smuggled out of the ghetto. Hiding with non-Jewish Lithuanians, Shalom managed to survive the war. When I interviewed him he explained that, "if I wanted to hear about his experiences during the war, I should read his book," as his book tells the story of his past. Respecting Shalom's wish, I have decided to present the prologue to his book, which I have translated, in which he describes the determining moment of his survival: his escape from the ghetto.

From his written account:

> I didn't really want to leave that morning, to emerge from the dim warmth of Mother and our only room, to prepare to depart. But I had to. All the arrangements had been made, and now everything depended on getting past the sentries successfully.
>
> It was a clear, crisp dawn in early spring and we may have had something to eat before setting out. Near the house I was befriended by a puppy which ran after us and I was torn — here at last was a dog that could be mine. I tried to plead with Mother to let me go back just long enough to

shut the pup in our room, so that if my escape failed again this morning, too, then at least I would have my very own dog, for the first time in years.

But this time my exit was fast and smooth. The German officer was absent, and the roll call was supervised only by our people, with no interference from the guards. A few more steps and we had already reached the riverbank. Oars cut through the calm water, and I looked around me, wonderstruck. After years in the ghetto, suddenly a river, so much space, and me to sail upon it, like long ago at summer camp.

As we neared the other bank, my mother quietly removed the two yellow patches, the threads of which she had previously cut, and which were now fastened only with a safety pin. Her instructions were clear: once we reached the other bank I was to march without stopping through the Lithuanians standing there, cross the road, and go up the path that led into the hills. All alone, I was to walk without raising suspicion and without looking back. Further up the path, a woman would meet me and tell me what to do.

Everything went as planned, except that I met no woman waiting for me on the path. I proceeded according to my instructions, going deeper into the hills, farther and farther from the riverbank and my mother. Only then did a figure with a sealed face approach me and as she passed me she whispered that I should continue slowly, she would soon return and join me. A short while later I was following her, up a steep path, and I soon found myself in the house of an elderly Lithuanian woman, Marija.

All this occurred so quickly and so easily that I scarcely grasped what had happened to me in such a short while. To tell the truth, I am not sure even today, after these many years, that I have fully digested what happened to me that morning. But the next day I received the first letter from my mother, written on a rolled-up scrap of paper, to be read and then burned: "I watched you move away, my child," she wrote, and I will never forget this, "climbing all by yourself onto the bank of the river, walking past guards and people on your way to freedom. A day will come when a film will be made about your miraculous escape from the ghetto."

Like Moses in the bulrushes I was cast by Mother onto the shore of life. I therefore dedicate this story to my mother, who gave me life twice, but was unable to save her own even once.[21]

Shalom was reunited only years later with his father. In 1946, Shalom left Europe for Israel. When Shalom arrived in Israel, he was determined to integrate quickly and build a 'normal life'. He explains that during his first years in Israel, "normal adolescence came, in the city, on *kibbutz*, and in the army." He was determined to become a pioneer and settle the land. Shalom dreamt of building a memorial for 'my friends from the ghetto'. Over the years, Shalom poured his energies into his studies, work, and his family. He began studying and, in 1962, married Miriam, a *sabra*. Together they have three children. He completed his doctorate and lectured in agricultural studies. Shalom has had many professional interests and changed his career numerous times over the years. Today Shalom is active, amongst other activities, in an organization for former Lithuanian Jews, under whose auspices he has been instrumental in arranging a reunion/meeting of the Child Survivors of the Kovno Ghetto.

Yafe

Yafe was born in Paris on March 9, 1931. When the war broke out, Yafe remembers her father resisting her mother's pleas to flee the Nazis. He insisted that because he was an honest, respected citizen, no harm would come to them. Yafe's father was forced to leave his family after he was conscripted into the French army. Yafe explains that once her father left, her mother fell into a depression and was not able to take care of the children. She recalls, "My sister was six months old and only ate from my mother's breast. The baby screamed, my brother cried. My brother did not want me to comb his hair. I was a big girl and I wanted his hair to be combed well, with his sailor outfit. He did not want his hair combed. My mother only cried. She lay down and lost any ability or motivation. The baby was crying and I heard the baby cry . . . my mother did not feed her. It was terrible. I found a bit of camembert cheese, I mixed it with a bit of sugar, and I forced my sister to eat it. Till this day she thanks me; she loves that cheese. Perhaps because of that I saved her. It was terrible." After some time, Yafe and her family eventually returned home to Trouville, where they were reunited with her father. Because of the lack of work in Trouville, Yafe's father moved to Paris alone. In the meantime Trouville was declared a closed zone. "My father could not come back and we could not get out. Later on my mother managed to send me and my brother with a non-Jewish woman to Paris." Yafe's father moved to Paris, and took Yafe and her brother with him, whilst Yafe's mother and baby sister, who had remained in Trouville, were rounded up and put into a concentration camp. Yafe explains that she remained in contact with her mother as, "My mother was able to write to us every week from the camp, and we could write to her. She even wrote that we could come and be in the camp too. This helped the Germans and many people went on their own accord into the camp. We did not go in. My father sent my mother a package every week."

One day, Yafe's father disappeared and was never seen again. Many years after the war, she found out that he had been deported to Auschwitz where he had been killed upon arrival. In the meantime, because Yafe and her brother were now completely alone, they were placed in an orphanage. She remembers the orphanage as a sad and depressing place where "everyone was dressed in the same clothes, and all the girls had the same haircut . . . with a fringe and they shaved the heads. And everyone had the same eyes. And I saw that all the girls looked like one another. Everyone was sad there." In 1943 the orphanage was closed. Yafe explains, "They sent the boys in one truck to one place and the girls to another. Thus, I was separated from my brother . . . " Yafe contracted a contagious disease and was placed in a hospital for a period until she recuperated and was taken into hiding by an elderly non-Jewish French woman. Yafe recalls the woman saying to her: "'From today I am your grandmother'. She was elderly. She brought with her a basket with red apricots and immediately I realized that she was a good French citizen. The woman was also hiding three other boys besides me. She did not have any children. She got money from the Jewish underground every month. It was forbidden for me to go to school, but I didn't have a yellow star there. The resistance always tried to connect siblings. I was given the address where my brother was and, in February, he sent me a postcard, which I still have till today. After the war, we found him living at that same place." Whilst in hiding with this couple, Yafe was sexually harassed by her male rescuer.

At some stage, Yafe managed to have her brother brought to her hiding place. At the end of the war, Yafe was reunited with her siblings, all of whom had been hidden with French families during the war. With the help of a Jewish organization, Yafe found her mother in an asylum, yet sadly she had become a broken woman. She recalls when she first saw her mother: "There was a long path and there were people who were banging their heads with shoes. There was a scared, disheveled woman who jumped out and said: '*sheindele meine sheindele!*' [my beauty, my beauty] She began to kiss me and cry and talk and talk . . . but I didn't understand. I couldn't believe that it was my mother. And I said to her '*leibe mame, zisse mame*' [sweet mother, good mother] . . . she had no teeth and she had no nails."

Yafe eventually managed to get her mother released from the institution and helped her reestablish their lives in Paris. However, in 1949 Yafe decided to move to Israel on her own to study. Her move was very difficult. She explains that, "I felt bad in Israel. I didn't know the language and I was used to going to the theatre and I read a lot of books, and I couldn't read books here. I had to read the material for the course and it was very difficult, despite the enormous help that my boyfriend gave me. I was a good student, because studying was very important to me. But I felt like a stranger." During her studies at a teacher's seminary, she met the man who was to be her husband. She explains that as a young couple, they struggled financially: "We had a hard life, we both worked very hard. Both of us were teachers. I wanted to study but my husband always said: 'When you're a grandmother you can study'. In the meantime we raised our children." Yafe has four children and 16 grandchildren. During the war, Yafe wrote a diary which she is now translating into Hebrew.

David

David was born in Kovno, Lithuania, in 1938. He tells of when the Nazis invaded Lithuania in 1941, and how riots erupted which were carried out by the Lithuanians themselves against the Jews, whilst the Nazis turned a blind eye. David explains that, "It's a bit ironic, as when the Germans invaded the Lithuanians began attacking the Jews and killed many of them. The Jews asked the Germans to defend them, and the Germans said that the Jews needed to move into the ghetto. The Jews saw the ghetto as some type of defense. I think that was very ironic." The Jewish community of Kovno was ghettoized in 1941.

David spent a few years in the ghetto together with his parents before being smuggled out. He was five years old when he was taken away from his parents and hidden with a Christian Lithuanian family, with whom he remained for the duration of the war. Because of his young age during the war, "I don't think that I remember things from the ghetto in an organized, ordered way." Thus, during our interview, David spoke very little about those years. His parents remained in the ghetto until it was "liquidated, and they were both taken to a concentration camp, where they were separated and, somehow, with a lot of luck, both of them managed to survive."

David does not remember his years in hiding as particularly traumatic, rather he recalls how well taken care of and loved he was by the families who hid him. He told me that, "when there was a noise in the corridors, they would put me in the linen closet. It seemed to me a natural thing to do. Not only that. I remember seeing it as a sign of their concern for me . . . that they cared for me more than for their own children. They managed to give me the feeling that they cared for me. Therefore, I did not feel that I was amongst strangers. My story is not the story of a child who lived amongst strangers and felt rejected."

After the war had ended, David was found by some of his parents' friends who, after locating him, decided to take him with them. He explains that, "We obviously didn't know if my parents survived or not, so they took me with them." So David joined this family on its trek across Europe, as they made their way towards Germany; at some point in that journey, he was reunited with his parents. He explains that, "after the war ended in Europe, there were all sorts of organizations which tried to identify survivors and reunite them with their families. That's how my parents found me. My parents were told that I was alive, and we were reunited two years later." David was first reunited with his mother, whom he met on the way to Germany, and later they met up with his father in Italy. He explains that, "from Italy we made *aliya* in 1948, and we settled in Israel." In Israel, David's parents had an extensive network of family and friends who helped them to establish themselves fairly quickly. David recalls that during the first few years, he experienced some difficulties integrating into Israeli society. However, after some two to three years, David felt that he belonged. He integrated almost completely into Israeli society and over the years developed a successful career in academia. Today he is a head of department at one of Israel's leading universities. He is married and has one daughter. Despite his almost complete integration into Israeli society, David's life has always been connected to the *Shoah*, mainly due to the prominent personality of his father, who was a distinguished member of the Jewish community before, during and after the war. After the war, his father wrote a history of the Kovno ghetto, which became one of the definitive works on the period.

In Death Camps These children were exceptions to the murder process of the Final Solution . . . because they were not killed immediately. "They had been awarded a temporary existence permit for the duration of which they functioned as slave laborers, or amused or entertained the SS," or because they were smuggled into the camps and hidden by adults. "Other children were exceptions to the assembly-line system of death not because they lived longer, but because they were murdered by another method: shot, beaten, suffocated, smashed or ripped apart. But, for the hundreds of thousands of children who passed through these murder mills, the common pattern prevailed. Essentially, there was no child life in Chelmno or the Operation Reinhard killing centers."[22]

Kalman

Kalman was born in May 1930, in the town of Balassagyarmat, situated on the Slovak–Hungarian border. Kalman was one of five children, three of whom survived the war, including his twin sister, Devorah. Kalman lost his father when he was two years old. At the age of twelve, Kalman was placed under his grandfather's care, in order to study at one of the most prestigious *Yeshivot* in Hungary. It was within the walls of the *Yeshiva* that Kalman discovered his passion for the Talmud – the Oral Law – a passion that has remained with him throughout his life. When the Nazis invaded Hungary on March 19, 1944, Kalman was on his way home for the *Pesach* vacation. Whilst traveling home, he was arrested and put into a detention center. He explains, "I was released because of my young age and I got home in time to find myself in a ghetto which was also happening all over Hungary . . . and three, four weeks later, in mid May, in the second half of May, we were kicked out of the ghetto too."

In the spring of 1944, Kalman, his family, and his entire village were evacuated from their homes, and sent in cattle cars to Auschwitz–Birkenau. In his interview, he explains his arrival there. "Birkenau. We have left off with the sliding doors of the cattle train sliding open and we are faced with a bunch of . . . pajamas-clad people speaking the coarse gutter Yiddish of Poland, all of it in harsh terms to . . . 'get the hell out of the box cars, pronto, don't touch the luggage, leave it there it will follow you. Get out and line up in rows of ten' . . . Then a voice shouted from the top of the column in German '*tzwillinge raus*' 'twins step out' . . . Mother called to *saba*, '*saba* give me the boy'. Mother held onto me and we stepped out. We were told to stand out and before our eyes our little *kehilla* . . . disappeared in the next thirty-five minutes." Kalman and his twin sister, Devorah, were spared the fate of the rest of his village because Mengele, who conducted medical experiments on twin prisoners, considered them to be 'useful'. During the course of his incarceration in Birkenau, Kalman was experimented upon twice. Kalman, unlike some of the other twins, managed to survive the experiments. In 1945, during the evacuation of Auschwitz–Birkenau, Kalman and his friend, Louis Bacci, decided not to join the rest of the camp on the death marches. Kalman explains that "they hid under their bunks," whilst the rest of the camp was evacuated, and remained there "until that Saturday that I maintain is the twentieth of January, when a *yankel*[23] with a white thing showed up in the afternoon with a sub-machine gun, and we understood it was a Russian soldier."

Soon after liberation, Kalman began to make his way back to Hungary on foot. Upon arrival Hungary he joined the *Bnei Akiva* Zionist Youth Movement and "by the fall of 1945 we were headed for Yugoslavia for the *Aliya Bet*, the ship . . . which I took was called *Knesset Yisrael*. On board there were some four thousand souls, including children. Not too far out of Haifa, we bumped into the British navy who then forced us off our ships and onto the British army ships. From there we were taken to detention camps in Cyprus . . . " Kalman eventually reached Israel in 1947, where he joined the Israeli air force. Kalman's sister, Devorah, also survived the war, and today they both live in Israel. Unfortunately, Kalman's mother did not survive the war. She died on the death marches from Auschwitz–Birkenau in January 1945. Kalman later married and has two sons. He worked in the commercial aircraft industry and has now retired. Soon after retirement, he decided to go 'home', to the Talmud Department at the University of Bar Ilan.

Sara

Sara was born to a religious family in 1931, in Carpathian Ruthenia. When the Nazis invaded Hungary in 1944, Sara was fourteen years old. Her family was ghettoized for a brief period before they were deported directly to Auschwitz–Birkenau. Sara explains that no ghetto was established in her village, "because there were too few Jews." Instead, they were confined to their houses. She explains that there was no food and because "I was small and ran fast, I left the house. I was the main provider. During the night, I would sneak into our fields, as we had been farmers, to steal potatoes and fruit and bring them home. It was forbidden to go to the store . . . This is one of my memories, stealing food so there would be food at home." Sara and her family did not remain in their homes for long before being deported to Auschwitz–Birkenau where she was separated from her parents. She explains that "the separation from my parents was very difficult. Mengele did not want to separate us and we all went together. But at some point a man came up to me and forcibly removed me from my family. He was one of the prisoners; one of those men who worked in the commandos whose job it was to help the Germans unload the trains. He removed both my sister and myself, and threw us to the other side. That was the separation from my family. I never saw them again."

Sara was imprisoned in Auschwitz–Birkenau for just less than a year before being evacuated in 1945 on a death march. She explains that between the time she was deported to Auschwitz–Birkenau and liberated from Bergen Belsen in April 1945, she had been incarcerated in five camps, "I was in Auschwitz, in Breslau, Mauthausen, Gross-Rosen and I was liberated from Bergen Belsen. What happened in each of those camps is difficult to describe in a few sentences. But Auschwitz was a very difficult place. Perhaps the worst place; despite the fact that at each place I arrived, I would say, 'This is the worst, this is the worst'." Sara explains that her survival was a miracle and indeed each story she tells demonstrates that astounding survival. In her narrative she even tells of her attempts to fast on *Yom Kippur* in the camp. Beyond luck, Sara also attributes her survival to her need to keep her sister alive throughout the war. Both sisters managed to survive the war, and after they were liberated they began to make their way back to their home-town in Hungry to see if any family members had survived. Sara explains that although she knew no one remained, nevertheless she was compelled to go back and check. They were fortunate enough to meet a cousin who had also survived the war and together they made their way across Europe. After spending some time in Europe, their cousin convinced them to make *aliya* and they left for Israel on an illegal ship. The ship was stopped by the British outside Haifa, though they were permitted to enter Palestine. They were detained in Atlit for a few months, until they received their immigration certificates. Sara and her sister moved to an Orthodox *kibbutz* where they remain to this day. Sara is a mother and grandmother to nineteen grandchildren and two great grandchildren.

Yitzhak

Yitzhak was born in 1932, in Katowice, Poland. When the war broke out in 1939 he, together with his family, was ghettoized in the first ghetto to be established in Poland: Piotrkow Trybunalski. He was in the ghetto for three years until his deportation to the Blyzin labor camp. Here Yitzhak witnessed from his bedroom window the gradual 'liquidation' of his community as it was deported to Treblinka. He explains that "in October 1942, they took all the Jews and I saw it all from my window. Thousands of Jews walking under the window. Suddenly my mother recognized her sister, and she began tearing her hair out of her head, because we knew that they were all going to die. We also knew it was Treblinka. People knew."

Yitzhak's family was spared temporarily because his father was considered to be a valuable worker, being fluent in German. Yitzhak and his brother even managed to escape the *kinderaktion* through the intervention of his parents. He recalls that "before we got onto the trains, two German trucks arrived and the Germans simply started selecting the children. How can they go to a labor camp? Children weren't productive. It was obvious. They took my brother and myself, and loaded us onto the truck. I was already on the truck when my mother began shouting: 'Ernst! Ernst! The children!' At the last minute, my father realized what was happening and he approached the SS man, the commander and began to speak to him in German. He bribed him with one hand and took me off the truck with the other, as I was standing at the edge of the truck. Then he pulled my brother off with other hand. He then took us to the train that was going to Blyzin. That was a real feeling of having been saved."

In 1943, Yitzhak and his family were deported to the labor camp, Blizjin, where they were incarcerated for a year. Yitzhak remembers this as a relatively good period, especially, as he explains, "in comparison to what the rest of the Jews of Poland were experiencing then." When the camp was eventually closed, Yitzhak, together with his mother and younger brother, were deported to Auschwitz–Birkenau on August 1, 1944. His father, who was left to dismantle the camp, arrived in Auschwitz–Birkenau later on. Upon arrival in the camp, Yitzhak was separated from his mother and brother. He was interned in the children's barrack together with other Jewish and non-Jewish Polish children. During the next few months, Yitzhak managed to stay alive and avoided *selektionen* for the gas chambers. On January 18, 1945 Yitzhak was evacuated with the rest of the camp and marched in the direction of Germany, on a death march. He was marched from Auschwitz to Gleiwitz from Gleiwitz by train to Sachsenhausen and from Sachsenhausen to Mauthausen and from Mauthausen on a death march to Gunskirchen in Austria. The 21st Infantry Division of the US Army liberated him in Gunskirchen on May 4, 1945.

Yitzhak made *aliya* in 1945, and was placed in the care of a surrogate family in Be'er Tuvia. In 1947, he was reunited with his mother, yet sadly both his younger brother, Eduard, and his father did not survive the war. In Israel, Yitzhak did not live with his mother, who had remarried, but in different institutional frameworks run by the state. He served proudly in the Israeli army and married a *sabra*, who is deeply involved in tracing her own family's past during the war. Today, Yitzhak lives in Haifa and has three children. He has recently retired, and he devotes a large part of his free time to reading about the *Shoah*. He attends conferences and lectures about the *Shoah* regularly, and is especially interested in the topics pertaining to Jewish armed resistance and the partisan movements during the war.

Shlomo

Shlomo was born in Southern Hungary, on the Yugoslavian border, in 1929. In 1939 he was sent by his parents to study in a *yeshiva* in a village in Slovakia. When the war broke out, Shlomo was arrested, as he did not have any identity papers. He explains that "My parents, may their memory be blessed, gave my [identity] papers, the papers which I should have had, to my cousin . . . Therefore he was able to escape from Slovakia, and that was that. My cousin's parents were taken to Majdanek . . . not Majdanek to Treblinka, sorry, they took the whole family to Treblinka, and my cousin lived . . . on my papers. So I was screwed. . . They caught me because I did not have Hungarian papers. I was not the only one. There were many of us in the same situation."[24] Shlomo was then deported from prison in Budapest to Auschwitz at the end of 1941, beginning of 1942. He explains that he was one of the first prisoners, as "then the Auschwitz complex was not so well developed, as it was in 1943. One can say that we built Auschwitz . . . what was called Birkenau."

Shlomo explains that he was interned in Auschwitz–Birkenau from the time he arrived in 1942, until its liquidation in January 1945. His narrative is the chilling story of a prisoner of Birkenau who 'lived' for over three years in the death camp. On January 17, 1945, Shlomo was evacuated from Auschwitz with the majority of the camp prisoners. He marched from January till the beginning of April, and was liberated in Breslau, by the Russians, on May 11, 1945, two days after the war ended. After being nursed back to health by the Russians, Shlomo was released. He explains: "When I was released I weighed twenty-seven kilograms. When I was released, I was only skin and bones and I didn't even know how to walk. I walked like an animal, I remember . . . and . . . he (G-d) helped me and I got healthy. I began to make my way back to Hungary to look for my family . . . " Shlomo managed to locate two of his sisters, and soon afterwards made *aliya*, married and had children. Shlomo divorced his first wife and has subsequently remarried. Today, Shlomo and Shoshana live on the fringe of the Ultra-Orthodox community in Geula, Jerusalem, where he is an active member of the community. Shlomo is a deeply religious man, yet he struggles with G-d because of what he went through and witnessed during the *Shoah*. Whilst talking to Shlomo about the past, Auschwitz seems to be constantly in front of his eyes.

In Work/Labor Camps   "Young people, who entered the slave labor network, whether through the selection at Auschwitz–Birkenau or because they were sent directly to a forced labor camp, shed their child-hood with their names. They were robbed of their youth as they were stripped of their packages, clothes, and hair. From the moment they joined the slave ranks they had no choice but to act as the adult laborers they were taken to be."[25]

Yaacov

Yaacov was born in 1933 in Olshani Lithuania. When the Nazis invaded the Soviet Union and his home town fell under Nazi Occupation, he was eight years old. Yaacov and his family were forced to live in the town's ghetto until its liquidation in 1942, and then trans-ferred to the Oszmiana ghetto. Yaacov explains that the most traumatic episode he remembers from the Oszmiana ghetto was the *Aktion*, carried out in October 1942 by the Jewish police of the Vilna Ghetto, under Nazi orders. Yaacov remembers that "they selected out six hundred people, not all of whom were old people. There were some young people amongst them, but they did not look good . . . because of everything that they had already endured . . . They took them. My family and I . . . we were locked into the synagogue . . . Those who were to be kept alive were packed into the synagogue. The synagogue was big, but they had packed nearly the entire ghetto into the synagogue. It was a big syna-gogue but it was packed . . . like sardines. It was difficult to stand, there was no air . . . " Out of the six hundred selected, 406 old people were handed over to the Nazis to be killed.

After surviving the *Aktion* in Oszmiana, Yaacov and his family were then transferred to the labor camp, Jiezmariai. Once again, they remained there for a brief time, before being transferred to the Kovno ghetto. Their stay in Kovno was also brief as, one day, the adults in the camp were ordered to assemble at the gate of the ghetto. Yaacov explains that: "I went with my parents . . . My whole family passed through the gate . . . there were Germans who were standing there together with the Jewish ghetto police. They stopped me and would not let me through the gate . . . because I was a child and they said that children were not allowed . . . My family tried to speak . . . but of course it didn't help . . . They tried to convince the police who were standing there to let me join them . . . but they did not want to listen . . . I began to look for a way to join them . . . to escape . . . I ran along the length of the ghetto fence and I found a hole in the fence. I crept through the hole and hid in the line of people. I stood next to my father. My father had a bag . . . I stood on the bag . . . They counted the people in the line and I stood on the bag. They didn't see. That's how I managed to go with my family." Yaacov managed to smuggle himself into the camp, where he was picked to work directly for the officer in charge of the camp, cleaning his boots and attending to the horses. On March 27, 1944, a *Kinderaktion* was carried out in the labor camp. Children were dragged away from their parents and hurled onto awaiting trucks. Yaacov was ordered to join the children, but was saved at the last minute by the head of the camp, who was a German soldier. This soldier approached one of the SS men and requested, "This is my oldest worker, I am asking you to leave him here."

The labor camp was eventually liquidated and Yaacov and his family were twice moved to two other labor camps. Yaacov explains that with the evacuation of each camp, thrse was a dark sense of foreboding, as they did not know where they would be taken to next and what would happen to them. When the Nazis announced that the last camp, Rudomplania, was to be evacuated, the prisoners, with the help of two Ukrainian guards, planned an escape. The SS planned to march the prisoners from the camp through a forest, to an awaiting train. Upon reaching the forest, the prisoners began to flee. As Yaacov explains, "Whilst we were walking to the train station my family walked together. But when the pandemonium began we simply lost one another . . . And I found myself completely alone."

Yaacov was reunited with his father and sister in the forest, yet his mother was never seen again. Yaacov and his surviving family remained in Lithuania for a short while before deciding to move to Poland. He explains that in Poland, "I studied there; I even managed to complete high school, the gymnasium. The moment I had completed my studies, we were given permission to make *aliya* to Israel. We arrived in Israel in 1950. At the beginning of 1951, I was too young to join the army, as I was seventeen years old. But, by December 1951, I was conscripted into the IDF. I did the army, completed my studies, work, family and that's it . . . that's more or less my history here in Israel." Yaacov explains that "the decision to come to Israel was not out of Zionist conviction; it was because we were convinced that we simply had no other place in the world to live . . . It was clear to us that we needed to have a piece of land. Those ravings of the anti-Semites: 'Jews to Palestine' with which every child was familiar even before the Germans entered. Thus the idea of Palestine was in every Jew's soul, even if he was or wasn't Zionist, and especially after what we had been through it was clear to us that we had nothing to find there anymore. There were people who went to America; those who had family there. We had family in the States who began to look for us after the war and even asked us to join them, but we decided that we were going to *Eretz Yisrael*, and that's how we got to Israel."

Yaacov is married and has two sons and grandchildren. He is currently retired and spends most of his time reading, like Yitzhak, about armed Jewish resistance during the Holocaust.

Michal

Michal was born in the midst of the *Shoah*: in 1941 in Radzivilov, Poland. A year after she was born, her father was killed by the *Gestapo*, and her mother, realizing the imminent danger facing her own life, decided to find a way to save her infant daughter. She approached one of the young Polish Catholic girls that worked for them and asked her for help.[26]

Michal explains that, "The next thing I remember is being with this young Polish couple . . . we were sitting outside . . . it was the country . . . it was a village and they had a small house and it was summer time and we were sitting outside in the yard of the house having a picnic . . . a dinner outside on the blanket and it was she, her husband and me . . . and . . . (silence). We heard the *Gestapo* coming, the marching . . . we heard the noise . . . They pushed me under the blanket we were sitting on and the *Gestapo* walked into the yard and shouted at them to get into the house. They stepped onto the blanket . . . but they were so angry, and so . . . They were convinced for some reason that this couple was hiding a Jewish child . . . It's a small village. I guess word got around. They knew that my mother had had a child and . . . it just became a matter of principle; of eliminating every Jewish person in the town . . . In a fit of anger or zealousness, I don't know what it was, one of them stepped on me and didn't realize it. They took the couple into the house . . . a few minutes later, I heard a gun shots and they . . . left the house . . . "

The next day, Michal was found by the young Polish woman's mother, who decided to hide Michal herself. Yet, after some time it became increasingly dangerous to hide her, as the family was being constantly harassed by the *Gestapo* who were convinced that the Polish family was hiding a Jewish child. All the time that Michal was in hiding, she was in contact with friends of her parents who had formed a partisan unit and were hiding in the forests. Sensing the imminent danger, they decided to take Michal out of the family's care. Michal explains: "They felt that this woman could not withstand any more. She had certainly sacrificed enough . . . and (Silence) one night they came to take me away with them, they came in a covered truck . . . they took me . . . They started driving with the truck into the forest and just as we got into the forest we were caught. We were put onto the trains . . . " Michal was imprisoned in a camp and remained there until the end of the war. At the end of the war, a woman who had also survived the camp took Michal to Berlin with her. "We finally got to Berlin and there was this sentry post someplace . . . there was . . . night time . . . and there was a full moon, and she was so excited on finally reaching Berlin that she stood up, and she was silhouetted against the moon. The sentry saw her and he shot her on the spot and she died . . . " Michal was not alone for long. She managed to attach herself to a group of orphaned children who roamed the streets of Berlin together in search of food and shelter.

Later, Michal was adopted by an American couple and went to live in the United States. Michal explains bitterly that, "They just handed us out to anybody that looked reasonable . . . this couple was an elderly couple and they were financially well off and I guess they made a good impression on the court and . . . so I was given to them in Philadelphia." Michal describes her adoption and life in America as a difficult and painful one. She never felt wanted by her adopted family, nor was she able to develop any sense of connection or belonging to anyone or anything in the United States.

However, at the age of sixteen, Michal found comfort and a sense of belonging in Israel. She explains that in Israel it "was the first time I felt whole and could be me." Consequently Michal decided to make Israel her home. She made *aliya*, married soon afterwards, and gave birth to two daughters. Michal then divorced after years of marriage. She felt that the wounds of her past prevented her from developing a trusting relationship, as she had always felt insecure in her relationship. Yet, being exceptionally bright and talented, Michal was able to develop a successful career in academia. Michal's narrative is laden with sadness and pain. She has struggled with her traumatic past, with both her war and post-war memories. Her experience of life has been difficult, but despite the difficulties and pain she has succeeded in building a family and a successful career, which have given her some degree of solace and satisfaction.

Fleeing with parents Whilst fleeing with their parents, children adapted to parental models. They depended on their parents to protect them from the threatening world. Children who were still with at least one of their parents at the beginning of the war continued to hope that their parents would help and save them. They permitted themselves to observe the horrible reality as complete chaos from which they were insulated and which did not touch them. "The feeling was that I am a child and my mother takes care of me, and if my mother will die, then I will die also." Or "I didn't think about the future. I trusted my mother. I had the security that my mother is next to me."[27] While parents were able to provide some physical or emotional protection, children stayed close and obeyed. "But when parents were helpless, children could reverse roles with them and rescue them."[28]

Rachel

At the beginning of her interview, Rachel said, "What I want to tell you is that my whole life has been alongside the *Shoah*. I was not only born in an atmosphere of war, but my whole childhood and my first memories are connected to the war. All the years, my whole life has been dedicated not to trying to understand the Holocaust, but at least trying to deal with it."

At the outbreak of war Rachel was four years old, and her family, which was living in Paris at the time, decided to flee to the countryside where they hid for the duration of the war. Hiding with her family in an isolated village, Rachel explains that she did not 'witness' the *Shoah* itself. However, 'knowing' the *Shoah* became a very real part of her experience after the war, when her family moved back to Paris and had to confront the reality of what had happened. Due to her young age, Rachel remembers very little from the war years; she only has flashes of memory.

She explains that, "My experiences after the war were more difficult than the war itself. Many others share this feeing. During the war, one had to survive. After the war, one had to confront the reality, all sorts of things, which were more and more terrible. It was a very difficult period. So, to say that the war ended in 1945, it did not; not for us. The war itself, if you look at it historically, did end. However, in terms of humanity, it certainly did not. Certainly not."

After the war, Rachel's sister made *aliya*, whilst Rachel and her parents remained in France. Rachel continued to study, completed her MA degree and, after working for some time at the university, decided to make *aliya*. She recalls that, "The moment I knew that I could support myself financially here in Israel, I made *aliya* . . . Whilst I was in France, I tried to understand what it meant to be a Jew. I came to the conclusion that being a believing and observant Jew was not enough. I came to the realization that the only way to be true to my Jewishness was to be in *Eretz Yisrael*, and so I made *aliya*."

Rachel's narrative was filled with passion, wisdom, and pain. She is truly a remarkable woman who has spent her life searching for meaning and growth, especially in relation to her experiences in the war and her Jewish identity. Rachel's parents, once they retired, also made *aliya*. Rachel, now a retired academic, spends most of her time taking care of her elderly mother.

Yehiel

Yehiel was born in 1933, in Fiume, Italy. Even though Italy was aligned with Nazi Germany, no harm came to the Jews until 1938 when Mussolini began to apply the Nazi's 'Racial laws' to the Jews. Yehiel describes how, despite a few changes, life in Fiume continued as normal until September 1943 with the German invasion. On September 27, 1943, Yehiel and his family left Fiume. He recalls, "The partisans had destroyed all the roads which led to the city . . . no automobile could pass there. Father decided to rent a horse and cart. We got onto the cart: My parents, myself, my two sisters, my aunt and my grandmother, and we left . . . We left our apartment, we left our store, we left everything . . . " After a few days, they reached a small village and found a non-Jewish family willing to take them in and hide them. At the end of 1943, as the situation became increasingly unstable, Yehiel and his family were spirited out of their hiding place by the anti-fascist underground. He explains that, "They took all of us, not all together, but in groups through the back roads to temporary hiding places where we would hide . . . until our false papers were ready. It was lucky that father had money, because the papers cost money. However, later we found out that even those who didn't have money were helped . . . We had to hide until our papers were ready." Whilst waiting for the false papers to be prepared, Yehiel, his sister and cousins were placed in a monastery in the town of Lugo. He recalls that, "The whole time that we were there, our parents never visited us . . . We learnt what we needed to learn in two days. We had to behave like non-Jews and to constantly be careful. It was not easy. It carried on for months."

Yehiel describes that at a certain point, his father began to feel uneasy; he felt that something was about to happen. Consequently, the family reunited and made their way to northern Italy. Once they reached the Swiss border, they hired smugglers to help them escape over the Alps into neutral Switzerland. After a treacherous climb, Yehiel and his immediate family made it over the border safely. In Switzerland, Yehiel and his siblings were placed in a *Kinderheim* run by the Joint Distribution Committee and UNRRA. According to Yehiel, life in Switzerland was not easy, as they were separated from their parents and their movements were restricted. After the war, Yehiel and his parents returned to their hometown, Fiume. But they decided not to remain there as it had fallen under Communist rule and the economic situation was dire. Yehiel made *aliya* in 1950, a year after his parents' *aliya*. Yehiel explains that "my mother, father, grandmother and aunt are all buried here in Israel . . . My grandmother was even blessed to see her great grandchildren . . . " All of Yehiel's immediate family survived the war, and moved to Israel.

Tamar

Tamar was born in Chernovitz, Romania, in 1936. In 1941, as the Russian army was retreating and before the Nazis had occupied Chernovitz, a power vacuum emerged during which riots broke out against the Jews. During that period, Tamar's sister, who was ill with dysentery at that time, died, as the family was unable to get her medical assistance. During the *Shiva*, Tamar recalls that rioters invaded their home and threatened to kill her grandfather on the spot unless he handed over all the valuables in the house. Tamar remembers that "There was screaming and shouting and they shouted at my mother and *safta* and . . . terrible . . . and they begged them not to hang *saba*. They took what they could and left."

Tamar and her family, together with the rest of the Jews of Chernovitz, were expelled from their homes and deported to Transnistria. At the train station Tamar lost sight of her parents. She recalls that, "I walked and cried and a German or Romanian officer, I don't know who, came up to me and asked me 'Why are you crying?' Now that I think of it, it was probably a German. I probably spoke to him in German, because it was my mother tongue. I said to him: 'I have lost my parents'. He took my hand and we walked the whole length of the platform . . . for a long time, back and forth looking for my parents . . . I remembered which direction we had walked in and . . . I found my parents. He brought me to my parents . . . do you see that! You know that sometimes . . . sometimes miracles do happen to people."

Tamar and her family were loaded onto the trains and traveled to Mogilev. When they arrived there, they were forced to run for kilometers in the snow. During the ordeal, Tamar remembers her father turning to her mother saying: " 'Now we are leaving the line' . . . My parents understood that they were leading us to our deaths . . . My parents decided to escape with a little girl. I was a little girl."

Tamar, together with her parents, spent the next few years running and hiding from the Nazis. They battled against hunger and disease, living under the constant threat that at any moment they could be betrayed and handed over to the Nazis. They managed to survive through the good will of strangers, and always managed to flee immediately at the first signs of danger. After the war, Tamar and her family made their way back to Chernovitz. When Chernovitz was taken over by the Communists and the factories began to be expropriated, Tamar's father decided that the time had come to leave once again. They then made their way to Bucharest where Tamar's uncle lived. Tamar explains, "We arrived in Bucharest and we stayed at my uncle's and after a period of time we got permission to make *aliya* to Israel."

Tamar and her parents arrived in Israel in the early 1950s, where they struggled together with a new language and in a difficult economic climate. Tamar explains that she had a difficult absorption, and she remembers that Israeli society was not particularly welcoming or empathetic to Holocaust survivors. Tamar married a *sabra* at an early age and had two children. Her dream was to study at university, but she was unable to do so because of the difficult economic situation in which the young couple found themselves. Unfortunately, her economic situation became even more strained when her husband passed away whilst her children were young and she was faced with the challenge of bringing them up alone, as a single parent. She worked to support them and, later on, remarried. Tamar has five grandchildren whom she describes as 'unusually talented'. Tamar seems to have found some security and comfort in her later years. She managed to fulfill her dream of studying at university. She explains, "I pounced on my studies like a hungry person. It was very important for me to study . . . It was something that was even more important to me than . . . a million dollars . . . I remember when I received my BA certificate it was if I had received a million dollars . . . an inheritance was not important to me like that . . . it was something . . . it was an achievement for me . . . it was big for me. In light of all the effort, all the history . . . this was what I saw as my greatest achievement."

Ruth

Ruth is Yehiel's younger sister. Born in 1938, she was five years old when Italy was invaded by the Nazis. Ruth explains that because she was very young during the war, she hardly remembers her experiences. She does, however, have flashes of memories, which relate to key episodes. Ruth nevertheless 'knows' her story as her brother Yehiel remembers almost everything and provides Ruth with 'missing details'.

Ruth is able to remember significant moments – moments when her reality was abruptly disrupted. "I remember when we were in hiding, us little cousins were playing together . . . because we were a few families of cousins together, and we exchanged shoes. I don't know what kind of game it was, but as children we played this game. And suddenly our parents came to fetch us – now I know, afterwards . . . I knew from the history my brother told me, because we had to flee because the . . . Germans knew that we were there and they were supposed to come and take us – so we had to flee and they came to fetch us very quickly. They were in a real hurry, and . . . I didn't have time to exchange back my shoes. So I remained with my cousin's shoes on, and he stayed with my shoes. I remember that my father was angry at me because my shoes were new and his shoes were old and had holes in the soles, and . . . we had a long way to go with these shoes. My shoes ended up in Auschwitz. That was the last time I saw that cousin of mine. This episode of exchanging shoes and of being fetched and taken, I remember." Throughout her narrative, Ruth refers to the final destination of her shoes. Ruth does not feel that she suffered particularly during the war, yet she is deeply affected by the 'randomness' of her survival.

Ruth's narrative is characteristic of the narrative of a young child survivor, as her memories are fragmented. She has strong memories of smells, tastes, and emotional responses. She recalls, "I'll never, never forget it. It's very vivid in my memory, I remember it very well . . . and the sound of the sirens, I was petrified of it. My mother said afterwards that I would go out of my mind when I heard sirens. I remember . . . when my father in one of the hiding places . . . shaved his beard. My father had a very Jewish face . . . We were outside playing, the children, and my mother and father called us in – they were laughing – they thought that it was a funny thing and I came in and I saw my father without his beard. He didn't have a real big beard, he had a little goatie, and I burst out crying." Ruth does not explain or understand her response. Previous research suggests that during the war, very small children often did not comprehend their new reality, which was constantly disrupted. Yolanda Gampel confirms that the narratives of child survivors are imbued with a feeling of how, in an instant, the world changed from being ordered and comprehensible to a new world of total chaos.[29]

Most of Ruth's narrative is centered on her *aliya* to Israel and her experiences as a new immigrant. She explains that most of her memories are from then as, "In Israel, I must say, maybe because I was older already and I remembered . . . I felt more." Ruth describes her immigration and absorption into Israeli society as particularly difficult. Her difficulties were not necessarily related to her traumatic past and her identity as a survivor, but rather are testimony to the difficulties experienced by immigrant youth. Ruth explains that in Israel she felt 'different', something she had rarely felt in Italy, even during and after the war. In the *Aliyat Hanoar* institution she felt like an outsider, especially because no one spoke Italian and her Hebrew was not good enough to communicate with other children.

Ruth says that her most challenging times were her school years. "When I went to school, I felt very much an outsider . . . although I spoke Hebrew, but I went to a school, to *Horev,* which was a very snobby school . . . they had been here many years and I felt very much an outsider. Also . . . my clothes were different . . . and maybe it's not true, but I felt then that I am poor and they are rich. Maybe because they were established already in Israel. Now, when I think back and I know these friends, I don't think they were all rich, but that was the feeling that I had. Also, they all lived in Rehavia. I lived in the suburbs, far away . . . so, at the beginning I felt very much an outsider. I never forget . . . a girl that today is my best friend, *really* my best friend. She said once, without thinking, that her mother said that she should never marry a . . . Holocaust refugee, because 'they all have problems'. I suppose things that children feel also when they come now from Russia, and so on. I felt that my parents were different, and I was ashamed of my parents. You know, because they didn't speak the language, and they weren't professors and doctors and so on. But that didn't last too long . . . "

Ruth's narrative is one that relates the "typical" difficulties that immigrant children have in socializing into a new country and into a different youth culture. Ruth is able to recognize this phenomenon when she makes the connection between her experiences as an immigrant and the experiences of Russian *olim* today. However, despite the initial difficulties, Ruth integrated very quickly into Israeli society; she married a *sabra,* and throughout her life no one ever knew that she was a child survivor as she had successfully camouflaged her past. Yet, her experiences during her first years in Israel continue to exist in painful memory.

Einsatzgruppen "Most of you know what it is like to see 100 corpses side by side, or 500 or 1000. To have stood fast through this and – except for cases of human weakness – to have stayed decent that has made us hard . . . All in all, however, we can say that we have carried out this most difficult of tasks in a spirit of love for our people. And we have suffered no harm to our inner being, our soul, our character . . . " Heinrich Himmler, from a "Speech by Himmler before Senior SS Officers in Ponzan", October 4, 1943.[50]

Dina

Dina was seven years old when the war broke out in Vilna. Her earliest memories of home are ones of music and song, as her family were professional musicians, her home a concert hall. In the early stages of the war, Dina's father was deported to Siberia and Dina's mother pleaded with the Soviet authorities to allow her and her family to join their father, but her request was denied. Thus, Dina, her mother, and two brothers were moved into the Vilna ghetto with the rest of the Vilna Jewish community. Dina is unsure as to how long they lived in the ghetto. She remembers that she was too young to work and instead had to stay at home all day. She describes 'her job' as making sure the Nazis did not take her away.

Dina and her family were hiding in a small cellar during one of the *aktionen*. Dina describes how the Nazis used dogs to find Jews who were in hiding. The dogs sniffed Dina and her family out of their hiding place, and they were led out onto the street to join crowds of Jews, waiting to be transported to an unknown work destination. As they reached the street, Dina was separated from her mother and brother. She walked with her grandmother, aunt, and second brother through the night until they reached the forest of Ponar. Dina describes a living hell as she watched the Jews of Vilna get undressed, line up in rows of ten, and then be shot falling into open pits. Then Dina's turn arrived and she recalls that, "There was our pit and a pit for the men. My brother was there and I saw him there, and that's how we parted. He was in another pit. It seems to me that I was amongst the last, because when I fell into the pit I was not at the bottom. The pit was full of people, to the top. When I fell into the pit, I sat up and saw what was there." Dina had been wounded in the leg, but had managed to stay alive by sitting up in the pit and not suffocating under the bodies. As darkness fell, she began to hear voices of people who were still alive. A woman who had also survived, called out to her to see if she was still alive and when darkness fell, the two of them climbed their way out of the pit and started running. They had no idea where to go, but kept running until the morning when they managed to find a village. No one was prepared to shelter them there. They eventually came across an isolated property and the woman agreed to take them in. Yet, she was only prepared to shelter Dina as she had been wounded in the leg. The woman directed the other survivor to a labor camp in the region, where other Jews were working. Dina was not able to stay with the woman for very long and, as soon as she could walk, she began to wander the countryside in search of food and shelter. This is how Dina survived the next three years; she took on a Christian name and spent the war years struggling on her own to survive. Her narrative of the war is one that screams of loneliness and vulnerability, which was only exacerbated after liberation. At the end of the war, Dina returned to Vilna in the hope of finding some of her relatives. Yet, no one returned. She explains how she sat in the synagogue, in a corner, waiting for someone to arrive, yet no one ever did, and she was left completely alone. Individual families took it upon themselves to take care of her, but they were unable to do this on a permanent basis. After some time the trauma of her experiences during the war began to affect her physically, eventually paralyzing one half of her body. Whilst in hospital, she met two young Jews, who took her under their wing and helped nurse her back to health. Once she had recovered, Dina decided she wanted to study and went to live in an orphanage in Vilna where she began to study and rebuild her life. Around this time she received word that her father was still alive and they began to correspond with each other. After graduating from high school, Dina married and had two children. The couple decided to leave Lithuania and make *aliya*. Delayed because of immigration restrictions, Dina and her family finally arrived in Israel in 1960.

Dina's story was especially difficult for her to tell and me to listen to. She found it hard to remember details of names and places, and there was no one around her who was able to validate the memories of the seven-year old child who had escaped death so narrowly. As Dina began telling about her experience at Ponar, she became increasingly anxious, and began reliving the experience. She breathed heavily, rubbed her hands roughly together, and rocked back and forth as she spoke. It was clear that she was pained by the experience of retelling, yet continued despite the difficulties. As interviewer, I felt responsible for her having to go through the anguish of remembering and visiting the painful past. Perhaps the most remarkable aspect of the interview is that Dina today is a warm, positive, happy woman. She has an amazing spirit and zest for life despite the horror she experienced as a young child.

In an interview with Eliezer, I asked him what motivated him to write a book about his experiences after decades of silence, to which he replied, "You are a young girl . . . (laughs) Look, first, man is complicated, at least I am. If you ask me who I am, I will tell you that I don't know. I am the strangest person that I know. Usually after talking to you for a few months, I can get to know you. I don't have the ability to know myself." Each individual behaves and responds in a particular way, sometimes conscious and sometimes not. Therefore, the explanations of the narratives to be presented in the chapters that follow cannot explore and describe all the elements behind each individual's 'silence and retelling'. Nevertheless, I hope that this work as a whole will contribute to the beginning of our understanding these processes.

The Protagonists

Found their voices	Resistant voices	Always spoken	Retreat away from specch
Dina	Shlomo	Kalman	Rachel
Yafe	Michal	Yitzchak	Sara
Ehud	Yaacov		
Yehiel	Eliezer		
Ruth	Avivit		
Rivka	David		
Ariala			
Naomi			
Shalom			
Noah			
Tamar			

Hidden Child Survivors Who Have Found Their Voice

Of the twenty-one child survivors included in this work, nineteen had chosen to remain silent for most of their adult lives about their experiences during the war. Their silence had not always been absolute, as some did share their experiences with significant others. Yet, generally, they did all that they could to hide their traumatic pasts from the outside world, suppressing and denying their identity as survivors. However, in the last few years, eleven of these individuals have begun to speak about their pasts openly and to identify publicly as child survivors. Interestingly, what characterizes this group is that the vast majority of them had survived the war in hiding, a survival strategy that itself demanded silence.

Silence as a Tool for Survival During the War

The intention of the Nazis was to annihilate European Jewry. Thus the Jewish child, the biological continuity of the Jewish people, was marked for elimination. In order to escape Nazi persecution, Jewish children had to be hidden. They were hidden either before deportation to concentration and death camps, or were smuggled into the camps and hidden. They were either hidden physically, or had their Jewish identity hidden. In most cases, the children could not survive on their own and were thus dependent upon adults for protection. Adults were responsible for their physical as well as emotional survival. Under Nazi occupation, Jews attempted to escape the ghettos, mass executions or deportations to death camps by hiding amongst the non-Jewish population. Only rarely could an entire family make an illegal move to the Christian world, as it was too risky to hide large groups of Jews. Some family members lacked the physical strength and language skills required for concealment in the 'forbidden world'. Others had no possibility of finding refuge or lacked the will and determination to try. Some had no idea of their fate and did not imagine there was any reason to part from their loved ones. Some decided that they would rather die together than attempt to survive apart. It must be emphasized that children were not the ones who made the decision to go into hiding. They had the decision made for them. Sometimes parents had disappeared and the children found themselves in a new, unrecognizable reality in which they had to fend for themselves. In other cases, the parents had explained the situation and the reason for their decision to seek refuge – for the family, or only for the children. Obviously, the age of the child at the time determined how much the child understood about his or her new reality.

Once the family had made the decision to hide amongst the non-Jewish population and had succeeded in escaping and finding shelter, they had to rely completely on the protection of their Christian rescuers. These were either private individuals or people connected to organizations. Most countries, among them Belgium, Holland and Poland, had special sections of the underground that were devoted to saving Jewish children. Frequently, both Jews and Christians ran these sections. Religious institutions, including churches, monasteries and orphanages, were also involved, acting independently in tandem with the underground; sometimes no arrangements were made, and the child simply went into hiding. In these cases, the child needed to be old enough to take care of him/herself. Children who arranged their own hiding had to spend the war years on the run, moving from place to place and constantly maintaining an existence outside of the law or, alternatively, by obtaining false papers, simply living and working illegally, 'passing' as a Gentile."[1]

Debórah Dwork writes that, "To go into hiding meant that all, or nearly all ties with society were severed. Whether in an attic in the city or a warren in the forest, the child was literally hidden from the mortal danger the rest of the world represented."[2] Children who had typically Jewish features were forced to hide physically. Nechama Tec, a hidden child survivor, writes that whilst she was in hiding, "our daily existence was tied to two components: giving up our Jewish identity and silence. Giving up our Jewish identity meant becoming someone else. The better we played the role, the safer we were. Sometimes we forgot who we were. Though helpful, this was emotionally costly. For many of us, giving up our true identity created an emotional void and made us feel anxious that we would never recapture our past. We also felt ashamed for giving up what had been cherished by our parents . . . We had to be silent about our past, present and future. We often had to listen to anti-

Semitic remarks in silence. Silence became deeply ingrained in all hidden children."[3] Robert Krell explains that silence continued to dominate the emotional and cognitive world of child survivors long after their liberation. He writes, "Of all voices from the Holocaust, ours has remained the most silent and the least noticed. For good reason. Many of us were raised in silence, enveloped in silence. A child not noticed might survive. We could not draw attention to ourselves, not in that world. In this world too, silence remains a companion of sorts. After the war we were discouraged to speak of it. In the interest of our future, mostly well-meaning persons unintentionally silenced us."[4] Thus, after liberation, hidden child survivors entered into another phase of silence – 'secondary silencing'.

After the War: Secondary Silencing

This second period of silence is connected to six issues: During the war in order to hide one's Jewish identity, children **learned silence** as a survival technique, a behavior that was transferred to their post-war environment. For many children, their **age at the time of persecution** was particularly important as in many instances the ability to speak about the past was dependent on the child survivor's ability to recall the events. Some child survivors were deterred from speaking because of the **pain involved in remembering** their traumatic past and their lost loved ones. Most significantly, many hidden child survivors felt that they did not have a story to tell because of the **hierarchy of suffering** that was established in the post-war environment, which validated to a greater or lesser degree the traumatic nature of different types of experience. Particularly powerful was the **conspiracy of silence** that was imposed both externally and internally whereby many well meaning adults felt that by remembering the past the children would be unable to adjust to their new lives. After the war, child survivors desperately tried to find a place of **belonging**. Thus, they themselves chose to remain silent as they feared that telling would hinder their absorption and integration. In their attempt to rebuild their lives many child survivors, like adult survivors, felt that they needed to pour their energies into rebuilding a new life and into remembering and mourning their lives before the war.

Learned Silence

The fear of exposure and the commitment to silence, learned and internalized during the war, continued to haunt the children even after liberation. Silence was 'learned' during the war and was thus difficult to 'unlearn'. It continued to dominate their emotional and cognitive world, especially in relation to their willingness and ability to speak about their pasts. Judith Kestenberg's research asserts that the experiences of children during the war are the most significant factor in their post-war adaptation. Ehud, a hidden child survivor I interviewed, wrote that for the hidden child survivor, "the deep scars created during formative years were to leave an enduring mark on his personality."[5]

Susan Zuccotti, in her book *The Holocaust, The French and the Jews*, writes that "In the historical reality of the Holocaust in France, especially as it applied to native Jews, silence was perhaps the most important factor in survival. In a situation in which Jews were not usually physically identifiable as such and where anti-Jewish police units were understaffed, Jews with false papers and ration cards could often survive by living quietly and taking occasional jobs. They needed, in most cases, one or two active benefactors, but they also equally required the passive goodwill of the neighbors who inevitably knew they were outsiders."[6]

Hiding with her family in an isolated French village throughout the war, Rachel was forced to live in silence for an extended period of time in order to survive. Even as a young child, four years old when the war broke out, Rachel understood the importance of silence, and the importance of her own behavior in saving her as well as her family's lives. Thus, for Rachel, memories from the war years are dominated by her experience of silence and being silenced, an experience which continued to pervade her life even after her liberation and throughout her adult years. Rachel presented this issue right at the beginning of her interview: "My personality is a talkative one. During the war, it was important to keep quiet. For me, keeping quiet did not exist. Therefore, what I internalized during the war years was the more I didn't exist, the better. I did not have wants. I was satisfied with what I had. What I remember about myself, and that other people told me, was that I cried a lot. That was the only way that I was allowed to express myself. That is what I did. It's a silence, but it's a roaring silence and it hurt me tremendously. From the moment [we were hidden] I had to keep silent because who knows, perhaps I would reveal something . . . and I have very painful memories from that. Once the French police came and asked me questions. I was small and I was already used to not saying things. If they forced me to speak, I would say very vague things . . . and that is a very, very painful memory, as after they left they came back again, but this time with my father between them. I thought they had caught him. I felt terribly guilt, as if I had given him away. It was very difficult. Till this day, it stirs something very painful in me. It was as if it wasn't enough that I controlled my speech . . . As a child, that silence was very difficult."

Silence may have helped to enable Jewish children to survive physically, yet, as Rachel explains, the years of silence wounded her emotionally. According to Rachel, silence went against her natural inclination. She describes herself as having a naturally 'talkative personality', and silence helped her to 'not exist'. Realizing the danger of speech, Rachel learned to express her feelings non-verbally, through her tears. Tears would not betray her identity, but would help her express her sadness and frustration. Thus, it is hardly surprising that Rachel's most precious memories of her experiences during the war were those times when she was able to break the silence, and speak freely to the trees, the sky and the birds, to express who she was, to reclaim her identity, her self.

"And in the forest I knew you could talk out loud. So, I would begin to speak. They used to call me 'kettle'; there was a Yiddish expression: 'the kettle begins to boil' . . . when I was in those places, I would speak non-stop. I remember it as an experience. If you ask what was good then – that was the only thing. It was good, because finally I had freedom. Something open, something safe. Because usually you had to keep quiet. But here I could talk about all sorts of nonsense, about all sorts of things. What could I talk about? But I could speak. That was joy for me."

Unlike Rachel, who was hidden throughout the war with her parents, Ariala was in hiding alone. Placed into hiding with a rabid anti-Semite who was not aware of her Jewish identity, Ariala not only had to hide her Jewish identity from the villagers, her schoolmates and teachers, but also from her rescuer – "*grandmère*". Ariala explains, "*Grandmère* did not know who I was, who my parents were, what my religion was. She did not know anything. She didn't ask anything either. I was an unwanted child; it was as if I had no past. And I don't tell her anything. Why not? I don't know."

Ariala quickly learned to conceal her Jewish identity from *grandmère* as, "There are two things that *grandmère* hates. She hates other people's children and she hates Jews. *Grandmère* says to me that the First World War was because of the Jews and *grandmère* says that the World War II was because of the Jews. *Grandmère* says to me that if there is suffering, it is because of the Jews, and she even says that when *grandpère* has asthma, it's because of the Jews. Why? Because the Jews steal the Catholic's medicine, so that's why the situation is very difficult, because of the Jews. So I was very afraid that *grandmère* would find out that I was Jewish. I know that I am Jewish, but I don't say anything, and everything that *grandmère* says, I believe. First, I don't have a family, I only have *grandmere* and everything that she says I want to be true and I want her to love me. Thus, everything that she says, I agree with. Besides that, everything that I studied in church, and what was written in the books, was exactly the same idea. They said that the Jews killed Jesus. The boy [Jesus] who so loved? So, *grandmère* was right. The Jews are really bad, so I hate Jews."[7]

Flora Hogman, who researched the experience of Jewish children in hiding, wrote that, for the child in hiding, identification with their biological parents was shattered, at least temporarily, "as identifications with new, different models in whom these children placed their trust, was formed . . . The learning that took place was not subject to their own choice but imposed on these children as a means to be safe and survive."[8] Thus Ariala identified with *grandmère*, seeing her as a 'maternal figure' because she was so reliant upon her, even if it meant internalizing *grandmère's* anti-Semitic ideas – themselves an attack on her own identity and her past. This is a painful testimony in that it highlights the degree to which children had no defenses against the hostile anti-Semitic environment, especially when they were reliant upon these people for their survival. Rationally, the anti-Semitic remarks and attitudes made sense to the children – they were suffering and thus were being punished for their sins.

Ariala also became increasingly drawn to Christianity as the Christian world and the church experience provided the sense of protection and physical safety for those children who had been separated from their families and lost the experience of a stable home. Particularly powerful for Ariala was the figure of Jesus, whom she identified with and saw as a protector.

Accordingly, Ariala realized that she was completely dependent on her *grandmère* for her physical and emotional security, and therefore dared not reveal her Jewish identity. Ariala was not only emotionally abused, but also physically abused by *grandmère*. She recalls regular beatings, as she became the victim of *grandmère's* rage. Thus Ariala learned compliance and silence, tools which were essential for her survival. Beyond physical survival, Ariala, as a young child, also had a strong need to be loved. No matter how cruel her caretaker was, she constantly tried to please *grandmère* and comply with her demands. She suffered in silence in order to survive physically and emotionally. Judith Herman explains that, in order to survive, the abused child needs to maintain an attachment to their caretaker.

Even after the war had ended, Ariala remained dependent upon *grandmère's* care and protection. For so many hidden child survivors, liberation did not always signify the end of their hiding or a changed or new reality as they continued to remain in their rescuers' homes. It was only after Ariala's father reappeared to claim her that she was able to emerge from hiding, and reclaim her identity. In her narrative, Ariala dramatically describes the moment when her 'shameful secret' was revealed to *grandmère*.

"*Grandmère* was running around the house, wanting to give my father food and drink. 'Mr. Shenkar, Mr. Shenkar', and she said to him: 'Mr. Shenkar, do you know you have a very sweet daughter. She is not such a good student at school, but she is the best at church'. Father listened and afterwards he said: 'Paulette, you won't be going back to church, because we are Jews'. At that moment, I preferred to return to the cellar with all the rats rather than let *grandmère* hear that we are Jews. For so many years, I had kept the secret . . . I had kept that secret for all those years, in order to be with *grandmère*, to hate Jews, and suddenly father, in front of everyone, her grandchild, and his parents who were also there, everyone hears that I am a Jew and my father is a Jew. I was so afraid. I grab father by the neck and say to him: 'Take me home. I don't want to stay here any longer. I am scared, I am scared'. And father said: 'What's there to be scared about? The war is over, and your father is here, why be scared?' I couldn't explain anything and I couldn't even explain anything to myself. After that, I don't remember what happened when *grandmère* heard that, I don't remember anything. But we went home."

The silence around Ariala's Jewish identity was broken in a threatening environment, in *grandmère's* home. It is telling that Ariala does not remember anything more after this dramatic episode. Her fear at that moment must have been so overwhelming that she forgot what transpired subsequently. This may be understood as a traumatic reaction, or 'psychogenic amnesia' a temporary loss of memory precipitated by a psychological trauma. When the amnesia is limited to a certain event, "it often serves the purpose of temporary escape from an intolerable situation."[9] Ariala appears to have suffered 'limited amnesia' around this episode, which highlights the emotional intensity of it.

As a result of these traumatic experiences, feelings of fear and vulnerability surrounding her Jewish identity continued for many years after the war. These feelings were reinforced even further after she discovered what had happened to the Jews during the *Shoah*. She explains that "it was very difficult with *grandmère*, but at her house there were no gas chambers; there was no torture; no crematorium. There were no such things. There was suffering that I could endure, but here [in her home after the war] it was too much for me, and I didn't know how to deal with it." Ariala chose to deal with the past by rejecting her Jewishness and ignoring her Jewish identity, thereby continuing to ensure her survival through silence. She was even attracted to her husband, a child survivor himself, because he had also rejected Judaism and Jews. Ariala, on one level, had internalized *grandmère's* anti-Semitism, but she had also internalized the silence around her identity. In her post-war environment, that same silence was the only way Ariala could cope with her survival and build a 'normal life', free of images of persecution, death, and destruction. By continuing to hide she felt that she was insulating herself from the Jewish fate.

As seen from Ariala's experience, children in hiding were not always cared for in a loving and nurturing environment. Their rescuers were sometimes cruel and demanding, and even physically and sexually abusive. Debórah Dwork suggests that, "Perhaps inevitably in such a situation of control and dependency, aggression was manifested sexually."[10] In the face of such abuse, child survivors remained silent both during and after the war. Yafe is a child survivor who was sexually harassed during the war. She explains that whilst protected by the woman rescuer, the husband threatened her. "The woman was a good woman, but her husband was not good. What happened? I was the only girl there. There were three other children. Everyone was younger than me. They did not have to work. Every time the woman was not at home, he tried to take advantage of me sexually. He would sit me down, and would stroke and hug me. He would sit me down on his sexual organ. When I would say to him: 'I will tell grandmother' . . . I called them grandmother and grandfather . . . he would laugh . . . 'you're going to tell grandmother . . . I have a greater weapon . . . I will tell on you to the Germans'. Thus, I had to keep quiet. I was lucky in that nothing really happened. But I saw his sexual organ . . . I did not tell my husband about it . . . only a few years ago. One night, in the middle of the night, I woke up and began to cry. I told him about it. It was recently, perhaps five years ago. And, he said to me: 'But it wasn't your fault. Nothing happened. I love you'. This had always been a secret, which I had not told anyone. Now I am not afraid to tell it."

In her narrative, Yafe tells that in order to survive during the war, she had to keep two secrets: that she was a Jewish child, and that she was being sexually harassed. Like all of these 'hidden children', she continued to remain silent about these experiences after the war and for most of her adult life. Yet, even after she had broken the silence around her past, she continued to hide her experiences of sexual harassment, as she 'was scared' to tell. Yafe does not explicitly state why she has been scared to talk about these specific incidents, yet it seems that her fear of exposure continued to be as real then as it had been in the past. Yafe's silence was perhaps built upon the 'shame' associated with sexual harassment and abuse generally – a shame which continues till today. Judith Herman explains, "The real conditions of women's lives were hidden in the sphere of the personal, in private life. The cherished value of privacy created a powerful barrier to consciousness and rendered women's reality as practically invisible. To speak about experiences in sexual or domestic life was to invite public humiliation, ridicule, and disbelief. Women were silenced by fear and shame . . . "[11] Yafe also lives within a religious community, which may have made it more difficult for her to share this piece of her story. Furthermore, researchers have noted that the issue of sexual harassment during the *Shoah* has been a silent issue. Only with the examination of the fate and experience of Jewish women as a distinct victimized group during the Holocaust have these 'private experiences' of women during that time entered public consciousness and become audible.[12] Thus, this widened academic discourse may also have encouraged Yafe to speak about her experiences. For forty years, Yafe was unable to find a forum in which to retell her story, to express her pain; her victimization was thereby sustained for many decades even after the *Shoah* had ended. Today, in an environment which discusses issues of women's suffering and exploitation more openly, Yafe feels more confident to speak about her own 'private' experiences.

Yafe's narrative is a clear example of how the narrator selects what will be revealed and what will remain hidden in their narration. The narrative is not a complete presentation of the individual's life, but rather a selection of episodes and stories. Furthermore, Yafe's narrative illustrates that for some survivors, the process of retelling may take many years, their stories unfolding as they gain the confidence and courage to relate different aspects of their experience.

Age during the war – Too young to remember?

Researchers have pointed to the age of the persecuted child as an important factor in determining their post-war adjustment. My research has found that the age of the child survivor is also significant in relation to their memory of the events, and in determining how the child relates to and articulates their past. Ruth, Rivka, Tamar, Rachel and Noah were all under the age of five when the war began. All explain that they do not remember the war clearly, only in fragments.

Ruth, born in 1938, was five years old when Italy was occupied by Nazi Germany. In her narrative, Ruth explains that due to her young age, she has no recollection of the first few years of the war. Rather her memory of the period is made up of fragments, which are organized around specific, emotive memories. Not only are her memories fragmented, but she is also unsure of the source of them. She explains, "I remember very vaguely and I also have very special memories. I am also not sure whether I really remember, or whether I think that I remember because I was told this story so many times that . . . I think that I can remember. But, I still think that I remember . . . you know, certain special things." Ruth and her entire family survived the war and she therefore had access to her story through the memories of others.

When I asked Ruth if this disturbed her, that she relied heavily on her brother's memory in recalling her own experiences of the war, she responded: "No. I was little . . . You can't expect a very young child to remember. I remember places. Yes, I went there and I remembered the places, but not as much as he [her brother] would remember. He was double . . . double my years then, which is a lot. I was 5, he was 10, so that's a big difference. And . . . no, on the contrary . . . He remembered dates . . . and he was also the first-born of the family, so he was with my father and he was the boy and he went to the synagogue more, so it's quite logical that he remembers better."

Over the years, Yehiel, Ruth's brother, has been much more vocal about the past than Ruth has. This is clearly related to their ages during the war and their ability to remember. Furthermore, the socio-cultural context has also played an important role in determining who is heard. As a result of the phenomenon whereby survivors have been cast as 'witnesses' to the tragedy and are invited to give accounts of their stories, those survivors who could provide 'testimony' in a chronological, comprehensive manner would be 'heard' more than those who had fragmented memories of their past. Ruth's interview demonstrates this phenomenon: She could not provide the testimony, so she could not be heard. On the subject of giving testimony at Yad Vashem, Ruth replied that she had never done so, "because my brother has done it and it's the same story . . . " Even today, Ruth does not always give testimony by herself. She explains, "There was a time when they asked my brother to say a few words at Yad Vashem about our *kehilla* in Fiume. Again, because he doesn't speak English and they were an English-speaking group, I came. He was there together with me, and he helped me write whatever I wanted to say about all these institutions in the *kehilla*. With my brother, mainly I think about history. The historical facts, and the dates, that he remembers and I don't. In addition, I asked him, 'Who helped this, and was this and who was that'." Ruth's narrative provides a clear example of how the individual constructs their personal memory and identity through the collective.

Likewise, in her narrative, Rivka explains that she was too young to remember. Furthermore, she was not able to glean any information from her mother, as it was too difficult for her mother to speak about her experiences. When I asked Rivka if she has any recollection of being separated from her parents during the war, she responded: "My younger brother was the first to go, and after some time I went.

Therefore, I had seen his separation. [After the war] We didn't ask questions, so I can't really tell you. I can't ask my mother about it because it was traumatic for her. She sent me away without knowing if she would see me the next day. Therefore, I cannot ask her how I reacted then. Do you understand me?"

Similarly, Rachel, who was four when the war broke out in France, does not have a chronological memory of the war itself. She explains, "Because I was young, my memories from the war are like flashes. There are small things. It's like drawings, like dots. My *Shoah* is almost like that. A lot of small things and that is, for me, the *Shoah*. It could be connected to food, to clothes, to all sorts of things." Indeed, Rachel's memories are connected to strong visual images, which in turn are connected strong feelings and emotions. Paul Valent explains that, "for us younger child survivors who remember primarily through the body, through emotions, 'atmosphere feels'."[13]

All these narratives reinforce the accepted notion that there are innate age limitations on the capacity to remember. Paul Valent points out that children between four and six remember only some images of childhood. The youngest children, either born just preceding or at the outbreak of the war, have "almost no visual memories at all of their traumatic childhoods. What memories they had were little fragments. Often the only memories were in the nature of seemingly irrational feelings and behavioral impulses."[14] Even though their vague memories of the past may have inhibited their retelling, when listening to child survivors' narratives, it is clear that their fragments of memory are nevertheless significant and meaningful. In many cases, they represent dramatic moments around which the rest of their narratives are organized. It seems that even if these memories have not been articulated, they have remained in the minds of these child survivors. Often the first "remembered memory represents an existence in nutshell."[15] In the case of child survivors who were relatively young during the war, and who find it difficult to remember the details of their past, it appears that the few fragments of memory that they do have of those years have made a major impact on the way they relate to their pasts and their lives.

Ehud's narrative differs greatly from the narratives of those child survivors presented previously. Despite his young age at the outbreak of the war, Ehud has a rich and detailed memory of his war-time experiences. However, Ehud explains, despite his strong memories the adult world did not trust his memory. In his words, "Many child survivors were told by their caretakers or other adults: 'You were too young to remember'." He responds to this by saying, "In terms of memory, children are much less likely to forget than adults. Adults know the connections, they have a greater ability to remember and it's true that children usually forget. Sometimes they may forget even long periods, years and months that they have experienced. But the impact of specific events was very great. Perhaps they had an even stronger impact than they did on adults, because the child was not able to understand them. He was not able to make the connections of the same traumatic events that the adult was. Sometimes it made a bigger impact on the child, and remains more firmly embedded in the child's memory." Ehud argues that the war was such a disorganizing event in the child's life that it was almost impossible to forget.

Adults may have found it difficult to trust the memory of children, perhaps because it was too difficult to contain and believe their stories. Consequently, children who were 'not believed', remained silent about their past. In some cases children anticipated the disbelief. Ehud remarks that child survivors remained silent, "because we knew that we would not be understood and we suspected that we would not be believed." Thus, Ehud chose to remain silent about his past, not because he did not remember, but rather in response to his post-war environment.

The Pain of Remembering

Robert Krell remarks that the "older survivor possesses a memory of family and tradition, daily life and habits, the smells and the sounds of the past."[16] From the interviews that I conducted with older child survivors it was clear that their capacity to remember details and chronology was far greater than for the younger child survivors. Thus, the ability to remember is not the issue for older child survivors. The pain of remembering might be. Remembering is painful because it "releases previously frozen feelings and meanings."[17] Child survivors who were older also had memories of their lives before the war. For some, this brings comfort, as they are able to recollect a safe, nurturing world. For others, however, remembering their parents, siblings and homes is a painful exercise. The pain of remembering may act as a powerful inhibitor to retelling. Furthermore, it may also influence what is said, as sometimes the narration "selects *in* what is 'human' or 'redemptive' . . . it selects *out* what is unredeemed and traumatic."[18] One of the memories I found to be commonly selected out by child survivors is the memory of their murdered parents, especially the moment of separation. In the case of older child survivors, their age during the war, unlike younger survivors, does not account for their silence. Rather, I found that they explain their silence as a reaction to the pain of remembering and in relation to their post-war environment.

Hidden child survivors usually spent the war years in isolation with little or no knowledge of the fate of their families and friends or of the murder operations being conducted by the Nazis. Even if children were hidden in convents or orphanages, they usually did not know the identities of the other children, as secrecy was paramount for survival. Thus, many hidden children speak of their experiences during the war as lonely. Once the child survivors came out of hiding, and began to reunite with their families or meet other survivors, they discovered that they had not been alone in their suffering and heard for the first time about the fate and experiences of their loved ones. For those children who had spent the war years in hiding, they were shocked when learning about the existence of the concentration and death camps, and the fate of those they loved in these camps. Keilson argues that the 'post Holocaust' – the stage of returning to find what no longer existed[19] – was most traumatic for child survivors as it was then that many understood the irreversibility of what had happened, and that everything dear to them was perhaps lost forever. Rachel and Ariala, two children who survived the war in hiding, explain that it was at this point, at the 'post Holocaust' stage, that the *Shoah* began for them.

Ariala was eleven and a half years old when the war ended, and upon returning to her home in Paris after years of hiding, expected to find everything as she had left it. Throughout the war she had remembered her father's promise: "Once mother recuperates, she will be brought home." Thus, when Ariala was eventually brought home three years later, she expected to find her mother there, healthy and able to take care of her again. She explains, "This is my story. For me, the *Shoah* begins when I ask the question: 'Where is mother?' Until that moment, I had known that there had been a war. I didn't know that anything was happening to the Jews. I didn't know anything. I only knew that I was a very miserable girl, but I didn't know why. And that's it. But . . . the *Shoah* – then they didn't say *Shoah*, they said 'holocaust, 'genocide'. I hadn't heard anything about it. Suddenly the war is over, the Jews do not have to go out wearing that sign, that *Magen David*, but for me the *Shoah* had just begun . . . So father answered me, 'You don't have a mother anymore', and I asked: 'Where is mother?' and he said: 'Mother was murdered'. Still I couldn't grasp it. I was eleven and a half years old. Nevertheless, I was a big girl. I can't grasp it. Father said: 'it's better if you don't ask any more questions, because we don't have a family anymore' . . . And then I began to ask about everyone, giving all their names, the names of all my cousins, uncles, aunts and grandparents on both sides and the same word. 'Murdered, murdered, murdered'. And I don't know what was going on."

Not only did children have to confront the loss of their loved ones, but also the brutal way in which they had been murdered. Ariala explains, "So people began to return and come up to our house. They begin to tell their stories, and for the first time I heard about gas chambers, crematoria, punishments, death, fire, everything. I thought that they were mad." Thus, once the war was over, children were exposed to the knowledge of the hideous world of the camps and mass murder. These stories were so shocking that the hidden children felt that their own experiences paled into insignificance, which only reinforced their silence. The hidden children did not want to hear about the suffering of other children and adults in the camps, and at the same time adults did not want to hear about the suffering of the hidden children.

The Hierarchy of Suffering

Once survivors began to speak to one another about their experiences, individual stories were compared and judged and some became seen as more traumatic, others less so. This 'relativity of trauma' is referred to as the hierarchy of suffering, which validated to a greater or lesser degree the traumatic nature of different types of experience. Consequently, only those survivors with 'valid' traumatic experiences felt entitled to speak after the war. Eva Fogelman writes, "for many years after the war only survivors of ghettos and concentration camps were considered the 'legitimate' Holocaust survivors. Hidden children therefore did not identify themselves as such, nor did others perceive them as Holocaust survivors."[20] Individuals need recognition from their communities for the crucial development of their identity formation. "Denial of the significance of the Holocaust for hidden children thus resulted in unresolved 'identity confusion'"[21] for many. After the war, hidden child survivors found themselves at the bottom of the hierarchy of suffering, which is one of the reasons why so many of them chose to remain silent about their past.

Thus, Ariala's silence, which had begun during the war, continued in her post-war life. Once she returned home she found that adult survivors, including her own father, were not willing to hear about her experiences during the war. They insisted that she had 'been lucky during the war', that she had not been in a camp, and that she survived whilst the majority of children had died. She explains that, "I wanted to speak with my father about it, to tell him that even if I had not been in the camps, I was beaten and that it had been difficult for me too. I wanted to tell him, but my father said: 'Keep quiet, you could have been like Elianne; you also could have been in a camp, in a crematoria and everything'. Therefore, I kept quiet. I heard that I had been lucky. I had a problem because, on the one hand, everyone told me that I was lucky, and I knew that I was lucky, but on the other hand, I knew that I had suffered. It was shameful to have suffered. It was shameful for me to think that I had it hard. I felt that I was not like everyone else, so I closed, really locked my story away. It was like it was an embarrassment that I had not been in a ghetto or camps. So I closed my mouth."

Ariala's silence can be attributed to a hierarchy of suffering that was operative amongst survivors themselves, in their own sub-communities. Amongst adult survivors, and especially those who had lost their own children in the Holocaust, Ariala was unable to speak about her experiences of pain and suffering. They invalidated her trauma and made her feel guilty for the 'relatively good' experience that she had had. Because the child's trauma was de-legitimized, Sara Moskowitz and Robert Krell observed, "the child survivor eventually felt that he/she was the bearer of a shameful secret too terrible to talk about. This evoked earlier feelings of shame, further sapping the child's confidence, initiative, and freedom to act. The stance of the silent or 'silenced' victim was strengthened and the opportunity to reflect on his or her survival was stifled."[22]

Not only did the adult survivor community make Ariala feel guilty for having a relatively 'good' war-time experience, some of them made her feel guilty for having survived at all. Ariala explains: "The most difficult was amongst those people who had children like me who had been sent to the camps and had not returned. They had been killed. It was usually one parent and they knew what had happened to their children, and they returned and saw me alive. I remember one of them saying: 'Ah so you are here?' and I said: 'Yes, I am here', and he said: 'You don't know how lucky you are, you could have been like my children who were burnt in the crematorium'. Afterwards, I heard that that's what happened to my cousin, Elianne. Elianne's father also returned after the war. He really loved me before the war, and suddenly I see that he hates me. It's in his eyes, because I lived and his daughter died. He wasn't the only one. The women who came back from the camps, who had lost their children, they hated me. I felt guilty that I was alive, and to live with those thoughts was very difficult."

For many bereaved parents, Ariala's survival was unbearable. It reminded them of what they had lost, and brought to the fore the issue of whether they could have done more to save their children from their ghastly fate. Ariala's narrative is important in that it demonstrates the unwillingness of survivors to listen to stories of other survivors. Hidden child survivors did not want to hear about the death and destruction of the world of the camps, whilst adult survivors who had lost their own children were reluctant to hear the stories of children who had survived.

Ariala's narrative reflects the role that the adult-survivor community had in determining who had the right to claim a traumatic past and, consequently, who had the right to speak about their experiences. Ariala's post-war environment was instrumental in reinforcing her silence. Consequently, she never felt that she had the right to call herself a Holocaust survivor, nor talk about her suffering. Instead, Ariala translated her experiences during the *Shoah* into a narrative of loss – the loss of her family – but not one which ever told of her own personal suffering during the war.

This hierarchy of suffering, established by survivors themselves after the war, in turn shaped the collective discourse about the Holocaust. Those voices which represented the cultural ideals of the time were also more audible, and were equally instrumental in shaping collective memory. In an address to the 'First Gathering of Child Survivors of the Kovno ghetto', held in Israel in 2000, psychologist and child survivor Shlomo Breznitz argued that the public discourse around the Holocaust was dominated by the 'big stories', which were considered to be more traumatic than the 'little stories'. He explains that the experiences of children, or the 'little stories', could only surface and be heard once the "big stories had been heard or those survivors no longer remained to tell their stories." He argues that his own personal story, of hiding during the war, was 'minor' in comparison to the stories of others. Whilst hiding in a convent, he said, "we were hungry, but we were not dying of hunger."[23]

Shalom, who was smuggled out of the Kovno ghetto and placed in the care of non-Jews, also attributes his silence to the hierarchy of suffering. He explains that there were certain voices in Israeli society which dominated the public discourse. He explains that, "During that time in Israel, there were so many dramatic stories: Elie Wiesel, Katzetnik fainting in the Eichmann Trial. I have no dramas to tell. Mengele did not torture me; I did not go through the chimneys. I have nothing special to tell. I was not in a concentration camp." As mentioned before, the Eichmann Trial was instrumental in heightening Israeli consciousness to the *Shoah* in general, yet it too validated certain types of experiences over others, thereby institutionalizing a specific type of memory regarding the *Shoah*. Dalia Ofer argued that the trial glorified resistance even more, yet it also seems to have put the camp experience, specifically the Auschwitz experience, at the center of Holocaust memory. As Shalom explained, because of the trial, he felt excluded from the collective narrative. He did not feel that his story was dramatic, especially in comparison to the stories of those who had survived Auschwitz.

Anita Shapira's work supports Shalom's experience when she writes that the *Shoah* in Israel was related to in great terms, where certain icons of the *Shoah*, which claimed to represent the total experience, dominated the public imagination. There was no room in collective memory for those who had not experienced the 'massive' events, for the memories of the individual, for narratives of personal pain. This dynamic not only influenced the child survivors' tendency to remain silent, it also influenced their relationship to their past. Due to the imposed hierarchy of suffering, Shalom now believes that suffering is relative, and that he suffered less in comparison to others. He explains, "I really still think that what each survivor went through is relative, and they each have their own story. If he didn't have a unique story, he wouldn't be a survivor. Let's say that if he is a survivor, he had a unique story. Of course, each person who perished has a unique story too, but he cannot tell it. So, relatively, I did not have a unique story."

Whilst the hierarchy of suffering may have 'relativized' trauma and suffering for some child survivors, for others it completely negated their experiences. Ruth, in her interview, explains, "I didn't feel that I was a, um . . . how do you call it, *a survivor?* I always thought that a survivor was somebody that was in Auschwitz. Somebody who has been in Auschwitz is a survivor. I didn't consider myself a survivor of the Holocaust."

When she arrived in Israel, Ruth noted, "Who were the survivors? The Auschwitz survivors. They were the survivors. They were felt, they were noticed, and they were the survivors. They underwent such terrible sufferings that I myself thought what I went through was nothing by comparison to what they went through. I did not think about the fact that I could have been taken to Auschwitz at any given minute . . . I thought about what happened to me . . . I always felt that in comparison to what these Auschwitz survivors went through, what did I have to speak about? Being in a convent? Being in hiding? Going over the Alps by night? . . . It wasn't the tendency in those days . . . until quite recently . . . the tendency was to talk about horrors of Auschwitz and the camps."

In this extract, Ruth describes how in the years immediately after the war, the collective memory of the Holocaust was built around the experience of camp survivors, specifically Auschwitz survivors. They were the 'dominant voices'; they were recognized as survivors, because, as she explains, "they had the mark."[24] As a young girl growing up in a highly charged and emotional environment, Ruth internalized the dominant messages in Israeli collective memory, which in turn defined her own relationship to her past and her identity as a survivor. Interestingly, Ruth identifies the survivors as those who survived the camps and does not mention the partisans and resistance fighters. Perhaps for her, the victims or the survivors of the *Shoah* are those who survived the camps, and the resistance fighters are the heroes of the period.

Both Ruth and Rivka explain that after listening to the stories of other survivors, they do not feel morally entitled to claim a similar experience. Rivka believes that there is an objective, qualitative difference between her experiences during the war and the experiences of others. She argues, "There was the issue of having a lot of parents, we were passed around . . . but we didn't see death in the streets. I do not know what that is, thank G-d. I have one trauma, but I don't have those kinds of traumas. Do you understand? And thank G-d, in that respect I didn't experience it . . . but my trauma was that I was passed between many families." For some hidden child survivors, what differentiates their trauma from the trauma of others is that they did not witness the atrocities of the Holocaust, that despite their own experiences of vulnerability, fear and powerlessness, they did not witness death and are thus not haunted by images of death and destruction. These narratives suggest that for some hidden children, the hierarchy of suffering is also connected to the degree of witnessing, or proximity to death, irrespective of the individuals' personal pain, suffering and loss during the war. The potency of the hierarchy of suffering suggests that whilst trauma was experienced internally, after the war it was defined and evaluated externally.

The Conspiracy of Silence

Whilst the hierarchy of suffering was established amongst the survivors themselves and reinforced by collective memory, the "conspiracy of silence,"[25] a concept defined by Yael Danieli, was constructed by those individuals who did not experience the *Shoah*, around the stories of Holocaust survivors. In the case of child survivors, the adult survivor community was also instrumental in constructing a 'conspiracy of silence' around their experiences. In her research, Yael Danieli argues that adult survivors remained silent about their war-time experiences because their post-war environments were not responsive to their stories; they had no empathic audience with whom to communicate their traumatic pasts. She explains that the accounts of survivors were too gruesome to listen to and that survivors were also faced with the pervasively held myths of passivity and the suspicion that they must have performed immoral acts in order to survive. The 'conspiracy of silence' can also explain the phenomenon of silence amongst child survivors. The adult community, which included adult survivors, saw silence as a way to protect the children from their traumatic pasts. Thus they refrained from speaking about the war in front of the children, and did not usually question the children about their experiences during the war. Many adults felt that they had been unable to protect the children from the Nazis, but perhaps now they would be able to protect them from their traumatic memories. Furthermore, they believed that the best course of action was for the children to move on and build new lives. Some researchers argue that the 'conspiracy of silence' was constructed in order to shield the adults from knowing the full extent of their own children's suffering. It was especially difficult to listen to the experiences of children, as their stories signified the desertion of children by the adult world. This inability on the parts of adults to listen to and contain the stories of child survivors resulted in their questioning the veracity of the children's accounts. Judith Kestenberg explains: "Many parents of children who were persecuted believe that the children did not suffer because they were too small to understand the danger. Feeling guilty that they were not able to safeguard their children against pain, hunger and premature aging, they tell their children that they were too young to remember what happened under the Nazis."[26]

After the war, Rachel's silence around her past and experiences during the war continued. Part of the explanation for such behavior was that she had internalized the belief that her survival was dependent on her silence. Rachel was taught that, in order to survive, one needed to remain silent. This strategy, which was reinforced by her parents, continued to guide her behavior in her post-war life. Rachel explains that, "For years after the end of the war, I personally experienced another period of silence, as I was excluded from what was going on around me. If they were amongst adults, my parents and others, the moment that I would appear, they said a word in Yiddish, which meant 'the little one'. When the little one would appear, a silence would fall amongst them. That means they stopped conveying information, facts, all sorts of things that they knew. That means that again I was amidst silence . . ."

After the war, Rachel's parents tried to shield Rachel from the terrible reality of the *Shoah*. They they tried to keep the *Shoah* a 'secret' from her, in the hope of not upsetting or traumatizing her. Rachel's parents hoped to protect her, yet the "conspiracy of silence" was not always protective, productive or rehabilitating. Rachel had learned that silence was vital for her physical survival, yet throughout the war and in her post-war environment she felt that it threatened her psychological and emotional well-being. Unable to articulate her feelings, Rachel expressed her distress through her body, through tears and illness. In order to break the silence that surrounded her after the war, Rachel became ill: "It took me 40 years to understand that that's how I managed to get recognition from my parents, that I exist. I had a high temperature, I was sick, therefore I exist, and I am here. It was silence; silence that continued for a long time."

The silence that Rachel was subject to after the war triggered and reinforced the feelings of vulnerability and isolation that she had felt during the war. As a result of this 'secondary silencing', Rachel felt that there was no essential difference between her life during and after the war, as she continued to remain in hiding. She continued to feel vulnerable and insecure, and unable to live 'normally'. However, Rachel's parents could not completely hide the *Shoah* from her. She absorbed the atmosphere of pain and terror through the hushed whispers of the survivors around her. Rachel describes how her home became a meeting place for survivors, and her parents tried to give these 'broken families, broken people' advice or simply an empathic ear. Rachel describes, "I internalized the pain of the people after the war. It's not only the war. I remember well a woman who my mother brought out of a mental institution. She was admitted there. The woman would come home and begin to speak. I remember that my mother would say: 'It's enough'. However, the woman would say: 'But you know it does me good to speak'. And she would begin to tell her stories again. So where could you run to? It was my home. I understand Yiddish, so I understood her stories. I listened and that's how I heard many stories . . . All sorts of things. You internalize the pain of others . . . if you ask me about the war, for me it's not only the war; it's also after the war as well."

Even though Rachel's home became a meeting point for survivors who came and told their stories, Rachel's family continued to remain silent about their own past and the fate of their family. I asked Rachel if her parents spoke about the past when she was young and she answered that they didn't, "For my parents it was a trauma. They had come from Poland, made it through France. Their whole family in France was killed. Their own family – my mother's parents, sisters, everyone." Silence became the mode of behavior regarding the past. The past was too traumatic and her parents decided to focus on the future. Thus the home became one of silence, where the past was not talked about, but silently mourned. Both Rachel and her parents chose to remain silent for most of their adult years. Rachel had learned to hide her past, although she continued to feel that she was denying a fundamental part of herself and her existence.

Whilst Ariala and Rachel were silenced by their parents, Tamar modeled her own behavior on her parent's silence. In her interview, Tamar explained that throughout the war she had shared the burden of survival with her parents. They had not shielded her from the terrifying reality and she was party to all of their decisions and deliberations. Thus her experiences during the war were inextricably bound to those of her parents, which in turn influenced the way that she related to her past after the war. Tamar explains that after the war, her parents hardly spoke about their pasts. Rather they focused on rebuilding their lives and their future. She explained that, "My parents were very strong people. Moreover, I don't think at any period that it influenced them because they were strong. They knew how to stand on their own two feet . . . they did not allow themselves to sink into the past . . . it's very easy to sink into the past and to close up and to go over it again and again all the time . . . they closed themselves off from it and continued on. They did not break down psychologically . . . they were not consumed by their sorrow or by self-pity . . . no! They fought hard for their daily existence. They never spoke about the past!"

Tamar remembers her parents as strong, determined people, who were committed to rebuilding their lives anew, not in the shadow of the past. She perceives their ability to move on from their war experiences as a testament to their remarkable strength. Like her parents, Tamar has also remained silent about her past, and has rarely spoken about it to anyone. What is fascinating about Tamar's story is that she has not only internalized her parent's reaction to their past, but also the way in which they perceived the past – as a period of weakness. Even today, she still finds it difficult to see herself as a survivor. This became apparent in her interview, after I had asked Tamar why she refused to watch the video testimony she had given recently, to which she replied, "Maybe, because I don't want to see myself as an unfortunate person, maybe that's the reason. My personality, which stems from my parents', is weakness and weakness is a negative thing . . . it is forbidden to be weak, as those who are weak break . . . and you need to be strong and keep on going. That's the motto . . . It is forbidden to be weak! Weak, and you cannot succeed; continue, and progress with life. If you are strong, you live! That's what I think . . . you have highlighted this for me. That's why I have not wanted to look at the film. I am scared to see myself as weak."

This extract represents a crucial stage in Tamar's interview, as she tries to come to terms with her own feelings regarding her identity as a Holocaust survivor. This part of the interview reflects what Ruthellen Josselson understands as the "the dialogical moment," which refers to "places within narrative where the self is most clearly in dialogue with itself. These moments of crisis represent nodes of change in which the individual becomes other than he or she was." Josselson explains, "In these dialogic moments, where the planes of self meet, the challenge to empathy and to our capacity to narrate is greatest and is also where our learning about the other is maximized. In contrast to a mere recitation of events (which in themselves are dialogic), we might conceive of dialogic moments expressed in narratives that are personal keys to meaning-making, the place where a person's self-understanding is put to a self imposed test."[77]

Tamar does emerge from this 'dialogical moment' with a new self-awareness – she understands that the way she views her past, as period of weakness, is an extension of her parents' attitudes towards their pasts. They concealed their pasts and their identities as survivors in order not to expose what they believed signified weakness and vulnerability. Furthermore, during the war they had learned that weakness threatened survival, conceptions which were reinforced by their post-war environment. Tamar explains that, "In Israel there was an atmosphere that the new immigrant and the survivor was weak . . . had some sort of stigma . . . he was not a *sabra* . . . he was not a member of the group . . . and no one wants to be placed in such a category which has such a stigma. So people became more and more closed." Thus, the lessons they learned and internalized during the war were reinforced by the socio-cultural values of their post-war community, which applauded stories of heroism and resistance and silenced stories of victimization and suffering. It is difficult to identify the source of Tamar's parents' attitudes: were their reactions a result of their own personality, their experience during the war, or the pressures and norms of their post-war environment? Tamar's parents perceived retelling as an exercise in self-pity, and chose to remain silent, and she followed their example.

Previous research has shown that the nature of the familial relationship was found to be an important factor in determining the child's ability to cope during the war. In my research, I found that the nature of the familial relationship also affected their post-war adjustment. This is powerfully illustrated in Rivka's narrative. When the war ended, Rivka's mother, who had survived the war, came to reclaim Rivka from her beloved rescuers. Her rescuers had prepared her for this possibility, yet the woman who claimed to be her mother was unrecognizable to her. Rivka explained that when she first saw her mother and brother, "Both of them were very, very thin or because of the hunger they swelled up and she looked terrible. I didn't recognize her and I didn't want her. Today as a mother, I think that if perhaps I would have sat quietly I would have recognized her. But a child could not understand the other side of the coin. He only sees one side, meaning: You didn't want me, you sent me away, now I don't want you. When I think about it today as a mother, it was a reaction. It wasn't that I didn't know her. It was that I didn't want her . . . The third time my mother came with my brother. He is five years older than me, I recognized him."

This is a particularly sensitive part in Rivka's narrative, as it reflects Rivka's continued struggle to come to terms with her initial reaction to her mother. This powerful extract demonstrates the retrospective nature of interviews, as interviewees, from the vantage point of today, continue to make meaning of their pasts. Rivka is trying to understand her reaction from the vantage point of her present role as a mother and not as a child. As a child, Rivka understood her rejection of her mother in terms of her mother's physical strangeness, yet today she views it as a reaction to what she perceived to be her mother's rejection of her during the war. Now she is also able to 'forgive' her mother, because she understands the complexity of the war situation, an understanding which was unavailable to her then.

Yet, despite their reunion, Rivka was unable to reconcile her relationship with her mother. She explains that they had experienced such different realities during the war that they had drifted apart and were unable to empathize with one another's experiences. Her siblings had been able to have a relationship with their mother as, "My two brothers had been with her in the camp, so the three of them were good friends. I had a good life during the war. I had not been hungry but . . . I did not have a mother, and with my mother, I could not return to being mother and daughter because of a certain distance . . . "

Researchers have pointed out that reunions between children and parents after the war were not always joyous occasions. Judith Kestenberg remarks that yearning for the restoration of the past, both parents and children "expected to find their families as they were at the moment of separation. Children blamed their parents for abandoning them; some thought that these strange adults pretended to be their parents."[28] In addition, parents and children had often not shared the same experiences and therefore found it very difficult to communicate. Communication was also sometimes hindered by language. There were cases in which children no longer understood and spoke the same language as their parents.

Thus Rivka found herself unable to communicate her experiences to her family, and was thus left alone with her memories. Moreover, Rivka felt guilty for having had what she described as a 'good life during the war', whilst her mother and brothers had been imprisoned in a camp. This also made it difficult for her to talk about her past as a traumatic event. In addition Rivka's mother refused to speak about her experiences during the war in an attempt to protect her children from the horrors of the past. Thus, Rivka, like Tamar, learned from her mother not to speak about the past.

It can be seen from some of the narratives presented above that the adult community was instrumental in shaping the ways in which child survivors related to their pasts. This is hardly surprising as child survivors, even after the war, were still dependent upon the care and guidance of adults. And these adults usually instructed them to bury their pasts and look forward to a new future. Silence was seen as a therapeutic response to trauma.

The Search for Belonging

For many child survivors any sense of belonging and security they had managed to build during the war – as artificial as it may be – crumbled upon liberation. Hence, liberation was not always a purely joyous event for child survivors (or for many adult survivors), as they were suddenly thrust into the 'normal' world, which was unfamiliar and in which they felt like strangers. In many cases the shock was exacerbated because the children did not understand their new reality, nor had anyone to explain it to them. Researchers write that, upon liberation, "a great many child survivors felt that they did not belong anywhere, not only in terms of country or social group, but also in terms of age. They did not feel understood by their parents and elders who had been persecuted as adults. Nor did they feel that they belonged to the children of survivors who had never been persecuted themselves."[29] Psychiatrist and child survivor Haim Dasberg explains that the survivor of trauma suffers from primary trauma, the traumatic event, and "secondary victimization following the re-entry into the post violent society."[30] In the survivors' re-entry into a post-traumatic society, the issue becomes their very belonging to that society. According to Dasberg, the transition from a victim to a survivor to a citizen in a free world is difficult for the individual.

Thus the post-war environment presented many challenges for child survivors. Alienated and traumatized, they felt a strong need to find stability, a home and an identity, and to 'belong'. Child survivors, like adult survivors, realized that in order to 'belong' they needed to direct their energies into rebuilding their lives; they needed to look forward and not back. They themselves needed to silence their past. It must be noted, however, that the struggle to belong is not exclusive to victims of trauma, it is endemic to the difficulties caused by emigration.

Eradicating difference   Ehud felt that he was different from other children almost immediately after the war, as he waited for his parents to return. He was eleven years old at the time. He recalls, "When the day of liberation came we felt a huge sense of relief, which was inexplicable, because we didn't know the facts. But we knew that something good was happening. And for a lot, for most people, that was the case. They found their family . . . I was waiting like everyone else, and what happened to everyone else? A father came, or two parents, or a brother, or a grandfather, or an uncle, and in the end I was left alone. No one came to take me. I stayed in Montinitin alone . . . and I returned to the Roza family." At this moment, Ehud realized that his life had changed irrevocably; he no longer had parents, or a home. He was an orphan. This is what Ehud considers to be his most traumatic war-time experience – waiting for his parents who never returned. From this distressing extract we learn that, for many child survivors, a clear demarcation between the war, and the post-war years does not always exist.

Ehud's feeling of being different was further accentuated in his post-war environment, amongst his adopted parents. Because they had not experienced the war, they could not understand or relate to his experiences, and were unable to help him make the transition from his past to his present. Even the most obvious things were strange to him, and needed an explanation. He recalls that, "They gave me a banana and they said to me: 'Eat, eat'. I didn't know that it had a skin that needed to be removed. When they laughed, I was hurt. That's the reception that I got. They had the best intentions. They wanted to help me, but that's what happened. I have tens of instances like that in my mind . . . For example, when I ate ice cream for the first time, they said to me that it was hot. Obviously, it was a joke . . . but a child is hurt by jokes that are made at his expense, for something he does not know, and everybody else knows about. It hurts. When I eat a banana or ice cream, I remember those things, till this day. They had the best intentions, but the change was too quick, too drastic. It did not allow me to make the transition peacefully."

Throughout his interview Ehud explains that he had felt like an alien in his new home. It was as if he had come from a different planet, and in a sense he had. Because feeling like an outsider was very painful for him, Ehud eventually took his adopted parent's advice: "Put the past behind you, and build a new life." In so doing, he hoped to construct a new identity and to become like everyone else. Although he was influenced by the sentiments of his adopted parents, Ehud sees his retreat into silence as essentially stemming from his own needs. He explained that, "In the beginning we did not speak; we were quiet. Not only because we were silenced, but because we had a need to be silent. This stemmed from the child's need to be part of the post-war society and not to feel and be seen as different." Ehud explains that he did not want everyone to know that he suffered, "to look like someone who came from there." Therefore, he chose to remain silent about his past. Therefore, "things developed very quickly. I had a *Bar Mitzvah*, the adoption process began, and my life took on a completely different direction to what I had imagined, or hoped, or even envisaged to myself. I was a boy living in Switzerland. I became Swiss, spoke Swiss, went to school, matriculated, and served in the Swiss army. Things flowed. But what needs to be said is, during that whole period, no one hid anything. But I certainly did not speak about the past to any of my friends in my class."

Ehud sees his need to silence his past and integrate into his post-war environment as a reaction to his experiences during the war. He explains, "The need to blend in well, to totally integrate themselves into society, is for child survivors directly related to their past. Then one had to adapt totally to conditions which were not normal, to difficult conditions, to conditions of struggles between life and death. In addition, it continued in their post-war lives as the need to deny, to forget what once was, and to become a new person, in a new period, continued under the new conditions . . . to be like everyone else. It wasn't only an objective need to integrate. It was also a mental need, to be like everyone else." Thus, he sees his experiences during the war as having shaped his behavior and personality, leaving an indelible mark on his life long after the war had ended.

Ehud also attributes his silence to his adopted parents. He explains that, "Even if I would speak about it, they would not hear, they would not listen, and they also would not understand. But there was another purpose in it, which today we are aware of: to repress, to forget, not to think about it, to forget it. My adopted parents wanted to help me, and they said it with sincerity: 'What was was, forget about it, you have a new life and that's it'." The literature has shown that adopted parents and other guardians often feared bringing up the child's past. In many instances, they supported the child's own tendencies to suppress the past. Some children spoke out too quickly and were taught to remain silent, often by well-meaning people not wishing to cause pain to the children by encouraging their preoccupation with tragedy. Other well-meaning people simply would not listen because of their own feelings of guilt and fear. They were not always sensitive to the child's experience and needs to mourn and remember loved ones. They may have felt that it threatened their relationship with their adopted child, or simply that it was better for the child to forget his or her past. After the war, children continued to be dependent on caretakers. Thus, just like during the war, they felt compelled to behave in the way dictated by their parents and caretakers.

In their post-war environments, child survivors wanted to belong, and silence became their main tool. Yet perhaps more significantly, they wanted to disassociate themselves from the image of the victim and survivor that had been constructed from within their post-war reality, and which may have matched their own painful reality. As Robert Krell explains, "There is comfort in our silence. We have blended into the appearance of normality."[31]

Aliya *to Israel: Building a new identity*   Most of the child survivors whom I interviewed made *aliya* to Israel immediately after the war had ended. They went to build a new home for themselves. Judith Shuval writes that, from its earliest stages, immigration to Israel has been socially constructed as a unique phenomenon. "Migrants to other destinations generally leave the place they consider home to find a new home; in the Israeli case, Jews were viewed as 'strangers' in their countries of origin and sought to find a new home by means of migration."[32] For many survivors of the Holocaust, whose homes and lives had been destroyed, Israel seemed to be the logical step towards building a new home and future for themselves, their families and the Jewish people. Zionism was seen as the logical response to the *Shoah*. Shamai Davidson observed that, "Palestine represented the old-new symbolic homeland Zion in the midst of the disappointing emptiness of the post-war reality in Europe around them. It was an expression of the overcoming of death and their uprooted existence and an attempt at renewed human spirituality."[33] Most of the child survivors whom I interviewed did not necessarily choose Israel as their new home. Instead it was chosen for them, either by their parents or the different organizations that took charge of orphaned Jewish children after the war. Seven of the child survivors decided to make Israel their home voluntarily, at a later stage in their lives. Most of them chose to come to Israel in search of a new home and to establish a sense of belonging.

One of the central goals of Israeli society since its inception has been to facilitate and encourage the immigration of Jews and make possible their full integration into the society. Yet, in its early years, Israeli society was less able to accept the ethnic traditions and particular behavior of its immigrants, viewing them as a threat to its new emerging culture. Therefore, the price for full integration was discarding one's past. The message to the child survivors upon their arrival in Israel was to integrate and assimilate into Israeli society.

Historically, the *Yishuv* first encountered child survivors of the *Shoah* with the arrival of the Teheran children in 1943. Hanna Yablonka says that the Israeli population was deeply affected by these children, "but of course, different criteria would have been used in judging children and orphans from those older survivors of the Holocaust. The sight of helpless children suffering always arouses feelings of sympathy, and of course, children are malleable, easily influenced, so there was always hope that it was not too late to instill in them the values and ethics of the indigenous population."[34] According to Hanna Yablonka, the *Yishuv* perceived the child survivor as someone who could be rehabilitated, molded, and absorbed effectively into Israeli society. This was also consistent with classical Zionist ideology, which sought to create young '*sabras*', 'new Jews'. Integration implied that the child survivors were meant to begin a new life in Israel, and forget their past; they were encouraged to "recreate the structures and techniques" [35] for membership in their new cultural environments. Their future, like the future of the state, was to be detached from the Diaspora and the horror of the Holocaust. Thus one can see that from the outset, child survivors in Israel were not necessarily seen in the same way as adult survivors were, but as children who had a traumatic past, yet could be rehabilitated, absorbed and transformed into 'new Israelis'.

As previously mentioned, the Youth Aliya movement was an organization that created a framework for the absorption of immigrant children and their integration into Israeli society. Some of the child survivors whom I interviewed spent some time in the movement after their arrival in Israel. Ruth, who spent a year in such an institution after her arrival from Italy, explains that, "I remember very much that in this *Aliyat Hanoar*, in this *Mossad Le'Aliyat Hanoar* here in Israel . . . I really wanted to be Israeli. I wanted so much to be Israeli. I don't know why . . . but maybe because I was older already, I don't know. But, I really wanted to be Israeli."

One of the main reasons as to why child survivors were so motivated to become *sabras* was because, as an identity, it was so empowering. Tamar encountered *sabras* for the first time on her voyage to Palestine. She recalls "I walked around the boat and I got very jealous because on the boat there was a group of Israelis. They were probably from a youth movement and they were taking Jewish youth from Romania [to Israel]. And they sang and danced. I looked at them with envy . . . how they danced! They were already about fifteen, sixteen, seventeen years old and I was still small, so I looked on with envy and I remember how they danced there and spoke about *Eretz Yisrael* . . . "

Tamar was envious of these young adults, as they were happy, carefree, and passionate about their identity. The image of dancing youth was an inspiring one for Tamar, especially after her own experiences during the war, and it is hardly surprising that she wanted to become one of them. She explains that most child survivors who came to Israel remained silent after the war, "Because they wanted to be like the rest of the children in the country. They wanted to be the same; they wanted some role model, and it was the *sabra*. The courageous, the beautiful, the fearless . . . the one who spoke straight, did not procrastinate, not shy . . . because of this they raised obnoxious children here . . . that was part of Zionism, the new youth that they created here."

From Tamar's narrative we learn that there are three key reasons for her maintained silence. First, as discussed earlier, was the role of her parents in shaping her relationship to the past. Second, Tamar was attracted to the energy and passion that the *sabra* youth exuded, and therefore wanted to become one of them, unshackled, by the past. Third, she dissociated herself from the 'survivor identity', because in her experience survivors were seen as weak and powerless by her parents as well as by Israeli society. They viewed the Holocaust experience as one of quintessential powerlessness, and thus sought to rehabilitate themselves and their history, by silencing their past and by transforming the weak, dependent Diaspora Jew into a powerful, independent *sabra*.

The *kibbutz* framework was particularly effective in integrating child survivors into the country as it provided them with an immediate sense of belonging and identity. This was clearly seen in the case of Noah, who integrated quickly into the new environment. Orphaned as a result of the war, the *kibbutz* provided him with a home and a surrogate family. It also helped him fashion a new identity, based on the cultural ideals of the *kibbutz* movement and the fledgling state. Within his new socio-cultural environment he was encouraged to forget his suffering past and focus on his bright and hopeful future. For most of his life Noah attempted to hide his identity as a survivor of the Holocaust, and poured his energies into becoming a *sabra*. Hillel Klein, in his work with Holocaust survivors who had been absorbed in *kibbutzim*, observed that after some time survivors ceased seeing themselves as survivors as their source of identity "shifted from the Holocaust experience to the *kibbutz* itself."[36] Their past was replaced by a positive identity which was mutually reinforced by their *kibbutz* community, as the *kibbutz* community did "not explicitly identify its members as holocaust survivors."[37] The socio-cultural environment of the *kibbutz*, as a microcosm of Israeli society, sought to integrate these young survivors as quickly as possible. Hillel Klein also writes that the ideology of the *kibbutz* was easily internalized by the young survivors as it "provided a rationale for surviving the Holocaust and a new self image of self-realization as pioneers and builders of a new society."[38] The *kibbutz* experience encapsulated the collective narrative of destruction and rebirth. Noah was highly responsive to his new environment, and over the years he stopped identifying with his past; his identity as a survivor became increasingly irrelevant. Hillel Klein writes that survivors in the *kibbutzim* used the *kibbutz* and the opportunities it presented to them to "sublimate their experiences."[39] Nevertheless, he cautions that the survivors have not forgotten their past sufferings. Noah's positive experience with Youth Aliya is not shared by all child survivors. Both child survivors and researchers have been critical of the organization, which they felt only exacerbated difference and antagonism between the child survivors and the children of the *kibbutzim*, and contributed to stigmatization and discrimination of child survivors.[40] Eliezer's experience, to be discussed later, is particularly relevant in this respect.

Lost Memories, Lost Voice

In her narrative, Dina recalls that one of her constant fears during the war was unintentionally revealing who she really was. "I was scared that I would say something in my sleep at night. I was scared the whole time that I would maybe dream about my mother, as I was all alone. The whole war I was alone. I had no one. I survived and I kept moving between the villages. Where didn't I go? I went all alone. I needed to eat, to clothe myself, to sleep. It's clear that they didn't give me any money. Did I think of money? Did I think that the war would ever end? Every night I dreamt that my mother said to me: 'You have to survive the war and you have to tell what you have been through and what they did to you'. All of those things were in my heart and mind, as if my mother had said: 'Be strong, you need to survive this and tell what happened to us and all that was done to us'."

During the war, Dina was afraid that her loneliness and longing for her mother would betray her identity and lead to her death. Yet, her dreams also gave her some comfort in the form of the company of her mother and some reprieve from her endless lonely struggle. While these memories of her mother during the war threatened her physically, emotionally they served to sustain her. In Dina's dreams, it was not only the image of her mother that sustained her, but also the mission her mother imposed on her: to live so as to become a witness to the mass murder of her family and the rest of the Jews murdered at Ponar. This is a recurrent theme in the narratives of child survivors who, at the moment of separation from their parents, were entreated with a specific message which sustained them throughout the war period. Even though Dina wanted to remember and retell her past, she was unable to do so, as she had 'lost her memories'.

In our interview, I asked Dina if she had ever spoken about her past to others, to which she replied, "We didn't speak about it . . . only after a long time . . . but what I did do . . . I didn't know how to read, but in the orphanage [after the war] I began to write. I wrote a diary. I began to write down what I had been through. I knew all the names of the people, and all the places I had been in. I remembered everything and wrote it all down. I came here [Israel] and I thought to myself, 'Maybe I will write a book'. And everyone said to me 'Yes, write a book, a book. But you will need help, so give it to someone to help you write it'." Thus, after the war, Dina was committed to retelling her past. She acknowledged her war-time experiences, was open about them, but was not prepared to let them engulf her. She wrote her diary in the orphanage, in a safe, supportive and nurturing environment, and when she arrived in Israel she decided to publish it.

She sought the assistance of a particular academic "in Tel Aviv. He was also a Doctor. I bought my diary to him and I asked him to take a look at it because I wanted to write a book. I really thought that it would happen. But he didn't return my diary. Nothing. We went there a few times and we asked for it. He said: 'I sent it. I sent it'. What hurts me most is that I don't have the names of the people. People also helped me during the war . . . that woman who went with me and helped me. I really want to thank her now. I don't remember the names. They made a joke out of us. That's what hurts. What they did there they did . . . but here . . . Jews?"

Dina has never recovered her diary, or her memories. In losing her diary, she also lost her testimony, and the testimony of her murdered family. She cannot fulfill her mother's wish, because she cannot remember. Devorah has come to understand this experience as one that typifies the general lack of care and consideration that Israelis had for Holocaust survivors. She remarks that, "They made a joke out of us." According to Dina, Israeli society took advantage of survivors' vulnerability and powerlessness. They stole their memories and wounded their pride. After this incident, Dina retreated into silence, realizing that her current struggle was to build a new life in Israel, where she would become independent, stable and secure. She explains that, "I wanted to achieve. I didn't want them to pity me. Never! I really worked very hard. In the beginning, I didn't know the language. I was a cleaner. So, I went to *ulpan* lessons. I had to take classes. I had to look after the children and then go to work too. It was all so that I could achieve what I needed to achieve . . ."

After many years of hard work, Dina is able to recognize her achievements. She turned to me and said, "My house is fine. I have two children. My son has six children; he is religious. I have a daughter who has four children. My daughter is the oldest. I even have a great grandchild now. That's my greatest pleasure and enjoyment. And that's what we did." Dina was not prepared to be intimidated by Israeli society, and the devastating loss of her diary only strengthened her resolve to be accepted, to 'be one of them'. At the end of her interview she explained that she believes she has managed to achieve this. "My children served in the army. Each one contributed. My granddaughter is also in the army now. All of those things, it's like everyone else. We are not different. We were not born here, but we did not contribute any less. We did the same as everybody else."

No Longer Bearing the Silence

Hidden child survivors have essentially remained hidden for the past fifty years. Nevertheless, they have constructed a relationship to the past, which in part is based on their age and experiences during the war itself, and in part in response to their post-war environment. Their experiences during the war had taught them that in order to survive, one needed to remain silent. This 'motto' was internalized by the children and continued to influence their behavior in their post-war environment. I have defined this as 'learned silence'. As Dan Bar-On states, "how individuals define that experience depends on their sense of the legitimacy of what they did or experienced as much as the legitimacy given to their feelings by the society around them."[41] In the case of hidden child survivors of the Holocaust, their suffering during the war was generally not recognized, validated or legitimized after the war; not by the adult survivor community, nor by the adult community in general. Silence was imposed upon them through, as Yael Danieli defined it a "conspiracy of silence" and a hierarchy of suffering. Thus while children experienced the trauma of the war internally, this experience was socio-culturally defined and evaluated. Their identity as survivors and their relationship to their pasts were constructed in relation to the values, judgments and guidance of their post-war environment. Thus, once the experience of hidden child survivors of the Holocaust was de-legitimized, they remained silent and as long as they were silent, their experiences could not be represented in the collective narrative of the *Shoah*.

It is important to point out that the silence of child survivors is also connected to their status as dependants after the war. During the war, they were vulnerable and dependent on their adult caretakers. After the war, their dependency on adults continued. And, essentially, the adult community felt that silence was the correct response to their trauma. Instead of focusing on the past, they were encouraged to look forward, to build a new future and forge a new identity, even if this course of action ran contrary to their emotional needs.

However, child survivors have been totally powerless or passive in constructing their relationships to their pasts. Many interviewers welcomed and actively chose silence, as it closed off the past and helped them in their search for belonging and integration into their new, post-war environments. This can be understood on a number of levels. First, many child survivors decided that they wanted to abandon their past in the hope of constructing a new future, and sense of belonging. Tired of being victimized and different, they wanted to shed their difference and become 'normal', like 'everybody else'. Second, child survivors who made *aliya* immediately following the war were greatly influenced by Zionism and struggled to fashion a new identity for themselves based on the cultural and ideological values of their new community, which demanded that they keep silent about their traumatic pasts. Third, child survivors were also influenced by the messages, meanings and contours of collective memory. They did not want to be identified as 'Holocaust survivors', who, they felt, were seen in a negative light by Israeli society. Young and impressionable, they had also internalized those messages which frowned upon and rejected the Diaspora experience. The *sabra* identity was particularly compelling for these youngsters as it was based on a positive Jewish identity and not one associated with persecution and suffering. Therefore, silence enabled these 'hidden children' to remain hidden; and with ingenious skill, they camouflaged themselves and integrated successfully into Israeli society. They had hidden themselves so well that I myself was astonished when I met them. Most of them did not have a trace of any foreign accent and were completely fluent in Hebrew. They had rebuilt their lives, married, had children and grandchildren, and were professionally successful. It was hard for me to believe that they had not been born and raised here, as their stories of suffering and trauma from 'then' seemed disconnected from their current persona, their 'now'. Their integration seemed to have been so successful that all of them considered themselves to be, first and foremost, Israelis. Clearly, the social environment strongly influences the rehabilitation of traumatized human beings. "The psychosocial structure of Israeli society, especially during the early years of the state, helped the majority of survivors and their children achieve genuine social integration. Especially for survivors who came to Israel in their late teens and early twenties, belonging, identification, and activity fused into a cohesive whole, creating new meaning in their lives as uprooted, traumatized persons."[42]

Be this as it may, despite their successes most of the hidden children whom I interviewed could no longer bear the silence. It seemed that this silence, which all had conspired to maintain, and that hed appeared to be the only way of overcoming the past in order to build a new future, had only been successful superficially. To create a wall of silence was not to deal with the past, rather it was to conceal it, in turn concealing a vital part of their identity. Consequently they have begun to gather their memories and find their individual voices, this group of hidden child survivors in particular, becoming increasingly vocal in their attempts to reclaim their past. Chapter 4 will examine the dynamics behind this recovery and articulation of their voice.

4

Finding Their Voices

Chapter 3 explored how hidden child survivors, in their post-war environments, were either silenced by others or silenced themselves in their struggle to build new lives. However, throughout their lives they have continued to face new challenges and changes: different events or phases in their life-cycle, which may have triggered visions or memories of their past, which as Eva Fogelman explains, "often . . . give rise to a child survivor's impulse to speak."[1] My research has found that these hidden child survivors have chosen to begin speaking about their pasts at a later stage in their lives.

Fifty years after the Holocaust, the 'older' survivors have passed away and child survivors are being increasingly seen as the 'last witnesses'. They are the only ones who are still able to tell their stories. Thus, the natural passing of time has pushed child survivors to the fore of Holocaust memory and commemoration. As one child survivor exclaimed, "The others are dead and now they are interested in us!" Paul Valent writes that, "The Holocaust is now only memories. Child survivors are living representatives of the Holocaust, and only their memories give it flesh and blood."[2] Thus, the openness of contemporary Israeli society towards the Holocaust, and the life-stage at which child survivors find themselves today, have provided a unique conjunction of circumstances encouraging child survivors to come out of hiding and articulate their experiences.

This chapter discusses the ways in which these hidden child survivors understand their own journey into a public telling of their pasts. For some, telling emerged from a deep, personal need, whilst others were encouraged to share their pasts by significant others or in response to the willingness of contemporary Israeli society to hear their stories. Chapter 3 demonstrated how the experiences of hidden children, and their identity as survivors, were not validated in their post-war environment. Denied their traumatic pasts, hidden children remained silent. However, once their stories and trauma were validated and their identity as survivors was legitimized, hidden children were encouraged to find their voices and began to reveal their pasts. Usually, the process of validation began with the individual finding an address-able other or an empathic audience – someone who was willing and able to hear and contain their story. As they were encouraged to speak, the process of silencing was reversed.

The process of validation and subsequent recalling and revealing was not instantaneous. Rather, for many hidden child survivors it was a painfully slow process. Retrieval of one's memories in the case of child survivors entailed a reversal of one's psyche, which requires negating past messages that child survivors 'could not' remember or 'should not' remember and what they did remember was 'not valid'. Claiming one's memories required assertiveness over such admonitions. Even the simple act of remembering is a difficult process as the memories them-selves are painful. Therefore, voicing their silenced pasts was dependent upon the individual's need and ability to tell, as well as the audience's ability and willingness to listen.

Occasions that Triggered a Telling

Identity Crisis

Silence was employed by both adult and child survivors as a tool for surviving survival. Child survivors, in their attempt to rebuild their lives after the war, silenced their past and built a new identity for them-selves. The hidden children continued to remain 'hidden' during their adult lives, and their silence helped them rebuild their lives. However, at some stage in their lives, these 'hidden children' began to feel a burning need to reclaim their former identities, which involved remem-bering their traumatic pasts. Ehud explains that the question of an integrated identity has become central to the experience of child survivors in their older years. He explains that in their post-war lives, child survivors lived with two parallel, un-integrated identities. Their 'first identity' is that of the child in their pre-war life and a victim during the war. According to Ehud, "This is the man who has memories; memo-ries which he is not always able to repress . . . which preserve the identity of the suffering child." The 'second identity' is the identity that the child created for him/herself after the war. This new, adopted identity was crucial for the child's integration and survival in their post-war envi-ronment. As Ehud explains, this identity is "another man, an addition, who lives his life from the late forties, fifties, sixties, seventies and eighties and nineties. He has created a new life; yet, he is essentially the same man as the first, but with two parallel identities. They are not always united and integrated harmoniously." Lawrence Langer identified this phenomenon in his study on the testimonies of Holocaust survivors. He writes that the self of Holocaust survivors "clearly operates on two levels, separated by an intervening, untranscendal loss,"[3] which becomes apparent in their telling. According to Ehud, at a certain point the person is unable to live with these two parallel, un-integrated identities, as the emotional and psychological burden is too great.

Ehud explains that, "The price that one pays for the adoption of a new identity, I think, is the eternal lying, putting up appearances, hiding things from even one's closest family members, and from one's partner. To behave in a way . . . to live and to make others believe and to change as if you are one man without the second identity (sic)[4] . . . that you are only the identity that you have adopted, that you fight for each day, the one that you want to show. It's an act that is done not only to survive, but because there is no choice. You cannot live with your past and with your memories. You have to overcome them; you have to turn them into something, which is positively constructive. But it does not mean that it disappears." Ehud suggests that child survivors constantly struggle over their identity, and this becomes an integral part of the nature of survival itself. For Sara Moskowitz, the identity crisis is not necessarily linked to the child survivor's post-war adaptation, but rather to the loss of their parents and their past at a very young age. She writes, "the loss of parents in early life means loss of the very nucleus of one's identity."[5]

Ehud's identity struggle, which began as a result of the war and the loss of his parents, continued in his post-war environment. Living in Switzerland for years he tried desperately to become Swiss. Yet, after all that he had experienced in Europe, he never felt a true sense of belonging there. He explains that, "In Switzerland, I had a comfortable life, a loving family, and I was not short of a thing. But the transition or the contrast from what I knew from the preceding years was so great, it did not let me rest." Ehud explains that "those who are abroad [outside of Israel], consciously or unconsciously continue to be hidden, directly or indirectly. They hide much more from their pasts . . . they hide the fact that they are not as acceptable as other citizens. They hide everything that they have endured and it influences them more than those in Israel. They are more likely to experience anti-Semitism . . . all of them who are here [in Israel] are more free. These are the obstacles for those children who live abroad." One of the difficulties Ehud faced whilst living in Europe was that he was unable to express himself freely, nor able to speak about his past, because, as he recalls, "Even if I would speak about it, they would not hear, they would not listen, and they also would not understand."

Aliya

Ehud explains that after the war, "I was fighting to be rooted, to be like everyone else. I really wanted to, and I tried, and to a certain degree, I achieved it . . . but I was a damaged person, a man who had been cut off from my roots. I didn't want to stay on European soil." Unable to achieve the sense of belonging he had hoped for in Europe with his adopted family, Ehud eventually moved to Israel in 1958. He was in search of a new home, and a place in which he would be able to be live and express himself freely.

Like Ehud, Rachel, Yafe, and Ariala are all hidden child survivors who remained in Europe after the war but did not feel they could make their homes there as they were unable to feel any sense of belonging. Ariala decided after the war to cut herself off from her Jewish past and, together with her husband, who was also a survivor, poured her energies into becoming French and raising their children to be proud French citizens. She recalls feeling after the war, "I have only one country, that is France, and I am a good French citizen. Besides that I want nothing . . . and that's how I will bring up my children, to be good French citizens." However, these feelings changed radically in June 1967, on the eve of the Six-Day War. Ariala explains that she only became aware of the political crisis in the Middle East, "when I saw that it bothered my father. I looked for Israel on a map. Suddenly I see a small spot on the map, surrounded by Arab countries . . . it was like an earthquake in my body. I felt that I was going to fall . . . It was like that country was Auschwitz and it was surrounded by Germans, Nazis . . . and soon that small spot will disappear and there will be a blood bath again. Everyone will disappear and nothing will remain. At that moment, everything that was in me that I had rejected, that I threw away so violently, came back to me. I said to myself: 'I am a Jew, I belong to that nation and if that nation disappears, so will I'. I simply could not continue to live in the same way that I had up until now. I was embarrassed that I hated Jews, that I believed all the Jewish victims were guilty, guilty for what happened to them because they killed Jesus, that it was their fault . . . and suddenly that feeling . . . I was embarrassed that I hated my people, myself. And here in that area, on that map, there are Jews in danger and I am out of the picture. I decided that I wanted to be with them."

Facing what she thought to be another potential Holocaust, Ariala felt reconnected to her Jewish roots, which she had abandoned after the war.

At this point in her life, married with children, she was independent enough to free herself from the anti-Semitic ideas of *grandmère*, and even became repulsed by her own 'anti-Semitic' thoughts. Furthermore, she was also no longer dependent upon the adult survivor community, which had helped alienate her from the Jewish community. Once Israel and the Jewish people were threatened, Ariala began to feel the need to be part of the Jewish people and take an active part in the Jewish experience. If Israel was a potential Auschwitz, she wanted to be there too, as she did not want to spend the next war 'in hiding' like she had during the Holocaust. Instead, she wanted to be with everyone else, to feel included, to find her place. As a result of the Six-Day War, Ariala decided that her place was in Israel, and she eventually managed to persuade her husband, who had also been deeply affected by the Six-Day War, to make *aliya*.

In the interview, Ariala, with tears in her eyes, dramatically recounts their boat journey from Europe to Israel, "One winter's day in January 1970 we find ourselves, the four of us, on the ship *Marseilles*. We are going to Israel. We are *olim chadashim*. We don't know the language, we don't have an apartment, we don't have an income, or a profession. The only thing we had was our last month's salary. But we know that it was the right step. My daughter was twelve and a half, my son was fourteen and a half. They were not small children. But I gave them the feeling that this was the right place to be. We know nothing about Israel, really nothing . . . On January 11, 1970 at four o'clock in the morning, we reach Haifa. There are four people on deck, my husband, my children, and me. It was very cold. I looked, and I can't believe what is in front of me. The sky is still cloudy, there are still stars, we don't move from where we are standing. And slowly we see the light rising and the sun begins to shine and suddenly it rises and I see the mountains, the Carmel, the sky and the sun and I say to myself: 'This is all mine! This is my country. I have come home'. At the same time I see my mother's face, I see Rivka, in my imagination I see my two grandmothers, two grandfathers, I see the whole family and I say to my mother: 'Mother do you see me? Are you proud of me? Grandmother, grandfather, is what I have done okay? Are you proud? Do you see that I have done it?'"

In making *aliya*, Ariala had begun her long journey home from after the war. She remembers the strong feelings of belonging that she felt when she reached the shores of Haifa, and the knowledge that she had finally made the right choice. By coming, as Ariala describes, 'home', she was finally confronting and owning the past, and was able face her murdered family and her losses. After years of suffering and hiding, both during and after the war, Ariala decided she wanted to come out of 'hiding'. For her that meant rejoining the Jewish people and their fate.

Her feelings of estrangement and guilt, which had begun in hiding and continued in her post-war environment, began to dissipate once she made *aliya* and found a new home.

Yet, for Ehud, Rachel and Ariala, *aliya* was only the beginning of their journey 'home'. Israel symbolized their physical home, but they still felt far away from their emotional homes – themselves and their pasts. As is clear from their narratives, *aliya* did not always soothe or heal the wounds of the past, or their identity conflicts. Nevertheless it was the first step. Ehud explains, "I acclimatized immediately. I left wealth, a comfortable life. I am not complaining about it today, but life there was certainly more comfortable in Switzerland. [In Israel] I found friends immediately, a way of life that suited me. I learnt the language immediately and I worked, established a family. My adaptation to the country was immediate . . . but the hardships remained. The same banana is the same banana . . . But my life had been created in the way I have wanted it to be, according to my own and my wife's spirit." Israel did not completely resolve Ehud's identity crisis; it merely anaesthetized it for a while.

Ehud, Rachel and Ariala did not start speaking about their past when they arrived in Israel. Instead they poured their energies into integrating into Israeli society, finding jobs and learning the language. In a sense, they were a few years behind those child survivors who had come immediately after the war. It would take Ehud, Rachel and Ariala a few more years, like other child survivors living in Israel, to confront the past and begin working through it. Meanwhile they continued to live with two un-integrated identities.

For those child survivors who came to Israel immediately after the war, their identity crisis was less apparent because Israel provided them with a Jewish environment and gave them an immediate sense of belonging and hope for a positive Jewish future. Although they did not suffer from an identity crisis in the same way as those who had lived in Europe after the war, they had also replaced one identity with another, and silenced and repressed their pasts. Thus, both groups of child survivors needed to embark on a journey of mourning and working through their losses. Both groups had to cope with memories of a painful past, the loss of loved ones, and an awareness that their parents and friends would never return.

Moments of Vulnerability and Tension

In character with other child survivors after the war, Shalom silenced the past and focused his energies on rebuilding his life and his future. Shamai Davidson writes that, "In this way, they (survivors) were socially acceptable and even became exemplary citizens in terms of personal, family and social advancement."[6] In our interview, I asked Shalom why he did not speak or write about the past for so many years, to which he replied, "Yes, it's interesting. For many years, it didn't concern me. I said to myself that once, I thought that when I reach pension age . . . One day on the horizon, I will summarize what happened to me, for the sake of my children, but not before. There was no reason." Shalom also believed that he had as he put it, 'no dramas to tell'. The hierarchy of suffering had also influenced his decision to remain silent. However, the primary motivation behind Shalom's silence was that he felt totally unaffected by the war; it did not seem to impinge on or influence his life. He did not feel any post-traumatic symptoms, and therefore had not felt the need to look back at his past.

He recalls, "I even remember that in the faculty for agriculture, we had to take a course. They wanted us to get a bit of humanities, and an introduction to psychology. So at the end of the lecture I went up to the lecturer and I said to him: 'Look at man's mind. I have been through so many things, and they don't even bother me. I don't think about it at all'. And he looked at me. I remember the look on his face when he said: 'Really?' It seems that he knew better than me. He had some sort of crystal ball . . . but I really thought that. Once I really tried. I took a vacation and I came to some friends in Jerusalem. They went away and they gave me their apartment for four days. I sat down and I really began to record it. So, an organized man begins with the first day of the war. For two days, I scribbled and scribbled, and I think that I had not even finished the first day. I saw that it wasn't working, so I left it. That was in 1966. Of course, I wrote about it in stories. I remember at school, shortly after coming to Palestine at the age of thirteen, I was very weak in Hebrew, so when we were asked to do creative writing, I decided to write about some *Aktion*. Something dramatic . . . good to sell. But I got very bad grades, because I didn't know how to write. So, that was some sort of testimony . . . "

Even though Shalom believed that the war had not affected him, and therefore he did not need to confront and work through his past, this extract reveals that he had tried to write about his experiences on a few occasions, yet found he was neither able nor encouraged to do so. It is unclear from his interview what motivated Shalom to record his past then for clearly an answer to this question would help us understand more clearly the process of his telling. Nevertheless, from 1977 Shalom once again decided to look backwards, at his past, and managed to record his memories in a masterful narrative. His memoir took him twenty years to write – twenty years to work through his past. After years of silence, Shalom explains that, in 1977, he found a 'reason' to write about the past. Perhaps more accurately, the reason found him.

He explains that, "In 1967, I had a few visions. I also met a psychologist for the first time. I had some difficulties in the family and so we went, the two of us, to a psychologist . . . to a social worker. And in between everything, he heard about my past, and said to me quietly: 'A boy who experienced such things from the age of 8 till 11, it's worthwhile that you write it down one day. After you have written it down you will see that it will be easier for you'. I remember that he recommended it, that it was worthwhile for me to write it once, and it could be an outlet for me, to make it somehow easier." Shalom does not elaborate on the visions that he had in 1967. Perhaps the tensions and anxieties that preceded the Six-Day War triggered some painful memories for him. Nevertheless, he gradually became aware that the *Shoah*, albeit over in actuality, continued to influence his life and his relationships. The critical turning point for Shalom took place in the summer of 1977, when he was confronted with the same feelings of vulnerability and loneliness that he had experienced during the war.

In 1977, Shalom went to study in America for the summer session at a university. He recalls, "I was in America and under great stress." Even though he had made significant professional accomplishments over the years, when classes began Shalom had difficulty in following the lectures. He had difficulty with the language. Although he knew English fluently, he could not follow conversational English. He had taken a heavy study load and was struggling to keep up with the classes. He felt that he was losing a race and for Shalom, to lose means to lose control, something he felt was unbearable. He explains that, "I had signed up for a lot of courses. I have big eyes. I felt that I was disgraced. I tried to cope with it, but the terminology – even to understand the language was difficult. Ironically, the lecturer was an ex-German. Even the Americans found it difficult to understand his English. I hardly understood anything. I did not know the bibliography. I was very pressured. In Yiddish, you say, 'It's nothing'. It wasn't nice. Suddenly, everyone is looking at me like I was in a showcase. It obviously stressed me. And I am alone. My wife and three kids are in Israel. And there is no phone. And everything is expensive. And that probably explains the next two things that happened to me."

In a stressful environment, in which his confidence was undermined, in which he felt powerless and vulnerable, Shalom began to have visions from the war. The first vision, he explains, happened when "I went to visit the White House and there was an orchestra playing there from Seattle. Every week there was to be a group from somewhere else. They were singing to people as the people were organized into groups to enter the White House. They stood waiting in a long line, as group after group went in. I waited in the line too, but I thought that the line was too long so I decided that I would rather watch. It was like a carnival. Groups would pass through like that and walk in silence. And, suddenly I felt like I was there, in the big *Aktion*. The only difference here was that the lines returned. I am seeing here something that I actually know. Shocked I ran away. Think about it, 1977, and what I am talking to you about happened in 1941. Thirty-six years have passed . . . and suddenly it comes out of me."

The second vision occurred when he "was sitting in the library, doing an assignment. From then on, I have hated that word. I am sitting in the library. The lesson began at nine o'clock and I came at eight o'clock. It was difficult getting there. I would have to change two buses in order to get there, walk a kilometer or two. I lived in a poor neighborhood, and you had to take two buses and walk quite a bit. I remember that by eight o'clock in the morning I was already sitting in the library, preparing for the class. Sitting opposite me were some other students, five or six of them. They were Americans, and they were preparing something in common. They were reading and laughing, and joking. They didn't seem to be concerned about what awaited us. There was a soldier there. An officer or two, one girl and a nun. I look at the nun, and suddenly the thought crosses my mind: 'She would not betray me'. I was astounded. Do you know that that was what we had to think about all the time? . . . that perhaps, in a difficult situation, there was hope that one such as her would permit me to hide in the church. The priest, the nuns, in the monastery . . . perhaps, despite the fact that they weren't always nice, but somehow it was still possible. I realized that after thirty-six years, everything was coming back to me. It is still in me. I didn't know that it was still in me. The demon knocks and wants to get out of the bottle."

Feeling vulnerable and powerless, Shalom's defenses were weakened and he could no longer defend himself against his traumatic memories. Each of the scenes that he describes are moments which epitomize the feelings he felt during the war: the helplessness, the *Aktion*, and the vulnerability – relying on the good will of non-Jews in order to be saved. Shamai Davidson writes that after some years of working with survivors, he recognized a specific group, "who were functioning well and who seemed well adjusted, but who in encountering various stressful life situations would react or decompensate with manifestations of the survivor syndrome[7] . . . A major vulnerability is related to the fact that chance occurrences in everyday life can arouse memories of the traumatic experiences and return the survivor to the horror of experiences deeply imprinted in memory."[8] Shamai Davidson's words seem particularly apt in describing Shalom's experience in America in

1977. After experiencing those traumatic memories, Shalom realized that he was still deeply affected by his experiences during the war. He realized that he had internalized certain fears and anxieties from the war years, which manifested themselves in his post-war life. Over the last three decades, Shalom has begun to contemplate how the *Shoah* had affected his personality, choice of wife and his parenting. Before that, however, Shalom began to feel the need to exorcize the past. He took the advice of the psychologist he had met a few years before, and began to write.

He explains that, "I eventually dropped most of the courses . . . afterwards I had two weeks to visit my wife's relatives. Eventually I arrived in Pennsylvania, at my uncle and aunt's house. And they were very nice, as they left me alone for half a day. I sat in the kitchen with a piece of paper and I wrote the first page of my memoir. I was strongly motivated. Perhaps it came from a logical understanding that this is what I had to do now. I had to continue to write my memoirs. I had written the first page in the kitchen. And I was relieved." Perhaps it was appropriate that Shalom began his confrontation with the past whilst he was still in America, in the place where his anxieties had surfaced so powerfully.

When Shalom returned to Israel, he continued writing. He recalls that, "Every page was an event. It was very emotional. Slowly, slowly I learned how to handle it." Shalom decided that it was best to write alone, to relive his memories alone, in an isolated apartment removed from his everyday life. He managed to do so by house-sitting his friends' apartments when they went away, "I went through sixteen apartments like that." He had learned that in order to confront the past, he needed to put the present aside.

It took Shalom seven years to write the first draft of his book, and then he began to re-work it, turning it into a moving literary piece. Writing triggered his memory and he was "shocked by how much I had inside of me that I didn't know. And I know that this was the first time that I had relived these events. I was emotional. I cried and I was enraptured." Shalom found it difficult to move between the past and the present. At first, he felt that he was living two lives, as he was revisiting a part of himself that, as he explained, he had "placed in an archive", that was foreign to his current persona. He explains that this was very taxing emotionally as, "One moment you are in an *Aktion*, the next you return to . . . hot cold, hot cold." Throughout the period of his writing, Shalom struggled to maintain the balance between 'then' and 'now', between his 'first' and 'second identity'. He was careful not to allow the little boy in the war to consume the adult man.

I asked Shalom if he felt that writing his book was a helpful experience, to which he replied, "Yes, of course it helped . . . I can now speak freely about the subject and subjects that are connected to it. I am my friends' historiographer. With the help of a calendar, I have ordered all the events. Intentionally, I didn't read about the *Shoah* in our region. I didn't want to do that so I wouldn't color my memories with other works. And that's one of the reasons why I have not been back to Lithuania. I don't want to see that the river that I remember is a small one, and the mountain is some small hill. I want to preserve my memories the way they are. Now I speak very freely about almost everything – something that I didn't do before. I see it in comparison to my friends who have not yet done this work. It is difficult for them to touch the past. They are too sensitive. They jump [between events] and get confused over when things happened, [it is difficult to determine] where is the beginning and where is the end. I made order out of it, without research and without documents, but with the help of a calendar. There is a book on the history of the ghetto, which helped me. I made order of many things, because you don't always remember what happened first and what happened afterwards. But I am able to speak about it freely, and I can even advise people. I have no doubt that it helped me. I became a 'normal person' in inverted commas, in a very obvious way."

Shalom reveals how the process of remembering and retelling has affected his life, as it has not only enabled him to confront his past and restore his memories, but it has also transformed his identity. Before writing his book, Shalom remarked, "I did speak about it from time to time. I also didn't hide the fact that I was a Holocaust survivor." However, it was not a central part of his identity and his life. Yet, once he began to confront and record the past, his identity as a survivor became more visible, and assumed a more prominent role in his life. He has become an 'adviser' to other survivors, encouraging others to confront their pasts, and create order and meaning out of their memories. Through his book, he has also become the 'historiographer' of their collective pasts, and assumed the role of 'historical witness'. Shalom has become a leading figure amongst child survivors from the Kovno ghetto. He has achieved this 'new life position' through the success of his book, his powerful personality, and his boundless energy. He has also achieved this 'new life position' because Israeli society has encouraged him to develop it as he is an inspiring role model. Albeit, once a victim, he managed to survive the war and rebuild his life. He was successful in his career and integrated well into Israeli society. His story is empowering as it represents the triumph of an individual over adversity and evil. Shalom has become an agent of memory for the larger collective and within his own community of survivors. His experience is a powerful example of the interaction between collective memory and personal memory and identity.

Nevertheless, Shalom is ambivalent over his new role. Whilst writing the book he struggled to maintain a balance between his 'post-war self' and the 'little boy' in the ghetto. The success of his book, *Crossing the River*, has only exacerbated this conflict. Shalom explains that, "writing connected me back to my past. Now I am even more of a Holocaust survivor than I once was. And it seems that it needed to be that way, and today I am more at peace with that chapter in my life. Sometimes I am shocked that I am too involved. I really don't want it to consume me, to let it get out of hand . . . A friend once gave me some advice. 'Listen, don't commit to anything after you have finished writing the book. Give yourself the option to close the chapter and to move on'. And, until this very moment, I am still debating. I don't know. It's not for nothing that I said that I don't know whether to carry on dealing with it or not. If I wanted to, I could be busy with it for the rest of my life. I will become one of the eulogists, lamenters, and speakers. I could be involved in this organization, be the head of it, and organize the memorials each year. It could become a full-time job. I would be a lamenter. I certainly don't want it. On the other hand, I do not see myself becoming free from it completely. We will see how it will develop in the coming years . . . This book has obligated me on a certain level. People invite me to speak and I make an appearance . . . because that's part of the message. That means I will become part of this whole thing even if I don't want to. Or I could announce one day that it's over . . . right now I don't see it, perhaps in another two to three years time, at some point, I will reach saturation point. So it's because of the book . . . the book has complicated my life: on the one hand it has made my life easier, and on the other it has committed me."

This is perhaps the most poignant dialogical moment in Shalom's narrative. His extract reveals an ongoing struggle in defining his identity and his relationship to his past, a struggle that has characterized his post-war experience. Shalom does not want the war to encroach upon his life, to take over his consciousness, identity, and destroy everything he has built subsequently. Yet, he also feels that he can no longer shut the door on the past; as he explained, he has 'let the demon out'. At this point, Shalom sees it as an 'either or' situation. He has not found a way to integrate or even balance the past and the present. Perhaps he does not see it as a possibility, because the very nature of the *Shoah* is all consuming, and the only way to balance it is by 'closing the door'. Lawrence Langer explains that this struggle is based on "the incompatibility between the 'impromptu self'" that endured the atrocity and the self that sought reintegration into society after liberation".[9]

Shalom recognizes that his book helped him to confront and work through his past. Yet he also recognizes that it has a role beyond his own particular needs, beyond his own working through. Inger Agger and Soern Jensen write that, "In the telling, the trauma story becomes a testimony . . . Testimony has both a private dimension, which is confessional and spiritual, and a public aspect, which is political and judicial. The use of the word *testimony* links both meanings, giving a new and larger dimension to the patient's individual experience."[10] The transformation of Shalom's 'telling' into 'testimony' is what now obligates Shalom to the past.

Despite the painful issues that writing the book has raised for him, Shalom does not regret writing it. He believes that it has granted him invaluable wisdom and has helped him develop a deeper level of self-understanding – of who he once was and of who he is today. Judith Herman would describe Shalom as entering the third and final stage of recovery in which "the survivor no longer feels possessed by her traumatic past; she is in possession of herself. She has some understanding of the person she used to be and of the damage done to that person by the traumatic event. Her task is to now become the person she wants to be."[11]

Writing the book has also allowed Shalom to mourn the loss of his mother and sister. He explains, "It seems that I have exhausted the topic, in terms of memories and chronology, but perhaps not in terms of emotions. But even in terms of emotions, I think that I never separated from my family who died, from my mother and my younger sister. I had never worked it through till the end. That was one of the hardest things for me when I wrote the book, and it was important to me. I made the separation; the mourning that a person needs to go through when a person dies. I had never experienced that before. For all of those years . . . at a person's grave you hear the *Kaddish* and it's hard, but that chapter is closed. There is meaning in the *Shiva*, the *Shloshim*, the *Yahrzeit*. However, that act was not performed in my case because I never got a clear, defined message saying, 'Your mother died on such a such day'. It is clear that she was no longer alive. The same thing with my sister. Until now I am still troubled by thoughts that she may still live as a Lithuanian somewhere in that country. So things carried on, and slowly, slowly, they never appeared so it seemed that they were no longer with us. There was never an act of mourning which is necessary for separation." The process of writing the book can be seen as Shalom's mourning process. In dedicating the book to his mother's memory, Shalom has built a monument in her memory, a *matzeva* and, perhaps, finally come to terms with her death.

The issue of mourning is central to the experience of survivors. Shamai Davidson remarks, "Every survivor of the Holocaust has to struggle to come to terms with massive losses from the moment of his realization that he has survived."[12] However, mourning is a difficult task due to the enormity of the loss and the nature of the murder. Loss during the *Shoah* is a global loss. As Shamai Davidson points out, it is "the loss of all or almost all the family and friends, home and possessions, community and country, ultimately of identity and meaning in life."[13] Mourning was also difficult because most deaths had no witnesses, there was no 'evidence', no grave, which made the death of loved ones very difficult to accept. This was especially difficult for children who had been hidden during the war and whose parents had disappeared, as they had no idea where their parents had disappeared to. They also usually believed that they would be reunited with their parents after the war. This hope kept many of them alive. "Fantasies of reunion and future life together with loved ones were indulged in by many of the victims as a coping strategy while in the grip of the genocidal machine."[14] Therefore, many child survivors also refused to mourn, as they did not want to accept the death of their parents and their families. Rather they clung to the lingering hope that they would yet return, as "to speak about it was to accept that they were dead."[15]

Ever since the publication of his book, Shalom has become a dominant voice amongst child survivors in Israel, and thereby an agent of public memory. Through his public lectures he began to direct and instruct other child survivors, constructing a *collective remembrance*, which would add to or challenge the existing public memory. On March 11, 2000, the Association of Lithuanian Jews organized a meeting for child survivors of the Kovno Ghetto, which was the first of its kind. The conference hall was filled with excitement as child survivors, now mature adults, began to meet one another and reminisce about their pasts. Shalom, as one of its chief organizers, opened the conference. His address to the survivors, in which he attempted to explain why the organizers had felt the necessity to arrange such an event, was very moving. He explained that the aim of the conference was first to give voice to the experiences of the children of the Kovno Ghetto, which up until then had not been heard. Second, he also saw the conference as creating an opportunity for those child survivors who had not previously spoken about their past, to begin speaking. Third, they wanted child survivors to know that they were not alone, and that they had support. Fourth they wanted to persuade individuals that speaking about their pasts was in their best interests, and would help their families greatly. Lastly, he asserted that the survivors represented a living monument for those who were not there and who died in the Holocaust, and therefore they had an obligation to speak. Essentially, Shalom charged his fellow survivors with a mission to become agents of memory: to embark on the same journey he had begun twenty years ago. He encouraged child survivors to come out of hiding, to face their past, and help build a collective memory of a once silent and silenced population.

Reuniting with one's rescuers

Throughout her adult life, Rivka's relationship with her mother continued to be a complicated one, as the process of estrangement, which began after the war, continued. Rivka explained that she even transferred these feelings to her children, as they found it difficult to relate to her mother as a grandmother. This dynamic became even more pronounced when Rivka's rescuers came back into her life, as she looked towards her rescuers as parental figures and her children looked to them as surrogate grandparents. They also helped Rivka find her past, her memories and her voice – something that her biological mother had not been willing or able to do. Daniel Schacter writes, "Re-experiencing ones personal past sometimes depends on chance encounters with objects that contain keys to unlocking memories that might otherwise be hidden forever."[16] Her rescuers and not her biological mother were the 'key' to her memories and her identity.

In the next passage, Rivka explains how she met her rescuers after decades of separation. She explains that, "When I was married and had three children, the Israeli government arranged for all those Dutch people who had hidden Jewish children during the war, to be honored by Yad Vashem. They invited all of those people who were able to travel to come to Israel for a two-week visit. My rescuers came on that trip and that's how we reconnected again. I didn't know how to write in Dutch, but I have a neighbor here who speaks Dutch and she wrote a letter to them for me. I wrote to them telling them about my children, and they began visiting me every Christmas, because they have three weeks of holidays then . . . When they used to come, they did not want to travel around the country; they only wanted to spend time with the children. They wanted to see them when they woke up in the morning, when they came home from kindergarten. They used to come to the kindergarten with me, and all the teachers knew their 'aunt and uncle' from Holland . . . then the *bar-mitzvot* started and then the weddings . . . they used to come to every *simcha*." From what Rivka describes, the relationship was one of the same warmth and giving that characterized their relationship during the war. Once they reappeared back into her life, they resumed their role as caretakers, providing the now adult Rivka with financial and emotional support. I got the feeling that Rivka, in reuniting with her rescuers, had found her parents again. Eva Fogelman explains this dynamic, "Rescuing is at least in part a maternal activity, and to be rescued one has to develop the dependence of a child in regard to his parents."[17] In Rivka's case, this relationship continued in her mind after the war had ended, and was reinforced once they reconnected.

When I asked Rivka when she had begun speaking about her past, she replied, "When my rescuers came to Israel . . . Once when they were here, I asked them if they could write about the period during the war when I was with them. They were very, very simple people, and they did not have the ability to write well . . . so we had an idea. He would tell the story in Dutch and I would translate it into Hebrew. That's how my children heard all the stories. All the time, each visit, it was like that, and I learned which questions to ask. When I asked questions, he would answer and I would record them. Afterwards we wrote the story down from the tape. After the story had been written, I felt more comfortable and freer to speak about my past. Also because I began to remember, because it was written . . . " Not only did Rivka's rescuers facilitate the telling of her own story, Rivka facilitated the telling of theirs.

Once Rivka's rescuers reappeared into her life, she rediscovered her past and her former 'identity' as a child. One event triggered a process of recall, identification, telling, and public commemoration. Her narrative is important in that it demonstrates how personal memory and identity contributes to the construction of collective memory. Rivka welcomed her past, because she had been loved and cared for by her rescuers, and she remembered the time she spent with them fondly. It is not clear from her narrative what the actual trigger behind Rivka's inquiry was; yet it is clear that she had a need to know more about her past. Rivka's past had been inaccessible to her for most of her life. Due to her young age during the war, once she was taken away from her rescuers, she lost her access to her memories. Moreover, her mother also refused to speak about the past after the war. Thus, after the war Rivka had no access to her memories of her past life and had no way to confirm or verify what she had experienced. Eva Fogelman writes that rescuers are "a source of information which can confirm the child's hidden past."[18] Thus, when Rivka was reunited with her rescuers, she began to discover who she was, and had the confidence to give voice to her story because she now had a story to tell.

Both Rivka and her children learned about her war-time experiences through the memories of her rescuer. Thus, her past is constructed from the memories of her rescuers and not from her own. The fact that she does not have her 'own story' does not bother Rivka. Rather, it is *having* memories that are important for her. Her narrative does contain a few of her own memories too, some of which predate her stay with this particular couple. Her own memories are predominantly sensory memories, memories of touch, sound, smell, and emotions, which are fragmented and lack coherence. Through listening to her rescuers' stories, Rivka was able to merge her own fragmented, sensory memories with the memories of her rescuer, thus creating a coherent, verified narrative of the past. Rivka's narrative clearly demonstrates that her memories of the war are a 'reconstruction' of the period, a reconstruction which has been co-constructed.

Furthermore, when Rivka was asked to speak to school students about her experiences during the war, she would arrange the meetings to coincide with her rescuers' visit to Israel. In co-telling, Rivka's story became further enmeshed with her rescuers; she did not have a separate story or a separate narrative identity. Rather, her own story is an extension of the narrative of her rescuers. As Rivka rediscovered her past and with help of her rescuers reconstructed a personal story, she assumed the role as an agent of memory and carried her story, and that of her rescuers, to a wider audience.

Once Rivka's biological mother broke her silence, after decades of silence, the relationship between the two of them began to improve. Rivka's mother began to speak about her own past, once her children began speaking about theirs, as she realized that she could no longer protect them from the past as some of them (though not Rivka) had remembered it clearly. Rivka's brother also wrote a book about his experiences during the war. Rivka and her brother combined both their stories and presented the book to their mother as a sign of their gratitude to her. Rivka remarks that they produced the book so that, "our children and grandchildren will remember what happened. So, through that, my children and my brother's children have got a different picture than they had whilst growing up. That was their grandmother . . . do you understand me? My mother is eighty-five today, nearly eighty-six years old. We all understand her more today and she has become closer to us, and she even speaks a bit about the past . . . you asked if she spoke about the past a lot . . . but today, because my brother spoke, all of us can ask her what we couldn't before . . . "

This extract is significant in that it reflects how silence became a barrier to fostering and developing familial relationships, not only between parents and children, but also between grandparents and grandchildren. It demonstrates how the process of retelling works to rebuild the bridges of misunderstanding and misconceptions, as individuals begin to know and understand each other better.

A large motivation behind Rivka's retelling is related to her need to thank and praise her rescuers for risking their lives to save her during the *Shoah*. Her testimony is public recognition of their heroic behavior. At the First International Gathering of Hidden Children During World War II, which was held in New York in 1991, Abe Foxman opened the conference relating to the issue of rescuers. "Above all, we want to say 'thank you' to those who saved our lives. Most of us never had the opportunity to say *dziekuje, merci,* or *danke schoen.* Most of us never had the opportunity to look into a face and say 'thank you'. We want to say to our loved ones: Thank you for understanding, thank you for being patient. Thank you for bearing our silence and thank you for bearing our anger."[19]

"Listening to my brother's story"

Ruth explains that there were a few reasons behind her telling. " [It occurred] much later in my life . . . I would say it happened ten years ago, fifteen years ago, not before. On one of my Sabbaticals – I am a teacher – I decided to do a course at Yad Vashem, and that is when I really started to get involved with the Holocaust again. Since then, I am always in touch with Yad Vashem. I did a course also of *Hadracha* for teenagers, for schools, and then I also took schools for a while, but then I stopped." Approximately ten to fifteen years ago, Ruth, the Israeli schoolteacher, began to reacquaint herself with the *Shoah.* She explains that she began to "learn about it in order to teach about it." During the course itself, Ruth revealed her own personal past. She explains that, "Up until ten years ago, I never told anybody – at school my friends didn't know, I don't know how it got started they got to know about it. Maybe when I went to Yad Vashem. Because the people there were amazed! And they said, 'Why don't you tell your pupils?' Up till then, I had never spoke to my pupils about it. Since then I always tell my pupils about it."

As Ruth learnt more about the *Shoah,* she began to find her own place within its narrative. Furthermore, 'significant others' validated her story and legitimized her identity as a Holocaust survivor – something which she had denied for over forty years. In Chapter 3 I discussed how part of Ruth's ambivalence towards her past was connected to the way in which the *Shoah* was presented in Israeli collective memory, where the 'authentic' Holocaust survivors were seen as those who survived the camps. Therefore, the fact that her story was validated in Yad Vashem is very significant when trying to understand the reasons behind Ruth's telling. She was silenced by collective memory after the war, and now the 'main architect' of collective memory in Israel was validating her past and encouraging her to tell her story – her story as a survivor of the Holocaust. Ruth's narrative is important in that it show how personal memory is not static, but can develop and change in reaction to both external and internal pressures. In the past few years, Ruth appears to have changed her personal story from the story of immigrant[20] to the

story of a child survivor – as a result of public legitimization of her identity as a child survivor. Yet, despite the difference, both are legitimate
and authentic voices.

Because of her young age during the war, Ruth usually remembered
her war experiences through the experiences of her brother. Therefore,
it is hardly surprising that whilst watching her brother's video testimony, she began to feel the need to speak about her own past. She
explains, "Then another thing happened. My brother also did a course
for survivors at Yad Vashem more or less at the same time, and he was
video-taped in Yad Vashem. And once I took this tape to look at it. I
looked at it by myself, and it really did something to me. It moved me
a lot. First of all I learned things I didn't know . . . " Thus, whilst listening to his story, she heard her *own* story being told and began to
acknowledge her own personal suffering during the war and to identify as a Holocaust survivor. Once Ruth was able to own her identity
and her past, she felt comfortable sharing it with others. Her first audience was her family. She explains that, "And I decided then that . . . I
will have an evening with the whole family here. We had an evening
here, the whole family – my children, their spouses, my brother's children and their spouses. I also have two grandchildren who are already
at an age at which they could understand, my cousin, the one who
looked after me and their children, my mother was still alive, and we
sat here and one of my children suggested that we should video tape
this meeting . . . but I was very skeptical, because it was a video where
he talks and I didn't know how the children would react. And also at
the beginning they asked and they said 'Oh, it is only talking, there is
no . . . ' – you know how they want to see things, so I really wasn't sure
how it is going to be. And it was an unbelievable evening . . . And
whenever one of the children – it was really the first time that my children, their children, heard the story and every time they wanted to ask
something, we stopped the video and they asked questions and my
mother could tell, my brother could tell, my cousin could tell, I could
tell. Each one gave his own point of view, yes? For example, the interviewer asked my brother 'How did you feel then, you know, without
your parents?' And so on. And each one of us gave our view. And I
remember we stayed here until one o'clock in the morning and the children didn't stop – they weren't children, they were big and married and
they didn't stop asking questions."

That evening, by each family member contributing their individual
memories, Ruth's family created their own collective remembrance of
their collective past. This experience was also particularly powerful for
Ruth as she realized that people, and in this case her children, were fasci-
nated by her story and wanted to know more. She had found an

empathic audience, first through Yad Vashem and now with her family, which encouraged her to retell her story publicly. Yet, despite the fact that this initiated Ruth's retelling, she continued to present her own story as part of her family's narrative, and not as her own individual experience. A possible explanation may be that, because she relies on the memories of her brother, she does not have the confidence to speak on her own. Her story is not entirely her own. Rather, like Rivka, her narrative of the war is made up of multiple memories. This is one of the reasons why she has not given personal testimony at Yad Vashem. She reasons that, "Because my brother has done it and it's the same story. It's the same story . . . " In the past few years, although Ruth has begun to own her identity as a survivor, she still does not believe that she has her own unique story to tell.

Aging

According to Ehud, the identity conflict experienced by child survivors becomes more acute during aging, at which stage, he cautions, "then one needs to deal with them [past memories]." Ehud's own narratives confirm the developmental theories of Erik Erikson, later expanded by Henry Krystal, on aging and integration, as presented in Chapter 1. Ehud explains that, "In the meantime we got older, and we have reached the stage where we know that we will die. We will die tomorrow or in another week or in another ten years time, and we want to try and close the circle, to tell our own versions, in a gentle way. Not so much to commemorate something, but with the feeling that perhaps our children or grandchildren, or our grandchildren through our children, can learn and know who we were and what we have experienced."

As Ehud enters the later years of his life, he begins to feel the need to revisit and retell his entire past, so that his 'entire' self will be remembered after he dies. What is fascinating is that Ehud has reasoned that in order to *live* after the war, he needed to conceal his biological identity. Yet he cannot cope with the thought of *dying* and being *remembered* as only half the individual that he was. In this extract, Ehud also explains that his need for integration is related to his own need for his grandchildren to know who he is, and who their grandparents were. If he fails to tell them before he dies, their memory will be lost forever.

Grandchildren: "Safta, were you in the Holocaust?"

Tamar began speaking about her past only three years ago. When asking Tamar what prompted her to begin speaking about her past, she replied, "About two years ago I began speaking on the subject. It happened to me on *Yom Hashoah*. Suddenly I felt that I have to speak. But before that, there was nothing . . . Coming up to *Yom Hashoah*, one of my grandchildren asked me '*Safta*, were you in the Holocaust?' and I said 'Yes'. They said, 'But you never spoke about the subject', and then something like broke inside of me, I said 'That's it', now I have to start speaking . . . "

Tamar's grandchild had asked a very confronting question, one that challenged her very identity: I know you are my *safta*, but don't you have another past too? Once the fact of her hidden past was revealed, Tamar could no longer keep up her disguise, especially from those nearest and dearest to her. Like Ehud, there came a moment when she could no longer hide her full identity, and she began to feel the need to acknowledge her past. Unlike Ehud, however, who as a result of his adoption had created two separate identities, there was some continuity in Tamar's identity as she had survived the war with her parents. Although she had concealed her war-time experiences, she had remained 'Tamar' throughout her life.

Tamar's "autobiographical occasion"[21] correlates with Dan Bar-On's theory that the third generation is able to facilitate telling amongst survivors. In his work *Fear and Hope*, Bar-On, quoting Cohler and Grunebaum, explains that the *Shoah* "wiped out the possibility of a *full life-cycle* of multigenerational families, where daughters learn how to be mothers, where grandchildren hear stories and get a sense of continuity from their grandparents."[22] However, with the birth of their grandchildren, this *full life-cycle* was established for survivors, and grandchildren may have introduced a new sense of hopefulness into the family, which facilitated an opening of communication between grandparents and grandchildren. Berlaziki explains, "survivors' fears about being able to rebuild normal lives for their children after what they had been through diminished as their grandchildren, the third generation, grew up. This success made it possible for them to open up and speak."[23] Furthermore, grandparents, reaching Erikson's "aging and integration" stage, began to feel the need to reminisce about their past and pass on their memories. As was clearly demonstrated in Ehud's narratives, child survivors are not only concerned with passing on their own memories and personal stories, but also the memories and legacies of their parents, grandparents, and other lost loved ones who the individual also wants to be remembered after they have died. The impluse to talk and give testimomy became greater than the need for silence.

It is also significant that Tamar's grandchild asked her about her past just before *Yom Hashoah*. During this period in Israel, there is a heightened consciousness about the *Shoah*. It is discussed constantly in the media and in schools, and Israeli school children, like Tamar's grandchild, become more familiar with the story of the *Shoah*. Thus for many school children, having grandparents who are survivors may be a source of pride. On the day itself, *Yom Hashoah* is commemorated by a variety of observances, including commemorative ceremonies and speeches, a moment of silence, and mass media programming, through which Israel attempts to create a ritually unified vision of the past. Thus, the timing of her 'autobiographical occasion' is also related to the heightened discourse about the *Shoah* during this particular calendar period in Israeli society. Tamar's narrative provides us with a powerful example of how collective memory and collective remembrances of the past influence the survivor and their relationship to their own pasts. For many survivors this period is particularly difficult as they are constantly confronted with painful images, and some feel the need to retreat away from the past. For others, like Tamar, this period triggers the past, and it becomes no longer concealable or escapable. There is also an increased pressure and demand on survivors to speak about their experiences during this time, to large audiences of school children, soldiers and at communal memorial services.

Even though Tamar felt the need to begin speaking, she could not do it alone. Rather, she needed a framework that would help her in this painful process. Tamar explains that, "Some time passed, and I saw an advertisement in the newspaper for *Yom Hashoah* for survivors to call AMCHA. Then I called AMCHA and spoke to a woman who happened to be my neighbor, and she has written a book, and it turns out that she had also been in Transnistria in the same town . . . village Shargarod, where I was during the war, only she was an orphan and I was with my parents. And then she started to tell me about Yad Vashem and all the courses that they give . . . they train people to speak . . . That wanted to impart a little knowledge about the *Shoah* . . . to people for the future generations . . . and that's how I got to Yad Vashem, which was, in fact, by chance . . . " The fact that Tamar spoke to a woman, who even happened to be her neighbor, who had had a similar experience during the war, must have further encouraged Tamar to begin this process; it validated her own experiences and reduced her feelings of isolation. These networks of communication between survivors (through personal relationships or support groups like AMCHA) are instrumental in helping survivors acknowledge and articulate their pasts.

Later on in the interview, Tamar explained that her own urge to tell was encouraged by a similar urge in her aged father. Tamar explains, "Only now, about half a year ago, I wrote our life history with my father. He was already old and he could not remember much. Only when I remembered did I remind him! He also repressed it." Tamar had modeled her own silence on her parent's silence. Because they were determined to build a new future and not look back on what they had experienced, the past was hardly ever mentioned in their home. However, at the end of his life, Tamar's father felt the need to recall his experiences and, with her help, they re-remembered their past together, co-constructing their story. Thus, by telling his past, Tamar's father sanctioned Tamar's telling of her own. The very dynamic that had been responsible for her silence all the years was now reversed, enabling Tamar to break her silence and begin to give voice to her past.

Public Recognition

In their post-war environments, child survivors and especially hidden child survivors were not recognized as a separate victim group by society. Their experiences were not validated and in some cases were not even believed. Yet, in the last decade, this has begun to change, as they are now being recognized as a distinct and separate group. Robert Krell states, "While there exist many articles in the psychiatric literature about Holocaust survivors and about their offspring, little mention is made of child survivors as a distinct group. All my life I have known such children, played and studied with them, argued and laughed with them. But it is only until recently that I became aware of their unique presence."[24] Robert Krell argues that, once child survivors were recognized as a distinct group, it facilitated their emergence from hiding and encouraged their retelling.

Perhaps the most significant event which validated experience of hidden child survivors was the First International Gathering of Hidden Children During World War II. This conference, held in New York in 1991, united more than 1,600 hidden child survivors. It recognized the uniqueness of the hidden child's story, and helped the participants form a collective identity. For many, this was the first time they met others who had shared similar pasts. As a result of the conference, the 'Hidden Child Foundation' of the Anti-Defamation League of New York City was created, and has since organized subsequent international conferences, which are attended by child survivors and their children, the second generation. Over the years, support groups for hidden children have began to emerge in various parts of the world in which communities of child survivors live.

Debórah Dwork attributes the break in the silence of child survivors to larger historical changes. She points to the fall of the Berlin Wall and the changing map of Europe, which has created a yearning for memory and continuity, both on a collective and individual level. She writes, "We see that not only for individual people, but for whole populations, the break or rupture with the past is merely superficial . . . those who experienced the war are reconnecting to their past and defying the imposed divide in their individual and collective histories. Both in the private lives and in the lives of nations we are witnessing the expression of a fundamental continuity between the post-war now, the pre-war and wartime then."[25]

This phenomenon whereby the experience of children during the war has begun to be recognized and written about can also be linked to the feminist turn in history which seeks to represent the voices of those who were traditionally silenced, marginalized or absent from traditional historical narratives. Feminist historians argue that historical narratives have largely written about the experiences of men, and have ignored the experiences of women and children. In the last decade, feminist critique has been levelled against Holocaust studies too. Researchers in this field argue that in order to get a fuller, more integrated understanding of the Holocaust, one needs to research the particular experiences of the Jewish victims, which includes gender. They argue that just as gender defines the individual's experience of the world, so too did it affect their experiences as victims of Nazism. Further, Joan Ringelheim argues, "To the Nazis, Jewish women were not simply Jews; they were Jewish women and they were treated accordingly in the system of annihilation."[26] As Ringelheim explains, "for Jewish women the Holocaust produced a set of experiences, responses, and memories that do not always parallel those of Jewish men . . . Therefore to ignore the plight of Jewish women is to ignore more than half of the Jewish population who were deported and murdered."[27] The aim of these researchers is to historiographically democratize the Holocaust experience, to represent the experiences of all its victims, which include the experiences of Jewish children during the war. As a result, the experience of Jewish children has begun to be recognized and written about as a separate victim group. Child survivors are thus becoming able to locate themselves within the history of the Holocaust, which serves to validate and legitimize their experiences as victims and survivors.

Survivor Groups: Finding an Empathic Audience

Child survivors in Israel have also begun to define themselves as a distinct group in the last few years. This has led to the formation of different child survivor groups and organizations. AMCHA in Jerusalem initiated one of the first child survivor groups. The first gathering of former hidden children on the premises of AMCHA took place in late 1992 following an advertisement in the local newspaper. The program adopted consisted of a regular monthly meeting in the framework of a narrative group, which was to be led by two professional therapists. The aim of the program was not only therapeutic, but also to encourage and facilitate retelling. In 1994 AMCHA initiated an autobiographical writing workshop for child survivors. It was in these groups that Ehud began learning how to speak about his past. "The trigger that caused me to open up, to bring up my memories, to develop them, to organize them, to express them, to try and understand them, was a small advert in one of the newspapers in Jerusalem, that AMCHA was starting a group for children who had been through the *Shoah*, for child survivors. That group began in 1992, and between fifteen and eighteen children joined. Slowly, slowly, we began to feel and see that we were among people who, despite the differences in birthplaces, professional life, educational training etc. had a something in common: our experiences during the *Shoah*. We quickly saw that everything that we had to tell, that we could bring up from our deepest memories, all the things that we had hidden from ourselves, from our partners, from our families, we were able to bring up in front of strangers who had experienced similar things. They had experienced the same things and they understood them. Because of this mutual understanding and shared experience, we could, each one of us tell what he sensed, what he feels, what he felt. We learnt that we were not the only ones. Everyone always thought that he was the only one that experienced it, thought, and suffered in the way he felt it."

Through what Dori Laub and Marjorie Allard have defined as an *empathic other*[28] in his support group, Ehud is given the strength to investigate his past. Not only does the group listen to what Ehud has to say, but also they *understand* what he is saying. Ehud does not feel 'alien' amongst the members of the group; they know where he comes from, and understand and empathize with his anxieties and behavior. The AMCHA group represents the antithesis of his adopted parents, who unknowingly made Ehud acutely aware of his difference. His difference was exacerbated in Israel, as an immigrant who as he remembers 'did not know Hebrew nursery rhymes to sing to his children'. In his group, Ehud no longer has to struggle with his feelings of alienation and loneliness; there he no longer feels different. Ehud's narrative affirms Judith Herman's findings that, "The core experiences of psychological trauma are disempowerment and disconnection from others. Recovery, therefore, is based upon the empowerment of the survivor and the creation of new connections . . . In her renewed connections with other people, the survivor recreates the psychological faculties that were damaged or deformed by the traumatic experience."[29] Therefore it is hardly surprising that Ehud began his telling within a group setting, as the group recreated a sense of belonging which had been destroyed both during and after the war.

Dori Laub and Marjorie Allard write that the experience of failed empathy during the *Shoah* is at the heart of the survivor's intolerable sense of aloneness. "It structures the survivor's need to find a good other who can combat this sense of aloneness and who can refigure the survivor as a human being who has a place in the world. The listener embodies the return of the other. Thus, the latent meaning of the desire to bear witness is reparation of the impaired dyad in the imagined or attempted act of communicating. The wish to reinvent the responsive other through testimony so as to reconstitute the self as *one who is heard*."[30]

Ehud continues, "Secondly, we found an empathic ear. We were encouraged by the knowledge that we were understood in a very dramatic way. With time, we learned how to raise our memories in an organized manner, to understand by our behavior, and ourselves, what had happened. The feeling that we felt when bringing up our memories and in the analysis of our emotional states, led to a certain ease – the satisfaction that we were able to deal with our memories, to understand them more objectively, by comparing them with the experiences of others. The feeling was that, even though the horrific nature of the experiences has not been lessened, at least now there is cooperation, comradeship, that there are others and that it is possible to share it with them. We were able to see things from a different perspective, yet still in a personal way. But the greatest ease was being able to deal with the past in a conscious way."

Ehud's narrative reflects on one of the fundamental principles of recovery: "the empowerment of the survivor. She must be the author and the arbiter of her own recovery."[31] The AMCHA group facilitators, who were mental health professionals, empowered Ehud and his group by assisting them to understand 'what had happened and our behavior', and through helping them deal with their memories in an organized manner. The professionals gave the group tools with which to work though and understand the past and their related behaviors. Both during and after the war, Ehud suffered from loneliness and isolation. These feelings continued right through his adult life and finally he decided to deal with them. Through belonging to the AMCHA group, Ehud finally found a place of belonging, where he could speak about his past and his former identity, through his current identity.

What is clear from Ehud's narrative is that the route of his 'recovery' is connected to the route of his trauma. Throughout his narrative, Ehud explains that "the words that encapsulate the entire period are: isolation and loneliness," and it is within a supportive group framework that Ehud is able to begin working through his past, and heal his 'damaged self'. Ehud has been involved in the workshop since 1992. It has been instrumental in helping him to confront his past and work through his losses. In his interview he explained, "A few days ago, in the middle of the night, I wrote some things out of mental anguish when I couldn't sleep. Recently I have been involved, out of choice, in translating documents, usually letters, which were written by people, especially in Germany, Austria and France, who were arrested, beaten, taken and imprisoned; who lost family members, who didn't know where they were, had lost their businesses, were exiled to places or even different countries, were arrested, and were found in various places. They don't know why this was happening to them, and they didn't know what their fate would be. On the other hand, in total contrast, on the opposite side, I am reading documents written by the *Gestapo* and the *Wermacht* and the local authorities, the collaborators. Documents that are organized, in order, exact, and what are told in these documents are the clear orders of arrests and deportations. And the end is known for those who were sent to the east, who were sent to the death camps. Those documents directly relate to those same letters that I read in German and France, of those same people. Amidst this anguish, there is my own mental anguish. I saw myself as peeping into two worlds – of the victims and of the murderous acts, of people who don't know what is happening to them and what would happen to them, and those who are planning and are carrying it out. In my anguish I see my family torn from the village, deported to a camp, in the transports to the death camps; only I survived. I don't know how and when exactly and for what reason, by what thought; they don't have a grave, and I don't visit the place where they died. Until today, until the year 2000, I haven't said *Kaddish*, so I wrote a few lines, as if they were *Kaddish*."

For Ehud, these documents which he was translating are the 'evidence' of his family's death. Even though there is no grave, he is finally able to come to terms with his loss and embark on a process of mourning. His mourning began in 1992. However, by saying *Kaddish* in 2000, Ehud has finally recognized and internalized his status as an orphan. Like Shalom, through writing Ehud has been able to mourn the loss of his biological parents. Thus, remembering and retelling one's Holocaust experiences can be an extremely valuable model of working through trauma experienced during and after the war.

In 1992, Ehud had found himself in a very different sociocultural environment to that of 1945. After the war, he was told to forget the past and he tried to do so. In 1992, he was invited to remember it once again. However, one cannot attribute his telling to the change in his sociocultural environment only. At a certain stage of his life, Ehud felt compelled to look back, reveal, and mourn his past.

Validation: "Your story is not nothing"

We previously saw how Ariala translated her experience during the *Shoah* into a narrative of loss. She continued to relate to her past in this way for many years, even after she had made *aliya* and raised a family of her own. Ariala's relationship to her past began to change only recently. She recalls attending a conference for hidden children that was held in Jerusalem only a few years ago "in the hope that I could meet someone who knew my family in Poland, or someone who knew someone in Treblinka or Auschwitz . . . I went only for that reason." Ariala did not attend the conference as a hidden child survivor, but rather as a child who had been orphaned during the war. Nevertheless, it is interesting that she chose that conference in particular. At the conference, Ariala met another French woman. The two women spent most of their time at the conference together, and got to know each other. At one point the woman turned to Ariala and asked her, "What happened to you during the war?" She answered, 'My story is nothing, I don't want to speak about it'. The woman said 'But you were in hiding . . . ' and I said, 'Yes' and she asked: 'Where?' and I said: 'I was in a village'. And then she began to ask me all sorts of questions and I answered her. Eventually she said to me: 'Your story is not nothing'. I said that I didn't want to talk about it." The woman suggested that they start an organization together, for child survivors. She explained that, "It will be for people to come and speak because no one wants to speak about it." Ariala agreed to participate.

Ariala only began to speak about her past when someone asked her about it. She did not volunteer any information, nor did she present herself as a survivor at the conference, even though the conference must have been filled with people who had had similar experiences during the war. This was the first time in her narrative that she recalls that someone had validated her war experience. However, Ariala was not ready to internalize it. Sometime later, Ariala received a phone call from a woman, a television director, who had received her number from the woman she had met at the conference. The television director asked Ariala if she would be willing to be interviewed. Ariala agreed to meet the woman. They met in Ariala's home.

"She came here and she was a very clever woman. She felt that I didn't want to speak. Therefore, she asked me some questions and I answered them. She stayed here for about two hours and then she left. After a few days she phoned me and said: 'Are you prepared to speak about what we spoke about in front of a camera?' I said: 'I am prepared to, but on one condition, that I don't see the camera. I want it to be as if I am talking only to you'. We were already friends, because after she had asked me questions, we went onto the roof and ate together. I had a connection with her, I don't know how to explain it. It was like I had known her for a long time. There was a connection. So when she phoned to find out if I was interested, I said 'yes'." Ariala had found someone whom she could trust and who understood her. This gave her the courage and confidence to begin telling her story publicly, for the first time since the war ended.

Ariala became anxious in the days preceding the filming, as filming crews were sent to her home to prepare for the shooting. The day of the filming arrived, together with a large film crew. Unnerved by all the people and the attention, Ariala became reluctant to go ahead with the interview. She began to have misgivings that her story was not interesting, and that so much money would be spent filming such an 'ordinary', 'mundane' story. After fifty years, Ariala was still not convinced that she had a worthwhile story to tell as she had internalized the response of other survivors to her story after the war. "But they came and everyone was really very nice. I did not see them. I said to the interviewer, 'Come close to me, the closest you can, so that it will be just the two of us, and so that I won't see the crew'. I really did not want to see them at all. The filming took four days, it was a lot of time. I only answered the questions. I didn't do anything else."

Ariala's process of recalling was slow. With much reassurance, Ariala gradually became convinced that she had something worthwhile to share. Ariala was validated by those who listened to her story, just as to those whom she tried to tell had invalidated her before. Fifty years later, she was still dependent upon the opinion of others, to define and evaluate her experience. Eventually Ariala was validated by an 'official source', Yad Vashem, Israel's National Holocaust Remembrance Authority.

"Yad Vashem sent me a letter asking me if I was prepared to participate in a seminar. I didn't want to do it. It took me two years till I agreed to participate. I got the invitation every year and I always thought that the people who attend these seminars are from Auschwitz, Treblinka, Majdanek, all those places, and my story would not be interesting to anyone. It's boring. I don't want to. In the end when I eventually went to the conference, Moshe Harel told me that I am crazy. He said to me, 'But you don't understand that your story is also important'. And when I started to speak, because everyone spoke for five minutes about his story, I realized that I was the only one who hadn't been in a camp. When I saw that all of those people who are really Holocaust survivors, really camp survivors . . . they listened to my story. They looked at me like I was one their children, as if their children had to go through what I went through and as if they had to sign like my father did. I don't understand, they were in Auschwitz; they saw things that I didn't see. It's not only what they saw, but the smell that was there . . . And that's how I learnt how to tell my story, with Moshe Harel and Ephraim."

Validation for Ariala's story was taking place on a few levels. First, Yad Vashem invited her to participate in its workshop and thus 'they' identified her as a survivor. She herself did not determine her survivor identity; rather society did. Further, Moshe Harel, a psychologist, validated her suffering and encouraged her to speak. As a psychologist, he was not comparing her suffering to the suffering of others; he recognized her own trauma and validated it. Probably the most significant aspect in this narrative is that Ariala was recognized and validated as an 'authentic survivor' by her fellow survivors, who she considered as the 'real survivors'. By them listening to her story, she felt accepted, recognized and validated by the survivor community. She felt that the survivor community had excluded her after the war, and now, fifty years later, they were including her. Through the course at Yad Vashem, Ariala began to work through her past. Only when the hierarchy of suffering, which was responsible for silencing her, began to disintegrate, could Ariala begin to reclaim her past and find her voice. The survivors in the seminar did not compare their experiences, but rather recognized and endorsed the plurality of experiences.

Ariala's telling takes place within a socio-cultural environment that is radically different from her post-war environment. Whereas survivors themselves immediately after the war created the hierarchy of suffering, this narrative reflects the changing attitudes of these survivors themselves. The passing of time creates a point of distance that facilitates new perspectives on the traumatic event both for the collective and for individuals.

Ariala was then ready to speak in front of large audiences, "One day I found myself in front of students, and from then on, ever year, I get an invitation to speak on army bases, at high schools, for religious audiences and at Yad Vashem when non-Jewish tourists come there. And that's how it started, but I learned how to speak. I felt that I had a right to speak because of Moshe Harel."

However, Ariala was initially silenced by her father and, fifty years later, her surviving family continued to remain 'unconvinced' that she had suffered. This remains a painful issue for her. The interview that Ariala had given for Israeli television was broadcast in France too. Ariala was sure that her family had seen it there, and she waited to hear their response.

"Do you think that any one of them called me? No one! It was quite some time ago, about five years ago. In Israel, I got phone calls from everyone . . . I called my family and asked them, 'Did you see the film?'

And they asked: 'Which film?' and I said 'The film about me, about my life'. And they said: 'Ah yes, yes'. It was very difficult for me. They didn't hear me. It's as if I was making up stories; it's as if I had a good time during the war."

After listening to Ariala intently for over three hours, I got the sense that she had begun to own her suffering. Ariala's narrative is also illuminating in that it describes in detail the process of her retelling. Due to her silence, Ariala had not created a 'story' of her experiences. Thus, when she first told her 'story' it was in response to the interviewer's questions. After sharing her memories for the first time, Ariala was then able to reconstruct a 'story' or a narrative of her past, which she was able to share. Dori Laub and Marjorie Allard write that testimony, "in essence is a progression from interpretation of fragmentary defensive reenactments – a personalized, arrested state of 'possessedness' by trauma – to a knowing of the realness of trauma that has occurred in a specific time and place, that allows for one to negotiate a place for trauma *vis-à-vis* one's life so that it can become part of the flow of life, and thus allow life, in turn to be more whole again."[32] It is clear that retelling her past and owning her suffering has helped Ariala to understand her experience and integrate it meaningfully into her life. Yet, the fact that her own family continues to question the severity of her suffering during the war is an issue which continues to pain her till today.

Self-Validation: "My story is something"

The course co-run by Yad Vashem and AMCHA appears to have made a lasting impact on the child survivors who participated. It encouraged them to speak about their pasts, affirming that they had a story to tell. It also helped them work through their feelings of isolation and loneliness. The course provided a protective environment for the child survivors. However, it was not able to prepare them for the challenges they would face once they began retelling publicly. Right at the beginning of her interview, Tamar explains her first public address.

"It was some official ceremony for *Yom Hashoah* and they made classes . . . classes in which there were lectures and I went into one of the classrooms. The classroom was full, there were maybe one hundred children . . . one hundred and fifty . . . it was terribly hot, and I lectured and I spoke and spoke and I thought that I was speaking and that they were not listening! The classroom was crammed! Full of people! After fifty minutes I asked, 'Do you want to still hear? It does not tire you out?' 'No, No! Carry on. After that I finished and there were questions. They bombarded me with questions! One of the questions was very hard. One boy asked me, 'So tell me, you were not in Auschwitz correct? You were not in Majdanek or in Auschwitz?' As if in Transnistria[33] people, did not, did not suffer as much. I was shocked at that moment . . . .after I had thought about the question, I said: 'It's possible to die in many ways. It's possible to die systematically by gas, or crematorium. We experienced terrible hunger . . . .people died from hunger, cold, from typhus, from beatings, murder, from shootings – from all sorts of things which nature does to them, or from man's actions. From hunger . . . there was absolutely no food! They threw people in desolate places, thousands of people without food, without water to wash, in minus thirty degrees cold. In the morning we would take out carts with frozen dead bodies, they were like tree trunks. That's how they would take out carts with the dead. People would sit together with the dead, the living, everyone, together. And people who still lived died from hunger'."

Tamar understood the boy's question to be one that challenged her suffering and identity as survivor. She was confronted with the hierarchy of suffering, like so many hidden child survivors had been. However, Tamar did not become intimidated by the question, and she did not retreat into silence. Rather the question motivated her to describe and speak about her experiences. By saying to the audience, "It's possible to die in many ways", Tamar is challenging the 'accepted' hierarchy of suffering, and attempting to modify it so that her experiences are included. Furthermore, the student's question pushed Tamar, probably for the first time in her life, to relate her traumatic memories and publicly assert that she was indeed an 'authentic survivor'. Furthermore, by her response she was validating the experience of all the Jews who were deported to Transnistria.

It is also significant that, at this point in her narrative, she departs from her coherent narrative as her traumatic memory begins to take over and she begins to re-remember and re-live her war experiences. Daniel Schacter, in his work on memory, explains that it is possible to differentiate between traumatic and non-traumatic memory in the telling. "Ordinary experiences that we mull over and discuss with others can be changed by the retelling; repressed memories of trauma may remain frozen in their original form . . . " He bases his research on the findings of Van der Kolk and his colleagues who report that "people who have experienced severe traumas re-experience them as isolated pictures or bodily sensations accompanied by intense feeling, whereas the same people recall personality significant (not traumatic) experiences in more story-like narrative form."[34] Once Tamar's story was challenged and her identity as a survivor threatened, her narrative plunges into traumatic memory. Perhaps the question signified for Tamar that the boy had not understood her experiences, that there was an unbridgeable gap between them, which threatened the effectiveness of her retelling and her ability to pass on the message. This motivated Tamar to try and explain it in more detail. However, once she began to explain it, she plunged into traumatic memory.

Tamar was not intimidated by this incident, rather it became the driving force behind her subsequent retelling. Tamar subsequently became devoted to research and educating society about the history of the Jews in Transnistria during the Holocaust. "As I said to you, only two years ago I began speaking about the *Shoah* and since then it has not left me. All the time I read about it, especially on the topic of Transnistria . . . in that place, close to 500,000 people died[35] . . . and there were years in which nothing was known about it and also because the Romanians tried to hide it . . . and afterwards the subject of Auschwitz and Majdanek and all those places that people came back from and spoke about it and told about it. It caught all the attention of the *Shoah* . . . so that the *Shoah* and Auschwitz go together and when the you talk about Transnistria it's nothing . . . as if someone made it up . . . nearly ninety percent of the Jews of Besserabia were killed there! . . . from the Jewish community and from Czernowitz, seventy percent were killed. So half a million people there! And there is no memorial . . . it's as if it has been wiped off from the face of the earth."

Tamar's interview tracks the development of her personal memory and identity over the years. Initially committed to silence, Tamar begins telling once she is confronted by her grandchildren. Once Tamar began her retelling, she would not be discouraged. She had found her voice after fifty years, rediscovered her memories, and had been validated by her fellow survivors and by Yad Vashem, and also by an audience who wanted to hear. Yet as she began to identify publicly as a survivor, she was confronted with the hierarchy of suffering and found herself defending her own trauma as well as the trauma of the Jews of Transnistria. Over the years, Tamar has committed herself as an agent of memory on behalf of the Jews of Transnistria and is determined to have their experiences incorporated into collective memory of the *Shoah*. Furthermore in telling their story, she is able to place her own story in a wider narrative.

From Tamar's experience, we can learn that perhaps one of the most powerful elements in the dynamic of silence and telling is recognition and validation. For many hidden survivors, survivor support groups have provided them with the validation that they were deprived of in the years immediately following the war. No longer isolated and alone, survivors joined groups: this helped create a sense of belonging and identity amongst its members and gave them the confidence to speak. Once the experience and identity of hidden child survivors was validated, they became empowered to speak about their past. However, Ariala's case demonstrates that the source of validation is also important. Survivor support groups perform a vital role in helping the survivors find their voices. However it is not always enough for the child survivor to own up to their trauma. Rather, they also need to be validated by the person or people who invalidated their trauma initially. This is most clearly seen in Ariala's case where her father continues to deny her trauma – a source of much frustration and pain.

"Because somebody asked"

The story behind Yafe's telling is similar to that of Ariala. During her first years in Israel, Yafe explains that she remained silent about her past because of the way Israeli society related to the *Shoah* and viewed its victims. She also explains that at the time there was limited awareness of the *Shoah* and a high level of self-absorption on the part of the *sabras*. Essentially no one asked Yafe about her past, and she explains that she was 'too embarrassed to tell'. During the interview, she says that she began speaking in 1971. I asked her if she is able to recall why. She replied, "At that time a girl from a high-school interviewed me. Later in 1990, there was a woman who was a teacher for the first grade. She had also taught at a school in Kfar HaRoeh, where my husband had one been the principal. She said to me: 'Tell me Yafe, for ten years you taught at Kfar HaRoeh, but you never told anything'. I said to her, 'Tell me, did anyone ask me? No one asked and I didn't tell'." Similar to Ariala, Yafe began to share her past only when someone asked her.

"And every year since then, I speak at school about the *Shoah*. I have received a lot of letters and it gives me strength to speak. Girls tell me that it's because of me that they believe that the *Shoah* happened. One girl in sixth grade wrote to me and said, 'It's the first time that I believe that the *Shoah* happened'. It's because I speak on their level. It is true that I wasn't in a concentration camp. But I tell stories, I don't speak about it. I don't speak to them about six million, because no child can comprehend what that is. I can't either." Once Yafe began to speak about her past, she has not stopped. Her decision to continue speaking was reinforced by the response of her students. Especially because "there are girls who say that it's because of me that they believe the *Shoah* happened." Thus, as an educator, Yafe feels that she has an obligation to teach, to educate, and to honor the memory of those who perished. Yafe has devoted the last thirty years to telling her story. She has even published her story in a children's book about the *Shoah*.

Yafe accepts the hierarchy of suffering, yet despite the fact that she wasn't in a camp she believes she also has the right to speak, especially since she is able to communicate the experience to others. She justifies her right to speak, and educate, because she feels that students can relate to her experiences, as opposed to the 'massive stories' which are too difficult, even for her, to comprehend. Therefore for Yafe, the hierarchy of suffering does not determine who has the right to speak. Rather for her, it is the ability to communicate the past which is important, and not what one experienced. This piece also reflects how resilient the hierarchy of suffering is, and the extent to which it dominated the thinking of hidden child survivors.

Shlomo Breznitz, who addressed a child survivor conference in Israel in 2000, reinforced understanding. He argued that society has changed in what it is able and willing to hear. The stories of child survivors are not too harrowing and thus society is more receptive to them now, more than the 'horror stories' of the typical survivor testimony to which society has been exposed to over the past sixty years. He argues that the mythological experiences of trauma and suffering often distanced the survivor from his/her audience, and the 'smaller', more personal stories have the ability to produce empathy between survivors and his/her audience.[36] Stories of child survivors are thus becoming more 'popular' in collective memory, because they are more 'hearable' and 'manageable' than the traditional narratives of adult survivors.

Yafe's retelling is an extension of her teaching. She does not relate to it as a working through of her past. Nor does it help her to recover lost memories, or to build a chronological life story. There are no signs of an identity conflict and an attempt to integrate her 'two lives'. Yafe's narrative is one of loss, and her inability to come to terms with the loss of her father. Retelling has not eased the pain, nor has it facilitated a mourning process in the way it did for Shalom and Ehud. Yafe explains, "In Paris, if I saw a man who looked like my father, I would chase him. I thought that maybe father didn't remember us; maybe he didn't know where we survived. All the time I hoped. I didn't go to shul when they remembered the dead. I didn't want to pray. When I said grace after meals I included my father as 'my teacher' in the blessing."

Yafe was constantly searching for her father, or for evidence of his death. "After the war when I saw pictures of bones, and in Yad Vashem when I saw pictures of piles of bones, I searched . . . perhaps that's my father's leg." However, once she received documentation stating that her father had been deported to Drancy, Yafe began mourning. And she refuses to stop. "I know what happened from documents. A long time after the war, when I was already in Israel, I went to find out exactly what happened to my father. And my brother found a telegram which he has, which was sent to Adolf Eichmann in Berlin that on such a such date they took these Jews, and there is my father's address, his birth date, his occupation, everything was correct. They took him on the same day to Drancy, which was a transit camp on the way to Auschwitz." Yafe explains, "I am in constant mourning over my father. I have not stopped mourning."

At the end of our interview, Yafe reveals that she is constantly struggling with her past. "The visits to Yad Vashem have helped me. I really want to go to Auschwitz but my husband won't let me. He says that I may not be able to handle it. I don't know. Maybe he is right. But he wants me to speak with a psychiatrist about it. I am in psychiatric treatment. I may appear to be normal to you, I do try. I raised four children, I have four daughters-in-law, and sixteen grandchildren." Yafe cautions me not to be misled by her seemingly 'normal' appearance and life, as her life continues to be filled with pain and interminable mourning. It has been argued by mental health professionals, specifically psychiatrists and psychologists, that retelling one's trauma in a supportive, trusting environment can facilitate a process of confronting and working through trauma. However, Yafe's testimony reflects something quite different. Her narrative shows how, in her retelling "the victim is still consumed by the past, a sealed pain, only recaptured through struggle."[37] Validation may have helped Yafe articulate her past, and her need to educate the future generation continues to motivate her to speak about it, yet telling has not eased the pain or restored her sense of belonging.

Retelling and Rebuilding

The breaking of the silence of hidden child survivors cannot be attributed to a single cause. Rather, hidden child survivors began to give voice to their pasts for all the reasons that have been discussed. However, the narratives presented in this chapter reveal that a particular relationship exists between silence and retelling: The very motivation behind the initial silence/silencing became the motivation behind their decision to tell.

If we take Ehud and Shalom, we recall that the main motivation behind their silence was to rebuild a 'normal life', and have a 'normal identity'. No longer wanting to be different, they silenced their past and built a new future. However, at some point the past disturbed their 'normal lives'. Shalom was revisited by traumatic memories and Ehud realized that he could no longer hide the *Shoah*. Ehud explains that the *Shoah* cannot be hidden because, "For the survivor it is the most fundamental event in his life, even if he forgets it, or tries to forget it and represses it, it still comes out." Ehud realized that silence had not given him a 'normal life'; rather it had created another lie, another false identity. This only reinforced his feelings of loneliness and isolation – feelings that he had tried to overcome through his silence. Shalom explains that through re-membering his past, he has become a 'normal person' once again. For Ehud, telling has enabled him to finally come out of hiding.

Adults silenced Ariala and Tamar after the war. Ariala's past was invalidated by the adult community, especially adult survivors, and Tamar's past was silenced by her parents. Furthermore, like Ehud and Shalom, they too wanted to leave the past behind and become 'normal'. Tamar's journey to telling began when her father began to speak about the past, thus giving her permission to speak. Ariala began speaking once someone took interest in and validated her story. Perhaps the most crucial moment for Ariala was when other survivors, who were adult survivors of the camps, validated her story. "I was the only one who hadn't been in a camp, when I saw all of those people who are really Holocaust survivors, really camp survivors, they listened to my story . . . " In Ariala's case, retelling began when others validated her experience as a survivor; specifically when adult survivors authenticated her story, as inevitably they had been responsible for de-legitimizing her experiences.

Living in Israel after the war, Yafe and Ruth felt embarrassed by their past. They had internalized the stigma that Israeli society imposed on Holocaust survivors, and they chose to hide their identity as child survivors. However, in the last few decades the image of the survivor has changed in Israeli collective memory. No longer blamed and judged, survivors are now greeted as "celebrants of life, redeemers of the human spirit, and voices of heroic affirmation."[38] It was within this new socio-cultural environment that Yafe and Ruth began their telling. Specifically, recalling the past was encouraged by individuals who worked in state institutions: Ruth was encouraged to speak by staff at Yad Vashem, and Yafe was encouraged to speak by one of her peers at a public school. The main motivation behind Yafe's retelling was the positive feedback that she received from the students whom she spoke too. "There are teachers who have heard me three years ago and hear me again five years later and they say: 'Listen, you have helped me so much. One woman said that she had had a miscarriage and my talk helped, I gave her so much faith. All sorts of things. It happens that I meet some of my students who are now rabbis in *yeshivot*. It gives me satisfaction, because children really want to hear about it'." The stories of child survivors are now welcomed and encouraged in contemporary Israeli society. Israel as a society has become an empathic audience to the stories and memories of child survivors of the *Shoah*. Furthermore, their memories and experiences have become an integral part of contemporary collective memory.

All of the narratives presented in this chapter also reflect a general theme: the experience of the hidden child needs to be validated in order for them to begin telling their pasts. They have needed the outside world to show an interest in their stories and validate their experiences, before they could find their voices. In the post-war years, their trauma was invalidated and they became silent. Only when their trauma was validated did they begin telling. Judith Herman writes, "to hold traumatic reality in consciousness requires a social context that affirms and protects the victim and joins the victim and witness in a common alliance. For the individual victim, this social context is created by relationships with friends, lovers, and family. For the larger society, the social context is created by political movements that give voice to the disempowered."[39] From the narratives of hidden child survivors presented above, it can be seen that their telling was facilitated largely by a supportive sociocultural environment which encouraged them to share their pasts and validated their suffering. Some of the child survivors found their empathic audience in other individuals, and others in support groups. From the narratives presented, we learn that the child survivor is only willing and able to tell those whom they feel are truly interested in their story.

The only exception to this group may be Shalom, who began telling because of what she described as 'personal reasons'. However, Shalom did not keep his writing as a journal, but rather decided to publish. His book was published in 1999, in a sociocultural context that validated the experiences of child survivors. His work gave child survivors a voice and he hoped that it would encourage other child survivors to begin speaking about their experiences. Furthermore, Shalom sees himself as a witness – for all his friends who died. "I think that I wrote this book, first of all, to make it easier for me. But I also see myself as a representative of all my childhood friends. I am not speaking about the whole community. I see myself as one member of a group, where everyone died."

Just as Shalom attempted to validate the experience of other child survivors, child survivors as a group were also instrumental in their own public validation. The Hidden Children Conference, which was held in 1991, officially named them as a group and validated their separate identity. The fact that they were officially named as 'survivors' encouraged many of them to end their silence and begin investigating their pasts. In chapter 2, we saw how trauma, even though internally experienced, is externally defined and validated. This idea holds true when trying to understand the dynamics behind telling. These hidden children only begin to give voice to their experiences once their story was validated externally. "Restoration of the breach between the traumatized person and the community depends, first, upon the some public acknowledgement of the traumatic event . . . "[40]

Even though these hidden child survivors continued to hide their past, they did not necessarily forget it. The older child survivors have rich and detailed memories of their past, which, after years of silence, have sometimes become disorganized and confusing. Telling has facilitated a re-remembering of the past, as well as a reorganization of their memories into a coherent narrative. Further, once they began to re-remember, other memories surfaced. During the actual interviews, especially younger child survivors often remembered things for the first time. As younger child survivors have begun to re-remember their pasts, they are not confident as there are significant gaps in their memories. Some have been able to 'fill their memories out' with the recollections of parents, rescuers, documents etc., which has resulted in a reconstruction of their memories. Collective memory may been powerful in silencing personal memory, yet it was not able to erase it.

Part of the motivation behind building a narrative relates to the theory of aging and integration. However, it seems that Israeli society has demanded that child survivors create a narrative from their experiences, as they have become the 'new witnesses' to the *Shoah*. This process is apparent in the aims of the course run by Yad Vashem and AMCHA. Their aim is to help survivors build a story, which they can then retell as witnesses before large audiences. This has encouraged many child survivors to begin retelling, as society has now sent out the message that they 'have an important story to tell'. In retelling, the child survivors hope to undo the damage caused to them by years of silence. They want to stop lying to themselves and to others; and they want to stop hiding from themselves and from others. Furthermore, telling also facilitates a working through process, where survivors are able to confront their past and mourn their losses. For most of the survivors presented in this chapter, speaking initiated mourning – which was both painful and healing. The telling of trauma inevitably plunges the survivor into profound grief as they revisit the traumatic past. Furthermore, many survivors fear that "successful mourning may lead to letting go and thereby forgetting the dead and committing them to oblivion."[41] Yet, retelling the past is also therapeutic as it functions as a commemorative act, and may provide for some the sense of *symbolic immortality*[42] for their lost loved ones. Furthermore, Judith Herman explains that "after many repetitions, the moment comes when the telling of the trauma story no longer arouses quite such an intense feeling. It has become a part of the survivors' experience, but only a part of it . . . When the 'action of telling a story' has come to its conclusions, the traumatic experience truly belongs to the past."[43] Survivors can now look forward and focus on their present and the future. However, for some, retelling does not provide peace of mind. For individuals like Yafe, even after years of retelling, the past is still too overwhelming as she is unable to come to terms with her losses.

5

Those Who Have Always Spoken

Primo Levi, in his work *Moments of Reprieve*, writes that, "it has been observed by psychologists that the survivors of traumatic events are divided into two well-defined groups: those who repress their past *en bloc*, and those whose memory of the offense persists, as though carved in stone, prevailing over all previous or subsequent experiences. Now, not by choice but by nature I belong to the second group. Of my two years of life outside of the law I have not forgotten a single thing. Without any deliberate effort, memory continues to restore me events, faces, words, sensations as if at that time my mind had gone through a period or exalted receptivity, during which not a detail was lost."[1]

When I interviewed Yitzhak and Kalman it was clear that they, like Primo Levi, belonged to the second group of survivors. They have become "storytellers in their own lives and that the worlds they provide us with have not been given to us alone."[2] This was reflected in the way in which they told their narratives, which were clear and coherent. They also had the ability to relate their experiences in minute detail, and were able to construct a general chronology of the events. In effect, both Yitzhak and Kalman created stories of their experiences.

During the course of their interviews, they also explained that, as survivors, they had committed themselves to retelling their stories. Being survivors of Auschwitz–Birkenau the war had come to occupy a central place in their life history, and was a salient part of their identity. Researchers have found that the nature of the war experience is an important factor in the child survivor's decision whether or not to talk about their pasts. Both Kalman and Yitzhak spent a part of their war years as prisoners in Auschwitz–Birkenau. Surviving this experience not only shaped the way that they defined and remembered their internal trauma, but also determined the way they were perceived by and treated in their post-war socio-cultural environment. Because

Auschwitz–Birkenau occupied a central place in collective memory of the *Shoah*, their identity as survivors was never doubted. Their trauma was never de-legitimized, and their retelling was always encouraged.

Their motivation to speak stemmed from their own personal need. They also feel a sense of communal obligation to remember and never forget. They not only wanted to bear witness, but also wished to preserve the memories of what had been destroyed. Annette Wieviorka points out that "the imperative of memory never exists for itself, does not suffice unto itself. The majority of those who write testimonies justify recording their experiences in terms of motives that go beyond the presentation of their own suffering. Sometimes remembering is an obligation towards their dead companions . . . "[3] In their testimonies, both Kalman and Yitzhak pay homage to those who did not survive.

From the time of their liberation until today, both Kalman and Yitzhak have devoted their lives to retelling the past. In telling their stories they drew on narrative structures to give form and meaning to their experiences. Essentially the narrative structures that they use have helped them "make a story" of what is "not a story".[4]

Kalman employs biblical and Talmudic narratives, which can be considered as archetypes or myths, to narrate and understand his past. Rollo May defines myths as "narrative patterns that give significance to our existence."[5] For traditional Jews, the flow of contemporary events is subsumed to familiar archetypes, with myths of the past serving as paradigm and leitmotif in interpreting both the past and the future.[6] Thus, the traditional narrative helps Kalman connect his past with his present and his future. It also provides him with a vision of the world and the vital meaning of his experience. Yitzhak constructs his past around the narrative of heroism, which is congruent with Israel's meta-narrative of heroism. Like Kalman, Yitzhak uses the heroic narrative to describe and make meaning of his past, but he also uses it to transcend his victim past and forge a place of belonging in the present. He uses the heroic narrative to have "a story within which to situate, and through which to retell his own",[7] to transcend his victimization and connect to his post-war socio-cultural context. Furthermore, over the years both Kalman and Yitzhak have busied themselves with collecting historical documents which 'prove' their accounts and provide a historical context for their personal stories. The historical narrative also functions as a means through which they are able to communicate their pasts to those who did not experience the war. Throughout the years, both of these individuals have concerned themselves with finding ways to communicate their war experiences in their new socio-cultural environment, Israel.

Yitzhak "the Soldier"

Yitzhak explains that the first time he began speaking about his past was "when I wrote about it. It was in 1946. In school in Be'er Tuvia [an agricultural community] the teacher asked us to write an essay on any topic. I wrote about my liberation from Gunskirchen and the story that I told you about the German woman that I stayed with and how we walked to the main road. I wrote that in 1946 and I got a 'very good' for it." From the outset, the socio-cultural environment encouraged Yitzhak's need to speak about his past. He remarks, "I did not wait for the Eichmann Trial. I spoke about it even when I was in Be'er Tuvia, before the War of Independence, and afterwards as a student in *Mikvei Yisrael*.[8] I always spoke about it to my friends in the army. For days and nights, I spoke about it. I was always very open. I had a friend who was in unit 101. I was very close to him. We had studied together in *Mikvei Yisrael*, and we are still in contact. Once he said to me: 'Itzik, it's only because of the stories that you told me that I enlisted into unit 101. So that things like that won't happen to the Jewish people again'."

Unit 101 was created in response to the terrorist incursions into Israel between 1951 and 1955, which claimed the lives of 967 Israelis. Ariel Sharon was asked to create and lead this highly trained anti-terrorist unit, which was to strike accurately and effectively at the villages and strongholds used by the terrorists to commit these atrocities. In his autobiography, Sharon refers to the unit's first 'successful' operation in Kibbya.[9] He writes, "what this meant for army morale can hardly be exaggerated. The past years had been a time of impotence and frustration. With Kibbya a new sense of confidence began to take root. Even more important, Israel's Jews began to feel they were not completely defenseless against the murders and maimings that had, by 1953, reached into every corner of the country."[10] Because of its military successes, the unit occupied a central place in the Israeli collective consciousness, representing Israel's ability to defend her civilians from being attacked and murdered – the antithesis of the story of the *Shoah*.

Thus, from the outset Yitzhak had an empathic audience with whom he could share his past. This is an important extract as it demonstrates how Yitzhak had managed to forge a place for himself amongst the young *sabras*. Moreover, according to his narrative, it was he who became the 'hero' and who inspired his friend, the young *sabra*, to join one of the most elite units in the Israeli army at that time – Unit 101. This piece is particularly illuminating as it demonstrates how Israel's conflict with her Arab neighbors was viewed as a potential Holocaust. Israel continued to see herself as the victim, yet unlike in the Diaspora, Jews would fight with honor to protect its citizens. Hanna Yablonka writes that, "by participating in battle with veteran Israelis, Holocaust survivors earned what became known as 'revenge through resurrection' and in this manner became 'Israelis', particularly in their own eyes."[11]

Furthermore, this piece demonstrates how Yitzhak's openness about his past also helped him develop deep and meaningful relationships with his peers, as "people knew exactly what I had gone through. I remember that even in *Mikveh Yisrael*, we were young, and at night, in the dark, we were ten boys to a room, I spoke . . . I integrated and acclimatized like a *sabra*, and I spoke and spoke. I was very open."

Yitzhak's narrative stands in strong contrast to the narratives of child survivors who were silenced in their post-war environment. His story was neither silenced, nor did he feel the need to hide his survivor identity in order to be accepted into Israeli youth culture. His narrative begs the question: what is it about Yitzhak's experience during and after the war that facilitated such a radical departure from the experience of other child survivors, whose experiences in their post-war society are characterized mainly by silencing and repression? My investigations point to two major factors: first, his experience during the war, and second the meaning he has created around his survival.

The Centrality of Auschwitz in the Narrative of the Shoah

As discussed in the Introduction, for many years survivors of ghettos and concentration camps were considered to be the 'legitimate' Holocaust survivors. Furthermore, Auschwitz became a symbol which dominated the collective memory of the *Shoah*, especially after the Eichmann Trial. In his book *Justice in Jerusalem*, Gidon Hausner referred to Auschwitz as the "the peak of all horror."[12] The issue of Auschwitz–Birkenau being the 'symbol' of the Holocaust is an interesting phenomenon, which demands further explanation. Unfortunately, a full explanation is beyond the scope of this work.[13]

Yitzhak does not explicitly attribute his retelling to his identity as an Auschwitz survivor, but the social validation of his experience was certainly an important factor. What is clear from his narrative is that his experiences in Auschwitz–Birkenau are at the center of his narrative and identify him as a survivor of the *Shoah*. This is evident right from the beginning of my interview with him. Yitzhak begins his narrative by briefly explaining his life before the war. He then progresses to tell his past chronologically, from the outbreak of the war in Poland in 1939, to his family's subsequent ghettoization in Pietrikow–Tribunalksi. After taking a few minutes to describe his life in the ghetto, a period of four years, Yitzhak jumps to 1944 and his arrival in Auschwitz–Birkenau.

Thus, it can be seen simply from the format of the interview, how central his experience in Auschwitz–Birkenau is for him; all other experiences are arranged in relation to this period. After a brief description of his daily routine Yitzhak suddenly becomes aware that he has jumped ahead, and he promptly returns to describing life in the Pietrikow–Tribunalksi ghetto. Nevertheless, Auschwitz continues to dominate his narrative, and he constantly returns to his memories of that period.

One of the reasons why Yitzhak hardly speaks about the four years he spent in the ghetto and the year in the labor camp of Blyzin is connected to the workings of memory. Yitzhak, who was seven years old when the war broke out, explains that, "I can't tell about specific incidents . . . one episode I can remember . . . once, during winter . . . probably winter, 1944, they made us stand for roll-call as two people had tried to escape. They caught them, and brought them to the yard of the roll-call. When the whole camp was standing for roll-call they shot them in front of the whole camp . . . What else can I tell?"

Besides this traumatic memory, Yitzhak has some good memories of the labor camp, in which his movements were more or less unrestricted and, as he explains, "relative to what was happening to Jews at the same time, I had it relatively good during that year, between August 1943 and July 1944. My father, my mother and I worked and we were completely cut off from the bonfire that was sweeping Poland."

Almost all of Yitzhak's memories of his experiences in the ghetto and the labor camp, unlike those of Auschwitz–Birkenau, are not organized chronologically. Rather they appear as flashes, which is characteristic of the memory of younger child survivors. He remembers scenes of murder, deportations, and his own miraculous escape. One of the most vivid memories that Yitzhak has is of being saved from deportation by his father. Despite the relatively 'good memories' that Yitzhak has of the labor camp, he remembers himself as a passive and vulnerable victim whilst incarcerated in the ghetto. Thus, his narrative of his experiences in the ghetto closely resemble the narratives of other child survivors, which are usually narratives of helplessness and vulnerability, and whose survival was completely dependent upon the assistance and intervention of adults. However, this image of himself changed once he reached Auschwitz, as his feelings of powerlessness disappear. He explains that from the moment he arrived in the camp, after having left his father in Blyzin, and being separated from his mother on the ramp at Auschwitz–Birkenau, he began to fight for his own survival alone.

Constructing a Narrative of Heroism

Yitzhak explains that his transformation from victim to soldier happened soon after his arrival in Auschwitz–Birkenau. "We stood on the ramp, my mother, my brother and me. The Germans separated the women from the men. Our transport was not going to be killed; they only divided the women from the men. We were standing there and an SS man approached us and separated us immediately. It was clear that my younger brother would go with my mother to the woman's camp, Lager B. One of the prisoners from our transport pushed me in the direction of the men even before the SS man had selected us. It seems that the SS man agreed with that decision and I was considered a man with all that which it entailed. From that date, August 1, 1944, I began my struggle for survival alone – without my father, without mother, I call this my 'heroic period' as I had to worry about my existence, and not only my existence, but to stay alive, to survive, because each day, every hour that one stayed alive was a victory. The danger was everywhere."

It is clear from his narrative that his self-image changes when he reaches Auschwitz. Separated from his family, he stands on the ramp alone without the care and support of adults. From that moment, he is no longer a dependent and vulnerable child, but is forced to take care of himself and actively struggle to survive. Yitzhak's experience of losing his childhood was a universal experience for children who were 'selected' to live in Auschwitz–Birkenau. Yitzhak may have lost his childhood after arrival, but he nevertheless remembers this period with pride as he managed to survive on his own. Thus, Yitzhak has arranged his memories of Auschwitz around a narrative of heroism, through which he has made meaning of his past. He has constructed, through a careful selection of episodes, a story which represents his heroic behavior in the camps. When Yitzhak describes the death camp, the scenes of suffering, horror, and death which characterized the camp, are noticeably absent. Rather, he chooses to relate those episodes in which he managed to save himself, which supports the heroic vision he has of himself.

One of the episodes he describes is a 'selection' of a group of boys, in which those individuals who were seen as 'unworthy of life' were sent to the gas chambers. Each boy was examined in turn, naked, by an SS official, and, "At the end he came to me . . . he stood before me and I knew exactly what I was supposed to do. I stood on my toes, my pants covered my legs, so I stood on my toes, and it added some centimeters to my height. I opened my chest. I was not thin, I was not a *musselman*. I looked good. But . . . I wasn't tall. He stood before me and asked me: 'How old are you?' and I said, 'Fourteen, *Herr*

Obersturmführer'. It seems that he liked my answer, as he hesitated a moment, and he let me live."

Yitzhak relates another episode where he outsmarted Mengele in a *selektion*. He explains that Mengele "brought a measuring stick of a one and a half meters. Those who did not reach it were to be gassed. I saw what was going on and before they measured me . . . when he turned around . . . I jumped to the other line in which those who had already passed the test, the big ones, stood. And that's how I stayed alive a second time. I managed to survive." Yitzhak also recalls his mother saying that if a Nazi were to ask how old he was, he should add two years onto his age.

It is revealing that Yitzhak has chosen to focus on the episodes in which he managed to save himself, and not on the random nature of life and death in the death camp. Yitzhak's feelings of personal power can be seen as a survival mechanism, adopted whilst in the camp. Deborah Dwork argues that "It is not surprising that inmates should have found a logical explanation for the behavior that they witnessed. They presumed a rational basis for their experience."[14] It can be argued that by attributing rationale to the behavior of their oppressors, victims were able to give order to the chaos in which they found themselves. Furthermore, claiming personal control over one's fate and circumstances protected the victims from feeling vulnerable and powerless. Without it, many victims would have surrendered quickly to the inevitability of death. According to Shamai Davidson, one of the choices that victims had to continually make was the decision to survive, which "was a conscious and continuous choice that emphasized existential freedom as a reality even in the inferno of the Nazi concentration camps. The survivors who decided to live in the camps represent the ultimate triumph over death."[15] However, most researchers of the period argue that victims of the *Shoah* lacked any real power to affect their fate, and that their survival was first and foremost luck. It is important to differentiate between the objective circumstances in which the victims found themselves in and their subjective experiences. During the *Shoah* there were objective circumstances, independent of the individual's own will, that determined their fate. However, within those circumstances the individual, as long as he or she remained alive and was not on the brink of death, hoped and believed that they were still able to influence their fate.

Yitzhak's narrative indicates that his feelings of control and his heroic self-image, which developed during the war, continue to influence the way he remembers the period. He explains that when he returned to Auschwitz–Birkenau many years after the war, he stood on the ramp on which the Jews were selected and he "felt good. I felt that I am standing here, and, as a young boy, I prevailed over the Nazi empire. Despite the fact that the nation was destroyed, I, a child, won. I am a citizen of a free country, and I am standing on the ramp . . . I felt like a soldier who has returned to the site of battle. I am here, and Mengele is somewhere in hiding."

Yitzhak's continued need to present and perceive himself as a hero originated as a survival mechanism during the war, and was reinforced by his post-war environment in which heroism was a dominant value. Furthermore, in constructing a narrative of heroism, Yitzhak has chosen to remember and represent his past with a view of what he would have *liked* to have been, a soldier, rather than what he *was* during the war, a victim. Reframing his past has helped Yitzhak in his search for acceptance within Israeli society. It also gave meaning to his suffering and helped him manage his traumatic memories. Furthermore, the creation of a narrative, specifically a heroic narrative, has enabled Yitzhak to tell his past proudly. The telling provides Yitzhak, particularly as he ages, with a sense of himself that is vital and powerful; an image which he curiously does not associate with adult survivors who he sees as diminished by their past.

The Post-War Environment

As discussed extensively in the previous chapters, for those survivors who arrived in Israel in the first two decades after the war, 'what was socially possible to speak of' were stories of resistance and heroism. In reframing his personal past into a narrative of heroism Yitzhak has been reinforced in his framing of his experiences as a heroic past, and has been able to give voice to his experiences in his post-war environment.

Research has shown that an individual's experience during the war not only affected their relationship to the past, but also the manner in which it was transmitted to the second generation. Researchers have found that, "on the whole, families of ex-partisans seemed more open and willing to discuss Holocaust related issues than were the families of ex-prisoners of concentration camps." They account for this phenomenon as, "it is easier for the parent to tell and for the child to ask, about events in which the parent can be thought of as a hero who displayed resistance despite the most dire consequences. But the parents who suffered the horrors of the concentration camps more likely perceive themselves and are perceived by their children as helpless victims – a role neither parents not children cherish." Furthermore, researchers argue that ex-partisans felt that they were more active during the Holocaust, whereas ex-concentration camp victims felt more passive, and "such a difference could be linked to a greater willingness to communicate about traumatic events."[16] Despite the fact that objectively Yitzhak is an ex-prisoner and not an ex-partisan or ex-resistance fighter, he has reframed his experiences as one in which he is a resister, a soldier fighting for his survival and not a powerless, passive victim. This enabled him to confidently retell his past to his peers, his wife, his children, and to Israeli society. Yitzhak created a narrative of heroism in a socio-cultural context that applauded heroism.

Rebuilding Identity and a Search for Belonging

Yitzhak began to internalize the dominant strains and values of Israeli collective memory immediately after the war through his encounter with the Jewish Brigade – "the Hebrew fighting unit that served in the British army and fought in Italy. After the war they came to look for survivors. They covered Europe and they got to us in Austria. For me it was an enormous revolution. A revolution that is impossible to describe. Suddenly I see a Jewish soldier! Do you know what it means to see a Jewish soldier with a weapon? Carrying a flag with a blue *Magen David* on a white background? To see a Jewish soldier with a Tommy gun? Two commanders approached us and began to tell us about *Eretz Yisrael*. Before I did not know much about *Eretz Yisrael,* despite the fact that my uncle, my mother's brother, had gone to Palestine before the war in the 1930s. My mother always told me that I had an uncle in Palestine, whose name is Moshe Yakobowicz. But we did not hold Zionist views . . . I was a child and I didn't think it to be so important. First I was a young boy and second I didn't have Zionist views. Suddenly when I saw those soldiers from the Jewish Brigade it was like a revolution. It was amazing. Why? Because all the time the symbol of the blue *Magen David* on a white background was a symbol of degradation. Suddenly I saw the symbol of the blue *Magen David* as a symbol of pride. And here were Jewish soldiers with that as their flag. Jewish soldiers with a weapon! It is hard to describe the revolution when that happened in the mind of a child, of a young boy. Suddenly he sees Jewish life. As I had thought that all the Jews had been murdered. There were no Jewish soldiers, everyone had died, everyone was destroyed. They began to organize us, they began to appear, and they came a few times. One time they came and organized us finally and they took us to Italy."

For a young boy who had suffered years of degradation and humiliation, the soldiers of the Jewish Brigade became powerful role models. They represented hope, strength and pride, and infused the young boy with optimism and idealism. In rebuilding his life, Yitzhak chose to rebuild himself in their image, as a heroic soldier. He did this by reframing his past in their image, according to the dominant values of his new socio-cultural environment. The image of the pioneer soldier is an intrinsic part of the Zionist narrative, as "The soldier pioneer who historically sacrificed his life for his country was the mirror opposite of the Zionist perception of the prototypical Jew of the Diaspora."[17] Moreover, as a result of this powerful encounter Yitzhak was determined to make Israel his new home; he wanted to become part of Israeli society. Zionism, personified by the Jewish soldier, gave him hope and meaning. Zionism and identification with the Brigade soldiers gave him a sense of heroic resistance, as he was able to transform his traumatic experiences of loss, suffering, and destruction into a military battle of sacrifice, and victory. Shamai Davidson explains that the Zionist ideology and the longing to go to Palestine was seen as an expression of the "overcoming of death" and an attempt at a "renewed human spirituality."[18] Similar to the other child survivors, Yitzhak wanted "be like everyone else. I wanted to be one of the gang. So I spoke Hebrew." It is clear that Yitzhak was intent on rebuilding his life in the *sabra* mould. However, unlike most hidden child survivors, he did not choose to abandon his past and hide his identity. As he explains, he "was not a conventional child survivor. I was very open about the past." Despite his openness, Yitzhak was careful not to identify with other survivors and gradually separated himself from them. He explains that, "I had a better connection with those who were born in Israel than those who came from 'there' . . . I didn't like the Diaspora mentality. I saw the *sabra* as the antithesis of the Diaspora."

From this last sentence it becomes clear that Yitzhak began to internalize the values of Israeli society. Yitzhak learned that in order to rebuild a positive identity and integrate quickly into Israeli society, he had to distance himself from the survivor community, both young and old. He explains that, "I am proud that I did it, that I survived it. I do not feel that I am less because I was in the *Shoah*. I was a soldier who fought and was captured. I survived it and I came out of the hell. I was there and I am still able to function, I still am able to think. There are people who after the *Shoah* do not function. They are 'out'. But I am still with it, I still function. I completed a BA and I still take courses, on the computer, on the internet . . . I survived it and I came out of the hell."

In Yitzhak's case, the negative image of the survivor prompts him to reframe and redefine his experiences into something positive and heroic, of which he can speak. In coopting the positive image of the soldier, Yitzhak distances himself from the negative image of the survivor, and instead aligns himself with the native population, which enables him to speak about his past. Later on in the interview, it becomes apparent that his heroic narrative was also a way of distancing himself from the negative stereotype of passivity and weakness that were attributed to survivors in Israel. He explains that this idea was prevalent in the early years of the state. "The whole atmosphere in Israel was different in the beginning. 'Like sheep to slaughter' . . . 'you walked like sheep to slaughter' . . . they only valued those who had held a weapon in their hands. *Shoah ve Gevurah.* The heroism was ninety-six percent and the four percent was *Shoah.*"

From this extract, we learn that Yitzhak himself understands his retelling as a testament to his survival and to his resilience. His narrative is proof that the Nazis did not destroy him or his ability to rebuild a meaningful life after the war. This extract also reveals that Yitzhak is sensitive as to how he is perceived as a survivor in Israeli society. By defining his war experiences as a military battle, in which he fought as a soldier, Yitzhak disassociates himself from the status of 'victim', and the associations connected to that label. Furthermore, by adopting a critical stance towards other survivors Yitzhak manages to distance himself from them and their experiences. As a result, Yitzhak stops identifying himself as a victim of the Holocaust. He reframes his experiences according to the dominant values and motifs in Israeli society. By using the military metaphor to define his experiences, Yitzhak is claiming a respectable place in Israeli society, as well as creating a common language between himself and Israeli society.

For a young child who was so eager to be accepted, it is hardly surprising that he chose to define himself and his experiences as heroic. Yitzhak not only reframed his experiences because he wanted to be accepted in Israeli society. In addition, his narrative suggests that he also internalized the values of collective memory. He explains that, "during the first period I was angry with the older generation of the *Shoah* . . . why didn't they resist? I was angry. I became embittered. How did it happen to them? I identified with the fighters of *Lochomei Hagetaot*, with the heroes, the partisans. I identified with them very much. I didn't understand the older survivors, why didn't they fight? Despite the fact that I was there, and despite the fact that I knew that it was impossible to do anything." This is a powerful example of the extent to which collective memory of the *Shoah* influenced Yitzhak's personal memory. His need to belong and identify with Zionist ideals and values was so powerful that he chose to internalize them as 'truths', despite his own experience which pointed to a different reality. Yitzhak's narrative of heroism also dovetails with his inner experience of defense against passivity. It can be argued that Yitzhak framed his own personal narrative into a personification of collective memory.

However, over time, Yitzhak changed his perception: "I became more and more convinced that it was impossible to do anything. Even those who did not have a weapon in their hands were heroes. Therefore, I called my period in Auschwitz my heroic period. The war of existence. To survive each day, that was . . . in a practical sense . . . also a war, even a heroic war!"

Interestingly, the change in Yitzhak's personal attitudes correlates with the change in collective memory regarding the definition and understanding of heroism and resistance. Myron Aronoff explains that, "as conditions in a society change, leaders interpret the meaning of myths in a manner appropriate to the changing context and their changing goals. The core myths of all cultures are multivocal and lend themselves to conflicting interpretations with even contradictory ideological messages."[19] Over the past fifty years, Israeli society began to reevaluate its assumptions about, and understanding of, the *Shoah*, especially in relation to the mythological narrative of heroism. Heroism was no longer defined in terms of resistance, but in terms of survival. Dina Porat argues that, by the 1990s, Israeli attitudes towards the Holocaust and specifically the notion of heroism had changed. As reflected in his narrative, Yitzhak also began to understand heroism in a broader context, within which he still sits comfortably.

The last few years have witnessed even further changes in Yitzhak's perception. He has become more critical of the heroic image of the Israelis, which has impacted on his own relationship with other survivors. Recently, Yitzhak has grown closer to fellow survivors. I asked him why he thought this had happened, to which he replied, "It is more comfortable for me now . . . Why? Because even the image of the *sabra* has deteriorated. The *sabra* has also come to have a Diaspora mentality . . . Certainly, the distinctions have blurred."

Yitzhak commented that his perception of the *sabra* was challenged during the Yom Kippur War as, then, for the first time, he saw the *sabra* as a victim and not as a hero. The change in perception of the *sabra* also takes place on a wider social level. As discussed in the Introduction, the Yom Kippur War represented a turning point in Israel's relationship to the *Shoah* and the construction of collective memory. From the shocking realization of vulnerability the war resulted in the loss of the collective image of invincibility. According to Shamai Davidson, the false images that existed between *sabras* and survivors was challenged and began to change "in which a new identity was forged for Israeli society, now neither heroes or victims, no longer cast in a harsh antithesis of being either heroes or victims."[20] Yitzhak exemplifies the way in which the relationship to the past and to identity has been influenced by Israeli society and its changing values. Dina Porat writes that the deconstruction of the hero myth is part of a larger process in Israeli society. "First, the more complicated wars in the Middle East became . . . empathy toward other Jews in distress increased."[21] Furthermore, the Gulf War (1991) was especially significant as Israel played a passive role in the war. This stance reminded Israelis of the situation in which Jewish communities in Nazi-occupied Europe were trapped, "and the question of former attitudes towards them was a central issue during those weeks."[22]

Dina Porat also argues that the deconstruction of the hero myth is part of a universal phenomenon and not restricted to the Israeli experience. Attention focused on the victims' predicaments as individuals and not only as representatives of a larger community or a nation. Social and political changes in Israel also contributed to the change. Ben-Gurion's ideas of 'statehood' which emphasized the rebirth of the "new Jew", a new generation, heroic and victorious, were gradually replaced. Israeli society began to return to Jewish roots, and value the culture created in the Diaspora. She also points to survivors' resilience and successful integration as a catalyst behind the deconstruction of the hero image as "this group is one of the strongest in society, having recovered, integrated, rebuilt their lives, and contributed to 'post-catastrophic Zionism'."[23] Survivors' involvement in Israeli life, on a public, political, and social level, is astounding. With the deconstruction of the hero myth in Israeli society, Yitzhak began to feel more comfortable with other survivors, and with his past as a victim.

Distancing Oneself from the Trauma

Just as Israeli collective memory of the *Shoah* was initially constructed around the narrative of resistance in order to protect it from confronting pain and loss, so too can Yitzhak's narrative of heroism be seen in this light – as a protective stance which shielded him from his own traumatic memory. Lawrence Langer explains that the witness employs "heroic memory", which is of course retrospective, because they "remain divided between the knowledge that during the ordeal they were deprived of moral agency by their circumstances and their present need to see themselves then and now as the responsible agents of their own destiny and of those around them."[24] Furthermore, Jerome Bruner suggests that distressing or arousing experiences 'demand' a story, and that imposing a narrative structure on emotionally charged or salient events is a means of managing them.

Yitzhak's efforts to manage his trauma are not only reflected in the narrative of heroism, but also in the manner in which he chooses to tell his story. He explains that, "I tell this story openly, as if I wasn't there. As if I read it in a terrible book or I had a nightmare. It's as if I am looking from the side, outside. As if I wasn't there; as if I am talking about someone else, but in actual fact, I was there . . . Otherwise, I would go mad. A man can go crazy. And, that's the reason why a lot of people, especially the adults who after they had survived, could not speak about it. Why couldn't they speak about it? Because they simply could not bring up again all those things. I have the strength to look at it like a bystander . . . and to tell the story of someone else, but in reality it's me."

Yitzhak recognizes that he is only able to speak about his past from a distance, in order to protect himself from being consumed by his traumatic memory. During his post-war years he has witnessed how retelling the past can be debilitating and harmful for survivors. From his experience in his mother's home after the war, Yitzhak realizes that traumatic memory consumes adult survivors, which prevents them from rebuilding their lives, and from functioning. Yitzhak explains that, "There was a period when I didn't understand the older people who had survived the Holocaust. I also distanced myself from them. I also did not have a common language with them. When I was at my mother's all sorts of Jews came by, as well as Holocaust survivors. I did not feel comfortable with them . . . "

During the interview, I asked Yitzhak if he spoke about the past with his mother after the war. He replied, "Yes, but I did not like it when she spoke. It was good that she spoke, but she exploded when she spoke about it, her emotions exploded. It didn't affect me. I preferred that she didn't speak about it. I wanted to hear stories from her, but it was a conflict . . . I suffered when she spoke. She suffered a lot because of the war. She lost her husband and she lost a child. She remarried a second time to a widower who had lost two children and a wife. I didn't live with my mother all the time. Maybe it was good, maybe it wasn't good. I don't know how I would have been if I had been with my mother all the time. My mother suffered a lot from the *Shoah*. Everyday. On the one hand she had it easy because she had someone, but on the other hand, there was the *Shoah*. They lived in a *Shoah* atmosphere."

Yitzhak's mother was open about her past, yet the manner in which she retold her past alienated Yitzhak. In his post-wars, Yitzhak learned that it was acceptable to be open about one's experiences. Nevertheless, he needed to think about the *way* he retold his experiences. Yitzhak has learned to retell his past in a detached, analytical manner. He speaks as a historian, presenting the life story of an individual within a historical context, and using historical documents to support his claims, unlike his mother who, he recalls, "exploded when she spoke about it." I found it remarkable that Yitzhak, over the years, has managed to collect historical documents, which support most of his story. The following extract about his arrival in Auschwitz–Birkenau illustrates how Yitzhak retells his traumatic past, yet puts it into a historical framework. "We were beaten and yelled at when we got out of the train. It was the night between July 31st and August 1st. There is Nazi documentation of all of this. A friend of mine faxed me after he got it from the museum at Auschwitz . . . We arrived at Auschwitz. They did not murder us as I have already told you. There are various reasons why they did not murder us. There are German documents that details all sorts of transports from August 1944. Next to our transport . . . next to each transport it is written 'gassed' or 'left alive'. Next to our transport, there is a question mark. The clerk that wrote the question mark was asking 'What happened here?' 'Why didn't they kill them?' There is an explanation for this, the crematorium was so busy during that period murdering Hungarian Jews and Gypsies, that they simply did not manage to kill us."

The above is characteristic of Yitzhak's narrative; he constantly provides a reason or an explanation for the events. He is not able to see the *Shoah* as an event without reason, or explanation, including his own survival. I asked Yitzhak what he thought he gained from collecting all the material, to which he replied, "I feel very good. I struggle with it and I am able to cope with it and arrange it and speak about it. I use the documents freely. To research it . . . I have made it into my small research . . . out of the general story . . . a bit of my own. I adapt it." Throughout his interview, Yitzhak defended himself from the horrors of the past, his mother's pain and his traumatic memories. This defense, which he built carefully over many years, is the only way he can stop himself from being overwhelmed by it.

Yitzhak's narrative teaches us that beyond the decision to retell lies the deliberation of *what* to tell. In our interview, he presents both parts of himself during the war: his victim self and his heroic self. Nevertheless, when deciding what to retell to the wider society, it is clear that he has chosen only to narrate his heroic story. Yitzhak's narrative is a prime example of how the socio-cultural context not only influences the individual's decision to communicate his or her past, but also guides what is said. By appropriating the narrative of heroism, Yitzhak is able to join his individual story to a larger historical narrative, which gives his story a sense of meaning and coherence.

At the same time, it does seem that Yitzhak's need to distance himself from the trauma of the past, by reframing his story and retelling it in a detached manner, is a way of protecting himself from being consumed by the past. Yitzhak's self-presentation stands in strong contrast to the way he presents his mother and other adult survivors whom he feels have been consumed by their past. The narrative of heroism enabled Yitzhak to speak about his past, yet maintain his self-esteem and psychological equilibrium and it demonstrates how child survivors, when deciding to speak about their pasts, were influenced by the way they perceived those adult survivors who also spoke about their pasts. For the most part, it seems that they were repelled by what they perceived as an unhealthy preoccupation with the past, which threatened the child survivor's desperate need to belong in the present. Yitzhak has managed to build and maintain his self-esteem by using a heroic narrative to frame his experiences.[25] As Rollo May explains, when we emulate a hero we strengthen our own self-esteem.[26] Furthermore, unlike those 'resistant speakers', Yitzhak does not silence his past in his search for belonging. Instead, he reframes it and makes use of it in establishing his post-war identity.

Kalman the "Witness"

When I asked Kalman if he had always spoken about his past, he replied, "Yes, yes, but why I don't know. You are not the first doctoral candidate to talk to me about this." During the interview, Kalman did not investigate or attempt to understand why he has always spoken about his past.

However, it became apparent throughout the interview that the way he has chosen to deal with his past stands in direct opposition to the way his sister, Devorah, has chosen to deal with hers. Devorah and Kalman were 'Mengele twins' who survived the war. However, unlike Kalman, Devorah refuses to speak about her experiences during the war. Despite the fact that Kalman has never questioned his need to retell, he is aware that his willingness and ability to recount the past is a rare phenomenon amongst survivors. In earlier chapters it has been argued that hidden child survivors have often refrained from speaking about the past because of the 'hierarchy of suffering' that was created around the experiences of survivors. It must also be noted that child survivors of camps – camps which were regarded as the symbols of suffering – have also chosen to remain silent about their experiences. Kalman reflects on the silence amongst former camp prisoners right at the beginning of his interview.

"I am relatively healthy, body, soul. Actually my bones are starting to act up . . . inside psychologically I am comparatively normal and most important I am ready to talk. The average *Ka-tzetnik* doesn't want to talk or cannot . . . I will explain my sister's problem in this area. Devorah refuses to talk to this day. She didn't talk to her husband, she didn't talk to her children or her grandchildren . . . she doesn't talk to me! I mention this because she constitutes the opposite of her twin brother. Are you ready to talk?"

This extract is a powerful example of how Kalman understands his ability to communicate Auschwitz. First, he considers himself 'normal'. The past has not engulfed his life or paralyzed his emotional and psychological world. Therefore, he is still able to communicate as a 'normal person' to other 'normal people'. Secondly, Kalman points out that he is willing to talk. Unlike other camp survivors, he is willing to revisit the past openly and include that part of his life in his post-war experience. Kalman's willingness to speak can also be understood in terms of Annette Wierviorka's theory that "many bore witness precisely because so many could never do so."[27]

Furthermore, Devorah's silence cuts Kalman off from his own past. Because she has chosen to remain silent all these years, he will never know how his mother spent her last days and how she died. Upon arrival in Auschwitz–Birkenau, Kalman was separated from his mother and sister; he only managed to see his mother one more time before she died.

His last meeting with his mother is remembered with great sadness, and is one of the most painful memories with which he has to deal. "On the spur of the moment, I asked the sergeant in German 'Could I please be allowed to visit my mom?' 'Where is she?' he asked. 'Inside'. I replied. '*Loss!*, Bugger off . . . Okay you can go . . . ' So I charged in there and I found out where they are, and we meet, we kiss, we hug, we cry and a few minutes later I have to leave and again we meet, we kiss, we cry . . . and this too I sort of throw it off as something simple, but it's not . . . and the next day as I throw the extra food to my sister over the fence, my sister said to me in Hungarian 'Mommy is angry with you' . . . I asked her, 'What have I done?' She replied, 'Listen, you didn't kiss mummy's hand when you came to the camp, neither did you kiss her hand when you left. *Ima* [mother] was embarrassed in front of the ladies of the barrack, that her son didn't remember his manners' . . . I didn't see Mama after that . . . She was a walking skeleton, but managed to keep going [for a while longer] because of her steely spirit."

Kalman has distressing memories of his last encounter with his mother; she was angry with him for his lack of manners. This memory is so painful that Kalman finds it impossible to communicate. He explains, "Can I tell you how I felt when Devorah told me that I shamed mother?" Sara Moskowitz and Robert Krell explain, "for older children fortunate to have had a close relationships with a parent or grandparent, lifelong surges of grief and anger recur when the last sight of that person is recalled."[28] This would be particularly true if their last meeting had been one of conflict.

Because Devorah has refused to speak about the past, Kalman can never know whether his mother forgave him. Instead, for the past fifty years he has carried unresolved feelings of sadness and guilt. Nevertheless, he has been able to understand and interpret this incident differently many years later, in contrast with his experiences in Auschwitz. Whilst still carrying the pain, he now manages to see her reaction as a reflection of her 'steely spirit'. That she would not abandon her manners and sense of self, even under the horrific conditions of Auschwitz–Birkenau. Nor would she succumb to the Nazi's policies of attempted dehumanization and humiliation. He explains that, "two things came to my mind since then. The second one came with quiet learning and age . . . the ladies in front of whom mother felt ill at ease were decaying, dying, crippled . . . females lying in their own excrement and urine, two and a half days away from death. But no, to my mother this one was a '*Frau doktor* Schwanz', another was '*Frau* Berkowich' . . . and mother was the wife of this . . . .a superimposition of normal society on the inferno, not of Dante, of Birkenau . . . what kind of completely mad thing it was!"

Devorah's silence also prevents Kalman from knowing how or when his mother died. In his interview, he explains that he knows that his mother and Devorah were evacuated from Auschwitz in January 1945, on the death marches across Europe and that, "Devorah walked with mother into the death march and apparently somewhere along the route, *ima*, along with others, collapsed. She fell into the ditch. I do not know what happened then as Devorah refuses to tell us . . . I gather bits and pieces from other people and I have surmised, I surmise, I cannot say that it's true for sure, but that the other grown ups had dragged Devorah away from mother, because it was obvious that if she remained there with mother that she would die too. So someone had the wherewithal to say, 'Miss your mom is finished, you come with us now!' I don't know . . . I'm unable to say that for sure . . . Devorah does not communicate."

Kalman has no way of really 'knowing' what happened to his mother on that grueling death march. His sister has remained silent. For both Devorah and Kalman the last meeting with their mother is particularly traumatic. For Devorah, her mother's death was so traumatic that she has never been able to speak about it, nor has she been able to speak of her own experiences during the war. Yet, Kalman has committed himself to sharing his past, perhaps in reaction to Devorah's silence, so that the story of the *Shoah* will be remembered and not become, as he explains, "a subject . . . that will disappear with us." Kalman's anxiety over the past disappearing into forgetfulness is reflected in the following extract. When I asked Kalman what he thought of Yad Vashem, he replied, "I have listed Yad Vashem as in the rubric . . . a million *havdalot* . . . in the rubric of oral law, calling it a necessary, important, and necessary drawer in the cupboard of the history of *Am Yisrael* [the children of Israel] . . . did I put that right? The more work they do, the more important it is. The *Shoah* must not become an Inquisition, where there are one and a half professors in the Jewish world and one half professors in the Christian world who know a thing or two about the Inquisition . . . this must not happen with the *Shoah*. Not because I have personal interest in it, but because it is too important to be forgotten. It's already forgotten, it's already dusty, where do you keep the old stuff, on the bottom or on the top. We are already on one of them . . . "

Although Kalman has not explicitly stated his motivation behind his retelling, one possible way of understanding his retelling is as a reaction against the silence of other survivors. Kalman does recognize the fact that some survivors are simply unable or unwilling to remember the past because of the pain that it generates for them. Nevertheless, he sees it as his duty to retell the horrors of Auschwitz–Birkenau, because he is as he says a "rare *Katzetnik*," someone who is both willing and able to do so. Kalman is a witness to the story of his family, to those victims of Auschwitz–Birkenau who are not able to tell their stories, and to those survivors who are unwilling to do so. In telling and giving testimony, Kalman is performing an act of remembrance, one of the social imperatives of collective memory. In a sense he has taken on the role as an agent of memory, representing those survivors who have chosen to remain silent.

Kalman and Devorah's different relationships to their pasts can also be understood in terms of the psychology of twinship. One of the psychological challenges for twins is the difficulty in differentiating between the self and the twin. Ricardo Ainslie has found that in "numerous interviews the twins had ways of describing themselves and their experiences which suggested the sense of themselves as members of a common entity."[29] Descriptions of their relationships imply a "sense of being incomplete, parts of a whole, or within a common boundary in which one's existence is inexorably linked to the other."[30] Thus, it is hardly surprising that Kalman presents himself in comparison to his sister Devorah. This not only impacts on their identity, but also on the way that these two individuals choose to deal with and relate to their past. According to Kalman, each twin has developed diametrically opposed responses to their past: he has chosen to speak, whilst Devorah remains silent. These opposing responses function as parts of a whole, as each response compensates for the other. Devorah does not need to speak as Kalman speaks, and Kalman does not need to be silent because Devorah remains silent. Through Devorah's silence, Kalman is able to hold some elements of experiences as 'silent' and 'unknowable'.

Conversely, through Kalman's retelling, Devorah is able to reveal her past to significant others. Kalman's narrative powerfully demonstrates that the act of telling is not only determined by the socio-cultural context, but also by the social-psychological dynamics and relationships operating in particular families.

The Talmud: A Means of Communicating and Understanding the Past

Like Yitzhak, Kalman also retells his past using a traditional narrative. He chooses to use traditional Jewish sources and texts as metaphors for his experiences, and as a tool for understanding his past. Whilst Yitzhak uses a narrative from his post-war socio-cultural environment, Kalman draws his narrative from the cultural and traditional world of his pre-war life. Alfred Adler proposed that the individual is guided by a personal myth, which is established early in life. It provides guidance for the child and orients him in the world. Adler called this construct the "guiding fiction".[31]

As related earlier, Kalman grew up in Hungary in a strictly Orthodox community. At a very young age, he was sent away from home to study in a famous *yeshiva*. At the age of twelve, Kalman explains that, "I found myself in a larger township in the south of Hungary in a very important *yeshiva*, with about eight hundred *bocherim* [students]. The schedule was tough, and difficult for children. The first lesson was at six o'clock in the morning, winter and summer, sometimes before six." In the *yeshiva* Kalman studied the Talmud. His *yeshiva* experience lasted until 1944, when the Nazis occupied Hungary, and his world was to change forever. He left the pages of the Talmud and only in his retirement he has found them again.

"And after retirement, I headed straight for Bar-Ilan University, for the Talmud department, which was my dream. To come back to the pages of the Talmud, without God . . . not in a negative sense . . . He doesn't need my respect, I have a hunch that He survives with or without my respect, but I am a student on my own, nobody interferes with me. In psychological terms, I really craved the rose garden of my childhood, of my *yeshiva*. Both of my grandfathers inculcated a love of oral law into me as in my older brother . . . but I wanted more, I wanted a proper grounding in oral law. That's why I spent four academic years working my fanny blue, I was not an average student, way above average . . . "

Returning to the pages of the Talmud not only represented a return to his past, to his home, it helped him deal with his past. It becomes apparent from his interview that Kalman believes that his personal story

158

is not unique, that it has already been told in the Talmud and the Bible. Therefore it is through the Talmud that he searches for ways to describe, understand and make sense of his suffering and to reclaim his past.

During the interview, Kalman struggles to find the words to describe his horrific memories of Birkenau. He explains that, "The situation inside the camp was also an inferno. Inside our camp there is this area, which I call the toilets. This is a huge latrine. They dug a huge hole, because there were thousands of people here, placed concrete slabs . . . with male sized holes, equi-distant and that was the public toilets. This place was not just bad smelling; there were gasses coming up . . . many many people committed suicide by throwing themselves in this place, that's why I said Dante was a *boy chick* . . . Penning silly exercises com-pared to the reality of Birkenau."

In order to explain to me the reality of Birkenau, Kalman turned to the Bible. "I will tell you something else. There are two series of laws in the books of Moses . . . The portion of *Bechukotai* [*My Laws* – Leviticus 26] is the last section in the book of Leviticus. There is a chapter there that says 'What I will do to you if you keep the *mitzvoth* and what I will do to you if you don't keep the *mitzvoth*'. It's a harsh, brutal description of what will happen to us. It has another parallel in the book of Deuteronomy . . . Look up those two chapters . . . and I say what happened to us in and around Birkenau is pretty well described in both [chapters] . . . It's not for nothing that I have this tremendous respect for the oral law. It is a storehouse of genuine quality. And I can even under-stand how some of my brethren could retain their faith."

What is fascinating about this part of the interview is that Kalman finds a way to communicate his past through the Bible. When he begins to describe the horror of the latrines, he searches for literary parallels that can create a bridge of understanding between him, the survivor and me, the interviewer, someone one who has not experi-enced the *Shoah*. He rejects Dante's work as inadequate in describing Birkenau, and instead turns to the Bible, a source closer to the Jewish experience. In using the Bible, Kalman is not preaching a religious message. He is no longer a religious man and rejects the message of the Bible, as nowhere in his narrative does he suggest that the *Shoah* was a punishment for the sins of Jewish people. Instead, he considers Jewish texts to be a rich literary storehouse that are able to relate and describe the condition of the Jewish people, including their experiences during the *Shoah*.

Throughout the interview, Kalman is not only giving testimony; he is telling a story. He is searching for the meaning of his experience and loss. During the interview he asks, "How come that I have I received a first-class ticket to every playing of this opera?" Judith Herman writes that, "Survivors of atrocity of every age and of every culture come to a point in their testimony where all questions are reduced to one, spoken more in bewilderment than in outrage: Why? . . . Beyond this unfathomable question, the survivor confronts another, equally incomprehensible question: Why me? The arbitrary, random quality of her fate defies the basic human faith in a just or even a predictable world order. In order to develop a full understanding of the trauma story, the survivor must examine the moral questions of guilt and responsibility and reconstruct a system of belief that makes sense of her undeserved suffering."[32]

Kalman finds the answer to his suffering in the Talmud. He quotes a passage of the Talmud, which he considers as a 'magnificent parable' to his own predicament: "Rab Judah said in the name of Rab, 'When Moses ascended on high he found the Holy One, blessed be He, engaged in affixing coronets to the letters'. Said Moses, 'Lord of the Universe, Who stays Thy hand? He answered, 'There will arise a man at the end of many generations, Akiba b. Joseph by name, who will expound on each title heaps and heaps of laws'. 'Lord of the Universe', said Moses; 'permit me to see him'. He replied, 'Turn thee round'. Moses went and sat down behind eight rows [and listened to the discourses upon the law]. Not being able to follow their arguments he was ill at ease, but when they came to a certain subject and the disciples said to the master, 'Whence do you know it?' and [when] the latter replied 'It is a law given unto Moses at Sinai', he was comforted. Thereupon he returned to the Holy One, Blessed be He, and said, 'Lord of the Universe, Thou hast such a man and Thou givest the Torah by me!' He replied, 'Be silent, for such is my decree'. Then said Moses, 'Lord of the Universe, Thou hast shown me his Torah, show me his reward'. 'Turn thee round', said He; and Moses turned round and saw them weighing out his flesh at the market-stalls. 'Lord of the Universe', cried Moses, 'such Torah, and such a reward!' He replied, 'Be silent, for such is My decree'."[33]

Kalman continues by saying, "Now take these two lines: '*Such Torah, and such a reward!*' Remember that I am the little guy who was forgotten in the opera . . . excuse me 'that's torah and its reward?' When we stood in Birkenau next to the farm house, with me . . . (cries) I have problems keeping the lid on . . . I heard this sentence on the wind, the place was quiet, nobody goes to Birkenau, and even less go to the farm house. They don't know what happened there . . . I do! I am the little boy that was left on the podium and I have my twin sons with me . . . huh! They didn't understand, they knew that I'm in trouble. How on earth do you want me to dish this out! For crying out loud! They sensed that I am . . . they just held onto me and I didn't have to explain . . . in a way and this is my Talmud grounding . . . He must have said: '*Shmock!*' Here is your solace, Udi and Amichai, what do you want from me? Didn't you get your bit out of this opera? . . . "

In the parable, God does not give an answer to Moses regarding Rabbi Akiva's suffering. Instead, he instructs Moses to accept his decree uncritically. The harshness of His judgment is to be soothed through trusting and accepting God's actions and decrees. In his narrative, Kalman is also bereft of an answer to his question: "why me?" However, he managed to find solace and comfort in his children. Eventually, Kalman is able to accept his past, because he sees it as part of his life's journey which has given him his sons. Kalman has created his own meaning of his life story, by using the traditional narrative and meaning – making of the Talmud.

Elie Wiesel writes, "The truth will never be written. Like the Talmud, it will be transmitted from mouth to ear, from eye to eye."[34] Kalman, like Elie Wiesel, views his telling as an extension of the Talmud, where the lessons of the past, and not necessarily its answers, are transmitted orally to the next generation. The Talmud is a familiar mode of communication, or a form, which helps Kalman communicate his past to non-survivors. As Henry Greenspan explains, "for in themselves the forms and the meanings on which survivors draw in their recounting are not at all a 'foreign language' to us. They are in fact entirely familiar – exactly the same kind of narrative structures and schema of meaning on which we ourselves draw when retelling what we have lived. What is unfamiliar is the fate of these forms: the ultimate incapacity of survivor's stories to convey what they remember; the failure of meaning in the face of what was enacted and endured."[35] Contrary to Henry Greenspan's thesis, Kalman not only uses the Talmud as a mode of communication, he also finds meaning through the Talmud as he manages to find himself and his story amongst its pages. Interestingly, Kalman is not always concerned with the inability to convey the world of Birkenau. He is more afraid of our inability as an audience to absorb and contain his descriptions. Throughout the interview, Kalman repeatedly asks me if he is 'hurting me' with his story.

Personal Stories and Mythological Narrative

Unlike hidden child survivors, Kalman and Yitzhak have never questioned their identities as survivors, neither have they felt un-entitled to their suffering as their experiences have been validated and legitimized by the collective. In fact, as Auschwitz survivors their stories have been considered dominant voices in collective memory, and their survival has been viewed by the post-war community with awe.

Kalman and Yitzhak's personal stories are important in that they teach us that collective memory is not only instrumental in determining who speaks, but also influences what is said. Both have selected specific narratives to help present their experiences. Kalman draws on a traditional narrative which emanates from the socio-cultural world of his childhood, whilst Yitzhak adopts the central myth of his post-war reality. The myth of the hero is also a basic metaphor to the life story in general as it represents achievement. Both narratives are shaped by the prevailing norms of discourse within which they operate. Through reframing their experiences in accordance with the larger narrative, they are able to join with the collective text. Furthermore, they used these narrative scripts to understand their pasts, as part of their identity formation, and in their search for belonging.

Through the use of narrative, Kalman and Yitzhak are able to express the quintessence of their experiences. They frame their pasts on traditional scripts or myths. According to May, myths have an important psychological function as, "myth is a way of orienting ourselves to the cosmos, it gives meaning to our relations with ourselves and others, it makes possible our experience of identity, and it carries the moral values of the person and society".[36] In joining their personal stories with a mythological narrative, both Kalman and Yitzhak are able to join their personal stories with a larger, transcendal meta-narrative, giving structure and meaning to their individual experiences. Kalman and Yitzhak's narratives teach us that the survivors' ability to retell their past in their post-war environment is also linked with their ability to represent and understand their experience as something greater than their own. The mythical narratives empower the survivor and help them restore their sense of belonging in the world. Using myths as the core of the individual's biographies is therapeutic, as it provides insight and meaning which was not present before. In Lévi Strauss's terms: "the aim of mythology is to ensure that as closely as possible . . . the future will remain faithful to the present and the past."[37] Therefore, their mythic narratives help them feel a sense of connectedness with the world. Their stories are no longer aberrations, they are part of the human narrative; they confirm their survival.

However, both Kalman and Yitzhak have discovered that narrative structures are limited in conveying the full experience of the Holocaust and they find it difficult to identify completely with these particular traditional narratives. In his later years, Yitzhak has come to reject the superficiality of the 'heroic image' which has come to dominate Israeli collective memory. Instead, he has begun to turn to fellow survivors for comfort and belonging. Kalman, whilst embracing his childhood world, ultimately rejects it because of the religious leadership's failure to warn

Hungarian Jewry of their imminent doom and ignoring them in their most desperate hour. "Dear rabbis," he exclaims, "wherever you are. You have failed, certainly my generation . . . each and every one of them a complete and utter failure." Kalman remains conflicted as, on the one hand he is not willing to abandon the rich cultural world of traditional Jewish texts, but on the other, "neither do I know what to do with this damn thing . . . I take the liberty and my right to enjoy oral law, because it's magnificent, beautiful stuff and it has not much to do with the God department. It's a brilliant social-cultural platform which I am proud to be part of. Does this mean that I have to go to the *mikveh*? . . . and if yes, who says? The *rav*? Bugger him! The average *rav* as far as I am concerned is a miserable religious clerk! He is not my leader, he is not my adviser, he is not the man I want to follow."

Kalman is struggling to return home; it is no longer the same place in which he grew up. Instead, all sense of home has been irrevocably changed by the Holocaust and returning there, even with the help of other narrative structures, is no longer possible. Attempts to find meaning through the mythological narratives around them often only reveal the failure of such narratives in their ability to fully represent the individual. This is perhaps most apparent in Yitzhak's story where, despite the heroic self he chooses to present, he also suggests the presence of another self – his victim self – which is rarely articulated, existing as it does outside all narrative.

6

Resistant Speakers

Once I had completed my interviewing and began to think about the people with whom I had spent countless hours, I realized that the manner in which they had received me as an interviewer was related to how they felt about speaking about their past. If they had agreed without hesitation to be interviewed, it usually transpired that they were eager to talk about their pasts in general. However, there were those individuals who were more apprehensive when I called to request an interview, which usually reflected their resistance towards recounting their pasts. Needless to say, this was not the only factor that shaped the interviewing relationship, but it was a sensitive indicator of the individual's relationship to his/her past and to the act of recounting. I also sensed their apprehension during the early stages of the interview. I found these interviews to be the most challenging for me as a researcher, as I was attempting to listen to the life stories of people who were resistant to sharing their pasts.

The narratives examined in this chapter tell of varied experiences both during and after the war. Resistance to recalling the past could be seen as connected to the nature of the war experience itself. Eliezer was hidden in a monastery in France during the war. David and Avivit both spent some time in the Kovno ghetto, before being smuggled out and placed in the care of Lithuanian non-Jews. Michal spent the first year in hiding with a Polish family, and was then incarcerated in a camp for the duration of the war. Both Michal and Avivit, who were witnesses to Nazi brutality and terror, are reluctant to recall their past due to the traumatic nature of their memories. David and Eliezer, who were hidden during the war, share many behavioral characteristics of hidden child survivors. During the war, they learned to keep silent and transferred this learned behavior to their post-war life. Because they had spent quite a few years hiding in what they remember to be relatively 'good' condi-

164

tions, they do not feel that they suffered during the war, and are reluctant to claim a traumatic past. Janice Haaken, in her work on memory of childhood sexual abuse, writes, "In negotiating the meaning of disturbing events, human consciousness is prone to two opposing sorts of social defenses: one involves denial and minimization of disturbing sources of knowledge and the other involves elaboration and amplifications of them."[1] Through minimizing their pasts, both David and Eliezer have managed to distance themselves from their survivor identity and have remained silent about their past for most of their lives.

In their post-war environments, David, Eliezer, Michal, and Avivit have chosen to keep their war experiences and their identity as Holocaust survivors hidden from the wider public. They have successfully distanced themselves from identifying as Holocaust survivors, largely in response to the image and treatment of Holocaust survivors in Israeli society. Instead, they have chosen to rebuild their identity around their post-war experiences, i.e. what they have managed to create out of the ruins of their traumatic pasts.

Eliezer: "It's not interesting – What should I talk about?"

When I came to meet Eliezer on the appointed day, I arrived to find him partially dressed, and surprised to see me. He had forgotten our appointment and did not have time to be interviewed. When he checked his diary, he found that he had not recorded our appointment. At that moment, I began to consider whether Eliezer had wanted to be interviewed at all. Nevertheless, we rescheduled the interview and instead of interviewing Eliezer, I spent the rest of the day interviewing his wife. As a result of this awkward first encounter, I became hesitant about the following interview. Nevertheless, the day before our scheduled meeting, I called to confirm our arrangement, and we met again for the second time.

Hierarchy of Suffering

Eliezer, for most of his life, has concealed his past from his wife and his children. In the last few years he has begun to speak about his experiences during the war and work through his loss. Despite the fact that the past has re-surfaced in his life, he continues to reject his identity as a survivor, and does not speak publicly about his past. His reluctance is first and foremost connected to his experiences during the war. Eliezer explains that, "One, my experience was unusual. I was a child in a

Christian environment. All of those survivors who survived camps, they are the 'nobility of the nobility'. I cannot come and 'sell' my wares to someone who survived a concentration camp, whose experiences were beyond my own. Despite the fact that I don't agree with this completely, there is no place for discussion here. So I never felt that I was a survivor with other survivors."

Robert Krell, writing about his own experiences, expresses the same sentiment as Eliezer, "I was with wonderful hiders and therefore assume that every other child's hiding experience was worse than mine, for mine was close to ideal."[2] Nevertheless, Eliezer does have some problems with the hierarchy of suffering. He explains, "I have to say one thing: you can't measure pain. He who measures it, comes from a position of weakness. In my hierarchy, I always go to the bottom quickly. I don't have a problem with that. Especially when you are talking about unpleasant things. Why be on top? I will leave it for others. Quite the opposite; it's good."

This is a wonderful example of a dialogical moment, in which Eliezer is struggling to make meaning of his personal pain. On the one hand, he feels that he cannot claim that he suffered during the war, especially in comparison to the suffering of those who survived the camps. However, he *knows* that he too suffered. Therefore, he argues that one cannot objectively measure or judge the extent of someone else's suffering. In this extract, Eliezer is struggling to come to terms with the reality of the hierarchy of suffering and its implications, which he feels, on a rational, 'moral' level, is justified, yet on the emotional level is meaningless. This sentiment is shared by Robert Krell, who later wrote, "and even my 'good' experience has had a continuous devastating effect on my life."[3]

As a result of this dialogical moment, Eliezer reaches a new level of understanding, where he comes to terms with his position in the hierarchy. He no longer feels that his low position invalidates his suffering. Rather he embraces it as it signifies his good fortune of having been spared more suffering. Eliezer rebels against the meaning that collective memory has attributed to the hierarchy of suffering, and creates his own.

Eliezer's silence, which was learned during his years of hiding, was reinforced after making *aliya*. After experiencing a difficult absorption process, he concluded at a very young age that being identified as a Holocaust survivor was a great disadvantage in Israel.

Eliezer explains that "In Israel, they didn't know how to absorb the young adults from there, who moved here. My experience in Israel was very, very difficult, for three reasons. When I arrived in Israel, despite the war etc., I was studying part-time. I was a student then. When I arrived in Israel, I felt like a member of the proletariat. And this was a very difficult adjustment for me to make, to being a member of the pro-letariat. For a boy of fifteen, after everything he has been through, not able to study, but needs to work and earn a living, it was a terrible situation. There was no framework which could help me. It's not their fault. But they disregarded children who had come from Europe after the *Shoah*, Who is he? What is he? Nothing! When I arrived in Israel, I did a psychometric test and they found out that I was indeed talented, talented enough to study whatever I wanted at university. They sent me to an occupational school in Safed, which also prepared students for their high school diploma. That was at the end of 1947. Meanwhile I was caught in the siege of Safed, and was enlisted into the army ... Therefore, instead of studying they enlisted me into *Gadna* and I became the commander's messenger. When they bombed the fortress, I was sent to relay messages . . . At the age of sixteen my hand was wounded, defending Safed. Today nobody remembers it. One of the things which I am still not able to digest is that we were in the framework of *Aliyat Hanoar*. The details are not important, and all of us refugee children participated in the operations . . . children my age . . . tens of them. Children of our age who were born here remained at home with their parents. And they sent us to fight. I was the youngest so I wasn't conscripted. About a third of them were killed in the war. They took the children who were refugees, looked down on them, and killed them. That's after the *Shoah*. It was also necessary because of the situation . . . it's true that 500,000 Jews fought against one million Arabs, so I suppose that it is justified."

Eliezer's personal narrative reflects one of the most sensitive debates that consumed the leadership of Youth *Aliya* during the War of Independence – the issue of evacuating Youth *Aliya* children from the border areas, which were unsafe. Another issue that arose was, as Hanoch Reinhold, a member of Youth *Aliya* asked, "Do we agree that the youths who have been in the country a few months only, under our auspices, should be digging trenches and fulfilling military orders? This question raises the problem: should a differentiation be made between local youth and young people who survived the Holocaust?"[4] The eventual decision to conscript the young survivors in the war effort, thus discontinuing their studies temporarily, was influenced "by the needs of war – 'survival'- and equalized between the local youth and the immigrant youth, with a commitment to reimburse the latter with a period of training [education] once the war was over."[5] Yet, as Hanna Yablonka writes, "The War of Independence had a very negative effect on the Holocaust youths' vocational training, since many of the kibbutz members were recruited into the war effort, departments were disbanded and people were needed to fill jobs that the times demanded . . ."[6]

Lacking the appropriate training and adequate equipment, survivors were conscripted to fight in the war almost immediately upon arrival in Palestine. The war also hindered the process of absorption as, once it began, there "was a convergence of the process of immigrant absorption and a desperate struggle for national survival. The pressure of events did not allow for sentiments. The painful past of the newcomer was largely ignored as many became fighters with the army which provided them with their first home in Israel."[7] According to Hanna Yablonka, towards the end of 1948, Holocaust survivors constituted about one-third of the IDF's combat power. "For these soldiers the army was their first encounter with Israel, both socially and institutionally . . . it was a harsh experience."[8] Furthermore, despite their involvement in the war, "the refugee soldiers did not become part of the myth of heroism of the War of Independence which was attributed wholly to Israeli youth."[9] Eliezer refers to this in his narrative when he explains that, in terms of the participation of young survivors in the war effort, "Today nobody remembers it." Despite their brave contribution, the survivors were not given the same credit as the *sabra* fighters. Eliezer's understanding of his own experience is echoed in Tom Segev's controversial book *The Seventh Million*, in which he writes, "The general opinion was that the human quality of the natives was higher than that of the immigrants, that the natives, not the immigrants were making the Israeli revolution."[10]

In his narrative Eliezer is able to accept Israel's need during the War of Independence to recruit child survivors. However, he is not able to accept the continued discrimination he felt was directed against survivors for years afterwards, particularly with regard to educational opportunities. He explains that, "I was shocked again when I was in the army, and an officer sent me to study for my high school diploma. I am talking about 1951. That man's name was Yitzhaki. He established all the army bands. A few months passed and I was still a boy, and I was studying with officers who complained that a simple soldier was studying with them. I would try and explain it to them. They stopped my studies. I could have completed my high school diploma in the army and then gone to university."

Hanna Yablonka explains the importance of education to child survivors in their post-war environments as it was seen by them as compensation for their having been so underprivileged due to the war. She writes that, "especially the study of Hebrew, also opened up for these youths a means by which they could catch up with the local youth and speed up their integration into their society. Furthermore, European communities had always placed great importance in education. Something of this moral message must have stayed with these children and their experience had taught them that the most valuable asset a person could have was his education, so that what had previously been an abstract value now took on a practical form. The young people who had received some education during the pre-war years associated this with memories of home, so that the act of obtaining an education held favorable connotations for them and they saw it as a means to their future security."[11]

In his narrative, Eliezer explains that because of his status as a child survivor, he was rejected, used and discriminated against by Israeli society, and prevented from receiving an education. According to Eliezer's narrative, *this* was his traumatic past. Realizing that his identity as a survivor was a disservice to him, he began to hide it. Unlike other child survivors who made *aliya* after the war, Eliezer did not find a real sense of belonging in Israel and has remained highly critical of Israeli society till this day. When I asked Eliezer if he wanted to make *aliya* after the war, he remarked: "No, I am here in Israel under protest. No one asked me."

Eliezer, like most child survivors, dedicated his life to rebuilding his future. This was another reason for silencing his past. I asked Eliezer if he had spoken about the past to his mother who had also survived the war, to which he replied: "No! I never spoke about it." *Never?* "It's not interesting. What should I talk about?" *Weren't you interested in what happened, or other people interested in you?* "No." *Did you speak about it with your wife?* "No – not until I wrote the book."

When I asked him why he waited so long to speak to his children about his past, he explained, "I am also not interested in it, and they are less. I didn't think like a father, I always did it intuitively. And today it no longer bothers them . . . a father has to be a strong figure, one that initiates . . . and to start telling them all about my sad past . . . I think that it is wrong. It does not add anything, and it does not help in any way. They can judge me according to what they see. I don't like speaking about the past. Have you noticed that even now I haven't spoken about the past? Only the present and the immediate past . . . next question."

Eliezer has chosen to distance himself from the past because he wants to be a 'strong figure' and not to be perceived as 'weak and vulnerable'. It is not clear from this extract what the source of this position is: Whether Eliezer has learned from his post-war experience that survivors are viewed as 'weak and vulnerable', or whether his own experience in remembering the past makes him feel weak and vulnerable', a side of him that he wants to avoid exposing, especially to his children. Later on in the interview, I learn that this attitude also came from his own experience in meeting other survivors. He explains that those child survivors whom he has met over the years and who speak about the past, "people who are my age and who went through what I did . . . Despite the fact that most have built their lives on the past, they ask immediately: 'Where were you? What did you do?'" Eliezer believes that retelling has been detrimental to the psychological well-being of survivors; that a constant preoccupation with the past has a debilitating effect on the individual, as it hinders them from recognizing and valuing their own resilience. It is also interesting how Eliezer's words echo the message of the collective, which pressured child survivors to bury their pasts in order to create a 'normal life'. However, it becomes clear later on in his narrative that this attitude is a projection of his own internal fears. Eliezer explains that although he remembers his past quite clearly, he avoids speaking about it so that he can 'keep a lid on' his own emotions. Therefore, by silencing the past, Eliezer is able to retain an emotionally balanced state of mind where he is able to stay in control. This is reflected in the following extract from his narrative. I asked Eliezer: *Do you read about the Shoah?* "Never." *Movies?* "I have not seen a movie on the *Shoah* . . . again, it stems from my weakness. I hate to identify one hundred percent with the *Shoah*. When I read a book or see a movie on the *Shoah*, I identify with it immediately. I don't like that. I have not read about it." *How do you explain that you don't want to identify with the Shoah one hundred percent?* "Perhaps I have some sort of psychological wound or something. I can't know. But I don't like to be in a situation in which I don't have full control over my feelings. I always have to control. It could be because of the *Shoah*. Perhaps its over the top, an exaggeration . . . During my childhood I had to control my thoughts all the time, otherwise I would have been lost. Perhaps. But that's just some nonsense. It's not serious. However, I have never identified with anything one hundred percent. I cannot be in a situation in which I cannot control my feelings."

Eliezer, like the other hidden child survivors, had learned during the war that silence was crucial for survival. In his post-war environment, he continued to silence his past in order to ensure both his physical and emotional survival. For years, many survivors kept their past hidden, "because of fears of being overwhelmed by their own emotions, and because of fears that their memories would be destructive to their new hard-won self-images and self-esteem."[12]

Despite years of silence and repression, Eliezer understood that he would not be able to repress the past indefinitely, and that at some point his past would resurface and present itself. He explains, "I am a stupid man. What do I mean by stupid? I think one is stronger than the past. Perhaps with aging and weakness, my ability to fight against it will become more difficult. After which people will say, 'You really are a Holocaust survivor'." This last sentence provides a key to understanding Eliezer's relationship to his past – he fears that by remembering and speaking about the past, it will overwhelm him and threaten the secure and strong base that he has created for himself. As a result, he will be become what he himself has come to identify as a Holocaust survivor – someone who is, as he describes, is 'not all there'.

However, Eliezer's need to confront the past came sooner than he expected, and resulted in the writing of his book. I asked Eliezer why he had decided to write the book. Initially he explained that essentially he didn't really understand it himself. He did manage to think of two possible reasons. "There are two things. I was very angry that my little brother died. He died because he was in the *Shoah*. That's one thing. The second thing, which is also coincidental, I participated in a group of artists, and when a man creates . . . There was something inside of me that wants to be released – and, through my art, I release it. It was both these things . . . " After years of silence, Eliezer, like Shalom, felt a strong need to release his past and to mourn his loss. Eliezer began his book as a series of drawings, to which he later added a script. His drawings, which are inspired by his childhood memories, are not realistic representations of the past, but rather symbolic abstractions through which he attempts to bring his repressed memories into consciousness. Thus, his work is a collection of surrealistic illustrations, through which he attempts to come to terms with his past and explore how it has shaped his identity. The surrealist drawings and abstract text poignantly reflect his relationship to the past. Over the years he had chosen to distance himself from it psychologically and emotionally, yet it remained an inescapable and integral part of himself.

A few lines later in his narrative, it became apparent that Eliezer was prompted to explore his past, like Shalom, after he found himself in a weak and vulnerable position; when he no longer had the strength to fight the past. Eliezer explains that some time ago, "I was also paralyzed completely . . . I couldn't reach the window, so I didn't throw myself out of it. That's not important, it's a small detail. When I was in this condition, a friend of mine brought me a book of poetry that he wrote. I hate to read poetry. I was scared that he would ask me what I thought of his poetry. Instead, I drew a picture for each poem and we printed it." Even in his weakened state, Eliezer struggled against the past consuming his emotional life and he chose to deal with it through art. His book also facilitated a process of mourning for his brother and working through his childhood trauma. Eliezer explains, "Through this project, I proved to myself that I was still able to function." Feeling empowered by the experience and confident in his ability to manage the past, Eliezer decided to participate in a course at Yad Vashem, which would prepare him to speak about his past publicly.

Being Discouraged to Speak

In our initial short-lived meeting, Eliezer did have half-an hour to spare, which was probably the most revealing part of our entire interview. He proceeded to tell me that when I called him and requested an interview, telling him that I had been given his telephone number by Yad Vashem, he was rather surprised, as Yad Vashem did not want him to represent them. Eliezer explained that during the course at Yad Vashem, he had an argument with one of the religious participants of the group over issues concerning theology and the Holocaust. He had even written a letter to the participant in which he explained his views further. Eliezer claims that because of this incident, and because of his strong anti-religious views, Yad Vashem did not want him to represent them.

I asked Eliezer if there was anything that he did get out of the course, to which he replied: "There was an excellent psychologist there, who understood that I wasn't suitable to lecture. I cannot lecture . . . The truth is that there were all sorts of people . . . take the woman who was Christian until 1967, she really enjoyed it . . . it gave her the opportunity to cry once a week. Many people whom I have met [at Yad Vashem] have turned it into their raison d'être. For them it is a positive step . . . if most people were like me, the Holocaust would have been forgotten yesterday. They have an important function. I think that it's very important, but I am not prepared to do it. I am not prepared to repeat the same sentences. I have heard how they repeat the same sentences, word for word, and they cry at the same moment. What they do is very important, don't misunderstand me. But it's not my cup of tea."

Because of his experience during and after the course at Yad Vashem, Eliezer has become even more estranged from the survivor community. The encounter at Yad Vashem reinforced his initial resistance to retelling. Eliezer remains a 'resistant speaker' for much the same reason that has determined his silence for most of his adult life. He does not want the *Shoah* to engulf his life; he does not want it to become his focus, his 'raison d'être'. Perhaps more importantly for the purposes of this work, Eliezer has been discouraged to speak by his socio-cultural environment. Today, in an era in which testimony is encouraged and survivors lauded, it appears that certain types of recounting are encouraged whilst others are suppressed. This incident suggests a new development in the collective memory of the Holocaust in Israel. In the early years of the state, the behavior of victims was judged and narratives of heroism were preferred over narratives of helplessness and suffering. Today, the 'messages' of survivors, independent of their war experiences, appear to be judged by the collective. Eliezer's narrative is important as it displays the potential conflict between the 'meaning making' of survivors and the institutions of commemoration. His narrative is a powerful example of how the socio-cultural environment continues to determine what is heard and what is not heard, and of how collective memory is created.

This experience of rejection confirms Eliezer's dislike of institutions, ideology and Israeli society, and reinforces his identity as a critic of the establishment. It also confirms the feelings of rejection by Israeli society that he felt as a survivor when he first came to Israel. Eliezer's narrative hints at the idea that even though Israel's collective memory of the *Shoah* has changed over the past fifty years, for some survivors it has not changed at all.

David: "The more I try and think about it . . . and try to reconstruct it, I find that generally, I was treated well"

The Normalization of a Traumatic Reality

With the invasion of the Nazis, Jewish children were thrust into an unrecognizable reality of war, destruction and death, which was beyond the realm of their understanding. Overnight their lives were transformed as they became targeted victims of Nazi persecution and terrorization. Anna Freud argued that children basically had a lack of understanding of their new reality. In her work with child survivors, she found that they used the proper words for the events without the proper meaning attached to them. For example "the word 'bombing' is often used indiscriminately for all manners of destruction of unwanted objects."[13]

The ability to comprehend the situation was also dependent on the age of the child, the stage of his or her cognitive development, as well as how the situation was explained to the child. The capacities for recouping, regrouping, for buffering and transcending are largely age and stage-dependent. Children who are older have more vivid memories of the past, and the ability to recall images of a loving, nurturing pre-war life. These memories help sustain the children through situations of prolonged distress and trauma, but they may hinder the child's transition and adaptation to the reality of the war. Younger children have fewer memories of the past and do not possess the positive images which insulate and sustain them. Researchers also argue that their naïveté helps them to adapt quickly to their new environment; younger children will "respond to a new and devoted caretaker more quickly than an eight year old."[14] Many if not most children adjusted to their threatening world by accepting it. David's narrative provides us with a wonderful illustration of how the age and stage of the child's cognitive development at the time of persecution affected his understanding of the reality during the war, and his subsequent memories of the past. David was three years old when the war broke out, and his memories of the ghetto are faint and disorganized. At the beginning of the interview, David relates, "I can't say that I have memories which are organized from my time in the ghetto. There are all sorts of pictures and things that I do remember, but I think that most of what I remember comes from stories that were told at home after the war." Furthermore, what he does remember of the ghetto are fragments of what he believed was 'normal life', nothing extraordinary. David explains that "then I didn't think about it, but today when I think about the things we spoke about, it's very interesting. Stories from there were essentially horror stories, but people turned them into regular things. Meaning, you are growing up and you know terrible things are happening which are part of one's everyday life. For me, those ideas, what happened in the camps, killings, and everything that happened there . . . you grow up as if it is part of you. Perhaps I absorbed that attitude in the ghetto. I don't remember, but it was clear that a certain atmosphere prevailed. A child who sees his parents behave in a certain way, who sees his surroundings in a certain way . . . absorbs it as something normal."

Ghetto life became his 'reality' because he was a young child, he did not know anything else, nor was he able to remember anything different. David Wdowinski, who was a psychiatrist and the head of the Zionist–Revisionist Organization in Poland for many years, was particularly concerned with the plight of children in the ghetto and noted, "The realities of ghetto life became the normal existence for children who did not know of any other way of living, and so they made up songs and games where 'action', blockade, sorrow, tears, hunger became the vocabulary of their make believe."[15] Young children, who were either born during the war or just before, had fewer memories of the past, experienced the calamities more passively than the older children. Normalizing the new reality was a survival tool for children during the *Shoah*, which in turn influenced the child survivor's perception of their past. As a result, David continues to remember his past as 'normal'. Furthermore, David explains that in order to cope emotionally during the war, one could not react to every traumatic event.

David's reluctance to talking about his past is connected to the way he has remembered it. David explains that, "The more I try and think about it and try to reconstruct it, I find that generally, I was treated well. In some instances, I can certainly say that they loved me. Perhaps I was a nice child, perhaps not. Perhaps I was treated well for no apparent reason. Perhaps it has to do with the personality of the people. Perhaps

I was lucky. I don't know why, but the fact remains that these people took care of me . . . "

David doesn't remember his years in hiding as particularly traumatic as he remembers that he was well taken care of and loved by the families who hid him. He recalls that, "when there was a noise in the corridors, they would put me in the linen closet. It seemed to me a natural thing to do. Not only that. I remember seeing it as a sign of their concern for me . . . that they cared for me more than for their own children. They managed to give me the feeling that they were caring for me. Thus, it was not a period in which I felt that I was amongst strangers, like the stories of a child who is a stranger and is rejected. Quite the opposite."

During the war, David did not understand his reality to be threatening because his loving and nurturing caretakers insulated him from the trauma of the war. Thus his experience of the war was not a traumatic one. Research that has been conducted with child survivors of the Holocaust is valuable in illuminating why the Holocaust did not seem to figure in David's conscious awareness as the major stress in his life. Joseph Westhermeyer and Karen Wahmanholm write, "A child can remain relatively secure and emotionally undisturbed in the midst of tumult if the family remains intact and the parents are able to discharge their parental responsibilities toward the child."[16] Thus, what was particularly traumatic for children, regardless of their age and stage of development, was the abrupt disappearance, removal or weakening of their familial support structures, without which they could not survive. Children themselves were subject or witness to murder, physical and mental abuse. Yet research points out that the effect of these traumas was graver when the child had lost his or her traditional support system. These findings are supported by literature dealing with trauma generally. Ronnie Janoff-Bulman, in his work on trauma, writes, "Although threats to survival are most apparent when the possibilities of serious physical injury or death are present, such threats may also be engendered in events that entail abandonment and separation. Real or threatened abandonment may mean personal annihilation; this is particularly the case for children for whom survival is intimately tied to care by others."[17]

Throughout almost the entire war period, David was insulated from the horror and devastation through the presence of loving and caring adults. As a result, he does not relate to his experiences as traumatic. However, later on in the interview, David begins to challenge his traditional perception and understanding of his past when he remembers a particular episode, which suggests moments of unhappiness or distress. He explains:

175

"Another thing which I have thought a lot about . . . before I met my mother, I was in a children's camp. However, I was connected to the family . . . I told you about them, the Jewish family. I really do think that they treated me well. But there are photos of me that were taken three weeks before I met my mother, and three weeks after, and it's a different person in those photos. You see it in the face. The first is of a miserable child with a long face, and the second is one of a child smiling. It's completely clear. It's a simple testament. But it did not leave me with the feeling that before that I suffered. It seems that they treated me well. That's all I can say. It seems that I was lucky that I was with people who gave whatever they could under the circumstances, to a boy without parents. But it's hard for me to recall it. It's all the thoughts of an adult man about a boy, who happens to be me. But I don't remember. Certainly a psychologist could make an interesting interpretation out of it."

This narrative is powerful in that it clearly shows the tension between memory and remembering. Over the past fifty years, David has constructed a particular memory of, and relationship to, his past – which may be quite different from the original episode. This reinforces the idea that narratives are a reconstruction of the past through the lens of the present. As an 'adult man', he remembers the experiences of a 'boy'. It is the remembering man that carves out the memory and meaning of the past. Lawrence Langer, in his work on Holocaust Testimonies, quotes Pam Bromberg to illustrate this dynamic: "Even as we recall the past our memories reshape it until it is hard to tell if we remember the original experience or only earlier memories of them. At the same time, the process of remembering is interpretive, and creates a new self-understanding, so that we change ourselves through our recollections. Any quest after objective truth which employs memory as the tool of vision must of necessity then be frustrated by both the internal selectivity of perceptions which later furnished memories; then by the gradual alteration of memory through repetition and interpretation; and finally by the particular configuration of the self at the moment of the actual recall."[18]

In his narrative, David recalls an episode which contradicts the narrative identity he has created throughout the interview. Yet, at the end of this particular extract David returns to his original position and his original understanding of the event remains unchanged. Despite contradictory memories, David continues to maintain a certain configuration of the self. However, the process of retelling has introduced contrary thoughts, and later on in his narrative David once again challenges his perception of his past. This can be seen in the following extract in which he explains: "I know that most of the people who I meet today and are survivors, are children from the ghetto, who were with their parents, or at least with one of them during the war. Relatively that was a better situation than mine. They were protected more. They took me, a child of five, and said – Go into the world! Go alone. Live amongst strangers, and find your place. Something like that. The main thing is to stay alive. Therefore, that was not the most comfortable beginning, as I understand it today. However, despite it all, I still cannot think of it as a bad period. Some things still stay in my memory, as I said, as a good period."

In this extract, David is in 'conversation with himself' over the meaning of his experience during the war. Throughout his life, he has not considered his past to be particularly traumatic. However, during his interview he begins to view it differently. Robinson and Hawpe in their work on narrative methodology explain that, "Retrospection, or reminiscing, can be viewed as a process of testing the continued validity of life experience stories. Sometimes new information relevant to an incident is discovered which creates discrepancies in the accepted story, but more often interpretative perspectives change prompting the reevaluation of the causal model which organized the original account."[19] This accurately describes David's narrative, where remembered material or retrospection threatened David's original interpretations. However, at the end of this extract, he remains unwilling to re-evaluate his original account; he remains reluctant to own a traumatic past.

A possible explanation for his persistence in remembering of past as a 'good period' is his strong sense of allegiance to his rescuers. Child survivors who survived at the hands of non-Jews – who risked their lives and the lives of their families in order to save them – feel that admitting that they had suffered in their care would be an ungrateful response to the sacrifices that were made on their behalf. Hidden child survivors developed a keen sense of loyalty to their rescuers, especially those who were kind and loving towards them. In some cases, child survivors came to view their rescuers as parental figures. By admitting that they had had difficult experiences during the war, the child survivor would not be able to preserve an idealized image of his or her 'parent', the rescuer. By claiming a traumatic past, hidden child survivors may be afraid of 'betraying' them. The rest of David's narrative supports this thesis in that allegiance and gratitude to his rescuers has become the focus of his relationship to his past. One of the main themes in his narrative is gratitude to those families who rescued him. He explains, "The more time that passes, the more I think about it, and I want more and more to give them [his rescuers] the credit. I am speaking about the way they treated me." By normalizing his experience during the war, David is able to preserve a good image of his rescuers and constantly feel grateful to them for their heroic behavior during the war.

David's narrative is a rich example of how the child survivors' experiences during the war have influenced their relationship to their past. During the war David 'normalized' his traumatic reality in order to survive, which has influenced the way he remembers the past. Furthermore, he understands that normalizing a traumatic reality is an important survival tool, one that he continues to use in his post-war reality. Furthermore, because David has few memories of the past and those that he does have are not remembered as 'traumatic' ones, he does not feel the need to share his past with others and he does not regard his 'survivor self' as the most salient element of his identity.[20]

Normalizing Continues in the Post-War Environment

In the first few years after the war, the *Shoah* was a constant topic of conversation in David's home. He grew up in a house similar to that of Ariella and Rachel's, in which he would be constantly listening to stories about the war. He explains that when his parents first arrived in Israel, they "tried to start a new life. They didn't want the *Shoah* to become the center of their lives. The tried to free themselves from it. However, it was not possible emotionally. Their experiences had been too powerful to put aside, and there were always reunions with people from 'there'. They would meet often. It came out of a strong social need, and that's something normal as far as I can understand . . . obviously I can't remember it . . . and as a child, many times I would sit there with them and listen. Moreover, they would say, 'We are not going to speak about the camps or about the ghettos'. Nevertheless, after half an hour that's what they would talk about. Each one with his own memories, his own things, and all sorts of stories. So if you ask how did I become exposed to the *Shoah*, perhaps that was the greatest source of exposure for me." David was never able to separate from the past as he grew up in an environment which was filled with stories of the past, and his parents were very well-known figures in the survivor community and in Israel. Before the war, his father was a member of the Lithuanian parliament and during the war he was a member of the ghetto *Judenrat*. After the war, he wrote one of the most important historical works on the Ghetto. Thus, David grew up in the shadow of his father's reputation, with the presence of *Shoah* ever present in their lives.

However difficult it was to contain the past, David's parents were determined to put it behind them and begin a new life. It is clear that David's parents' decision was influenced by the socio-cultural context at the time. Nevertheless, on a private level, David explains that it was important for his parents to record and remember the past. He explains that, "From the beginning, after he arrived in Israel, my father began writing his book and it occupied a lot of his time and attention. However, he really tried not to turn it into his whole life. He had work, he had a community and a family, and he wanted to live a normal life. Through writing, he was able to try and work through all sorts of things. However, there was no need to turn it into the focus of our family life. He believed that it was part of his rehabilitation. I think that it made a big impact on me, and I think that he was correct. Because life needed to carry on, and not only with the new problems that it brought, but also with the new successes and all the good things which a new life brought. To be over-involved with the past in those days . . . there were some people who were unable to disconnect themselves from the past, and it had a bad impact on their lives. Perhaps it bothered them. That's what they thought and that's how it looked, to begin again . . . it was as if they had left their souls there, and it was clear that that was not the way for them to rehabilitate themselves."

Following his parents' example, David learned to resist the encroachment of the past into his present and he was instructed to direct his energy into rebuilding a successful and meaningful future. This passage is the key to understanding David's resistance to speaking about the past. In David's case the past was not silenced, but was rather put aside 'to make way' for life after the war. This philosophy was reinforced by his encounters with other survivors as it became clear to David, as it was to Eliezer, that those survivors who were unable to disconnect from their pasts were unable to lead 'normal lives'. When I asked David if he had ever spoken publicly about the past, he replied, "I don't think that I want to busy myself with it, and anyway, I don't deal with it a lot. It is not something that occupies my present thoughts. Of course, it's connected to how I assess the world. But I think that if someone survived the *Shoah* and sees the need to keep living and thinks that he must continue living, like I do, that's the answer to the *Shoah*. We need to first of all remember the *Shoah* as an historical event, and we need to relate to it . . . on the other hand, our answer to the *Shoah* is to remain alive. The *Shoah* intended to destroy us, so the answer is – people need to lead normal lives. I don't think that by dealing with one's memories all the time is the right thing to do."

Therefore, for David, 'moving on' and building a 'normal life' was not only a strategy for rehabilitation, it also had an existential dimension to it. Once again, these ideas originated in his parent's home. David explains that, "My parents believed that that was the answer to the Nazis. That we would continue to live, despite what happened. We would start new lives, a new state, and rebuild ourselves personally as well as collectively. That they had not succeeded to break us . . . It is important to show that life continues on and that we are building and creating new things and succeeding not only to carry on from where we stopped, but to accomplish new things, despite the Nazis' attempt to destroy the existence of the Jewish people. I think that that was certainly one of the things that I remember, that there were quite a few people in our circle who thought that that was the right way." Aaron Hass, in his work on survivors, writes that this is a common attitude amongst survivors, as they "must reassure themselves that their enemies did not succeed. To admit to irreparable damage, to admit that their tormentors' reach has extended to their new lives, would imply that, ultimately they had lost. And so survivors acknowledge isolated symptoms . . . but assert their victory."[21] Rebuilding successful and meaningful lives thus came to be seen as their 'survivor mission'.

David's memories of the past have also been filtered and organized by his parents. David remarks, "I think that most of what I remember comes from stories that were told at home after the war." After the war, David's parents also made an effort to meet most of the families who had rescued him. This enabled them to gather more information about his past, and he was able to re-construct a chronology of his life. I asked David if he had spoken to his parents about his own experience during the war. He replied that "They spoke about theirs and certainly when I met my parents after the war, I assume that they spoke to me quite a lot about it. I can't remember exactly, but they clearly wanted to know what I had been through. However, after a certain period, it stopped being a topic that we spoke about a lot . . . So, all in all, I think that they knew a lot and they spoke to me about the different experiences. But at a certain stage they decided, or it happened naturally, to stop." Thus, throughout his life David had access to his past and to his pre-war identity through his parents. As a result, he is not bothered by his lack of memories. He explains that, "I am always curious to know more. But, I don't think that it bothers me. Meaning if I was able to remember more, I don't think that it would be more meaningful or different, or that it would do something special for me. I think that what I know is enough for me. I don't have burning questions that a better memory would help me resolve . . . but an incident that made an impression on me was a television program of a boy who was adopted and he really wanted to know who his parents were. It would help him with his life. I can understand him. I don't feel that I have an existential question that I can't ask. If, G-d forbid, one of my parents had not survived, I would very much want to know. But thank God both of them stayed alive and that's that. I was lucky that I knew then, and I had a good relationship with them. That's not something that I am missing." Because David's parents survived the war and were also willing to speak about the past, they helped him integrate his past with his present, giving him the foundations upon which to build his future.

Like most of the child survivors whom I interviewed, David chose to silence his past because he wanted to integrate into Israeli society and become a *sabra* like everybody else. After making *aliya*, David recalls being ridiculed by his peers because of his past, which encouraged him to repress it. David explains, "On the other hand, in relation to me, as a young boy who came to Israel, the environment responded to me with indifference or, on a certain level, mockery towards people who were in ghettos. 'You were soap', 'You didn't do anything, you didn't resist'. 'Where were you and what did you do?' 'What, you remained there?' I don't think that children in my surroundings thought much about it, but that's how they translated the things that they had heard. We were refugees." David explains that he encountered these attitudes even before he came to Israel. Whilst still in Europe, before making *aliya*, David was taught by Israeli emissaries. He explains, "Even then it was clear that it had been a mistake to stay in Europe and not come to Israel. They had a certain message. It wasn't always too strong, but it gave us the feeling . . . emissaries that came from here and told us that coming to Israel was the right thing to do and that here they were building free people, not like those who went like sheep to the slaughter." Besides the mockery and the ridicule, David explains that the subject of the *Shoah* was simply not spoken about and "it was not part of the educational curriculum, as they wanted to focus on rebuilding. That's the atmosphere that I felt here in Israel . . . and if I would bring up the subject of the *Shoah*, in the best of situations, it would not be acceptable or even desired." In response to the atmosphere he encountered in Israel, David repressed his experiences. He explains that, "There was no motivation to express it. In addition, I think that it's a natural thing for a young man who needs to get on with life. It's natural for him to face the future and not face the past."

Despite the fact that David became a *sabra*, he was always connected to his past through his parents, who also encouraged him to integrate into Israeli society. Nowhere in David's narrative is the issue of an identity crisis apparent. Quite the opposite, David's narrative reflects an integrated identity, where the past and the present sit together comfortably on the same page. Over the years, David has not experienced conflict over his identity, as the values of the socio-cultural context (the outer reality) matched his inner reality (the values of his parents and his own internal need to belong).

David's experiences during the war may not be at the center of his identity; yet in his narrative he does acknowledge that his past is always with him. I asked David how he felt on *Yom Hashoah,* to which he replied, "*Yom Hashoah* is a day of remembrance. I don't think that it's a special day . . . as somewhere the *Shoah* is always with me. I can't live without it. It's important that they have a ceremony and remember, but it's not a special day because of that, because it's something that is always with me, and thus it is a day no different from other days. The subject always returns in flashes, in small portions, but it's always there." We learn that for David, while the past is not the focus of his identity, it is as he describes 'always with him'. It has influenced his personal ideology and strengthened his commitment to building a just and moral world.

Michal: "I don't want validation, I want acceptance"

Children in Camps: The Trauma of Witnessing

Just as Jewish children were rare in the prisoner population of the extermination camps in Poland, they were also an infrequent presence in the original concentration camps in Germany. There too, the young were smuggled in, and either found themselves amongst the adult slave labor, or were hidden by the adult prisoners for as long as possible. There were also some concentration camps which permitted Jewish children to 'live' and die alongside their parents. The 'unknown destination' to which young people and their families were deported was their entry into hell. However horrendous their lives had been in hiding, in transit camps or ghettos, this was a new and unprecedented stage of misery. Whereas hidden children had learned to remain silent in order to conceal their identity during the war, for children incarcerated in Nazi camps, silence became a response to the trauma of witnessing.

Michal's narrative is characterized by a deep silence around her experiences as a prisoner in the camp. From the beginning of the interview, Michal tells a chronological life-story, yet a fragmented one; having been born in 1941, she was only an infant during the Holocaust period. She first describes an early memory of her mother, her experiences in hiding with Polish families, and her eventual capture by the Nazis. She then begins to describe the train journey to the camp. Her memories of the train are sharp and vivid, and resemble what we referred to previously as traumatic memory. This is also the only place in her narrative where she begins to describe in detail her experiences during the *Shoah.*

"... the trains were crowded ... it was unbelievable how many people were squeezed onto those trains. You could barely breathe. People died on the train. A woman gave birth on the train. Once a day they would stop and open the doors of the train and throw the dead people out. And then we came to the camp . . . I was there until the end of the war . . . it was some place near the Polish Russian border . . . " At this point her telling stops and she remains silent for a while. In fact, her entire camp experience is not told: she refers to her arrival in the camp and then skips to her liberation. The camp is represented in her narrative by its absence.

Michal has not 'forgotten' her incarceration; rather she chooses not to talk about it. I was aware of this prior to our interview, as a few days before we were scheduled to meet, Michal had called me. She sounded quite agitated on the phone and said that if I wanted to hear about the camps, "I shouldn't come," that "I would be wasting my time" because she does not like talking about it. I was taken aback, but attempted to reassure her that I was interested in hearing about her life as a whole and not about her camp experience specifically. In fact, I did not know the details of her story when I first called her. This was a learning experience for me as, for the first time, I was told directly that there were certain experiences that the interviewee was not prepared to speak about and would be omitted from her story. I obviously had to contain my heightened curiosity and respect the boundary that Michal had constructed. I encountered first-hand what I had learned from the literature: that silence was a tool for self-preservation and that some things were too difficult or painful to tell.

Post-War Environment: Subsequent Traumatization

Robert Krell explains that "a poor post-war environment could intensify the preceding traumatic events and, conversely, a good environment mitigate some of the traumatic effects."[22] This cannot be seen more clearly than in Michal's experience with her adopted family after the war. According to Michal, her adopted parents in the United States were quite unprepared for her arrival. She certainly was not the type of child they had wanted, and they were not the type of parents she had dreamed of.

She recalls that "I insisted on sleeping on the floor. I used to curl up by the bed on the floor and I wouldn't part with my orphanage clothes because they were . . . this was really the only continuity I had in my life, I wore these orphanage clothes all the time and they were very embarrassed . . . I think what they wanted was a child . . . yes, a little girl who would be like Shirley Temple. I don't know if you know who Shirley Temple is . . . she is just a cute little obnoxious movie star at the time who had curls, long curls and was very sweet. I had . . . this sweetness, I had dimples and I smiled all the time and I was really a cute little kid and . . . so they just thought, I was meant to be the epitome of this Shirley Temple but they were very disappointed from the first day!"

Michal felt that her adopted parents did not attempt to understand who she was, what she had experienced, or how difficult the transition was for her. Instead, they were intent on remolding her, in creating a 'Shirley Temple'. They were not interested in her past and they disregarded her experiences. She explains that, "They just expected me to forget . . . to 'put the past behind me'. They used to say to me, 'You ought to be so grateful we brought you from Germany and for giving you this life', and I always used to say that 'Germany was better than living with you'. And, in any case, then I learned to hide the Holocaust."

Having no Credibility

Michal continues to explain that even when she did find an audience, they usually did not believe her story. She explains, "When I talked about it, nobody believed me. They thought I was making this up and that I was lying and how could such a young child understand and how could such a young child remember and could this have happened?"

Michal's survival is truly remarkable. Born in 1941 in the midst of the war in Poland she survived the war in hiding and in a camp. Michal was four years old when she was liberated. One of the most fascinating elements of her narrative is that despite her very young age, Michal says she has vivid memories from the war. During the interview, she explains that very few people actually believe that she is able to remember her experiences, because she had been so young. She explains that this disbelief has continued, "And of course today, you know, people say how could you remember? In two more days, I am going to be fifty-nine. They say, 'How could you remember?' The only thing that I can say to them is that when something so traumatic happens to you, you can't forget, you just can't forget. A child who experiences anything so traumatic is not a child like other children. It is very vivid and it has always been . . . but nobody believes me."

Whilst growing up the reaction of disbelief certainly discouraged Michal from talking about her past. Today, however, Michal believes in and trusts her own memories, and she retells her war experience with confidence and self-assurance. Michal has built a chronological narrative of her life during and after the war, where one of the earliest memories is of being held by her mother. She recalls, "What I still remember of my mother is being held by her and seeing somebody with black hair . . . " The only memory that Michal has of her mother is the color of her mother's hair and the feeling of being held by her in a protective embrace. Judith Kestenberg's research with child survivors helps us understand Michal's memory of her mother. She explains, "Sensations and feelings are also more primordial and elementary than external perceptions."[23] Therefore, the memory of movement, a face, or the physicality of relationship is imprinted on the memory of the child.

The next memory that Michal presents in her recounting is the murder of her rescuers and her own narrow escape. She recalls, "I remember being with this young Polish couple . . . sitting outside in the yard of the house . . . We heard the *Gestapo* coming, we heard the marching . . . we heard the noise (silence) they pushed me under the blanket we were sitting on and the *Gestapo* walked into the yard and shouted at them to get into the house . . . They were so angry . . . they were convinced for some reason that this couple was hiding a Jewish child . . . (silence) . . . A few minutes later I heard a gun shot and they left the house . . . when it got dark, I walked into the house and saw the couple lying on the floor next to each other . . . I walked out of the house and I hid in the bushes. The next morning the mother of the young girl came . . . and found me among the bushes. I must have been three years old (silence)."

Michal is able to remember in detail the sequence of events. In her retelling, she has woven fragments of memory into a coherent, chronological, narrative. Over time Michal has managed to arrange her three-year old memories, and place them in a larger context of understanding. Ruthellen Josselson writes, "Narratives are not records of facts, of how things actually were, but of a meaning making system that makes sense out of the chaotic mass of perceptions and experiences of a life."[24] Michal's re-construction of her past can be categorized as the storyteller approach to memory "which places memory processes in the context of narratives and social relationships. This approach tends to focus on constellations of preserved knowledge – on how things 'hook together' rather than on constituent elements of memory."[25]

Michal's memories are also typical of the memories of very young children for whom memories of bodily and auditory sensations are salient. Charlotte Kahn, in an article on child survivors writes, "Contrary to the popular belief that children have no memory of their early experiences, infant traumatic experiences are stored, albeit in sensory-motor (not semantic and conceptual) form. Unavailable to conscious recall, these early stored experiences nonetheless influence behavior, even in adulthood. By contrast, frequent, sudden, terror experienced at a later age (that is after two-and-a-half to three years old) can be re-aroused by related stimuli (visual, auditory, or olfactory) and then retrieved. This is feasible because very early 'affectively charged experiences' are characterized by indelibility."[26]

Throughout her narrative, Michal describes her vivid memories of her frightful experiences during the war. Some of the memories are clearly hers, as she was the only witness. However, there are times in her narrative when it becomes apparent that there are other, external sources for her memory – friends of her parents who had remained in contact with her both during and after the war, who were committed to maintaining her memories and connection to the pre-war past of her family.

She explains, "And friends of my parents who had survived and had gone into the woods into hiding and had joined the underground . . . The militia . . . used to come round sometimes and visit me. They wanted me to know that I belonged. It seemed important to them to keep a tie with me so I wouldn't . . . well, today I can articulate it as 'losing my identity' . . . but basically they wanted me to know that I belonged to them and to have some sense of identity with them and belonging and so forth . . . "

This group of people eventually removed Michal from her hiding place with the Polish family, as "they felt that this woman could just not withstand the pressure anymore as the *Gestapo* came every day . . . and they started interviewing her children and questioning them and taking them down to their office and so forth. She had certainly sacrificed enough . . . and (silence) one night they came to take me away with them. They came in a covered truck . . . they started driving with the truck into the forest and just as we got into the forest we were caught and we were put onto the trains . . . (silence)."

The group was incarcerated in a camp for the duration of the war, and Michal was separated from them after liberation when she fled the camp with another woman who had decided to take care of her. Nevertheless, they were able to reconnect in Berlin and maintained contact even in America. Michal explains, "But I spent a lot of the war years and after the war in Germany with people who had been in the underground and in the partisans, who had been friends with my parents and who also turned up in Berlin. They found me and we were able to make the connection; later they came to the United States and looked me up. Actually, they wanted to adopt me . . . but by then the adoption with the American couple had gone through and there was nothing legally to do, but they did keep in touch with me."

Thus, Michal's parent's friends were in constant contact with her throughout her life, and were able to provide her with information and memories of her past. Despite the fact that she had lost her parents, these people provided her with a link to her past. They strengthened her memories and gave her a sense of connection. In fact, these individuals helped Michal feel an unwavering sense of rootedness, a rare experience for orphaned child survivors. Michal affirms this when she says, "I feel my roots, I know my roots . . . I don't feel that there are blank spaces anywhere in my history . . . I remember enough and as I said I have the ability to be in touch with some of those people in America who I remember from my childhood . . . Our paths cross every now and then."

Despite the confidence Michal had in her own memories, she had nobody to communicate them with. Even at school, Michal was silenced. She recalls an episode when, "We were having a drawing class and the teacher asked children to draw whatever they liked to draw and I remember looking around and everybody was drawing flowers and birds and bees and so forth and I just filled up page after page after page of swastikas. And she came over to me and she said, 'You can't do that' (Silence.) I didn't know what she was talking about. I didn't know what was not nice about drawing swastikas, she said draw whatever you want to draw about and that's all I ever knew what I wanted to draw about! So that . . . was not (laugh) a successful way to deal with all of this."

Michal remarks, later on in the interview, that it was at that moment that she realized that she was forbidden to speak about her past. Silence had been imposed on her by her adopted parents as well as her school-teacher. This episode represented a turning point for Michal, where she realized that in order to 'survive' she needed to conceal her past and reinvent herself. Acquiescence as a tool for survival was not foreign to Michal. During the war Michal had learnt that in order to survive, she needed to be a 'good little girl'. She explains, "I think that it was there that I learned that a way to survive is to make yourself useful . . . to make yourself appealing, to be acquiescent . . . to be anyone's definition of a good little girl and of course the definition of a good little girl changes in context . . . " In her post-war context that meant silencing the past and adopting a new identity – Shirley Temple.

She explains that, "I've learned to be very adaptive. When my hair started growing, and these awful Shirley Temple curls, and I had these dimples and I had all these sweet dresses . . . Once I lost my accent and once I learned to speak English I (silence), . . . nobody ever knew . . . there are people who I grew up with all those years and **nobody** ever knew because . . . I learned very fast from that incident with the swastikas that you don't talk about the war, you don't talk about the *Gestapo*, you don't talk about the camps, you don't talk about death, you don't talk about anything. You just needed to be the sweet little girl that everybody wants you to be and all the rest you just . . . hide. I learned to do it very well." Her narrative is fascinating in that it reveals how Michal continued to respond to her new reality in the same way that she had responded during the war. She had learned to be acquiescent in order to survive.

Over the years, with her new persona, Michal began to feel more 'acceptable'. Yet she also continued to feel misunderstood. Furthermore, the material comfort and security that her post-war environment provided her did not initially dispel her feelings of insecurity and vulnerability. Rather, these anxieties were exacerbated by her emotional deprivation and the de-legitimization of her suffering. As a result, at the age of sixteen, Michal began to feel depressed and alone with her pain. She recalls, "Once in the United States, when I was sixteen and I saw this depression starting, I asked my adopted mother to let me go to a doctor and deal with this depression. She said, 'Nice little girls don't get depressed and go to the doctor. What will people say and what are you going to talk about all this stuff for! Forget it. It happened a long time ago'." Just as Michal's war trauma had been de-legitimized in her post-war environment, so was her post-war depression.

It is clear from her narrative that one of the causes of her depression stemmed from her 'adopted identity'. Just like Ehud, she reached a point where she could no longer stand lying about her past. Neither could she maintain the façade she had painfully constructed for herself. She explains, "All of this hiding of the Holocaust in the States began to take its toll, and I mean most of the time I felt that I was living a double life . . . there was this American life, there was this person, this young girl, who presented . . . who developed this American persona and then there was the real me who had all this Holocaust stuff and who had no one to speak with and . . . that she had to hide . . . That was really my true self . . . " The distance Michal felt from this 'American persona' is even reflected in the language she uses – she uses the third person – when describing her. Not only did Michal long to express herself freely, she also wanted to reveal her past. Michal wanted her suffering to be acknowledged and validated, and her trauma legitimized. Michal was looking for an empathic audience – something that her adopted home and socio-cultural environment failed to provide.

Michal's opportunity to express herself came in her teenage years, when she participated in a summer trip to Israel. She recalls, "It was the first time I could breathe. It was the first time I could be me. It was the first time that all these parts of this persona come together. In Israel I could talk about the Holocaust and people did not think I was lying . . . In Israel I could be me! Without people criticizing, with having people accept and understand, and I think that was the one place where that was the first time I felt whole and could be me." Thus, it was in Israel that Michal experienced freedom for the first time since the war. The Israeli socio-cultural context enabled her to open up and gave her the freedom to explore her identity. Realizing that it was only in Israel that she could maintain her personal freedom, she decided to make Israel her permanent home. As was seen in previous narratives *aliya* was an important healing step for child survivors who suffered from a con-flicted identity, because Israel presented itself as a collective family, and many child survivors were able, by living in Israel, to overcome their feelings of isolation, alienation, and identity conflicts.

Michal explains, "When I came to Israel I was able to put the two parts together, I mean the three major periods in my life, the Holocaust, and then America which was so different but was basically a de-legitimizing of the Holocaust. That's really the only way that I can say it, it de-legit-imized all my experiences before . . . the period when I came to Israel, which is very different from America and from the Holocaust. I think that if there was any integration, it happened here . . . because here I could express both parts of my past . . . I could be this American, a young American, and I could talk about the Holocaust and people believed me."

Michal attributes this validation to the values of the socio-cultural environment, "In Israel it's part of society . . . it's part of the social life here . . . the fact that there is a Holocaust memorial day . . . it's part of this social identity of Israel. The Holocaust is a major Israeli event. Politicians talk about it, everybody talks about it . . . it's a reality in Israel." As was discussed in the Introduction, the *Shoah* has occupied a central place in Israeli society, unlike in the United States, where until 1978, it remained outside of public discourse. Michal's words are signif-icant as they illustrate the role that the socio-cultural context plays in validating traumatic experience. The socio-cultural context in Israel, in contrast to the United States, encouraged Michal to speak about and reclaim her past. Another factor that may have been instrumental in Michal's identity development was that she was far away from her adopted parents. She was beyond their reach, and no longer under their control, Michal could start defining her own identity, and determine who she was and who she wanted to be.

However, similar to the experiences of Ariella and Ehud, coming to Israel did not help Michal 'recover' from her traumatic past or alleviate her depression. Rather, her anxieties and fears continued to plague her life and dominate her relationships. Michal explains that when she got married, her past became too overwhelming. She explains that, "I came here and I met the man that I married and if you talk about before the war and after the war and this artificial sort of demarcation between this or compartmentalization between what happened before the war and after, this compartmentalization doesn't really work, it is a convenient way to define the periods historically . . . but it is not reality. As I said it

. . . the Holocaust does not just end. It just goes on and on and once I married these problems continued . . . the depression that I had started when I was nineteen, this business of not being able to be me, not being . . . not having anyone to talk to about the Holocaust, not having anyone to talk to about personality problems . . . I had feelings of insecurity, this driven need to be liked all the time by everyone . . . it made marriage very difficult (silence)."

Despite the fact that Israel helped Michal 'own' the two parts of her identity, she continued to feel uncomfortable speaking openly about her past and identifying herself as a Holocaust survivor. She explains that one of the reasons for her continued disguise was so that she could get on with her life. Yet, in the interview she explains that whilst this disguise was external, the past continued to plague her daily consciousness as she struggled with feelings of pain, fear and anxiety. To some extent she has even been able to keep these feelings "masked, because you go about your life and you do what you're supposed to do and nobody knows, except for you [referring to me, the interviewer], and the two other people who sent you to me . . . very few people, of course my close friends, but mostly, nobody knows and especially here I walk around with this American accent and I am relatively young and people don't believe that I lived through that and half the time I can't believe it myself."

Rejecting the Survivor Identity

Later on in her narrative, Michal gives another explanation for her silence. She does not want to be identified as a Holocaust survivor, because of the way the Holocaust survivor is perceived and represented in Israeli society. In the interview, I asked Michal why she does not like being identified as a survivor, to which she replied, "I don't like it, I mean as I say, it's a socially constructed category . . . Israeli society has constructed this type or this historical figure. For Israel, it is part of the construction of Israel's identity, it's part of the history of Israel and Israel has constructed this in many ways. All this survivor stuff is . . . I must say nonsense . . . just getting through the day, and getting up tomorrow and facing a new day makes everybody a survivor. In addition, there are no charmed lives and everybody has their own cross to bear, and life is not easy and life is long and all kinds of things happen and I don't like this label . . . I don't identify with it particularly. I mean I know, of course, that I lived through the Holocaust and it has made me different . . . in major ways from people who have not . . . but I don't like the label. It's almost offensive. It's been created to serve a social need . . . I think that its a verbal shortcut . . . I don't know if it's a stereotype but when you say 'Holocaust survivor' it conjures up a image of a personality . . . which isn't particularly attractive."

Michal does not want to be identified as a Holocaust survivor for many reasons. First, Michal rejects 'labels', as they rob the individual of their own experience and individuality. Janice Haaken explains that the contemporary use of the term 'survivor' imposes a diffuse sameness, "erasing vital differences."[27] By distancing herself from her survivor identity, Michal is asserting her individuality and the fact that she is more than just a Holocaust survivor. This idea has become one of the central issues facing survivors: claiming their identity and the risk of being identified as *only* a survivor, which has been constructed negatively in the collective discourse. This phenomenon is also echoed in the literature on sexual abuse. Carol Ronai, writing about child sexual abuse, explains: "People who claim the status of child sexual abuse victim receive from society a problematic set of categories with which to define themselves. Existing disclosure dictates to the children that they have been violated and that, as such, they are deviant – pariahs. They have no alternative to be other in the eyes of society; the status ascribed to them."[28] Ruthellen Josselson writes, "When we aggregate people, treating diversity as error variance, in the search of what is common to all, we often learn about what is true of no one in particular."[29] Furthermore, Michal's words reflect Henry Greenspan's argument that since the war, Holocaust survivors have been instrumentalized and objectified for social–political needs.

Michal does not want to be perceived as different from the rest of Israeli society. In fact she believes that everybody is a survivor of the challenges of their everyday life. However, she does recognize that her life-story is inherently different from other people who did not live through the *Shoah*. In this extract, Michal is struggling to define her point of view, to make meaning of her strong resistance to identifying publicly as a survivor. She begins by giving an academic, 'professional' answer, and in the end gives a personal one. In the last sentence, she touches on the core of her resistance, which is very difficult for her to articulate. "I don't know if it's a stereotype but it's, you know, when you say 'Holocaust survivor' it conjures up an image of a personality . . . which isn't particularly attractive." For Michal, the survivor identity as constructed and presented in Israeli society is 'offensive', and 'unattractive', and therefore she resists being identified as such.

The stigmatization of Holocaust survivor in Israel's collective memory has been discussed at length throughout this work. Michal's interview confirms that the sociocultural context which "characterized the survivors as 'weak', 'helpless', 'bad', 'guilt ridden', 'envious', 'greedy for compensation', 'imposters', 'overbearing', etc."[30] was instrumental in silencing them. Because of the way that she feels survivors are perceived in Israel, she resists 'exposing' her past, as she is unsure how people will relate to her once they 'know'.

Israel as a sociocultural environment may have helped Michal reconnect to her past. Yet it did not help her 'own' it publicly. Michal's experience of coming to terms with her past is an ongoing process and her narrative reflects Ruthellen Josselson's assertion that "the individual is always in process,"[31] constantly evolving and re-evaluating itself in light of the changing socio-cultural context.

Unlike the hidden child survivors we encountered in chapter 5 Michal has not been looking for validation of her trauma and her past. Rather, she claims to have been searching for 'acceptance'. She explains that, "What Israel has given me is acceptance. I don't need validation of the experience. I needed the acceptance. I needed to be accepted in the sense that I could . . . express and talk about my personality without it being de-legitimized. I don't need the validation on a social level." Unlike her adopted parents, 'Israel' accepted Michal for who she was. However, she continues to feel that her experience as a survivor is misunderstood in contemporary Israeli society. Today, Michal is looking for acceptance based on an intimate understanding of and sensitivity towards her past. She wants to be recognized as 'not normal', by which she means "different, rather than sick".[32] Michal acknowledges that the *Shoah* has left an indelible mark on her and that she has suffered and continues to suffer because of it. Yet she rejects the way Israeli society understands and portrays her 'difference'. Michal feels that the wider public cannot understand her experience, because it holds an insensitive and superficial understanding of the Holocaust and its survivors.

Michal has managed to find the type of acceptance she needs in a therapeutic environment, which 'understands' her past and listens empathically and non-judgmentally to her story. When I interviewed her in 2000 Michal had been in therapy with AMCHA for the previous five years. She explains that she didn't go to AMCHA to 'be cured', in fact she does not consider her therapy to be treatment. Rather, she goes there to find an empathic audience with whom she can explore, make meaning of her past and cope with her present. She explains, "People go to psychotherapy or psychological counseling or whatever you call it, therapy . . . therapy implies the ability to be cured . . . you go for treatment to be cured . . . but what's good about them . . . I mean I don't know how other people . . . but the person I meet there and talk to there . . . we've talked about it several times about the fact that it's not a question of becoming normal . . . it's certain . . . it's really just support . . . but what I think that AMCHA gives me is the ability . . . the knowledge that I have a place where I can go . . . that I can talk about the things without the expectation that I can be cured if being treated . . . They know that I can never be like everyone else and they know that the Holocaust, people who lived through the Holocaust, are different and I guess they know why they are different."

Aliya helped Michal re-connect to her past: AMCHA has enabled Michal to claim her 'wounded self'. AMCHA provided Michal with an empathic audience, which recognized and validated her fears, anxieties, and behavior. Within this environment, which represents the antithesis of her post-war environment, Michal feels that she can reveal and claim her wounded self, without being judged. Her experience with AMCHA also helped Michal to understand that many of her past and current issues and anxieties stemmed from her traumatic past. Right at the beginning of our interview, Michal stated, "I think that one of the important things for people to know is that the separation or the delineation between before and after is very much an artificial one. Places change, the geography changes . . . The social context changes . . . but basically the Holocaust doesn't really stop . . . I know that that sounds very dramatic . . . it doesn't really stop, it's not something that just happened and was over and then you just go on about your business. It's something that is always with you in various ways. It changes with different stages in your life or with different life cycles. It changes with the different roles you take upon yourself as you progress into adulthood and into middle age and beyond middle age . . . But it is really something that's always with you . . . "

Michal's narrative had a deep and profound affect on me. I was confronted with a bright and successful woman, mother and grandmother, who despite her achievements still felt insecure and vulnerable. Michal seemed to live in constant emotional pain, in constant fear that at any moment she could lose everything she has. Indeed, her experiences both during and after the war have reinforced her feelings of vulnerability and helplessness. As a mother, Michal nearly lost her daughter to cancer. She explained that for three years "it was total uncertainty . . . overcoming her cancer only became clear after three years . . . it was like another Holocaust, but much worse for some reason. I never understood why . . . but I always used to say that this experience with her cancer was a hundred times worse than . . . I used to say that I would relive the Holocaust a million times before I would relive . . . those three years." Michal's narrative centers on the themes of loss and uncertainty, yet the nature of the loss – the loss of one's parents and the loss of one's child – is inherently different. As a result of the war, Michal, the child, lost her parents and her past. After the war, Michal, the mother, nearly lost her daughter and her future. The parameters of

Michal's life seem to have been framed by the extreme circumstances of the war, and have been reinforced by subsequent traumas.

From her narrative, it is clear that throughout her life Michal has searched for a safe place for herself – a place in which she will be accepted unconditionally. AMCHA has provided her with such a place. Yet she is still resistant to retelling publicly, as she is afraid, based on her past experiences, of how society will respond to her. Michal's narrative vacillates between the need for recognition, acceptance, comfort, and the fear of exposure. Her narrative represents her search for an empathic audience; for an individual or group who will be able to listen and believe her, accept and not stigmatize her. Initially Michal found this empathic audience in Israel because of the relative openness of Israeli society, which enabled her to begin speaking about her past. Yet, over time she began to experience Israeli society as a critical and judgmental one, and no longer felt comfortable in exposing her survivor identity openly. Michal rejects Israeli society's perception of her suffering and of the survivor's experience in general, and therefore refuses to identify herself publicly as a Holocaust survivor. Michal's narrative reflects the basic distrust that survivors have of Israeli society's understanding of the *Shoah* in general, and the survivor experience in particular. Michal's narrative is a search for acceptance, for a forum in which she can express her memory openly and publicly without being labeled, stigmatized or de-legitimized. Throughout her narrative, Michal begs to be recognized and accepted as she describes, "one who has suffered and continues to suffer because of her past," not someone who is 'sick'. This acceptance she has begun to find in AMCHA.

On a wider level, Michal's narrative can be seen as a plea for a more sensitive, empathic, and knowledgeable understanding of the *Shoah* and of its few remaining survivors. Henry Greenspan's words are truly reflected in Michal's narrative. He explains that in survivors' accounts of their ongoing lives, "they attempt to retell not only their experiences during the Holocaust, or their identities as recounters, but the status of their survival itself."[33]

Avivit: "I am a person like everyone else"

I found Avivit to be the most 'resistant speaker' that I interviewed for my research. From the moment we met, she was very resistant to the interview, which reflected her general reluctance to sharing her past. My interview with Avivit began on a difficult footing. This can be seen from our opening exchange.

A: What do you want to start with?

S: Could you divide your life into a few chapters and . . .

A: What does that mean? Divide you life into a few chapters?

S: How do you see your life? Are there a few chapters that you can describe or is it one continual . . .

A: I can't answer a question like that. I am a person like everyone else. Do you ask yourself to divide your life into a few chapters?

S: No . . .

A: You should know. I am against when people put those people who went through the *Shoah* into boxes. Every time it is discussed on television, I call in and I am angry. We are ordinary people like everyone else. I have integrated very well and became just like a *sabra*. My mother tongue is Hebrew; I did not have any difficulties in my absorption. I have a problem that I didn't have a childhood and I don't have a family. I don't have any aunts or uncles, cousins. I don't have that. But, what I created afterwards . . . but to divide into chapters, is unacceptable to me. It is unacceptable to put people into boxes and they do that to people who experienced the *Shoah*. With every war, they say that for those who have been through the *Shoah*, finds the war more difficult. That's nonsense. It's unacceptable to me. I am an ordinary person like everyone else. The only thing is that I don't have family. It hurts me, and it is getting even more painful. I have children, grandchildren, everything, and I have my husband's family in Jerusalem. But what we are missing is family.

This exchange can be seen as a microcosm of Avivit's entire narrative, and is powerful in explaining her resistance to retelling. Like Michal, she does not want to be related to as a 'survivor', a stereotype, and lose her individuality. Avivit is fearful that once she reveals her past, the listener will *only* perceive her as a survivor, with all of its socio-cultural connotations, and other vital elements of her self will be lost. Beyond claiming her individuality, this exchange also reflects how powerful collective memory of the *Shoah* is in the mind's eye of the survivor. Avivit, like Michal, still feels that collective memory of the *Shoah* ostracizes and stigmatizes the survivor. As a result, they want to disassociate themselves from the 'survivor identity', and silence their past.

Avivit's decision to conceal her identity as a survivor is in response to the negative image that has been projected in Israeli society surrounding Holocaust survivors, and not due to her own feelings of weakness and vulnerability. Avivit does not feel damaged. Rather she is reacting against being defined as 'damaged'. Her narrative can be understood as a response against the cultural claim that survivors are 'damaged people', as she constantly asserts that she does not want to be seen as a victim who has been permanently damaged by the war. Through her narrative she transforms herself into one who has been 'unaffected' by her experiences during the war. Avivit wants to be recognized as someone who is resilient, who despite her traumatic past was able to rebuild a normal life. This is powerfully presented in the following extract, where Avivit's daughter, the proof of her rehabilitation, testifies to her 'normality'. She relates that, "when my younger daughter wrote a final project in high school, she wanted to write her project on my life story. I didn't really agree. So, she did it on that children's institution in Italy . . . but she began to read about . . . what children went through during the *Shoah*, about people who had experienced it. After she had read all that literature, she came to me and said: 'I don't understand what they are writing here'. Today she is a psychologist. She said: 'I don't understand what these people are writing here . . . You have no sign that you . . . everything that they write about those people who had experienced the *Shoah*, does not fit you'. So I am telling you that it is forbidden to put people into boxes."

Thus, from the outset, Avivit's resistance to the interview reflects her resistance to being interviewed *as* a survivor. Rather, she insists on being interviewed as an individual, as an Israeli and as someone who is 'normal'. This requires her to silence her past, because she feels the negative image of the survivor presented in collective memory still dominates the imagination of 'possible audiences'. It must be emphasized that Avivit does not feel that she has been 'damaged' by her past. This is not the way that she sees or experiences herself. Rather, in her desperate attempt to be accepted and belong, she refuses to identify publicly as a Holocaust survivor because of what she feels it has come to symbolize in Israeli society

The Inability to Retell

After our initial difficulties, I began to ask Avivit more specific questions. I asked her: "When were you born?" Avivit was more responsive to this type of question, and she gave me a short biography of her life. However, her responses were very general and unemotional. Pamela Ballinger, in her article on survivors, writes, "repression of emotion rather than memory"[34] characterizes survivors of collective trauma. Her responses confirmed my sense that Avivit really did not want to speak about the past at all. At this point, I began to feel more uncomfortable. I began to ask myself, "What am I doing here?" I wasn't quite sure, but something kept me there. Once I began to analyze her narrative, I began to discover that Avivit's reluctance towards retelling was not only connected to her fear of being labeled as a survivor. In addition she didn't want to speak about the past to someone who she felt could not understand her experiences. Throughout the interview, Avivit questioned my professional and academic abilities. She was trying to gauge how much I knew about the *Shoah*, in order to assess my ability to hear and understand her. From the nature of her responses to my questions, I realized that her resistance was to *me* interviewing *her* about her past. Lawrence Langer explains that, "From the point of view of the witness, the urge to tell meets resistance from the certainty that one's audience will not understand. The anxiety of futility lurks beneath the surface of many of those narratives, erupting occasionally and rousing us to an appraisal of our own stance that we cannot afford to ignore."[35] This dynamic is illustrated in the following extract. I had asked Avivit if she could relate a few specific incidents from her time spent in the ghetto.

S: Do you have memories from the period of the Shoah?
A: Of course I have. I have memories.
S: Could you tell me some of them?
A: What for example? What do you want to know?
S: Memories that are more dominant, that are with you all the time or perhaps, with time, you have remembered certain things more or less . . .
A: I remember everything.
S: Are there certain memories that . . .
A: I don't remember the names of children. That I don't remember. Only those who live in Israel. We have started to meet other children where each one tells how he/she survived. How each one of them fled from the ghetto . . . .
S: Are there things you remember as happier moments or . . .
A: I don't understand what you mean.
S: I simply want to hear some of your memories from the ghetto, from your home . . .
A: That's a very difficult question for me. Have you already interviewed people?
S: Yes.
A: What have they said?
S: Everyone has his or her own story.
A: I don't understand what you want.
S: To hear about your experiences . . .
A: What type of experiences does a girl of five, six, or seven have? That she knows that the Germans are coming and they say, 'to work' and she needs to go and find refuge. We were older children, we didn't have a childhood. We knew that we had to stay

alive whatever it took. We simply did not go through the childhood stage. We didn't have a childhood. We were big children. So
essentially that is what is missing. I have told you that a stage of
my life is missing, childhood.

This exchange reflects what survivors have often described as their
inability to relate their phantasmagoric experiences of the war to people
who have not experienced the *Shoah*, within "the logical framework of
today's realities, in which some semblance of comprehensible order
seems to prevail in society, is an impossible task of language."[36]

My interview questions were formulated in a different reality to that
to which the questions referred. Therefore, Avivit resisted answering
my questions about the past, because she felt that her answers would
only betray her experiences. Avivit did not seem to want to try and go
beyond this invisible boundary of un-shared experience, and her challenging responses only serve to reinforce the divide between us. Avivit
seems to be convinced, based on her years of experience as a 'survivor
of the Holocaust', that conversation about the past between survivors
and non-survivors is impossible. Lawrence Langer writes, "For the
survivor and the non- survivor, normal ideas of time, space, and identity oppose a remote experience that stubbornly eludes attempts to
bring it into familiar focus." Nevertheless, Langer does not believe that
communication is impossible, but that there exists "a more fluid image
of the ordeal, which permits certain modes of conduct to link the individual with normality and to reduce the sense of alienation between the
world of the death camps and our own."[37]

What remains clear from Avivit's narrative is that she does not recognize any link or shared understanding that she may have with her
current socio-cultural context, which may facilitate an understanding of
and communication about her past. Based on her experiences as a
Holocaust survivor in Israel, in which she has felt misunderstood and
misrepresented, Avivit does not see a possible link between her world
'then' and our world 'now'. Therefore, she refrains from presenting
herself as a survivor to Israeli society. Instead, she chooses to keep her
past a private matter, or shares it with those with whom which she feels
she has a shared language of experience. In the context of our interview,
Avivit viewed me as a representative of Israeli society, the 'now' who
could not possibly understand the 'then'.

Finding an Empathic Audience

At a certain point in the interview, the tension eased between Avivit and
myself, as we both began to feel more comfortable with each another.

Even though she did not want to speak about her past, she was more open and willing to share her life story with me. I had also learned to stop asking questions about the past, as it was clear that she did not want to speak about it, and was more comfortable with speaking about her present. As trust developed between the two of us, so too did the interview. Avivit slowly let down her defenses, as she was assured that I was not going to push her. I had given her the freedom to control the conversation. This reassured her that I was not trying to categorize her and that I was genuinely interested in what she wanted to say. It became clear both during and after the interview that, in order for Avivit to speak, she needed to feel in control, comfortable, and that she was in the presence of an empathic audience who did not judge or label her.

Like Michal, Avivit has recently found an empathic audience. Participating in a child survivors' group, she has begun speaking about her past with other child survivors from Kovno. I asked Avivit how she felt participating in this group, to which she replied, "Very good. Suddenly things connect; for example, in the last meeting we were shown a map of Kovno and especially the part where the ghetto was, and everyone looked to see where they lived. I feel okay. Everyone recollects about his or her childhood and it is wonderful. The last time I spoke . . . and we are trying to get it taped. They told me that there were meetings in which some people cried." Avivit's child survivor group is an informal support group, in which a feeling of "universality"[38] is created amongst the participants. This feeling of 'universality', where members of the group are able to identify and empathize with one another's story, worked against Avivit's feelings of isolation and stigmatization, which she experienced as a survivor in Israeli society. Within these groups the participants reinforce each other's normal reactions, because collectively they represent the very norm from which, individually, they deviate. Thus, it is hardly surprising that the child survivor group has made Avivit comfortable with retelling her past. Moreover, within this group she even feels safe reminiscing about her childhood.

Avivit's interview was a challenging experience for me, as it was the first time that I had been confronted with an individual who was so resistant to speaking about their past. For the first time I felt that I had been denied access to the past, because of my status as a non-survivor. My educational training failed to reassure her that I was *able* to listen to her war experiences. This interview was powerful in demonstrating the gap between the individual's personal experience and the collective's ability to understand and interpret their experiences. Furthermore, Avivit's attitude is also unique as most of my interviewees felt that despite my status as a non-survivor, they were still able to tell me *some-*

thing about their past. However, my empathy as a listener facilitated an open conversation, in which she shared with me her hopes and anxieties of her present reality.

Perceptions, Remembrance and Achievement

For these 'resistant speakers', there are clear limitations to their retelling. None of them are retelling as 'Holocaust survivors', but rather as individuals who have survived the *Shoah*. Unlike the child survivors whom we encountered in chapter 5, they do not want to be identified as Holocaust survivors, neither do they want their experiences validated. Rather, as in the words of Michal, they want to be 'accepted' as individuals who have survived the war, but who are not 'sick'.

These individuals' reluctance to retelling has developed and been reinforced over the past fifty years. As Jewish children under Nazi occupation, they had learned that in order to survive they needed to go unnoticed, and remain silent. After witnessing terrible scenes of suffering and destruction, they blocked the scenes from their minds in order to carry on and survive the horror. David and Eliezer have normalized their traumatic experiences, which has helped them survive the war and prevented them from becoming 'affected' by their past. Interestingly, these survival tools, which were learned during the war years, appear to have been internalized and continued to present themselves as adaptive behaviors in their post-war lives. Furthermore, for David and Eliezer, their encounter with other survivors, whom they perceive as damaged because of their constant preoccupation with the past, has acted as an important inhibitor in their recounting.

Nevertheless, one of the most striking insights from this material is that these child survivors are resistant to talk about their pasts *as a reaction* to the way the Holocaust survivor has been presented in and is perceived by Israeli society. Michal, Avivit and Eliezer do not want to be identified as 'Holocaust survivors', they prefer to keep their past to themselves. Charles Taylor in his work on multiculturalism writes, "We define our identity always in dialogue with, sometimes in struggle against, the things significant others want to see in us."[39] For these individuals, their experience of Israeli society and with collective memory of the *Shoah*, has alienated them from publicly owning their pasts. Furthermore, because they felt that the survivor experience was stigmatized and misrepresented, they have felt misunderstood. Their post-war experience has been one in which they have not found an empathic audience to whom they can retell their pasts, with the certainty that they will be understood. In relation to this issue, Henry

Greenspan writes, "Survivors do not recount in a vacuum but always to an actual or imagined audience of listeners. What survivors say, how they say it, whether they say it at all, will depend, in part, on their perceptions of those listeners, as well as on the ways the listeners have made their own hopes, fears, and expectations known. A consideration of listeners – like a consideration of meaning and form – thus becomes essential to the interpretation of survivors' recounting."[40] After many years of silence, Avivit has managed to find an empathic audience with other survivors and Michal has found her listeners within a therapeutic setting. David still does not feel the need to work through his past, and Eliezer feels rejected by his audience.

These four voices emphatically state that they do not want to be perceived or remembered through and by their victimization, but rather by their own achievements. Furthermore, both groups of child survivors – those who have found their voices, and those who remain reluctant to share their pasts – share the same need: to define their own experience and trauma. Both groups are reacting against the way that they perceive the Israeli socio-cultural context has defined and evaluated their trauma. Through retelling, hidden child survivors are trying to define themselves and validate their traumatic past, and through silence, these four child survivors are trying to maintain their own identity and self-understanding.

7

Retreat away from Speech

Judith Herman maintains that "sharing traumatic experience with others is a precondition for the restitution of a sense of a meaningful world."[1] According to Herman, recounting is an important step in the eventual working through of the traumatic event. This chapter is concerned with the opposite phenomenon. It focuses on the narratives of two child survivors who, after years of silence found their voices, and yet, in the past few years, have retreated away from speech once again. For Sara and Rachel, the act of telling their pasts has led to an intensification of their trauma, rather than a working through of it. They have retreated away from speech in order to shield themselves from their invasive memories of the past and the pain of remembering.

Sara: "I am going to stop . . . because I don't have any energy for it anymore"

When I met Sara on her *kibbutz*, she welcomed me warmly. However, as we walked to her home she kept repeating to me that she was not suitable for my study, because she did not consider herself to be a child survivor. Occasionally, throughout the interview, she remarked that her story was not a 'child's story' and thus unsuitable for the purposes of my research. Sara explained that she does not consider herself a child survivor, because from the moment she arrived in Auschwitz–Birkenau she was not treated like an child. Rather, she was made to work and suffer like an adult. Therefore she did not want to be categorized as something she did not consider herself or experience herself to be.[2] However, after a close analysis of the interview text I understood that her repeated statements regarding her unsuitability as a subject signaled another concern: Sara was no longer comfortable speaking about the past. This dynamic is reflected in the following exchange: I had asked Sara if she remembered her parents from whom she had been separated on the ramp on their arrival in Birkenau. She replied: "No. Not really. That's what hurts the most. This is a bit of my story. You didn't plan for this. You wanted children, the stories of children." In this extract, Sara touches upon what she describes as the most difficult aspect of her experience . . . her inability to remember her parents. This issue is so painful for her that she was quick to silence it. Not wanting to speak about her parents, she claimed once again that her story was unsuitable for my research. I therefore came to understand Sara's repeated statements to be a way of signaling to me that she was generally ambivalent with regard to speaking about her past.

Post-War Silence

Sara is a survivor of Auschwitz–Birkenau and of the Death Marches. The period of her victimization was relatively short as she was taken from her home in 1944 and deported straight to the death camp. Thus her story closely resembles Kalman's. However, unlike Kalman and Yitzhak, who have always spoken about their past, Sara at first chose to remain silent. Her decision was largely a response to the socio-cultural context in which she found herself after the war. Upon arrival in Israel, Sara, and her surviving sister, Leah, were taken to a *kibbutz* where they have remained members till today. Sara is an integral member of the *kibbutz*, and her story is well-known amongst her fellow *kibbutz* members. However, this was not always the case. When she first arrived she found that no one was willing to listen to her story. Sara explains that, "It was very difficult here in Israel, because the people here did not know what happened in Europe . . . They knew there was a war and that it had been bad for the Jews, but they had no idea of what happened there. Do you know that no one asked us? We came to the *kibbutz* with nothing. No one asked us: 'Do you need something to wear? Do you have a change of underwear? Do you need something?' They did not know what had happened."

This extract powerfully exemplifies the experience of the survivor in their post-war environment. Because the absorbing community had no awareness or understanding of the survivor's traumatic past, they were ineffectual in providing the survivors with even their basic needs. Beyond failing to fulfill her physical needs, her post-war environment failed to address her emotional needs, as her community showed no interest in hearing about her past. Hanna Yablonka, in her work on Holocaust survivors in Israel, claims that "documentation shows that the declarations of the Holocaust youth were significantly affected by the position taken by the *kibbutz* into which they were integrated."[3] Thus, in her first years in Israel, Sara did not find an empathic audience with whom she could communicate her past, which inhibited her talking about it. This extract resembles the narratives of the child survivors discussed in earlier chapters. However, it also introduces another, new dimension: that Israeli society's refusal to 'hear' the stories of survivors stemmed from what she considered as not only a lack of knowledge, but also a lack of desire to know about the *Shoah*.

November 1942 was a turning point in the understanding both by the *Yishuv* and the Allies of the fate of European Jewry. In 1942, an exchange agreement was made with Germany that allowed Jewish men, women and children who were citizens of Palestine to return to Palestine from the ghettos and labor camps in Eastern Europe in exchange for the return of German citizens from Palestine to Germany. This exchange provided the outside world, and the *Yishuv* in particular, with the earliest eyewitness testimonies from the victims themselves. Information and knowledge about the *Shoah* was available to the *Yishuv* and the general population as early as 1942. Yet, despite the availability of information, there appeared to be an inability to comprehend the situation on the part of the local Jewish population. Many people "still hoped that the annihilation of the Jews would not really be total"[4] and that death camps did not exist.

As mentioned in the Introduction, the main representatives of the Holocaust survivors' community – until the large wave during the War of Independence – to arrive in Israel were those Jews who had taken part in armed resistance and not the survivors of the death and concentration camps. Therefore only a certain type of experience was transmitted to Israeli society, which influenced what was known about the Shoah. Many survivors were also sensitive to the fact that little interest was shown in them or in their traumatic pasts. Generally people did not want to know how they had survived the Holocaust except for a few survivors who were fortunate enough to have fought as partisans or been involved in active armed resistance. Historians have also offered other explanations for what they consider to be the lack of any desire to know. Hanna Yablonka proposes that the Jews in Palestine were afraid of hurting the survivors. Dina Porat suggests that the War of Independence and the newly created state displaced all other experiences or concerns. The security and stability of the young of Israel was precarious. Six thousand men and women, one percent of its population, were killed in combat. Furthermore, over the next three and a half years, the population doubled and food, housing, and employment were sorely lacking. Moreover, governmental and army authorities were not yet properly functioning. "So preoccupied was the state with its struggle to survive that there was not even sufficient time to count or register the survivors of the Holocaust."[5]

Thus, in the first few years after the war, Sara chose not to speak about her past because she was unable to find an empathic audience within the fledgling state. Ronnie Janoff-Bulman's work is useful in explaining the role of the psychosocial context of Sara's silence. He writes, "expressions of caring, affection and a willingness to listen also help establish an environment that feels sufficiently safe to allow the victim to confront and consider the traumatic experience, rather than avoid it."[6] According to Sara, these responses were not available in her post-war environment, which helps to explain her silence and avoidance of her past.[7]

Too Embarrassed to Tell

From Sara's narrative it becomes apparent that her silence was not only a response to the absence of an empathic audience, it was also self-imposed. Later on in the interview, she explains that, "I was also very happy that they did not ask, because I didn't want to tell them. I didn't want to tell them where I had come from. I was embarrassed. I was so embarrassed of it."

Thus, another source of Sara's silence is her own sense of shame around her experiences. In his work on Holocaust testimonies, Lawrence Langer referred to this feeling amongst survivors as 'humiliated memory'. Humiliated memory, according to Lawrence Langer, refers to experiences which are too 'miserable' to recall, as "the humiliations endured in the camps were often worse than death".[8] This feeling of humiliation is also connected to the assault on the victim's sense of self that was endured because of their victimization. Furthermore, as an immigrant into a foreign society, Sara did not want to expose her feelings of humiliation and weakness. Instead, she was determined to integrate into Israeli society and become a contributing member of the new state, so much so that she wanted to volunteer for army service during the War of Independence.

Sara recalls that, "there was a man here who was in charge, and he said to me: 'Miss, you have fought in enough wars. Now you are to stay here, you are not going to join any army. You have finished fighting your war'. So, he would not allow me to go. But the *kibbutz* was on the front. We did all sorts of training, that included all the women who remained behind, who did not want to be enlisted. We took turns to guard during the night." Even though Sara had found her absorption into Israeli society difficult, she nonetheless wanted to join the fighting. Aya Shacham explains that "to become part of that same Zionist ethos that disparaged them, these youngsters sought a new name, a new identity, and a new future. Thus they welcomed the opportunity to fight."[9]

Furthermore, the literature on trauma suggests that victims may also have chosen to remain silent about their pasts out of embarrassment of their 'passivity' during their period of victimization. These feelings were reinforced by Israeli society, which frowned upon passivity and applauded heroism. Therefore, Sara chose not to talk about her past, in order to protect herself from the humiliation of exposing her 'victim self' in a society that was particularly critical of Jewish behavior during the Holocaust. Lawrence Langer explains that an integral part of 'humili-ated memory', is that the "witnesses inhabit two worlds simultaneously: the one of 'choiceless choice' *then*, the other of 'moral evaluation', *now*."[10] Thus, the victim's shame is also related to their fears about being misunderstood and judged by their post-war community. These feelings of humiliation are exacerbated if the survivor perceives his/her audience as both ignorant of and uninterested in the event itself.

Wanting to understand more about these feelings, I then asked Sara, "Why do you think that you were embarrassed to tell others about your past?" To which she replied: "I don't know why. I did not want to tell anyone what had happened to me. I didn't want anything. It took years until they wanted to know . . . people were not interested. Do you know, when they gave me a tattoo it didn't really work. I nearly fainted when they did it to me. But Hanna has one here, and it's big. Some people have a big tattoo here [pointing to her forearm]. I had a friend who had a large, bold tattoo and she would always walk with a long sleeve so they wouldn't see it. Once, somehow, she turned up her sleeve and they saw it, and said to her: 'What? Are you from there? You are so nice'. Do you understand? You're from there and you are nice? How can that be? They did not know what it was; they did not know how to digest it at all. Today there are still people who don't understand. And I know they don't understand. But today at least they know that it happened. They somehow know the truth."

This extract bears strong resemblance to the narratives of Avivit and Michal who have silenced their pasts in order to avoid stigmatization, as they "are regarded as 'deviants' because they have been marked by misfortune."[11] Ronnie Janoff-Bulman's work provides us with a wonderful commentary on the experience of Sara's friend. He explains that, "In the overwhelming majority of cases involving traumatic life events, survivors do not physically appear different from before. Yet all too often their victim status sets them apart; it's information rather than appearance or behavior that typically marks them as different. Victims carry with them a social stigma, for they are now viewed as somehow flawed or blemished."[12]

This extract painfully portrays the manner in which survivors were treated by seemingly insensitive individuals. The woman's words, "What? Are you from there? You are so nice," reflects one of the accusations that were hurled at survivors after the war: "What did you do to survive?" Sara's narrative powerfully conveys the struggle of survivors in Israeli society in the years immediately following the war. Particularly painful for her was the insensitivity, the lack of interest in her past, and the accusations made regarding the victim's behavior during the war. In Sara's case, Israeli society did not provide her with a nurturing environment in which there was a concern, empathy, affection, and a readiness to listen, conditions which are vital in encouraging the victim to articulate and work through their trauma. Judith Herman points out that, "The survivor's shame and guilt may be exacerbated by harsh judgment of others . . . From those who bear witness, the survivor seeks not absolution but fairness, compassion, and the willingness to share guilty knowledge of what happens to people in extremity."[13] Thus, Sara's experience with Israeli society in the early post-war years contributed to and reinforced her humiliated memory, which in turn inhibited her revealing her past.

The fact that Sara chose not to speak about her past does not mean that she did not think about it. During the interview, Sara explained that, "During the first years I didn't speak, but I didn't stop dreaming about it. The nightmares where the hardest. After I began speaking, the nightmares disappeared. I remember the last one, it was something . . . When my youngest son was born, today he is 37, he is a pilot . . . I was in the camp with a child behind me . . . I dreamed that I was very weak. I don't know, it was very difficult for me . . . one night I had terrible dreams. One night I dreamed . . . and he was a very small baby, he had just been born. I dreamed that I was leading him by the hand like I was dragging him in the air and the Nazis were running after us and shooting, and I was fleeing and I reached the abyss where I could no longer walk any further and he was dragging as if he was caught in the abyss. And I was holding his hand and I was not able to pull him out of the abyss. And I woke up. That dream has haunted me my whole life. I can remember it clearly. I can see it in front of my eyes. It was terrible. It is so difficult. It's impossible to explain. It was the last dream that I dreamt. I still dream a lot, but I don't remember anything when I wake up." Dori Laub explains that "the 'not telling' of the story serves as a perpetuation of its tyranny. The events become more and more distorted in their silent retention and pervasively invade and contaminate the survivor's daily life."[14]

Researchers argue that following victimization, survivors commonly re-experience the traumatic event through "intrusive recollections or distressing dreams. Even as they 'try' to avoid trauma-related thoughts and feel little, victims suddenly feel or act as if the traumatic event were recurring, as if they are reliving the experience."[15]

The content of Sara's dream is important as it reflects her fears and anxieties as a victim, which she has projected onto her contemporary reality. Sara's dream suggests that she has not been able to rid herself of her 'victim self'. Judith Herman explains that, "Even after release from captivity, the victim cannot assume her former identity. Whatever the new identity she develops in freedom must include the memory of the enslaved self. Her image of her body must include a body that cannot be controlled and is violated. Her image of herself in relation to others must include a person who can lose and be lost to others. And her moral ideals must co-exist with the knowledge of the capacity for evil, both within others and within herself."[16] After having experienced powerlessness and vulnerability, Sara's dream indicates that unconsciously she still sees herself as a powerless and vulnerable victim, who fears that she is unable to protect her children. Alternatively, the child in Sara's dream may represent her own experience in the war, where as a child, her mother was unable to protect her from the horror of the camps. It is clear from her narrative that the imminent birth of her last child triggers her feelings of vulnerability and danger, which she experienced as a child during the war.

Perhaps the most fascinating element of this extract is that Sara's nightmares cease, or rather she ceases to remember them, when she begins speaking about her past. Speaking may have helped Sara assimilate her traumatic experiences, making them more tolerable. Speaking imposes order on the experience, "which may be far more reassuring than the disjointed images often forced upon them".[17] James Pennebaker argues that the advantages of disclosure can be understood physiologically and cognitively. "Physiologically, disclosure reduces the work of active inhibition, and inhibition is associated with short-term autonomic activity and long-term stress-related disease . . . By confronting trauma, individuals are able to reframe and assimilate their experience. The translation into language may make a traumatic experience more understandable and circumscribed."[18] Talking about one's traumatic experiences may also be adaptive in that, when one shares trauma with empathic others, the social support may help the individual feel less alone with their pain, and help re-establish their sense of belonging and connection. Sara is convinced that retelling has been beneficial for her. As she explains, it "freed me a bit. It's a huge burden. It's very hard to keep in. How do I know that? There is something that I still haven't told anyone, and it is a huge burden. I will have to tell it someday, but I don't know to whom. It's very difficult. There are very difficult things . . . this is only a taste."

Telling

For thirty years after the war, Sara refrained from speaking about her past publicly, yet throughout that period she was committed to sharing her past with her children. Even though she decided to tell them about her past, she was always careful about what she told and how she told her story. She explains that she "always told them little bits. Like you ought to tell children. For example there are [other peoples'] houses in which they live the *Shoah*. They raised their kids with the *Shoah*. That was a terrible thing to do. My children had joy. They had a joyous home, with a lot of happiness. I told them about the past, but in a way you tell children. A little when they were small . . . " Sara is here reacting to the discourse around the impact of the war on the second generation, which is a highly sensitive issue in the narratives of some of the child survivors whom I interviewed. This issue will not be discussed in great detail as it lies beyond the scope of the present book. Nevertheless, what we can glean from this statement is that it was important for Sara that her children not be traumatized by her past. Furthermore, she was motivated to tell them because she "wanted them to know who their grandparents were. What happened to them, but in words that were suitable for children." Thus, Sara's telling functioned as a commemorative act and not necessarily as a working through of her own terrifying past.

After many years of silence, Sara began to speak about her past beyond the framework of her family. Sara explains that one day, "I was approached by the principal of a school who said to me: 'Please come and speak to the children in one of my classes'. My third son was in the eighth grade, so I said to him: 'But how can I stand in front of a class and tell such a story?' Eventually, he managed to convince me. I told my story, but not the whole one, perhaps a quarter of what happened to me. So I began to tell my story slowly, and today I realize that I am able to tell the whole thing. But there are still things which I still haven't spoken about. Things which are too difficult to say. I have also written a booklet, which has been translated into English too. It took me years to write. If I had to write it today I would expand it, for sure. But I wrote it very carefully. I also have a translation of it in English."

The trigger behind Sara's telling was external. Contrary to her experiences after the war, someone was interested in and willing to hear about her past. Yet, even when she was asked to tell her story, she still questioned whether she could tell such a story to children. However, despite her reservations, the school principal eventually persuaded her to address the school. In her narrative, Sara explains that she did not reveal her entire story in the first telling. Rather, her story gradually unfolded over many years, and, with countless retellings, she managed

209

to construct an almost complete narrative of her past. At some stage, she even decided to write it down, thereby committing her personal memories to public memory. Sara's narrative reflects the evolution of a life story. In Sara's case, her life story or narrative of the past is not revealed in one sitting. Rather it developed over time, which in turn influenced her own relationship to her past and her identity as a survivor. Unfortunately, her narrative does not reveal what she withheld and later added to her life story.

With each retelling, she uncovers and unburdens herself of another moment or experience, which she gradually constructs into a seemingly coherent narrative of the past. Once she had created a narrative, Sara began to retell it on countless occasions, thereby transforming her personal narrative into 'testimony', or a witness statement. As Sara begins to give testimony, she assumes the role of a historical witness, whose testimony commemorates her personal, familial, and communal past. Sara's retelling has been a slow process through which her past has been articulated, then told, then transmitted, and finally heard.

Sara explains that this process was instigated and influenced by the socio-cultural environment in which she has lived. She points to the openness of Israeli society in the last two decades regarding the Holocaust, and its willingness to hear her story, as factors which have encouraged her to relate her past. She explains that, "Now they know. Now they look at it differently. They plan for it, I go on every *aserah be'tevet* after Pesach, and I go to schools, to the army, and to the *kibbutzim* with my stories. They organize me to go to schools. Now they want to know everything. Everything is documented at Yad Vashem. They organize and request testimonials and documents and stories – everything."

Sara's experiences reflect how Israeli society's relationship to the *Shoah* has changed over the past fifty years. Furthermore, her narrative dramatically portrays how these changes have impacted on her own relationship to the past, and her decision to give voice to her past. When Sara first arrived in Israel, in reaction to what she perceived as a collective lack of interest in the *Shoah*, she chose to remain silent. Yet, it was the willingness of the collective to hear her story, thirty years later, that became the catalyst behind her telling. Sara is able to speak about her past, because she has found an addressable other.

One of the reasons Sara gives for her constant involvement with the subject is that "Now there are not many left who can tell. I am in the minority. My generation is getting smaller. I am amongst the younger ones, and I am already over seventy years old. There are no longer many who speak." Sara's words insinuate that as long as she is alive, she feels that she has an obligation to speak, as she is one of the last people who are able to 'tell the story'; she is one of the last survivors.

Sara's narrative reveals that there are multiple reasons behind her decision to tell and to continue telling. Initially, Sara was motivated to speak so that she could commemorate her family. Later on she realized that retelling also helped her work through her trauma. Today, Sara feels committed to retelling because she sees herself as one of the 'last witnesses', as someone who is still able to give first-person testimony about the past. Sara's changing motivations are consistent with a larger phenomenon. As Annette Wieviorka writes, "The nature of testimony itself has changed. There is no longer an internal logic which impels the survivor of the deportations to tell her story in front of a camera. Now what matters is a social imperative."[19] In the last twenty years, Sara's relationship to her past and the nature of her testimony have changed, in reaction to her own personal needs as well as in response to the changing socio-cultural environment in Israel.

Yet, despite her repeated retellings and her willingness to share her past, Sara explains that, "there is something that I still haven't told, and it is a huge burden. I will have to tell it someday, but I don't know to whom. It's very difficult. There are very difficult things . . . this is only a taste." Silence continues to occupy a place in her narrative. These words reflect Sara's continued search for an empathic audience, for someone "who hears".[20] Thus, Sara's silence suggests that she has still not found someone who hears with whom she can share those things, which are too difficult to say. Even within the context of our interview, she did not feel that she was able to reveal these experiences. This extract also supports Lawrence Langer's theory that humiliated memory is still present in survivor testimony. Even after years of retelling and of a supposed working through of the past, it can never be fully redeemed.

The Burden of Memory

At some point in the interview, it became clear that Sara was tired, and that she wanted the interview to end. This dynamic, which took place on a micro level – within our conversation – also represented a larger issue. Recently, Sara has tired of speaking about her past. She explains that, "it's difficult for me to understand why it's more difficult for me now that it was a few years ago. I also think that soon I will stop speaking about it. It's already not so . . . you need a lot of emotional strength for it, and I have lost a bit. I gave testimony at Yad Vashem and at *Beit Eidut* nearly every week. I am going to stop that because I don't have any energy for it anymore."

Sara reveals that over time, retelling has become more difficult – a phenomenon she finds difficult to understand. It also suggests that retelling no longer helps her deal with and manage her past. Sara's narrative may suggest that even though retelling has helped her work through her trauma, it has not necessarily alleviated her suffering or led to healing. Rather, the repetition of trauma through constant retelling may work to maintain and reinforce traumatic memories. Shlomith Rimmon Keinan, in *Discourse in Literature and Psychoanalysis*, suggests that "narration-as-repetition seems to me to be similarly double-edged: it may lead to a working through and an overcoming, but it may also imprison the narrative in a kind of textual neurosis, an issueless re-enactment of the traumatic events it narrates and conceals."[21] Keinan's theory suggests that Sara's retreat away from speech may be a reaction to her constant retelling, through which her narrative has become fixed and rigid, and has prevented her from telling or revealing her deeper truth. This view is also reflected in research done with Holocaust survivors. Furst writes, "Massive Trauma, such as experienced by concentration camp inmates [is] usually dealt with by recapitulation [but] it fails in its purpose . . . The repetitive reliving of these experiences represents a continuing but vain attempt at mastery. In other words, recapitulations persist because it fails, and instead of mastery and resolution, there is a fixation to the trauma, i.e: a traumatic neurosis."[22]

These theories seem apt in explaining Sara's experiences. I was especially convinced after hearing how often Sara does give testimony to different groups. She explains that, "Every year, and even this year, I have already received ten invitations, and I never commit myself. I write them down first, second and third, but I ask them to phone me a week before to confirm. How can I know what will happen in two to three months' time? Even a young person can't know that. Certainly not. I am always in demand like that. I have been to all of my granddaughter's schools. Now, I have another granddaughter who has asked me to come to her school. I have invitations to all sorts of places. I am already booked out. They know that if they don't book early, I will be busy."

This extract reflects Henry Greenspan's thesis that "the interest in testimony . . . continues to accelerate, and its collection and distribution – in the greatest possible quantity, through the most contemporary possible means – have become a modern crusade."[23] Sara's narrative suggests that the demands made on survivors today, to give testimony and narrate their pasts for educational purposes, may have become burdensome for the survivors themselves, as it imprisons them in the trauma of their pasts through constant repetition. Furthermore, Sara's narrative suggests that her story seems to have been co-opted by society, as they keep demanding that she 'performs' it for their own needs and not necessarily her own.

Sara's retreat away from speech can also be understood as a function of aging, where the benefits of retelling may not serve their initial purposes as the survivor enters old age. According to Yael Danieli, the aging process introduces additional stressful events including various losses and disappointments, and confrontation with one's own mortality. She writes that, "First, old age intensifies and magnifies the 'post-traumatic constellations' . . . Second, many survivors experience the normal phenomenon of old age as a recapitulation of Holocaust experiences. Thus, they experience their children having left home and their spouses' and friends' deaths as a reliving of their massive losses during the war."[24] Confronting one's mortality may trigger the same feelings of powerlessness and vulnerability that survivors felt as victims under Nazi terror. These feelings of vulnerability and anxiety, which are brought on by aging, may diminish the survivor's ability to deal with and ward off their intrusive memories. Thus, retelling during aging may reopen the wounds of the past, and diminish the survivor's psychological strength to deal with their invasive memories.

Emmanuel Sivan and Jay Winter, in their work *War and Rememberance*, argue that "Mourning is an essential part of the story of remembrance of war, but there is much evidence that it is problematic to consider remembrance in Freudian terms, as the work of mourning, leading to healing, reconciliation, and separation of the living from the lost loved-one. Our story is less optimistic and less redemptive. Even when some healing occurs, it is at best healing for a while, and when old age sets in, healing may cease altogether and wounds may reopen. Mourning may never end, and even when it seems to be completed, it may re-emerge. This form of mourning is usually termed 'melancholia'. One case in point is the suicide forty years after the World War II – and decades after the publication of his apparently healing memoirs – of the Italian writer, Primo Levi."[25]

Sara explains that even though she struggles with the past more now than she did earlier, it has always been a burden. She exclaims, "It's not been an easy life. It's a constant struggle to remain OK. To be OK with the children." Sara reveals that she has battled with her past. Her struggle to remain 'okay' and to prevent the past from affecting her everyday functioning has been a constant negotiation, both during her years of silence and during her years of telling. Therefore, the generative effect of each strategy was limited, as the traumatic past never become manageable, or worked through. Cathy Caruth explains that the irreconcilable element of trauma lies in the nature of trauma itself, "that the impact of the traumatic event lies precisely in its belatedness, in its refusal to be simply located, in its insistent appearance outside the boundaries of any single place or time . . . trauma is not a simple or single experience of events . . . but insofar as they are traumatic, [these events] assume their force precisely in their temporal delay."[26]

Sara's aging has forced her to re-evaluate her relationship to the past. Now, she is no longer motivated to reveal her past and share it with the world. Rather, she feels the need to turn inward, to stop telling, to silence the past, as she no longer feels that she has the strength to deal with it. It seems that Sara is suffering from 'witness burn-out', and her decision to stop speaking is a step towards self-preservation. Sara's life demonstrates that retelling is not only contingent upon an empathic audience and the openness and willingness of society to *hear* their experiences, but it is also dependent upon the individuals' own needs: their willingness and ability to confront their past and to constantly revisit the loss and devastation of their childhood. Sara's narrative aptly reflects her struggle to live *with* her Holocaust experiences, and survivor identity. Sara's interview stands in contrast with the interviews of most of the participants in this study. For most of the interviewees, the process of aging triggered their need to look back and speak their pasts. Yet for Sara, aging has begun to thwart this process.

Our interview ended rather abruptly, as Sara no longer wanted the interview to continue. Sensing her needs, I did not try and push the conversation any further. Nevertheless, we remained together for a while longer, as she invited me to eat lunch with her in the *kibbutz* dining-room. I agreed, and we sat eating our lunch together, in silence. I noticed that Sara appeared to be still preoccupied with the past; it was as if visions of the past remained in front of her eyes. I realized that the transition between *then* and *here* was not easy, and did not take place instantly. At some point Sara's daughter-in-law joined us, and her mood changed dramatically. Her daughter-in-law's presence pulled her back into the present, as she enthusiastically explained to her daughter-in-law who I was.

Rachel: "I don't know what to say to people"

Post-War Silence

The beginning of Rachel's story was related in chapters 2 and 3. As a hidden child survivor Rachel had learned to be silent about her past during the war in order to protect herself physically. Rachel had 'learned silence', a behavior that was difficult to unlearn since it was reinforced by her parents in her post-war environment. Furthermore, living in France after the war, she found it difficult to speak about her past to others, even to Jewish children who had had similar experiences during the *Shoah*. She describes post-war French society as a world of silence and continued hiding because "you needed to deal with non-Jewish Frenchmen who experienced the war but did not have the wounds that you had. Therefore, I was not successful in establishing a connection with the children at school, besides of course the Jewish children. Interestingly we had a good connection, but we never spoke about the war. Until today, I do not know what a few of my friends went through. I have no idea. We didn't speak about it, but we had a connection."

Rachel's narrative is better understood within the wider historical context. David Weinberg writes that after the war "efforts to discuss or remember the tragic events of the war were ridiculed or suppressed. Many Frenchman undoubtedly shared the view of the French philosopher Emmanuel Mounier that returning deportees were a 'nuisance' to most Frenchmen, "whose only wish is to return as quickly as possible to peace and quiet. Memories of Nazi brutalities also clashed with the desire of European leaders to enlist West Germany in the Cold War struggle against Soviet Communism."[27] He also argues that "most disturbing was the refusal to recognize the distinctive nature of the Jewish genocide. Jewish deportees were not allowed to march as a separate group during commemorations." Weinberg also explains that "nor was there much discussion of the Holocaust within the French Jewish community. Few Eastern European Jews had survived the ordeal; those who had seemed reticent to talk about their experiences . . . There was also intense opposition on the part of the Jewish community to the establishment to a Memorial to the Unknown Jewish Martyr near the historic Jewish area of the 'pletzl' in Paris . . . Community opposition to the memorial reflected the fact that despite the revelations of atrocities, many French Jews, like Frenchmen in general, simply could not grasp the immensity of the tragedy." Thus, public commemorations and rallies attracted few supporters. Weinberg explains this phenomenon as, "Like the French government itself, the French Jewish community was concerned with reconstruction and did not want to dwell on the past."[28] Thus, the French socio-cultural context encouraged silence and rebuilding.

Whilst living in France, Rachel felt increasingly silenced, not only in terms of her past, but also in terms of her Jewishness. David Weinberg writes that after the war many French Jews decided to hide their Jewish identities, as a result of the revival of anti-Semitism in the years immediately following the war. The rise in anti-Semitism was linked to Jewish communal attempts to rescue orphaned Jewish children and regain lost property. He writes, "Many thought that the *Shoah* had begun again, and decided to conceal their identities." Jewish journals between the years 1944 and 1950 were filled with articles "condemning intermarriage, conversion and name changing."[29] Weinberg also points to the opposite phenomenon where, as a result of the war, there was an intensification and strengthening of Jewish identity and consciousness. Yet, with the creation of the State of Israel in 1948, a debate arose amongst French Jewry as to whether or not make *aliya* to Israel. This became a great issue in France after the French publication of Arthur Koestler's controversial book *Promise and Fulfillment* (1949). Koestler argued that the creation of Israel signified the end of the Diaspora. Furthermore, remaining in France involved a terrible denial of Jewish identity, which would invariably lead to their assimilation into European society.

Within this conflictual atmosphere, Rachel seemed to have internalized the Zionist sentiments of the time. She felt that if she remained in France, she would not be able to actualize her Judaism. She explains that, "whilst I was in France I tried to understand what it meant to be a Jew. I concluded that being a Jew who believed and kept the laws was not enough. The only way to be true to my Jewishness was to be in *Eretz Yisrael*, and so I made *aliya*." Once Rachel completed her graduate studies in France, she made *aliya*, arriving in Israel in 1964. *Aliya* for Rachel, as for other child survivors, represented a 'returning home' – a place in which they could identify openly, freely, and positively as Jews. Israel offered a non-conflictual environment for child survivors who were searching to belong and build a new life.

Once Rachel arrived in Israel, she immediately began to feel a deep sense of belonging and connection. She felt connected to the Jewish people. Furthermore, because of the nature of Israeli society, Rachel felt that she could finally begin to break the years of silence. She explains that "The solution, or the opening, began when I came to *Eretz Yisrael*. Because here people had been through so much, at the very least emotionally, and others had a huge load, not necessarily those that survived the *Shoah*, but they experienced other types of difficulties. I don't know if it's pain, I don't know what it is, that made it possible that there was someone to talk to. Here it's possible. If you are talking about silence, then I can almost certainly say that until my *aliya* I was in a world of silence. And since I have been in *Eretz Yisrael*, it has been a different story. It is not that I stopped speaking in France. I spoke. But in terms of expressing my inner thoughts or something like that – only here."

Rachel's narrative provides us with an important insight as to how Israeli society, because it was a traumatized society, enabled her to achieve a sense of belonging. Because loss was an integral part of the socio-cultural environment, Rachel was able to find, within this community of mourners, a socio-cultural context that articulated and shared loss publicly, a place in which she could express her own losses.

To sum up, so far we have discussed the difficulties encountered by survivors in Israel, including the establishment of the 'conspiracy of silence', the 'hierarchy of suffering' and, in general, the negative image of Holocaust victims and survivors that pervaded Israeli society. Nonetheless, as we can see from Rachel's testimony, it appears survivors had more of a responsive audience in Israel then in Europe. Furthermore, in comparison to the European context, from the beginning in Israeli society, "at community and national levels, the Holocaust has always been given central significance and expression in annual memorial meetings for destroyed communities, the annual Holocaust Memorial Day, teaching programs in the schools, and through the newspapers, radio and television."[30] Commemoration is a step in the rehabilitation process; according to Emmanuel Sivan, it is a rehabilitation of a special kind, "in that it intends to contribute to society at large while at the same time endowing the death in question with meaning. It does not seek to divert one's mind from the dear departed or to provide substitutes for them . . . It rather endeavors, by objectifying their individuality, to transfer their memory to a wider social circle."[31] The memory and significance of the Holocaust were kept alive in the social consciousness of the people. Within this context of commemoration, Rachel was able to feel that her experiences were given a voice. It must be noted that in 1964, Israeli society was far more responsive to the Holocaust, because of the Eichmann Trial in 1961, than it had been when Sara first arrived in 1948. Thus, Sara and Rachel had very different experiences of Israeli society when they each first arrived in the country, which was connected to the developing relationship between Israel and the Holocaust. Although in the first decade of statehood the Holocaust was commemorated as a public event, the voice of individual survivors was nevertheless hardly audible. The more 'powerful voices', which were made representative of the Holocaust, belonged to the ghetto fighters and former members of the underground and resistance movements, and not to the child camp survivors or hidden child survivors, like Sara and Rachel.

Telling

Despite the fact that the Holocaust was granted a central significance from the establishment of the state and at important institutional levels, the experiences of the survivors as individuals, and especially of child survivors, went largely unheard. This is reflected powerfully in Rachel's narrative. Even though Rachel had found a place where her losses were articulated and mourned publicly, she was still reluctant to talk about her own personal story after she arrived in Israel.

She decided to to speak, "only at the end of the eighties . . . I don't remember exactly when it was. I think on the fortieth anniversary of the Warsaw Ghetto uprising or something like that. There was a gathering here and I went. They asked us to fill in some forms and there were questions: were you in the camps, in the partisans, or in hiding? I was not in any of the categories. I am also not second generation (there was a question regarding second generation). I was in none of the categories. As if again I do not exist. I don't belong . . . At a certain point, I don't know how to say this, but it emphasized the silence. Despite this, as I said in the beginning, I feel wounded by the *Shoah* from the beginning. I am wounded by the *Shoah*. Thus, I experienced the *Shoah* and I do belong. That's my life story." *Did that motivate you to begin to speak about it?* "That event [the fortieth Anniversary of the Warsaw Ghetto uprising] was a hard awakening for me. Like an 'enlightenment'. I felt that I had to so something. I was a teacher and on the day that was *Yom Hashoah* I made up my mind and I said to the students: 'Today I am not able to teach the usual material, I was a child during the *Shoah,* and then I would speak, I would say something'."

After decades of silence, just twenty years ago, Rachel decided to identify openly as a survivor of the Holocaust. The autobiographical occasion for Rachel was an external event, the public commemoration of the Warsaw Ghetto Uprising, held in Israel. Dalia Ofer explains that these public commemorations, in the 1970s and 1980s, enabled the survivors to identify openly as survivors. Despite the fact that this event motivated her to identity publicly as a survivor, it also reinforced her isolation as she found her experience excluded from the larger narrative of the *Shoah*. Nevertheless, despite this difficult experience, Rachel did not recoil into silence as she had learned to do. Rather, this incident motivated her even more to speak about her own past. This decision to speak, regardless of her socio-cultural context, represented a turning point in Rachel's life. For the first time she became active in defining herself and her relationship to the past. No longer wanting to live in silence, she wanted to be visible, noticed and feel alive. She believed that she could achieve this by giving voice to her past, by reversing her silencing. Relatively soon thereafter, Rachel joined a survivors group, '*Alumim'*, which, as she explains, is "our organization of children who were hidden in France." Within their own support groups, survivors began to carve out their own category of Holocaust experience and thus their place in the larger narrative of the *Shoah*.

After participating in the group, Rachel was then encouraged by the group founder to "participate in a workshop at Yad Vashem, a workshop for survivors to give testimony. That was something very powerful for me. I had never done anything like what is called psychological therapy or psychoanalysis . . . I don't know what. But I have the feeling that what they did to me, freed me from I don't know what. It was a terrible week, a week without sleep. I don't know how I managed

It was from Sunday till Thursday night. It was a powerful therapy and, to this day, I recommend that everyone should do it. But not everyone is able to deal with such a difficult thing. But what they do there is very powerful."

Amongst other survivors, Rachel found a supportive framework in which she could face her own past and give voice to her experiences. This group helped her work through her painful memories, which included memories of silence, isolation and loneliness. Thus, the group represented the antithesis of her experiences during and after the war. Furthermore, the survivor group also helped Rachel forge a place of belonging in the collective memory of the *Shoah*. Within the group, amongst themselves, through the sharing of their own personal memories, they created their own collective memory. Emmanuel Sivan writes that within the group of rememberers, "personal memories intermingle, influence each other and thus create a collective memory, feed it, and maintain its continuity. A collective memory enables a group to attain a consciousness based on a sort of 'network of complementarity'."[32]

What in Rachel's view was so powerful about the group was that, "the connections that we make between us are very special. Very, very, special. I don't know how to explain it to you. It's beyond comprehension. Its like with those who were in a Youth Movement together and one knows the other through shared memories. Or with those people who were in the same school together or something else. There is something in common. So here there is something in common between us. You can say a word that is connected to that time and we are immediately on the same wavelength. It's wonderful. It gives a lot of strength. For me personally it has given me a lot, a lot of . . . not encouragement . . . I can't actually say encouragement. It's good for me, it really is. Maybe it's funny, like those old war veterans who have memories, despite the fact that we were not in the same place. I, at least, was not with them. Some were in the same places, in the same institutions. But I was not with them, yet even so I still feel that I have something in common with them. Something very strong."

The importance of survivor support groups features prominently in the narratives of other child survivors. According to Haim Dasberg, the first child survivor support group in Israel began in 1986 under the guidance of Dr Yolanda Gampel. Dr Gampel became interested in listening to the stories of child survivors because of her therapeutic work with the second generation. "It seemed meaningful to her that there was a parallel in the progress of her patients' capacity to deal with the subject and to investigate the family's past and her own growing ability to overcome the countertransferential fear that she sensed when she first confronted the horrors of the *Shoah*."[33] As a result, Dr Gampel

219

began interviewing child survivors of the Holocaust, and was soon inundated with requests to interview more people. "As a consequence of the interviews, Dr Gampel writes, "we felt that we must provide a space for our interviewees where they could continue to think, remember, and express themselves in front of a listener. We established an open group that each interviewee was invited to join after the personal interviews had been concluded."[34] The group met regularly over six years. Haim Dasberg explained that subsequent child survivor support groups in Israel began to function in the 1990s, as this population group reached their fifties or sixties, and entered into the last developmental stage, which requires that they establish a sense of personal integration of their life. Thus, it is not coincidental that the first Child Survivor Conference . . . for Hidden Child Survivors – took place in 1991. In 1992, AMCHA organized the first gathering of former hidden children in Israel, following an advertisement in a local newspaper. The project of regular monthly meetings in the framework of a narrative group, led by two professional therapists, was discussed and adopted. This group met for five and a half consecutive years. This was the first but certainly not the last child survivor group that AMCHA established. Since then, various child survivor groups have emerged in Israel and overseas, and given a voice to the experiences of children during the Holocaust – "how they coped with the horror of irrational adult atrocities and what became of mundane, day-to-day experiences of normal childhood."[35]

In addition to being a locus of belonging and mutual understanding, the survivor support group "offers a place for abreaction and catharsis as well as a multiplicity of options for expressing feelings – naming and verbalizing, and modulating them. It also encourages mutual caring, which ultimately enhances self-care in the survivors and their offspring."[36] Thus these groups encourage and empower their members to confront and speak about their pasts. Furthermore, the experiences of others help child survivors corroborate their own past, especially in the case of child survivors who have weak and fragmented memories of the past. These groups are also important in that through the sharing of memories and stories these individuals are able to construct a sense of community, friendship and belonging that was destroyed because of the war. Within the group, Rachel also feels that she is able to reclaim her lost childhood.

She explains that: "What is also true, and I feel it in our group, is that we are all messed up. All of us have remained at the approximate age we were during the war. So, amongst ourselves we can behave like children. In that we are messed up. I see it. It's also a disability. It's something that is simply not normal." *Why a disability?* "All of us are around sixty years old. And we act like . . . I remember that once there was some story, like you read to a group of children, things like that. It was something . . . Like we were there . . . then. In terms of our behavior, I think that we behaved crazily." *How do you explain this?* My explanation is that I did not have a childhood. It seems that I still want something from then . . . now you have reminded me of the subject, now it is much less. Now it is not a burden for me, but I had the feeling, especially in those years in France, that they took my childhood away from me. I did not play, I did not enjoy. All those things that one is supposed to do during their childhood."

From Rachel's narrative, we learn that one of the important functions of these survivor groups is their attempt to replace what was lost during the war. In Rachel's case, her loss, in addition to the loss of her extended family, included the loss of her childhood. This sense of loss was greatly accentuated in her post-war environment, where her 'difference' stood out, and her feelings of disability intensified. However, amongst other survivors, people who had experienced similar experiences and suffered similar losses, Rachel felt 'normal'. Furthermore, because the participants were able to empathize with each other, they were responsive to each other's needs.

The survivor support group serves as a bridge between the survivors' experiences during the war and their post-war community. It is through this sub-community that survivors are able to integrate both worlds. The survivor group enables the survivor to recapture his or her past, and offers temporary relief to the gnawing losses of the past. However, the group does not have the power to *cure* the survivor of their feelings of loss and isolation, as it cannot alter the past and bring back murdered loved ones, or the survivors' lost childhood. Yet, it does offer a temporary respite, or a safe haven for survivors who, amongst themselves, can share moments of the past and recapture some of the loss. Yet, once the survivors leave the group their sense of loss and isolation returns, as they are confronted once again with an environment that fails to understand and empathize with their experiences. This is powerfully illustrated in Rachel's narrative, and is one of the main reasons behind her retreat away from speech.

Retreat away from Speech

Despite the heightened social consciousness regarding the Holocaust in Israeli society, survivors were not always willing or able to speak about their experiences. Nor were they always encouraged to do so. Rachel explains that, "In the beginning I continued to speak and in the last few years – again silence. I cannot do it, because I don't know what to say to people. I do not want sympathy. Absolutely not. I never looked for any sympathy. I did want to transmit something to them. I don't know what they are sensitive to. I am not prepared to . . . "

Rachel says that she finds it particularly difficult to speak about her past with 'the younger generation'. She explains, "I don't know how to talk to them. Something is not right here. I don't know what . . . I leave it to those who are younger than me to talk to them."

Despite the fact that Rachel has been trained as a teacher and trained teachers for many years, she has found it increasingly difficult to communicate her war experiences with the younger generation. In her interview, Rachel relates a difficult memory that she has from the war, perhaps the most traumatic part of her story. She brings this memory into the interview as a means of explaining the difficulties she has in communicating her past with the younger generation. She begins by saying, "It's a whole story that I don't want to go into because it is too painful. My parents were ordered to go to a place from which it was almost certain that they would probably not return from. I had long hair, blond hair. My mother decided that they would probably not return and she said to my sister that if they did not return, we were to be moved to live with some people in the village who had a farm. My mother cut my hair. Until this day, I remember it. I remember the noise of the scissors. It still pounds in me. This story is that after two days my parents returned and they brought me a clip to hold my hair. You cannot describe how much this clip was worth to me, till this day. It is a fifty-seven year-old story and I remember it. It was a regular clip, but with a flower. Something blue with a small flower. Why do I see it as such a big thing? Such a story it was! When I talk to young children I always tell them this story, 'Look at what luck I had . . . this really is the story of everyone'. But I got a present and I don't know what that was. I didn't understand that the clip was bought for me. How can you explain something like that to young children today? What will they understand? Once I told the story and someone said to me: 'So what? They cut your hair because they were afraid that you would get lice. What's the problem? They do it to children today as well. So what?' Where is there suffering here? There is none. What does a child understand about getting a clip? To get a present? What? He is short of things these days? What can he understand? So how would you like me to talk to youth? I don't know how to speak to them. Because for me, this story, to cut my hair, my first hair that I had . . . it's like removing a limb. Today the youth shave hair. But I am still from the generation that does not cut little girls' hair. You could have kept your hair until you married or something like that. It was a terrible feeling. What is very interesting is that in Yad Vashem, someone told me that in the camp they shaved her hair. She understood me. With her, there was an understanding. But today, I cannot relay that story; we are not on the same level here. I don't know how. Therefore, I don't know how to relate those things, which are related to feelings."

This is a particularly painful episode for Rachel. First, her audience does not see her story as 'traumatic', as they are unable to recognize and validate her pain. This is similar to what Rachel experienced after the war. As a child who had survived with her parents in hiding, she was placed on the lowest rung of the hierarchy of suffering. This extract is important in that it reveals that this notion of the hierarchy of suffering is still present within the contemporary socio-cultural context, within the imagination of the audience. Second, Rachel attributes this lack of empathy and validation to a cultural and experiential divide that exists between her and the younger generation. This notion of the inability to communicate one's emotional experience, or as Rachel says, 'feelings', is reflected in the work of Shlomo Breznitz, a child survivor and professor of psychology. He argues that only those who were *there* are able to *know* what happened.[37] Breznitz uses Tulving's (1970) differentiation between episodic and semantic memory to argue that the nature of memory itself hinders people from identifying with each other's experiences. He argued that today there exists a lot of information about the *Shoah*. This is referred to as semantic memory – "the intricate network of concepts, associations and facts that constitute our general knowledge of the world."[38] Semantic memory of the *Shoah* has been created around the event, and thus is accessible to those who have never experienced it. Episodic memory refers to a memory system which allows us to recollect specific incidents from our past, including the sensory and emotional elements of the experience. Thus, only those who experienced the event have access to this type of memory, which is memory of the experience itself. This sentiment is corroborated in Rachel's narrative.

Throughout her narrative, Rachel mourns the loss of her childhood, which she feels has disabled her. Unlike the youth of today, she is still not able to enjoy or receive gifts, finds wasting food sinful, and her ability to enjoy herself at parties and festive occasions is limited. These feelings of 'disability' and loss are accentuated when she meets younger people, who are unable to empathize with her experience as they do not understand that, "You don't throw things away, because everything has a value. It's very difficult with this generation. How can you throw food away? Finish what's on your plate. I don't know what it is not to finish food on my plate. I would not leave a piece of bread. If I began to eat a piece of bread and was no longer hungry, I would finish it. I would not throw it away. That's impossible. Maximum I would give it to an animal. But not to throw it away. So, I don't know how to talk to teenagers. Because, if for me the subject of food was so dominant in my life during the war, what can they understand about it today?"

Furthermore, the un-empathic response of her audience when hearing her story may serve to reinforce her feelings of loss, deprivation and alienation that she experienced both during the war as a victim, and after the war as a survivor. Thus, in Rachel's case, the act of retelling to the younger generation, people who are unable to understand her pain and whose lives serve as a direct reminder of what she has lost because of the war, has only intensified her trauma. Therefore, she has chosen to stop speaking about her past publicly. From Rachel's narrative we learn how "the listening stance of the other can either alienate and depersonalize,"[39] how sensitive the survivor is to the reactions of their audiences, and how their relationship to the past and talking about it is shaped in reaction to the audience's responses.

The lack of empathy for her story displayed on the part of her audience is not the only issue which troubles Rachel. She also is pained by what she considers her audience's general disinterest in the *Shoah*. She explains that, "Perhaps one of the hardest things was that nearly the last time I spoke, I felt that there are those who are not interested. I don't feel personally hurt, but hurt for all those who died, who perished. And I am not prepared to tolerate that. I am not speaking on behalf of myself. I am still active, but mainly for the cause of 'don't forget us'. And if I continue to speak, it is so that they won't be forgotten. And if there are people who it does not interest, I cannot do it. I cannot cope with that. I don't know . . . perhaps I need to do another workshop and ask them how to deal with such a situation . . . but right now, I can't do it."

The lack of interest in the fate of European Jewry during the *Shoah* is particularly painful for survivors, as "many prisoners' will to survive was based on their determination to let the world know. The thousands of reports buried in Warsaw, Terezin, and Auschwitz, and Birkenau were all born out of the same longing not to be forgotten."[40] Furthermore, after the war, survivors saw as their obligation and 'price' of their survival, the giving of testimony and bearing witness to the murder of the millions of nameless and faceless Jews. Annette Wieviorka writes that today collective memory demands that, "The survivors must still perform an act of remembrance. They are still summoned to tell the story, to preserve for history their evidence for the generations to come after their deaths."[41] Thus, it is hardly surprising that Rachel feels pained by her inability to communicate the past to the younger generation, as it implies that she has failed in her duty as a survivor. Furthermore, transmitting to future generations the knowledge of what happened and what could happen, provides the survivor with a sense of consensual validation. Rachel's experience exemplifies Dori Laub and Marjorie Allard's powerful statement, that "the absence of an empathic listener, or more radically, the absence of an *addressable* other, an other who can hear the anguish of one's memories and thus recognize their realness, annihilates the story and destroys the survivor once again."[42]

Rachel's narrative is one of constant negotiation. Throughout her life she has struggled to break the silence learned during the war and to express herself without inhibition. Rachel has been sensitive to the responses of the outside world, and her willingness to talk openly about the past in public has been determined largely by the way the socio-cultural context has responded to her story. Her sensitivity to the audience's response even presented itself within the context of our interview. At the end of the interview, Rachel hinted that her silence might not be permanent, and that she might begin to retell her past if she received enough encouragement. This is reflected in the last sentence of the interview where she explained, "You have come to encourage me that I do have something to say perhaps. Maybe if you tell me in the end that it was worthwhile, maybe it will give me a push, perhaps it is worthwhile that I continue." This extract reveals that despite the disappointments and obstacles, Rachel has not given up her mission to recount, as even in the context of our interview she looked to me for encouragement. In a sense, recounting symbolizes the 'correcting' of her childhood and her affirmation that she exists. Thus, perhaps as long as she lives, she will not abandon this mission, and will continue to search for an empathic audience and a way to recount her past. I would therefore argue that Rachel has not fully retreated away from speech. She is continually looking for reasons to justify and encourage her in her telling, to carry on herself role as an agent of memory.

The Trauma of Bearing Witness

Sara and Rachel had very different experiences during the war. Sara was orphaned because of the war and was a survivor of death and concentration camps, while Rachel survived the war in hiding with her family. Sara never doubted her identity as a survivor of the *Shoah*, yet was, as she explained, 'too embarrassed' to speak about her past for many years. Rachel's identity as a survivor was never validated and therefore silenced. As a result, both chose to remain silent about their pasts for most of their adult years. Despite the difference in their experiences, both women were not encouraged by their socio-cultural environment to relate their pasts. In their post-war environments, neither found an empathic audience with whom they could share their pasts. Nevertheless, at a later stage in their lives, both began to speak. Their decisions to tell can be seen as a direct response to the change in their socio-cultural environment, which during the 1970s and 1980s began to encourage Holocaust survivors to give testimony about their experiences during the *Shoah*. Survivors moved out of their worlds of silence and began to identify openly in their new role as 'historical witnesses'. Sara began to tell her story and, as a result, work though her pain. She became deeply involved with her past and she began to speak regularly about her experiences. Rachel's narrative is different from Sara's in that, even though survivors were encouraged to speak in the 1980s, there were still certain types of stories that were heard, while others continued to be silenced. Rachel's story, the story of a child in hiding, was still not included in the accepted collective narrative of the *Shoah*, and she remained unrepresented. Nevertheless, she remained committed to retelling. Sadly, however, Rachel was unable to find an empathic audience amongst Israelis who had not experienced the *Shoah*. However, she did manage to find an empathic audience amongst other survivors, who had had similar experiences. Within this supportive environment, Rachel began to work through her past and was encouraged to retell her past. Thus, both Sara and Rachel began to retell their pasts once they found an empathic audience that was willing and able to hear their stories. Nevertheless, silence eventually found its way back into their lives, for different reasons. Sara became tired of recounting, whilst Rachel became frustrated by her inability to recount effectively. Both women were also reacting to the demands of their socio-cultural context: while Sara has become burdened by her role as 'historical witness', Rachel is pained by her inadequacy as a 'historical witness'. For Rachel, the lack of empathy on the part of the younger generation has only emphasized the trauma of the past. For Sara, the painful memories of the past, which are brought up during telling, have become too difficult to deal with.

Perhaps these two narratives suggest that the demand made on survivors today to give testimony, to 'bear witness', to 'perform' is too much for them to bear, and the result has been as traumatic as the years of imposed silence. 'Bearing witness' and giving testimony often ignores the emotional element of that witnessing. Their retreat away from speech can also be viewed as an act of self-preservation; they protect themselves against the pain of remembering, and of not being heard.

8

Reflections and Conclusions

From Freedom to Victimization

Child survivors were not always child survivors. Neither were they always victims. This is something that they find important to remind us, the audience, each time they begin their life stories. In their interviews, child survivors begin with the words, "I was born in ____ to ____ in the city of ____. " All of them, except for Michal, were born into freedom, with one or both of their parents. They had a name, an identity, and every opportunity to develop a 'normal', stable life. Those individuals whom we consider to be child survivors, were born into a reality not so different from that of our own. Yet, *their* world was destroyed and irrevocably changed in an instant.

The survival of these children was indeed extraordinary. In order to survive, Jewish children had to become invisible; they had to disappear into cupboards, under floorboards, underground, or in pigsties. Alternatively, they had to re-invent themselves as Christian children, with new names, new parents, new families, and new identities. Children were told that their parents had taken ill, could no longer take care of them, or had chosen to abandon them; in order to survive the war their biological identity and their physical presence as Jewish children was erased. There were also Jewish children who managed to survive because they concealed their age so as to be considered 'useful' by the Nazis. These children became adults overnight, and were used as slave labor, or as guinea pigs in pseudo-scientific experimentation. Some spent years under Nazi occupation, others just months. Nevertheless, for all of them their biological identity and their assumptions about the world were shattered by their experiences, and they emerged from their period of victimization wounded, maimed, often orphaned, traumatized, and lost.

Confronting the Free World

When emerging from camps, forests, ghettos and hiding, victims became survivors and needed to confront the challenge of survival, of re-entering and rejoining the 'normal world' after their narrow escape from death. The difficulty for many, as they stood face to face with their liberators, was how to re-enter the world of the living, and integrate their experiences, from the moment that their liberators "stare[d] at me, bewildered by fright".[1] In 'surviving the survival', survivors were forced to confront their own nightmarish past, as well as the fears, revulsion and guilt that the post-war community harbored in regard to them.

The end of the war did not necessarily mean the end of suffering. In the case of child survivors of the Holocaust, liberation presented many other challenges. Many child survivors were not told explicitly that the war was over, that their reality had changed. And for many, it did not. Other children realized that the war was over, but did not necessarily think that their personal reality would change. The transition into the post-war reality was particularly difficult as many child survivors had either been born into or grown up in the chaos of the war, and had not known or could not remember a different reality. Behavior patterns they had adopted in order to survive during the war (which were not always appropriate to their post-war environment) were sometimes difficult to unlearn. One of these behaviors was 'learned silence'.

The transition from the war years into freedom was particularly difficult for the children. Especially difficult was their confrontation with their new status as orphans. Throughout the war, many children had kept hoping that their parents were alive and would return after the war. Yet this was not always the case. For orphaned survivors, it was particularly difficult to meet their 'new parents', and develop a sense of belonging and closeness to these strangers. In these first few months after the war, many child survivors were adopted or placed into the care of surrogate caretakers, or in institutions where their lives and identities were again irrevocably changed. Even if their biological parents did return, some parents were unrecognizable or unable to provide the security and nurturance that the children so desperately needed. The way the new reality was translated to the children affected the way these children adapted to and understood the 'free world'. Because in most cases the trauma of the war, and their liberation, was not confronted cognitively, individuals were not able to reframe and assimilate their experiences. This process of 'translation', and the individuals' consequent cognitive restructuring, is an area of research that calls for further investigation.

The Search for Belonging

Unlike adult survivors, child survivors, in the years immediately following the war, did not necessarily define or relate to themselves as 'survivors'. Instead, they tried quickly to adapt themselves to their new environments and integrate as quickly as possible into their post-war societies. This reaction stemmed from a strong need to belong. The destruction of a sense of belonging is not unique to child survivors of the Holocaust. It is endemic to survivors of trauma, whose connection to the world has been shattered or altered radically as a result of their traumatic experiences. The psychiatrist William Niederland, in his study of survivors of the Nazi Holocaust, observed that alterations of personal identity were a constant feature of 'survival syndrome'. While the majority of his patients asserted that, "I am now a different person," the most severely harmed stated simply, "I am not a person."[2] In the case of child survivors of the Holocaust, researchers argue that one of the fundamental attacks on the psyche of these victimized children was related to their sense of belonging. This began during the war and continued in their post-war environments.

According to psychologists, the sense of belonging is instilled in the individual from infancy. For these child survivors, this very early sense would have been uprooted by their experiences during the war as they were torn away from their homes and their families, and had to survive on their own. Their sense of belonging was further challenged after their liberation, as child survivors were forced to confront the finality of the loss of their families, emigration, acclimatization and integration into new societies and foreign cultures. Child survivors had an intense need to rejoin 'humanity'. They no longer wanted to be singled out, ostracized and victimized. Rather they wanted to become 'like everyone else', to be 'normal', which entailed a particular type of silencing of their experiences.

Integration into Israeli Society

Child survivors realized both on their own and with the guidance of their adult community, that they needed to look forward and not backwards; that the pain of the past could debilitate them and hinder their post-war adaptation. This realization was also an adaptation to the parameters of Israeli collective memory. It was hoped that the child survivors would become new *sabras*, which involved their abandoning their Diaspora identity and mentality, and assimilating into the Israeli society. This was congruent with the dominant values of Israeli society at the time, which emphasized reconstruction and renewal, "*Shoah u'Tekumah*". Furthermore, the silence of both adult and child survivors was also a reaction to the values and judgments of the post-war socio-cultural context, which encouraged certain types of narratives. In the early years of the state, Israeli society emphasized the notions of 'heroism and resistance', and suppressed narratives of vulnerability and victimization. Ariala explained that, "But we didn't experience it like . . . we are not soldiers; we were embarrassed because we were passive, and we had no story. So, that's the second problem; [that] we didn't have a story; that we couldn't brag about our accomplishments. We didn't do anything, we only hid."

This notion of 'heroism versus passivity' not only determined the patterns of speech and silence, it also affected the individuals' relationship to their pasts and their identity as survivors. The image of Holocaust survivors, especially in the early years of the state, was hardly complimentary. These attitudes influenced some of child survivors' decision not to publicly identify as survivors. This was particularly clear in the narratives of those whom I have defined as 'reluctant speakers'. Thus in many instances the relationship of survivors to their past was constructed in reaction to the values, judgments and guidance of their post-war socio-cultural environment. Interestingly, child survivors often chose to remain silent only after witnessing the effect that telling had on those who chose to share their pasts. Many of the interviewees explained that these adults, some of whom were their parents, were consumed by the past and were not able to move forward and develop relatively 'normal lives'. The child survivors believed that a constant preoccupation with the past hindered their feeling of belonging and connectedness to the post-Holocaust world.

Although this study has not focused on demonstrating the pervasiveness of these attitudes in Israeli society, the narratives presented do attest to the fact that child survivors themselves had experience of them in their daily interactions with individuals who had not experienced the *Shoah*. In order to get a more comprehensive understanding of this dynamic, more research needs to be done amongst the *sabra* population, in order to ascertain how the survivors were perceived and why.

The transition from 'victim' to an 'accepted' free citizen therefore demanded a silencing of the 'victim' and 'survivor' self, unless the individual could reframe their experiences in such a way that they were able to attain a deep sense of belonging despite or perhaps because of their survivor identity. This dynamic was clearly reflected in the narratives of those whom I have categorized as 'those who have always spoken'. By connecting to larger, traditional, and accepted narratives, individuals such as Yitzhak and Kalman managed to weave their 'victim' status into the 'normal' range of human experience, thereby not remaining on the fringe, or being considered 'abnormal', or different.

Despite the difficulties encountered by survivors in Israel, for those child survivors who made *aliya* at a later stage of their lives, the Israeli cultural context provided survivors with a more responsive audience, a greater sense of belonging and social recognition, than the European context. Most significantly, living in Israel gave these child survivors a greater sense of purpose and meaning, not only to their past but also to their present.

Professional Identity

Through silence and suppression of their pasts, most of the interviewees had managed to integrate themselves so successfully into their post-war environments that they had become indistinguishable from the rest of the population. Even whilst growing up, the interviewees explained, most of their friends at school did not know that they were survivors. In their adult years, most of them have become successful, contributing members of Israeli society. All of my interviewees have been and continue to be active and involved citizens; they hold passionate beliefs about the country, have busied themselves with the betterment of Israeli society, and work to alleviate the suffering of others.

Furthermore, the professions that many of the child survivors have chosen are also a response to their pasts. Many are involved in education and the caring professions, which they see as a corrective experience or as the 'price they pay for their survival'. Rachel explains that her work as a lecturer for pre-school teachers is her way of dealing with the *Shoah*. She says that being a lecturer in early childhood education "is more than comfort [for the experience of the *Shoah*]. I have said it often to my students . . . they wanted to kill me as a Jewish girl. I was awarded the privilege of training Jewish kindergarten teachers for Jewish children here in *Eretz Yisrael*. What could be greater than that? For me it is immense."

Naomi has worked as a nurse, and Shalom has devoted a large part of his life to ecological conservation in Israel. Michal, Ehud, David and Shalom all became academics in leading Israeli universities. Some of the interviewees have devoted their retirement years to doing volunteer work. Both Ehud and Yehiel volunteer their time to helping elderly Holocaust survivors by keeping them company and helping them with some of the difficulties that they face on a day-to-day basis. Naomi is intensely involved with Holocaust education. She has written a book for children about her experiences during the war which, she hopes, will sensitize the next generation to the subject. Because of the book's success, she now spends a significant amount of her time responding to the countless letters that she receives from children all over the country who have read her work. Rivka, a deeply religious woman, gives counseling to young brides before marriage. She has also recently retrained as a naturopath, and seeks to alleviate the physical suffering of people through non-conventional medicine.

Social Action

Marveling at the generosity of these individuals and their commitment to improving the world, I was helped by Michal to understand their instinct to care for and help other people. She explains, "There's no reason why I survived and six million didn't. There's no reason why they were murdered and I wasn't. It is just all so random . . . I think it's hard to live with the feeling that life is tenuous and random. But if I can find any meaning in any of it or a feeling of victory in any of it, it is that I've tried to make a difference in the world, I've tried to make it a better place."

Yafe also expresses this same sentiment in her narrative. She explains that, "I survived because I have a function. G-d did not randomly keep me alive. It seems that I needed to build a family. It seems that I needed to educate my children according to my beliefs. It seems that I had to educate a lot of children and, thank G-d, a lot of children remember me fondly. I ran a group with parents, to help parents educate their children, so that they would be good parents. So, it seems that this was my function in this world. It seems that I also have to pass on the message of the *Shoah*. I see this as an important function too."

Judith Herman explains that the need on the part of survivors to contribute to and improve the world is prevalent amongst survivors of trauma generally: "most survivors seek the resolution of their traumatic experience within the confines of their personal lives. But a significant minority, as a result of their trauma, feel called upon to engage in a wider world. These survivors recognize a political or religious dimension in their misfortune and discover that they can transform the meaning of their personal tragedy by making it the basis for social action. While there is no way to compensate for an atrocity, there is a way to transcend it, by making it a gift to others. The trauma is redeemed only when it becomes the source of a survivor mission."[3] Furthermore, their contribution to the well-being of their community has also enabled them to develop a more acute sense of belonging and connection

What is significant here is that the child survivors are attempting to give purpose to their survival through their activities in their subsequent lives. Brian Schiff relates to this phenomenon as "reading backwards,"[4] which "is a movement in the retelling of a life-history" whereby stories and events are perceived, told and understood from narratively later experiences, which are used to interpret the past. "All understanding is formed in what has taken place in life since."[5] This is a crucial point to consider, especially for historians. The narratives of survivors, or of any living witnesses, about their pasts may not necessarily be an 'accurate description of the events'. That is to say, there is a difference between the way we understand experience whilst it is happening, the way we remember it, and the way we tell it. The way we tell it may not match the way we experienced it at the time. Yet, for the narrator, the life story as it is told is still a truthful representation of the past and of who he/she *is*.

My work has focused on the story as told, in one telling, or sometimes two, and has tracked the effect of the socio-cultural context on a life story as it is interpreted at a particular time in history. It would be interesting to compare the testimonies of survivors diachronically, over their entire life-span, in order to track this dynamic, and understand even more deeply the social, historical and cultural processes which have affected the construction of the individual's perception of and relationship towards his or her past.

Secondary Silencing

Silencing of the past did not mean that it was necessarily forgotten. Contrary to Maurice Halbwachs'[6] approach to autobiographical memory, in which he argues that autobiographical memory tends to fade with time, and may even be lost, if it is not reinforced periodically through contact with persons with whom one shared the experiences in the past. Yet, the narratives of most of the child survivors whom I interviewed, not including those who say they were 'too young to remember', attest to the fact that despite the silence and silencing, their memories remained with them. Society was instrumental in framing their memories and imbuing them with meaning, and impacting the creation of their identities. Because the collective did not view hidden child survivors as 'survivors', they ceased to identify themselves as such. The 'real survivors', as Ruth explained, were those who survived Auschwitz. Furthermore, for most of their lives, child survivors did not create groups of *remembering communities* either; they remained alone with their memories. Instead, they mourned their personal past privately, while identifying with the collective memory and (sometimes) became part of the official ceremonies and rituals of mourning.

Reclaiming the Traumatic Past

Today, however, their challenge is quite different, for child survivors have not always found that deep sense of belonging for which they have been searching. Many of them have begun to feel that an essential part of them is missing, unclaimed, and unexpressed. Thus, in their later years, many have begun to look back towards the past in order to reclaim those aspects of themselves, those parts of their selves which were the foundations of their lives. Child survivors have recently begun to recall their memories and their pasts in order to give voice to the silenced parts of their selves and to reclaim their biological identities. In the case of younger child survivors, they have begun to search actively for memories, in an attempt to create a biological identity. Whilst silence was utilized in their search for normalcy and belonging in their postwar environment, now retelling is employed in their attempt at integration and in their 'search to belong to themselves'. Life stories or narratives are the individual's attempt to integrate seemingly different parts of themselves in the presentation of a coherent, meaningful self. Thus, through retelling, child survivors attempt to reclaim all parts of themselves, to tell us, and themselves, who they are.

The child survivors' need to look back at their personal pasts parallels the development of collective memory of the Holocaust in Israel. In the last few decades, Israeli society has demonstrated an openness and willingness to look back at the past and hear the stories of child survivors. After having established themselves as an integral part of Israeli society, in which their belonging and allegiance is no longer questioned, many have felt more comfortable revisiting their personal histories and talking about their experiences openly. In terms of national identity, the willingness and openness of Israeli society to listen to all aspects of the past perhaps reflects its own need to construct a continual narrative of its own history. This would include the experience of Jewish life in the Diaspora and the stories of personal loss, suffering, and sacrifice as well as those stories of resistance and strength during the *Shoah*.

Integration of Identity?

Some of my interviewees felt that in the last few years, by confronting their pasts, they have indeed managed to create a consistent sense of self. Ehud, after nearly fifty years of silence and the suppression of his survivor identity, is now able to present and give voice to his entire life history, claiming all parts of his identity. In a poem written on January 19, 1999 he signs off as:

"Herbert Odenheimer, Hiber Odenheimer, Hiber Odeh, Herbert Loeb, Ehud Lev. Born, expelled, incarcerated, orphan, in hiding, survived, adopted, married, father, grandfather, will die. His sons will say kaddish."

The need for many child survivors, Ehud included, to reflect upon and give voice to the past is also connected to their need to mourn and commemorate their lost loved ones. As child survivors, they have begun to realize that they are indeed the last witnesses, and fear that if they fail to remember now, the history and memory of their murdered loved ones, friends, acquaintances and communities will disappear with them.

Yet, unlike for Ehud, for other child survivors it is precisely this integration of identity that remains problematic. The challenge for these individuals is negotiating between their pasts and their current identities. Most of my interviewees struggle with the question, 'How can I hold onto all parts of myself? How can I be the person I was born, the child who was persecuted and survived, and the Israeli I have become? I am not *only* a survivor, but *all* of these other things too'. Some of my interviewees felt that they have been able to integrate the past into their lives, whilst others continue to experience what Haim Dasberg has defined as a 'split' in their personalities, a "feature of incomplete and postponed mourning, and also [a split] between a traumatized inner core and outward adaptedness."[7]

As Shalom revealed, the writing of his book, which brings to the fore his survivor identity in an attempt to integrate his silenced past, now threatens his post-war identity. Sara's narrative reveals that whilst retelling was initially therapeutic, it now threatens her post-war identity, her psychological equilibrium, and her emotional well-being. Remembering the victim self and what it implies can destroy the feelings of empowerment and accomplishment that survivors have fought to achieve in their post-war lives, as the "benevolent past will always be associated with the circumstances of its destruction and loss."[8]

The Limits of Telling and Knowing

Another obstacle to integration is connected to the notion of telling trauma. Despite their valiant efforts to give voice to their histories, there are still some aspects of the child survivors' experiences which will never be told. In terms of survivors of trauma, experiences may remain 'unknowable', either because they can never be fully *known*, or because they cannot be articulated and told. Kalman's narrative dramatically exemplifies the former. Because of his sister's silence, he is unable to *know* about the fate of his mother, or if she ever forgave him for embarrassing her in front of the ladies in the camp. Thus, as long as survivors remain silent, the 'whole' story can never be fully *known*. The past may also be unknowable because child survivors may have very little memory or proof of their pasts. The absence of memory may be connected to their age during persecution; many were too young to remember, and suffer psychogenic amnesia. And indeed, and because the Holocaust "is itself a crime perpetrated against the existence of the past and the possibility of a future. There were to be no traces of the crime left, no traces of the bodies burned, no traces of the thriving Jewish life that had existed for generations. There was to be no future for the Jewish people, continuity was to be broken, all places were to be destroyed."[9]

Sara's narrative teaches us that even if survivors do choose to tell their stories, repeatedly and over many years, it does not imply that their entire story will be told. Sara explains that there are still things which she has not told to anyone, as she is still looking for the 'other' to whom she can reveal those silenced parts of herself, those stories which have not become part of her voiced narrative. Thus, even once a survivor decides to retell their past, this occurs within a negotiated space, between the 'audience' and the survivor. Within this negotiated space the survivor chooses what he or she will tell, at the moment of retelling.

Survivors have their own limitations in knowing and articulating their past. This impacts our ability as researchers to *know* about the period we are researching. From this we learn that there are limitations of what we can know about the historical period we are examining. As I left Sara's *kibbutz*, I felt that I had 'failed' professionally and even interpersonally; that I was not that 'empathic other' with whom which she felt that she could share those silenced memories. Yet, upon reflection, I began to feel humbled by the experience. I began to realize that Sara had shared with me as much as she could, in that particular context. Interviewing allowed me to understand that the participants of my research, child survivors, were not objects of my research, but individuals who trusted me enough to let me into their lives, and whose boundaries I needed to respect. Thus, in listening to individual life stories, historians and social scientists may have to confront and accept the limits of *fully* knowing.

Another aspect of the silence surrounding the narratives of survivors is connected to the issue of the unsayable and indescribable, which has been discussed extensively in previous research and literature.[10] Most of the child survivors whom I interviewed found, at some point, that their experiences during the war were unsayable or indescribable. Ironically, this feature was most present in the narratives of those two individuals who 'have always spoken'. Even though they have always been able and willing to retell their pasts publicly and in their smaller sub-communities, there are aspects of their experiences which they find impossible to articulate. Unlike Sara, who has not found the right person to whom to tell her whole story, Kalman and Yitzhak cannot find the words to describe their experiences, which appear before their eyes as they speak. As Kalman states after trying to explain a traumatic event in the camp, "those bone chilling experiences . . . how am I going to make you guys understand this? How . . . how can you?! All I can do is make the noises . . . you can understand . . . you can swallow this, you don't swallow it . . . I am very . . . "

Haim Dasberg understands "the paradigm of the unfinished story," as "only one facet of the more encompassing paradigm of alienation of the traumatized person from his society."[11] Thus, according to Dasberg, gaps in the survivors' stories, or their unfinished tales, reflects their inability, due to the nature of trauma, to fully rejoin their post-war community. They are unable to become a part of their communities fully because they are unable to regain and communicate those parts of themselves that were lost or destroyed because of their victimization. Thus, the untellable or the unknowable aspects of survivor testimony attests to the fundamental sense of alienation and non-belonging that survivors of trauma feel in their post-war environment. Despite these feelings of alienation, most of the child survivors whom I interviewed felt a strong connection to Israel, and had strong identities as Israelis. It was belonging as child survivors within Israeli society which was more of a challenge for them. This has begun to change in the last few years, as they have been able to create their own sub-communities of belonging within Israeli society.

The Space in the Middle: Child Survivor Groups

Beyond remembering the past, child survivor support groups have enabled many to finally create a sense of belonging amongst their fellow child survivors. It is within these sub-communities that the individual is able to join the collective. The power of these groups cannot and must not be underestimated, as they work to undo much of the damage and loss that their members have experienced as a result of their traumatic pasts. They work to restore the child survivor's sense of belonging and connectedness to the world. Amongst themselves, they manage to recapture moments of their lost childhood; at times they feel like a reunited family, and allow themselves the freedom to reminisce because they know how to lead each other back from the past to the present. As Ehud describes his own experience with his support group: "The feeling was that, even though the horrific nature of the experiences has not been lessened, at least now there is cooperation, comradeship, that there are others and that it is possible to share it with them." For child survivors specifically, survivor support groups have helped individuals 'find their voice' through mutual validation and encouragement. Furthermore, it is within these groups that the child survivors feel most able to express the 'indescribable' and explore together the 'unknowable'. This has wider implications for research on victims of any trauma, as it begs the question of whether it is only amongst themselves that survivors of trauma can find a place of belonging, of companionship, and of empathy.

Individual Stories and Collective Memory

Besides functioning as a place of 'belonging', survivor groups also serve as a remembering community, which gives voice to their collective experience. This remembering community facilitates an integration of the individual's narrative into the collective narrative. Collective memory has been instrumental in determining which stories are to *be* told, and what *is* told during the telling. This has not only affected the individuals' relationship to their past and their identity as survivors, it has also shaped the writing of history.

The silence in historical representation around the experience of child survivors is powerfully demonstrated in Rachel's narrative when she explains, "The moment one is silent, there are no publications, there are no testimonies, there are no works, there is nothing. Look at what happened at Yad Vashem . . . it's only in the last few years, because I remember that I looked in the Pedagogical Center and I found almost nothing. There was nothing on France. Now I think that there is a little more. There are a few books and other things around, but I feel that it's because we started to draw attention to it. It's really only our own little group that has begun to draw attention to it. Here and there are people who have begun to publish material on it." Rachel sees a direct connection between the individual's silence and the collective silence. Once individuals create their own remembering community, they create an alternative narrative, which enters and is woven into the larger historical narrative of the Holocaust. According to Rachel, due to the work of her group, or remembering community, the experience of French Jewish children who were hidden during the war has begun to enter Israeli public consciousness and historical research. Thus, the remembering community, or in this case the child survivor support group, allows the individual to join, and to carve out a place of belonging within the wider historical narrative.

Whilst Rachel attributes the lack of historical writing on the experience of French children in hiding to their own silence, Ariala tells another story. She attributes the absence of historical writing on French Jewry during the war to the disproportionate attention paid by historians to the Eastern European Jewish experience. Her strong feelings on this matter were expressed even before I interviewed her. Yad Vashem had given me her name, but they had not given me the details of her past. When I called Ariala to make an appointment, I asked her a few questions to gauge whether she would be a suitable participant for my research. When I asked her where she was born, she said that she was born in Paris. I was somewhat disappointed in that I had interviewed quite a number of survivors from France and I was hoping to interview survivors from other countries in order to balance out the research sample. Unfortunately, Ariala became aware of my disappointment. I tried to explain to her that I had interviewed a number of survivors from France already, and that I needed to interview more people from Eastern Europe. Ariala became upset, and began to explain that she and her family suffered no less than those who had experienced the war in Poland. She declared that she was tired of what she saw as an obsession by Holocaust researchers in focusing on what had transpired in Poland. She felt that the suffering of French Jewry was ignored and marginalized in the story of the *Shoah*. She exclaimed that she and her family had suffered and died in the same way as had Polish Jews. It was a difficult but a revealing exchange, as it became clear that the hierarchy of suffering was experienced with regard to geographical location too. Ariala impressed upon me the importance of her story, and I felt that I was obligated to interview her, especially since I was investigating the very issue she was accusing me of – silencing narratives. Her interview was indeed fascinating and has come to occupy a central place in my work. This encounter reveals that while collective memory is instrumental in shaping and creating personal narratives, these individual narratives, in turn, have the power to shape the larger historical narrative. Through Ariala's own insistence, her narrative made her way into my research. Once other narratives are allowed to enter the public space, they add, contribute, challenge and change the traditional narrative and understanding of the past.

Perhaps more significantly, this extract illustrates the relationship between public memory, recognition, legitimization and belonging. Throughout her narrative, Ariala tells of the difficulties of not being recognized as one who suffered during the war. For Ariala, the hierarchy of suffering was so powerful that her experiences as a hidden child during the war were not regarded as traumatic. Instead she was told that she was not to speak about the past, and to consider herself, as she describes, 'lucky' that she survived at all. Ariala explained that the hierarchy of suffering also operated and continues to operate in terms of geographical location during the war: the collective experience of French Jewry during the war has been silenced and has remained on the periphery of historical research, whilst the experience of Eastern European Jewry has been central. Because of the proximity to the death camps and the number of victims, a public image has been generated in which the experience of Eastern European Jewry has occupied the center of Holocaust memory. In contrast, the experience of French Jewry has remained on the periphery – in terms of historical memory, survival, and suffering sustained. According to Ariala, this lack of recognition of the experiences and sufferings of French Jewry during the Holocaust has resulted not only in an absence of historical memory, but also a silencing of personal memory. This experience has been so powerful for Ariala that she has even come to anticipate disinterest from researchers. After hearing the disappointment in my voice over the phone, she immediately assumed that I was not interested in researching the experiences of French Jewry during the *Shoah*, even though I was trying to tell her that I had already interviewed quite a number of child survivors from France. She proceeded to tell me that *her family had suffered and died in the same way as had Polish Jews* and that her story was worth listening to.

In their struggle for recognition, child survivors are not only struggling to carve out a place of belonging, they are also attempting to re-appropriate the story of the *Shoah*, so that *they* will be able to tell their *own* stories. Through telling their stories, survivors will be able to determine the way their story and themselves will be heard, understood and remembered, especially after they are no longer able to do so. Henry Greenspan argues that in order to understand the experience of Holocaust survivors, one needs to engage in conversation *with* them, and not *about* them. He explains that in the past fifty years, survivors have became the 'objects' of our research. Their role as protagonists in their own stories has been dissolved, and they have not been allowed to make their own meaning. Inspired by Henry Greenspan's compelling work, I examined the narratives of child survivors of the Holocaust, in an attempt to understand how *they* have made sense of their own pasts and relate to their identity as survivors of the Holocaust. From their narratives, I heard repeatedly that their lives, their relationship to their past, and their identity as survivors are in constant negotiation. This process or negotiation of 'survival', which began during the war as they struggled to survive physically, has continued in their post-war lives in their struggle to survive emotionally and psychologically. For most of the child survivors whom I interviewed, understanding who they are and their relationship to their past has been an intricate and complicated process of pain, self-discovery and self-development. Yet, whilst the voices of my interviewees articulate feelings of defeat and loss, loneliness and abandonment, they nevertheless continue to seek ways to build and create meaningful lives, for themselves and their children. They continue to search for the strength to remember, to find the words, to give voice; they struggle with courage to work through their pasts.

When forging their relationship to their past and their identity, child survivors have not only responded to their own internal, individual needs and inhibitions – to remember or forget, to remain silent or to speak. They have also been influenced by external forces, including the nature of their experiences during the war, and the social-cultural context in which they have lived after the war. Charles Taylor writes that the "discovering my own identity doesn't mean that I work it out in isolation, but that I negotiate it through dialogue, partly overt, partly internal, with others. That is why the development of an ideal of inwardly generated identity gives a new importance to recognition. My own identity crucially depends on my dialogical relations with others."[12] For the twenty-one child survivors interviewed, their identity as survivors of the Holocaust, and their relationship to their past, has been constructed in reaction to the values, judgments and guidance of their post-war socio-cultural environment. Thus, the narratives of child survivors should be understood as more than simply memories, 'facts', or the life story of an individual. They are mirrors of larger social cultural concerns. Their individual trauma has been internally experienced, yet it has been externally defined and evaluated. However, through telling, "they are attempting to make the world look at you from my eyes. And if that's not power, then what is?"[13]

Notes

1 Introduction – Inhabiting Three Separate Worlds

1 H. Yablonka, "50 years of an encounter between Survivors and Israelis as reflected through Literature, Memory and Historiography," *Yalkut Moreshet* (1998): 84 (in Hebrew).

2 A. Shapira, "The Holocaust: Private Memories, Public Memory", *Jewish Social Studies* 4, 2 (1998): 47.

3 This phrase can be translated as "Holocaust and Redemption".

4 M. Friedman, "The Haredim and the Holocaust", *The Jerusalem Quarterly* 53 (1990): 90.

5 H. Yablonka, *Survivors of the Holocaust: Israel After the War* (London: Macmillan Press, 1999), 145.

6 A. Shapira, *Land and Power: The Zionist Resort to Force: 1881–1948* (New York: Oxford University Press, 1992), 332–4.

7 S. Bar-Gil, *Searching for a Home, Finding a Homeland. Youth Aliya: Education and Rehabilitation of She'rit Hapleitah* (Jerusalem: Yitzhak Ben Zvi, 1999), 17 (in Hebrew).

8 M. Kol, *Youth Aliya: Past, Present and Future* (Jerusalem: Jerusalem Post Press, 1957), 22.

9 Moshe Kol was appointed as head of Youth *Aliya* in 1948.

10 M. Kol, *Youth Aliya*, 23.

11 Bar Gil, *Searching for a Home*, 14.

12 Kol, *Youth Aliya*, 26.

13 Kol, *Youth Aliya*, 29.

14 According to Shlomo Bar-Gil, 52.7% were absorbed into *Kibbutzim* and 47.3% in other institutions. Bar-Gil, *Searching for a Home*, 136.

15 Kol, *Youth Aliya*, 56.

16 C. Schatzker, "The Role of *Aliyat Hanoar* in the Rescue, Absorption and Rehabilitation of Refugee Children", in *She'erit Hapletah, 1944–1948; Rehabilitation and Political Struggle. Proceedings of the Sixth Yad Vashem International Conference*, ed. Y. Gutman and A. Saf (Jerusalem: Yad Vashem. 1990), 380.

17 Shapira, *Land and Power*, 334.

18 G. Halasz, "Memories of Silence: Trauma Transmission in Holocaust Survivor Families and the Exiled Self", in *Remembering for The Future: The Holocaust in an Age of Genocide. Volume 3: Memory*, ed. J. K Roth and E. Maxwell (Basingstoke: Palgrave, 2001), 129.

19 Y. Gutman, "*She'erit Hapletah* – The problems, some elucidation", in *She'erit HaPletah 1944–1948*, 519–20.

20 H. Yablonka, *Survivors of the Holocaust*, 69.

21 Z. Solomon, "Oscillating Between Denial and Recognition of PTSD: Why Are Lessons Learned and Forgotten?" *Journal of Traumatic Stress* 8, 2 (1995): 276.

22 Z. Solomon, "From Denial to Recognition: Attitudes Toward Holocaust Survivors from World War II to the Present", *Journal of Traumatic Stress* 8, 2 (1995): 217.

23 Yablonka, *Survivors of the Holocaust*, 57.

24 D. Porat, "Attitudes of the Young State of Israel to the Holocaust and Its Survivors: A Debate over Identity and Values", in *New Perspectives on Israeli History: The Early Years of the State*, ed. L. J Silberstein (New York: New York University Press, 1991), 162.

25 Z. Solomon (1995): 218.

26 T. Segev, *The Seventh Million: The Israelis and the Holocaust* (New York: Hill and Wang, 1993), 155.

27 Z. Solomon, "Trauma and Society." *Journal of Traumatic Stress* 8, 2 (1995): 213.

28 C. Taylor, *Multiculturalism. Examining the Politics of Recognition* (Princeton, New Jersey: Princeton University Press, 1994), 25.

29 P. Levi, *The Drowned and the Saved* (London: Abacus, 1998), 62.

30 Gutman, *She'erit Hapletah*, 520.

31 Shapira (1998): 51.

32 Shapira (1998): 50.

33 D. Bar-On, *Fear and Hope: Three Generations of the Holocaust* (Cambridge, MA: Harvard University Press, 1995), 348–9.

34 Y. Danieli, "Families of survivors of the Nazi Holocaust: Some short – and long term – effects." *Stress and Anxiety* 8 (1982)

35 Shmuel Krakowski, quoted in D. Ofer, "Israel", in *The World Reacts to the Holocaust*, ed. D. S. Wyman (Baltimore: John Hopkins University Press, 1996), 857.

36 Ofer, *The World Reacts to the Holocaust*, 856.

37 Yablonka, *Survivors of the Holocaust*, 49.

38 Y. Weitz, "Shaping the Memory of the Holocaust in Israeli Society of the 1950's", in *Major Changes within the Jewish People in the Wake of the Holocaust. Proceedings of the Ninth Yad Vashem International Historical Conference*, ed. Y. Gutman and A. Saf (Jerusalem: Yad Vashem, 1993), 519.

39 D. Ofer, "The Strength of Remembrance: Commemorating the Holocaust During the First Decade of Israel", *Jewish Social Studies* 6, 2 (2000): 48. Dalia Ofer also points out that during the 1950's especially after the large scale immigration to Israel of Jews from Arab countries, there were voices which contested the traditional connection between the Diaspora, the Holocaust

and the new State of Israel. Their position shifted the focus from negation of the Diaspora to the centrality of life in Israel. "Alongside the criticism expressed about life in the Diaspora, there was also an intense feeling of loss . . . The Jewish experience in the Diaspora was presented as having bequeathed to the Jews a heritage of love and yearning for freedom. The aspiration for freedom was the burden that the Jewish people carried, and it was also the cause for the murderous and total war of Nazism against them . . . This expressed the desire to find a reason for the murder of the Jewish people and to give it some universal significance – namely, the Jews as the symbolic People of Freedom who must be embedded in a renewed life in Israel. " D. Ofer (2000): 44.

40   Ofer, *The World Reacts to the Holocaust*, 872.
41   Ofer, *The World Reacts to the Holocaust*, 876.
42   Ofer, *The World Reacts to the Holocaust*, 877–8.
43   Shapira (1998): 52.
44   H. Greenspan, *On Listening to Holocaust Survivors: Recounting and Life History* (Westport: Praeger Publishers, 1998), 44.
45   J. Winter and E. Sivan, "Setting the Framework" in *War and Remembrance in the Twentieth Century*, ed. J. Winter and E. Sivan (Cambridge: Cambridge University Press, 1999), 27–8.
46   Shapira (1998): 53.
47   *The Seventh Million* was first published in 1991.
48   Shapira (1998): 49.
49   Shapira (1998): 54.
50   E. Fogelman and H. Bass-Wichelhaus, "The Role of Group Experiences in the Healing Process of Massive Childhood Holocaust Trauma", *Journal of Applied Psychoanalytic Studies* 4,1 (2002): 35.
51   Ibid.
52   E. Fogelman and H. Bass-Wichelhaus (2002): 34.
53   E. Fogelman, quoted in J. S. Kestenberg, "Children of Survivors and Child Survivors", *Echoes of the Holocaust* 1 (1992): 40.
54   A. Wieviorka, "On Testimony", in *Holocaust Remembrance; The Shapes of Memory*, ed. G. Hartman (Cambridge: Blackwell Publishers, 1994), 24.
55   S. Breznitz, "The Holocaust as a State of Mind", in *Celebrating Elie Wiesel: Stories, Essays and Reflections*, ed. A. Rosen (Indiana: University of Notre Dame Press, 1998), 329.
56   Inscription on the Pillar of Heroism at Yad Vashem.
57   Y. Bauer, *The Jewish Emergence from Powerlessness* (Toronto: University of Toronto Press, 1979), 27.
58   In 1975 information reached the United States Department of Justice that John Iwan Demjanjuk, a resident of Cleveland, Ohio, had collaborated with the SS, and had served as a guard in the Sobibor death camp. In Israel, survivors identified him also as being "Ivan the Terrible", a Ukrainian staff member in Treblinka. On June 23, 1981, after a series of trials, the Northern District Court of the State of Ohio, ruled that Demjanjuk had lied when filling out his immigration application form in 1951, had concealed his membership in the SS, had been in the Trawniki SS training camp, and had

served in both Treblinka and Sobibor. His American citizenship was annulled and he was in effect sentenced to deportation. In October 1983, after Demjanjuk's appeals had failed, the State of Israel requested his extradition. At the end of 1985 the request was granted and on February 28, 1987 he was taken to Israel. On February 16, 1987, the trial of Demjanjuk began in Jerusalem, where he was charged with crimes against the Jewish people, crimes against humanity, war crimes, crimes against persecuted individuals, and murder. The defense did not deny what had taken place during the Holocaust or the killings at Treblinka, but it repudiated the identification of the defendant, claiming John Demjanjuk was not "Ivan the Terrible" of Treblinka. With the aid of psychological experts, the prosecution refuted the argument that the human memory could not be relied upon after such a long time; by means of the testimony of experts in criminal identification it rejected the argument that a document from Trawniki, with Demjanjuk's photograph, was forged; and with the aid of historians they refuted Demjanjuk's alibi. On April 18, 1988, the judges found Demjanjuk guilty of all the charges in the indictment and sentenced him to death. The defense lodged an appeal in the Israeli Supreme Court. The Israeli Supreme Court acquitted Demjanjuk, by virtue of doubt, of being "Ivan the Terrible" of Treblinka. However, the court did find that Demjanjuk served as a "wachmann" guard at Sobibor, Flossenburg and Regensburg concentration camps. Seeing that under the original indictment he had not been given the opportunity to defend himself against these charges, the court set him free.<http://www.yad-vashem.org.il/search/index_search.html>.

59 E. Zuroff, quoted in D. Horwitz, "After Demjanjuk: Is the Hunt for Nazis Over?" *The Jerusalem Report* 4, 7 (1993): 30.

60 B. Wilkomirski, *Fragments: Memoirs of a Wartime Childhood* (Frankfurt Am Main: Judischer Verlag, 1995).

61 See the *The Baltimore Sun*, June 22, 2000; *The Baltimore Jewish Times*, June 6, 2000 and *The Washington Post*, September 24, 2000.

62 *The Washington Times*, June 23, 2000.

63 Greenspan, *On Listening to Holocaust Survivors*, 48.

64 Ofer, *The World Reacts to the Holocaust*, 909.

65 Bar On, *Fear and Hope*.

66 A. Mazor, Y. Gampel, E. D. Enright and R. Orenstein, "Holocaust Survivors: Coping with Post-Traumatic memories in childhood and forty years later", *Journal of Traumatic Stress* 3 (1990).

67 P. Valent, "Resilience in Child Survivors of the Holocaust: Toward the Concept of Resilience", *Psychoanalytic Review* 85 (1998): 526.

68 M. S. Bergmann and M. E. Jucovy, ed. *Generations of the Holocaust* (New York: Basic Books, 1982).

69 Valent (1998): 527.

70 E. H Erikson, "Identity and the Life Cycle", *Psychological Issues* 1 (New York: International University Press, 1959).

71 H. Krystal, "Integration and Self-Healing in Post-Traumatic States: A Ten Year Retrospective", *American Imago* 48 (1991):102.

72 Krystal (1991):101.

73   Ibid.
74   R. Krell, "Therapeutic Value of Documenting Child Survivors", *Journal of the American Academy of Child Psychiatry* 24 (1985): 400.
75   S. Davidson, *Holding onto Humanity – The Message of Holocaust Survivors: The Shamai Davidson Papers*, ed. I. W. Charny (New York: New York University Press, 1992), 147.
76   C. Caruth, *Unclaimed Experience: Trauma, Narrative and History* (Baltimore: Johns Hopkins University Press, 1996).
77   J. Bruner, "Narrative and Paradigmatic Modes of Thought", in *Learning and Teaching the Ways of Knowing. 84th Yearbook of The National Society for the Study of Education*, ed. E. Eisner (Chicago: University of Chicago Press, 1985), 97.
78   R. Behar, *Translated Women: Crossing the Border with Esperanza's Story* (Boston: Beacon Press, 1993), 14.
79   J. L. Herman, *Trauma and Recovery* (New York: Basic Books, 1992), 241.
80   R. Josselson, "Imagining the Real: Empathy, Narrative, and the Dialogic Self". In *Narrative Study of Lives* 3, ed. R. Josselson and A. Lieblich (California: Thousand Oaks, Sage Publications, 1995), 32.
81   Josselson (1995): 32–3.

2   *The Protagonists*

1   I. Clendinnen, *Reading the Holocaust* (Melbourne: Text Publishing, 1998), 56.
2   'Katzetnik' refers to a camp inmate.
3   H. Greenspan, *On Listening to Holocaust Survivors. Recounting and Life History* (Westport, CT: Praeger Publishers, 1988), xix–xx.
4   M. Marrus, *The Holocaust in History* (London: Penguin Books, 1989), 65.
5   Marrus, *The Holocaust in History*, 65.
6   <http://www.yad-vashem.org.il/search/index_search.html>.
7   L. Lazare, *Rescue as Resistance: How Jewish Organizations Fought the Holocaust in France* (New York: Columbia University Press, 1996), 202–3.
8   <http://www.yad-vashem.org.il/search/index_search.html>.
9   Y. Bauer, *A History of the Holocaust* (Danbury: Franklin Watts, 1982), 290.
10   Bauer, *A History of the Holocaust*, 306–7.
11   Antonescu was made Regent of Romania in 1940 and lost power in a dramatic coup in 1944.
12   Bauer, *A History of the Holocaust*, 309.
13   M. Kaplan, *Between Dignity and Despair: Jewish Life in Nazi Germany* (Oxford: Oxford University Press, 1998), 228.
14   S. Davidson, *Holding onto Humanity – The Message of Holocaust Survivors: The Shamai Davidson Papers*, ed. I. W. Charny (New York: New York University Press, 1992), 59.
15   B. Schiff, *Telling Survival and the Holocaust* (University of Chicago, Ph.D. thesis. University Microfilms International, 1997), 70.
16   S. Moskowitz, and R. Krell, "Child Survivors of the Holocaust: Psychological Adaptations to Survival", *Israel Journal of Psychiatry and Related Sciences* 27, 2 (1990): 90–1.

17 D. Dwork, *Children with a Star: Jewish Youth in Nazi Occupied Europe* (New Haven and London: Yale University Press, 1991), 65.
18 R. Behar, *Translated Woman: Crossing the Border with Esperanza's Story* (Boston: Beacon Press, 1993), 7.
19 The spelling of all the East European towns mentioned is taken from: C. G. Cohen, *Shtetl Finder Gazatteer* (Los Angeles: Periday, 1980).
20 The *Kinderaktion* took place on 27–8 March, 1944.
21 S. Eilati, *Crossing the River* (Jerusalem: Yad Vashem, 1999), 11–12 (in Hebrew).
22 Dwork, *Children with a Star*, 215.
23 *Yankel* is the Yiddish expression for a buffoon. F. Kogos, *A Dictionary of Yiddish Slang and Idioms* (New York: The Citadel Press, 1966).
24 It must be noted that events described in this extract are not always clear; the extract is a reflection of the entire interview. This could be attributed to the fact that this interview was the first 'formal' interview that Shlomo had given. Furthermore, it was clear throughout the interview that Shlomo is still tormented by his past. His interview is made up of a random sequence of visual imprints, rather than a narration of events. This indicates that the past trauma has not been grasped and integrated into his present; instead, his traumatic past is experienced as part of his present. Shlomo's narrative is an example of traumatic memory, whereby his narrative is disrupted constantly as it dissolves in the face of the horrific visions of the past.
25 Dwork, *Children with a Star*, 228.
26 Perhaps one of the most startling aspects of Michal's narrative is her ability to recall her war-time experiences despite her young age. Furthermore there were no other living witnesses to most of the events she described who could have helped her verify her memories. Throughout her interview Michal insists that she remembers her past; that in fact it was too traumatic to forget. She explains that throughout her life she has had to defend her memories against accusations made by people who do not believe that she could have remembered anything from the period. The issue of age and memory will be discussed in more detail in later chapters.
27 Y. Gampel, "Facing War, Murder, Torture, and Death in Latency", *Psychoanalytic Review* 75, 4 (1988): 503.
28 P. Valent, *Child Survivors: Adults Living with Childhood Trauma* (Australia: William Heinemann, 1993), 272.
29 Gampel (1988).
30 H. Himmler, "Evacuation of the Jews", in *Documents of the Holocaust: Selected Sources on the Destruction of the Jews of Germany and Austria and the Soviet Union*, ed. Y. Arad, Y. Gutman, and A. Margaliot (Jerusalem: Yad Vashem, 1981), 344–5.

3 *Hidden Child Survivors Who have Found Their Voices*

1 D. Dwork, *Children with a Star: Jewish Youth in Nazi Europe* (New Haven and London: Yale University Press, 1991), 32.
2 Dwork, *Children with a Star*, 68.

3   N. Tec, "A Historical Perspective: Tracing the History of the Hidden Child", in *The Hidden Children: The Secret Survivors of the Holocaust*, ed. J. Marks (London: Piatkus, 1993), 285.

4   R. Krell (ed.), *Messages and Memories: Reflections on Child Survivors of the Holocaust* (Vancouver: Memory Press, 1999), 33.

5   E. Lev, "Expressing Childhood Experiences – A Writing Workshop, 1994–1999", *Remembering for the Future: The Holocaust in an Age of Genocide. Volume 3: Memory*, ed. J. K Roth and E. Maxwell (Hampshire: Palgrave, 2001), 152.

6   S. Zuccotti, *The Holocaust, The French and The Jews* (New York: Basic Books, 1993), 246.

7   It is interesting that throughout Ariala's narrative, she retells her past in the present tense – telling it as it is happening. Yet, her reflections on her past and the interpretation that she gives to her and other peoples' behavior and reactions, are all told in the past tense. This dynamic may be understood as an acting out of her story whilst retelling.

8   F. Hogman, "The Experience of Catholicism for Jewish Children During World War II", *Psychoanalytic Review* 75, 4 (1988): 524.

9   D. L Schacter, *Searching for Memory: The Brain, the Mind, and the Past* (New York: Basic Books, 1996), 223.

10 Dwork, *Children with a Star*, 80.

11 J. L. Herman, *Trauma and Recovery* (New York: Basic Books, 1992), 28.

12 For an in-depth discussion of the plight of women in the Holocaust see: *Women in the Holocaust*, ed. D. Ofer and L. J. Weitzman (London: Yale University Press, 1998).

13 P. Valent, "A Child Survivor's Appraisal of His Own Interview", in *Children During the Nazi Reign: Psychological Perspectives on the Interview Process*, ed. J. S. Kestenberg and E. Fogelman (Westport: Praeger Publishers, 1994), 125.

14 Valent, *Child Survivors: Adults Living with Childhood Trauma* (Melbourne: William Heinemann, Australia, 1993), 281.

15 Sual et al. 1956; Martin 1959, quoted in J. S. Kestenberg, "Overview of the Effect of Psychological Research Interviews on Child Survivors", *Children During the Nazi Reign*, 16.

16 R. Krell, "Child Survivors of the Holocaust: 40 Years Later", *Journal of the American Academy of Child Psychiatry* 24, 4 (1985): 379.

17 Valent, *Child Survivors*, 282.

18 H. Greenspan, *On Listening to Holocaust Survivors: Recounting and Life History* (Westport: Praeger Publishers, 1998), 157.

19 H. Keilson, *Sequential Traumatization in Children. A Clinical and Statistical follow-up study of the fate of the Jewish War Orphans in the Netherlands* (Jerusalem: The Magnes Press, 1979), 55.

20 E. Fogelman, "The Psychology behind the Hidden Child", in *The Hidden Children*, 302.

21 Ibid.

22 S. Moskowitz, and R. Krell, "Child Survivors of the Holocaust: Psychological Adaptations to Survival", *Israel Journal of Psychiatry and Related Sciences* 27, 2 (1990): 84.

23 S. Breznitz, in an address given to the Conference of Child Survivors of the Kovno Ghetto. April 2000, Israel.

24 Ruth is referring to the numbers tattooed onto the forearms of prisoners of Auschwitz. Only prisoners in Auschwitz were tattooed.

25 Y. Danieli, "Families of survivors of the Nazi Holocaust: Some short-and long term-effects," *Stress and Anxiety* 8 (1982).

26 J. S. Kestenberg, "Children of Survivors and Child Survivors", *Echoes of the Holocaust* 1 (1992): 37.

27 R. Josselson, "Imagining the Real: Empathy, Narrative, and the Dialogic Self", in *Narrative Study of Lives* 3, ed. R. Josselson and A. Lieblich (California: Thousand Oaks, Sage Publications, 1995), 37.

28 J. S Kestenberg and Y. Gampel, "Growing up in a Holocaust Culture", *Israel Journal of Psychiatry and Related Sciences* 20, 1–2 (1983): 142.

29 Grayzel, 1985 and Silber, 1985, quoted in M. Kestenberg and J. S Kestenberg, "The Sense of Belonging and Altruism in Children who Survived the Holocaust", *Psychoanalytic Review* 75, 4 (1988): 534.

30 H. Dasberg, "The Unfinished Story of Trauma as a paradigm for Psychotherapists", *Israel Journal of Psychiatry and Related Sciences* 29, 1 (1992): 46.

31 Krell, *Messages and Memories*, 33.

32 J. Shuval, "Israel in the Center of Post-Industrial Migration. The Mythology of 'Uniqueness'", in *Roots and Routes: Ethnicity and Migration in Global Perspective,* ed. S. Weil (Jerusalem: Magnes Press, 1995), 230–1.

33 S. Davidson, *Holding onto Humanity – The Message of Holocaust Survivors: The Shamai Davidson Papers,* ed. I. W. Charny (New York: New York University Press, 1992), 73–4.

34 H. Yablonka, *Survivors of the Holocaust: Israel After the War* (London: Macmillan Press, 1999), 45.

35 J. S. Kestenberg and Y. Gampel (1983): 143–4.

36 H. Klein, "Holocaust Survivors in Kibbutzim: Re-adaptation and Reintegration", *Israel Annals of Psychiatry and Related Disciplines* 10, 1 (1972): 8.

37 Klein (1972): 86.

38 Klein (1972): 85.

39 Klein (1972): 87.

40 For more on this issue see: A. Appelfeld, *Searing Light* (Tel Aviv: Kibbutz HaMeuchad, 1980) in Hebrew; S. Bar-Gil, *Searching for a Home, Finding a Homeland. Youth Aliya: Education and Rehabilitation of She'rit Hapleitah* (Jerusalem: Yitzhak Ben Zvi, 1999) in Hebrew; C. Schatzker, "The Role of *Aliyat Hanoar* in the Rescue, Absorption and Rehabilitation of Refugee Children", *She'erit Hapletah 1944–1948 Rehabilitation and Political Struggle Proceedings of the Sixth Yad Vashem International Conference,* ed. Y. Gutman and A. Saf (Jerusalem: Yad Vashem, 1990); Yablonka, *Survivors of the Holocaust.*

41 D. Bar On, *Fear and Hope: Three Generations of the Holocaust* (Cambridge, MA: Harvard University Press, 1995), 23.

42 Davidson, *Holding onto Humanity,* 150.

4 *Hidden Child Survivors Who Have Found Their Voice*

1   E. Fogelman, "Effects of Interviews with Rescued Child Survivors", in *Children During the Nazi Reign. Psychological Perspective on the Interview Process*, ed. J. S. Kestenberg and E. Fogelman (Westport, Connecticut: Praeger, 1994), 82.

2   P. Valent, "A Child Survivor's Appraisal of His Own Interview", in *Children During the Nazi Reign*, 281.

3   L. Langer, "Redefining Heroic Behavior: The Impromptu Self and the Holocaust", in *Lessons and Legacies*, ed. P. Hayes (Illinois: North Western University Press, 1991), 236.

4   Ehud said 'second identity' in the interview, but from the context it appears that he meant first identity.

5   S. Moskowitz, quoted in R. Krell, "Child Survivors of the Holocaust: 40 Years Later", *Journal of the American Academy of Child Psychiatry* 24, 4 (1985): 379.

6   S. Davidson, *Holding onto Humanity – The Message of Holocaust Survivors: The Shamai Davidson Papers*, ed. I. W. Charny (New York: New York University Press, 1992), 146.

7   "Survivor syndrome" is defined by psychiatrists William Niederland and Henry Krystal. They write, "Over the last 20 years, in the diagnosis and treatment of concentration – and extermination – camp survivors, indicates that we are dealing here with victims of a traumatization of such magnitude, severity, and duration as to produce a recognizable clinical syndrome . . . We have learned to recognize a syndrome characterized by the persistence of symptoms of withdrawal from social life, insomnia, nightmares, chronic depressive and anxiety reaction, and far-reaching somatization. H. Krystal and W. G. Niederland, "Clinical Observations on the Survivor Syndrome", *Massive Psychic Trauma* (New York: International Universities Press, 1968), 327.

8   Davidson, *Holding onto Humanity*, 48.

9   L. Langer, *Holocaust Testimonies: The Ruins of Memory* (New Haven: Yale University Press, 1991), 238.

10   I. Agger and S. Jensen 1990, quoted in J. L. Herman, *Trauma and Recovery* (New York: Basic Books, 1992), 181.

11   Herman, *Trauma and Recovery*, 202.

12   Davidson, *Holding onto Humanity*, 160.

13   Ibid.

14   Davidson, *Holding onto Humanity*, 161.

15   Davidson, *Holding onto Humanity*, 162.

16   D. L. Schacter, *Searching for Memory: The Brain, The Mind, and The Past* (New York: Basic Books, 1996), 27.

17   E. Fogelman, quoted in J. S. Kestenberg, "The Response of the Child to the Rescuer", *Echoes of the Holocaust* 4 (1995): 7.

18   E. Fogelman, "The Psychology behind the Hidden Child", in *The Hidden Children: The Secret Survivors of the Holocaust*, ed. J. Marks (London: Piatkus, 1993), 304.

19 A. H. Foxman, "A Broken Silence", *Dimensions* 6 (1991): 12–13.

20 In order to be certain of this, I would have needed to interview Ruth before her interaction with Yad Vashem.

21 V. Vinitzky-Seroussi, *After Pomp and Circumstance: high school reunion as an autobiographical occasion* (Chicago: University of Chicago Press, 1998).

22 B. J. Cohler and H. U. Grunebaum 1981, quoted in D. Bar-On, *Fear and Hope: Three Generations of the Holocaust* (Cambridge, MA: Harvard University Press, 1995), 30.

23 I. Berlazki 1991, quoted in Bar-On, *Fear and Hope*, 20.

24 R. Krell, "Child Survivors of the Holocaust: 40 Years Later", *Journal of the American Academy of Child Psychiatry* 24, 4 (1985): 378.

25 D. Dwork, *Children with a Star: Jewish Youth in Nazi Europe* (New Haven and London: Yale University Press, 1991), 19.

26 J. Ringelheim, "Gender Reconsidered", in *Women in the Holocaust*, ed. D. Ofer and L. J. Weitzman (New Haven: Yale University Press, 1998), 349.

27 Ringelheim, *Women in the Holocaust*, 346.

28 D. Laub and M. Allard, "History, memory and Truth: Defining the Place of the Survivor", in *The Holocaust and History: The Known, Unknown, and Disputed and the Reexamined*, ed. M. Berenbaum and A. J. Peck (Bloomington: Indiana University Press, 1998), 809.

29 Herman, *Trauma and Recovery*, 133.

30 Laub and Allard, *The Holocaust and History*, 808.

31 Herman, *Trauma and Recovery*, 133.

32 Laub and Allard, *The Holocaust in History*, 809.

33 Transnistria is an artificial geographic term, created in World War II, refer-ring to the part of the Ukraine conquered by German and Romanian troops in the summer of 1941. Before the war, this area had a Jewish population of 300,000. Tens of thousands of Jews were slaughtered by *Einsatzgruppe D*, and by German and Romanian forces. When Transnistria was occupied, it was used as a concentration point for the Jews of Bessarabia, Bukovina, and northern Moldavia who were expelled on the direct order of Ion Antonescu. Most of the Jews who survived the mass killings carried out in Bessarabia and Bukovina were deported to Transnistria by the end of 1941. Also deported to Transnistria were political prisoners and Jews who had evaded the existing regulations on forced labor. The total number of deportees was apparently 150,000 although German sources put the figure at 185,000. <http://www.yad-vashem.org.il/search/index_search.html>.

34 Schacter, *Searching for Memory*, 265.

35 Out of a total of 145,000–150,000 deported to Transnistria, some 90,000 perished there. <http://www.yad-vashem.org.il/search/ index_search. html>.

36 S. Breznitz, In an address given to the Conference of Child Survivors of the Kovno Ghetto. April 2000, Israel.

37 Langer, *Holocaust Testimonies*, 228.

38 H. Greenspan, *On Listening to Holocaust Survivors. Recounting and Life History* (Westport, CT: Praeger Publishers, 1988), 44.

39 Herman, *Trauma and Recovery*, 9.

40 Herman, *Trauma and Recovery*, 70.
41 Y. Danieli, "The Aging Survivor of the Holocaust: Discussion on the Achievement of Integration in Aging Survivors of the Nazi Holocaust", *Journal of Geriatric Psychiatry* 14 (1981): 207.
42 R. J. Lifton, quoted in Danieli (1981): 208.
43 Heman, *Trauma and Recovery*, 195.

5 *Those Who Have Always Spoken*

1 P. Levi, *Moments of Reprieve: A Memoir of Auschwitz* (New York: Penguin Books, 1995), viii–ix.
2 L. Kendall, *The Life and Hard Times of a Korean Shaman: Of Tales and the Telling of Tales* (Honolulu: University of Hawaii Press, 1998), 13.
3 A. Wieviorka, "On Testimony", in *Holocaust Remembrance: The Shapes of Memory*, ed. G. Hartman (Oxford: Blackwell, 1994), 30.
4 H. Greenspan, *On Listening to Holocaust Survivors. Recounting and Life History* (Westport, CT: Praeger Publishers, 1988), 43.
5 R. May, *Cry for Myth* (New York: W.W Norton & Co, 1991), 15.
6 L. D. Loeb, "Time, Myth and History in Judaism", *Conservative Judaism* 42, 3 (1990).
7 Greenspan, On *Listening to Holocaust Survivors*, 23.
8 Once child survivors began to be absorbed into Palestine, Henrietta Szold made an agreement with *Mikveh Yisrael* – the first agricultural school established in Palestine – for child survivors to be absorbed into the school. The school was first established in 1870 in respose to pogroms in Russia. The idea was revolutionary in those days – to separate children from their parents – in order to give them a secure future as farmers in *Eretz Yisrael*. Because agricultural training was the school's priority, it accepted both religious and non-religious children. This made it a unique institution in the Youth Aliya movement.
9 The first attack of the unit 101 was against the village of Kibbiya, a Palestinian village near the border in which 69 civilians were killed. The attack was in retaliation for the murder of a young mother, Susan Kanias, and her two children in the town of Yehud. The police investigation, indicated that the killers had infiltrated Yehud from the direction of Kibbiya. In his autobiography Sharon, wrote, "while the civilian deaths were a tragedy, the Kibbya raid was also a turning point." A. Sharon and D. Chanoff, *Warrior: The Autobiography of Ariel Sharon* (New York: Simon and Schuster, 1989), 85.
10 Ibid.
11 H. Yablonka, "The Silent Partner: Holocaust Survivors in the IDF", in *Israel: The First Decade of Independence*, ed. S. I. Toren and N. Lucas (Albany: State University Press of Albany, 1995), 566.
12 G. Hausner, *Justice in Jerusalem* (New York: Schocken Books, 1966), 169.
13 Stanisław Krajewski in his article, suggests a few reasons as to why Auschwitz has become the symbol of the *Shoah*. First, because of the number of people murdered there it was a 'true death factory'. Second,

there was the impeccable organization, large-scale transport and and infamous camouflage measures. Third, because of the modern scientific methods of organization of labor, and the technical innovations. Krajewsk writes that "It is extremely important that the Auschwitz survivors included such greatly talented men of letters as Tadeusz Borowski, Primo Levi, Elie Wiesel and others. Is the presence of so much excellent literature among Auschwitz the prime reason for endowing the camp with the rank of symbol?" S. Krajewski, "Auschwitz at the threshold of the New Millenium", in *Remembering for the Future: 2001, 3: Memory*, ed. J. K. Roth and E. Maxwell (Hampshire: Palgrave, 2001), 322–3.

14 D. Dwork, *Children with a Star: Jewish Youth in Nazi Europe* (New Haven and London: Yale University Press, 1991), 239.

15 S. Davidson, *Holding onto Humanity – The Message of Holocaust Survivors: The Shamai Davidson Papers*, ed. I. W. Charny (New York: New York University Press, 1992), 56.

16 S. Kav Venaki, A. Nadler and H. Gershoni, "Sharing the Holocaust Experience: Communication behaviors and their consequences in families of ex-partisans and ex-prisoners of concentration camps", *Family Process* 24, 2 (1985): 280–1.

17 M. J. Aronoff, "Myths, Symbols, and Rituals of the Emerging State", in *New Perspectives on Israeli History: The Early Years of the State*, ed. L. J. Silberstein (New York: New York University Press, 1991), 176.

18 Davidson, *Holding onto Humanity*, 74.

19 Aronoff, *New Perspectives on Israeli History*, 179.

20 Davidson, *Holding onto Humanity*, 211.

21 D. Porat, "Attitudes of the Young State of Israel toward the Holocaust and its survivors: A Debate over Identity and Values", in *New Perspectives on Israeli History*, 795.

22 Ibid.

23 Ibid.

24 L. Langer, *Holocaust Testimonies: The Ruins of Memory* (New Haven: Yale University Press, 1991), 185.

25 Lawrence Langer rejects the notion that heroic memory is part of survivor testimony. He writes, "Heroic memory is virtually unavailable to such witnesses, because for them remembering is invariably associated with a jumbled terminology and morality that confuse staying alive with the intrepid will to survive." Langer, *Holocaust Testimonies*, 185.

26 R. May, *Cry for Myth* (New York: W.W. Norton & Company, 1991), 58.

27 A. Wieviorka, "From Survivor to Witness: Voices from the Shoah," in *War and Remembrance in the Twentieth Century*, ed. J. Winter and E. Sivan (Cambridge: Cambridge University Press, 1999), 128.

28 S. Moskowitz, and R. Krell, "Child Survivors of the Holocaust: Psychological Adaptations to Survival", *Israel Journal of Psychiatry and Related Sciences* 27, 2 (1990): 83.

29 R. C. Ainslie, *The Psychology of Twinship* (Lincoln and London: University of Nebraska Press, 1985), 93.

30 Ainslie, *The Psychology of Twinship*, 94.

31 May (1975): 704.

32 J. L. Herman, *Trauma and Recovery* (New York: Basic Books, 1992), 178.

33 Kalman began to recite the passage in English, after a short time he asked me to look up the rest in the Talmud. The extract quoted above is the entire passage from: *Menahot*. Translated into English with Notes, Glossary and Indices by E. Cashdan (London: The Soncino Press, 1948): 29b, 190.

34 E. Wiesel, quoted in Greenspan, *On Listening to Holocaust Survivors*, 27.

35 H. Greenspan, *Who can retell? On the Recounting of Life History by Holocaust Survivors* (Brandeis University, Ph.D. thesis (University Microfilms International, 1986), 6.

36 May (1975): 704.

37 C. Lévi-Strauss, *Myth and Meaning* (New York: Schocken Books, 1979).

6 Resistant Speakers

1 J. Haaken, *Pillar of Salt: Gender, Memory, and the Perils of Looking Back* (New Jersey: Rutgers University Press, 1998), 83.

2 R. Krell (ed.), *Messages and Memories: Reflections on Child Survivors of the Holocaust* (Vancouver: Memory Press, 1999), 34.

3 R. Krell, *Messages and Memories*, 60.

4 H. Yablonka, *Survivors of the Holocaust: Israel After the War* (London: Macmillan Press, 1999), 206–7.

5 Yablonka, *Survivors of the Holocaust*, 207.

6 Yablonka, *Survivors of the Holocaust*, 212.

7 Yablonka, "The Silent Partner: Holocaust Survivors in the IDF", in *Israel: The First Decade of Independence*, ed. S. I. Toren and N. Lucas (Albany: State University Press of Albany, 1995), 557.

8 Yablonka (1995): 557–8.

9 Yablonka (1995): 566.

10 T. Segev, *The Seventh Million: The Israelis and the Holocaust* (United States: Harper Collins, 1993), 178–9.

11 Yablonka, *Survivors of the Holocaust*, 211.

12 S. Davidson, *Holding onto Humanity – The Message of Holocaust Survivors: The Shamai Davidson Papers*, ed. I. W. Charny (New York: New York University Press, 1992), 187.

13 A. Freud and D. T. Burlingham, *War and Children* (Connecticut: Greenwood Press Publishers, 1943), 18.

14 R. J. Apfel and B. Simon, *Minefields in Their Hearts: The Mental Health of Children in War and Communal Violence* (New Haven and London: Yale University Press, 1996), 8.

15 D. Wdowniski quoted in D. Dwork, *Children with a Star: Jewish Youth in Nazi Europe* (New Haven and London: Yale University Press, 1991), 189.

16 J. Westhermeyer and K. Wahmanholm, "Refugee Children", *Minefields in Their Hearts*, 83.

17 R. Janoff-Bulman, *Shattered Assumptions: Toward a New Psychology of Trauma* (New York: The Free Press, 1992), 58–9.

18   P. Bromberg quoted by L. Langer, *Versions of Survival: the Holocaust and the Human Spirit* (Albany: State University of New York Press, 1982), xi.

19   J. A. Robinson and L. Hawpe, "Narrative Thinking as a Heuristic Process", in *Narrative Psychology: The Storied Nature of Human Conduct*, ed. T. R. Sarbin (New York: Praeger Special Studies, 1986), 123.

20   Perhaps it would be more accurate to call David a "reluctant speaker" rather than a "resistant speaker."

21   A. Hass, *The Aftermath: Living with the Holocaust* (Cambridge: Cambridge University Press, 1995), 69.

22   R. Krell, "Child Survivors of the Holocaust: 40 Years Later", *Journal of the American Academy of Child Psychiatry* 24, 4 (1985): 380.

23   J. S Kestenberg, "Imagining and Remembering", *Israel Journal of Psychiatry and Related Sciences* 24, 2 (1987): 231.

24   R. Josselson, "Imagining the Real: Empathy, Narrative, and the Dialogic Self", in *Narrative Study of Lives* 3, ed. R. Josselson and A. Lieblich (California: Thousand Oaks, Sage Publications, 1995), 33.

25   Haaken, *Pillar of Salt*, 43.

26   C. Kahn, "Children's Responses to Persecution", in *Children Surviving Persecution: An International Study of Trauma and Healing*, ed. J. S. Kestenberg and C. Kahn (Westport: Praeger Publishers, 1998), 104.

27   Haaken, *Pillar of Salt*, 178.

28   C. R. Ronai, "Multiple Reflections of Child Sex Abuse: An Argument for a Layered Account", *Journal of Contemporary Ethnography* 23, 4 (1995): 418.

29   Josselson (1995): 32.

30   Davidson, *Holding onto Humanity*, 209.

31   Josselson (1995): 36.

32   H. Klein, "Holocaust Survivors in Kibbutzim: Re-adaptation and Reintegration", *Israel Annals of Psychiatry and Related Disciplines* 10, 1 (1972): 86.

33   H. Greenspan, *On Listening to Holocaust Survivors: Recounting and Life History* (Westport: Praeger Publishers, 1998), 19.

34   P. Ballinger, "The Culture of Survivors: Post Traumatic Stress Disorder and Traumatic Memory", *History and Memory* 10, 1 (1998): 122.

35   L. Langer, *Holocaust Testimonies: The Ruins of Memory* (New Haven: Yale University Press, 1991), xiii.

36   Davidson, *Holding onto Humanity*, 212.

37   Langer, *Versions of Survival*, 7.

38   A term used by Irvin Yalom, an authority on group psychology, to describe support groups, quoted from J. L. Herman, *Trauma and Recovery* (New York: Basic Books, 1992), 215.

39   C. Taylor, *Multiculturalism, Examining the Politics of Recognition* (Princeton, New Jersey: Princeton University Press, 1994),

7 *Retreat away from Speech*

1   J. L. Herman, *Trauma and Recovery* (New York: Basic Books, 1992), 70.

2   Sara is correct when she says that her story was not a 'child story'. She was

15 years old at the time and was subject to the same treatment as adults. This extract is important in that it reminds the researcher of the potential discrepency that may arise between the way individuals understand their own experiences, and the way researchers have chosen to define and interpret them.

3 H. Yablonka, *Survivors of the Holocaust: Israel After the War* (London: Macmillan Press, 1999), 218.

4 Ofer D., "Israel", in *The World Reacts to the Holocaust*, ed. D. S. Wyman (Baltimore: Johns Hopkins University Press, 1996), 848–9.

5 D. Porat, "Attitudes of the Young State of Israel toward the Holocaust and its survivors: A Debate over Identity and Values", in *New Perspectives on Israeli History: The Early Years of the State*, ed. L. J. Silberstein (New York: New York University Press, 1991), 168.

6 R. Janoff-Bulman, *Shattered Assumptions: Toward a New Psychology of Trauma* (New York: The Free Press, 1992), 158.

7 Even though there appears to have been little interest shown in the stories of individual survivors, especially those who survived the camps, on a meta-level the Holocaust and its meaning did in the 1940s and 1950s "capture the attention of Israelis – including the political leadership and the intellectual elite" Dalia Ofer argues that there was "a significant involvement in the 1940s and 1950s and an ongoing process of negotiation between Israelis and the events of the Holocaust. The discourse of the Holocaust and its conceptualization was intensively explored during the first decade and a half after World War II." D. Ofer, "The Strength of Remembrance: Commemorating the Holocaust During the First Decade of Israel", *Jewish Social Studies* 6, 2 (2000): 27 & 46.

8 L. Langer, *Holocaust Testimonies: The Ruins of Memory* (New Haven: Yale University Press, 1991), 77.

9 A. Shacham, quoted in Porat, *New Perspectives*, 167.

10 Langer, *Holocaust Testimonies*, 83.

11 Janoff-Bulman, *Shattered Assumptions*, 148.

12 Ibid.

13 Herman, *Trauma and Recovery*, 69.

14 D. Laub, "An Event without a Witness", in *Testimony: Crises of Witnessing in Literature, Psychoanalysis, and History*, ed. S. Felman and D. Laub (New York: Routledge, 1992), 79.

15 Janoff-Bulman, *Shattered Assumptions*, 104.

16 Herman, *Trauma and Recovery*, 93.

17 Janoff-Bulman, *Shattered Assumptions*, 108.

18 J. Pennebaker, quoted in Janoff-Bulman, *Shattered Assumptions*, 109.

19 A. Wieviorka, "From Survivor to Witness: Voices from the Shoah", in *War and Remembrance in the Twentieth Century*, ed. J. Winter and E. Sivan (Cambridge: Cambridge University Press, 1999), 138.

20 D. Laub, "Bearing Witness or the Vicissitudes of Listening", in *Testimony*, 70.

21 S. Rimmon-Keinan, *Discourse in Psychoanalysis and Literature* (London: Methuen, 1987), 178.

22 S. S. Furst, "The Stimulus barrier and the pathogenicity of trauma", *International Journal of Psychoanalysis* 59 (1978): 351.
23 H. Greenspan, *On Listening to Holocaust Survivors: Recounting and Life History* (Westport: Praeger Publishers, 1998), 48.
24 Y. Danieli, "The Aging Survivor of the Holocaust: Discussion on the Achievement of Integration in Aging Survivors of the Nazi Holocaust", *Journal of Geriatric Psychiatry* 14 (1981): 197.
25 J. M. Winter and E. Sivan, *War and Remembrance*, 32.
26 C. Caruth, *Trauma: Explorations in Memory*, ed. C. Caruth (Baltimore: Johns Hopkins University Press, 1995), 9.
27 D. Weinberg, "France", *The World Reacts to the Holocaust*, 20.
28 Weinberg, *The World Reacts to the Holocaust*, 20–1.
29 D. Weinberg, "The Reconstruction of the French Jewish Community After World War II", in *She'erit Hapletah 1944–1948 Rehabilitation and Political Struggle. Proccedings of the Sixth Yad Vashem International Historical Conference*, ed. Y. Gutman and A. Saf (Jerusalem, Israel: Yad Vashem, 1990), 174.
30 Davidson, *Holding onto Humanity*, 150.
31 E. Sivan, "Private Pain and Public Commemoration in Israel", *War and Remembrance*, 183.
32 Sivan, *War and Rememberance*, 190.
33 Y. Gampel and A. Mazor, "The Effects of Interviews on Child Survivors and on the Interviewers in Israel", in *Children During the Nazi Reign. Psychological Perspective on the Interview Process*, ed. J. S. Kestenberg and E. Fogelman (Westport, CT: Praeger, 1994), 162.
34 Gampel and Mazor, *Children During the Nazi Reign*, 164.
35 Gampel and Mazor, *Children During the Nazi Reign*, 163.
36 Danieli (1981): 205. This group was formed in 1975.
37 Emphasis mine. These ideas were put forth at a conference on Child Survivors held in April 2000 at the University of Haifa, Israel.
38 D. L. Schacter, *Searching for Memory: The Brain, The Mind, and The Past* (Basic Books, New York, 1996), 169.
39 D. Laub and M. Allard, "History, Memory and Truth: Defining the Place of the Survivor", in *The Holocaust and History: The Known, Unknown, and Disputed and the Reexamined*, ed. M. Berenbaum and A. J. Peck (Bloomington: Indiana University Press, 1998), 809.
40 L. Ettinger, "Holocaust Survivors in Past and Present", *The Holocaust and History*, 775.

8 *Reflections and Conclusions*

1 J. Semprun, *Literature or Life* (New York: Penguin Books, 1998), 3–5.
2 J. L. Herman, *Trauma and Recovery* (New York: Basic Books, 1992), 94.
3 Herman, *Trauma and Recovery*, 207.
4 B. Schiff, *Telling Survival and the Holocaust* (University of Chicago, Ph.D. thesis, University Microfilms International, 1997).
5 Schiff, *Telling Survival and the Holocaust*, 95.

6   M. Halbwachs, *On Collective Memory* (Chicago and London: University of Chicago Press, 1992).

7   H. Dasberg, "Adult Child Survivor Syndrome", *Israel Journal of Psychiatry and Related Sciences* 38 (2001): 23.

8   D. Laub and M. Allard, "History, memory and Truth: Defining the Place of the Survivor", in *The Holocaust and History: The Known, Unknown, and Disputed and the Reexamined*, ed. M. Berenbaum and A. J. Peck (Bloomington: Indiana University Press, 1998), 801.

9   Laub and Allard, *The Holocaust and History*, 800–1.

10 For some references on this issue see: G. Steiner, *Language and Silence: Essays on Language, Literature and the Inhuman* (New York: Atheneum, 1977); L. Langer, *"The Divided Voice" Confronting the Holocaust: The Impact of Elie Wiesel*, ed. A. H Rosenfeld and I. Greenberg (Bloomington: Indiana University Press, 1978); *Probing the Limits of Representation, Nazism and the "Final Solution"*, ed. S. Friedlander (Cambridge, Massachusetts: Harvard University Press, 1992); D. Bar On, *The Indescribable and the Undiscussable: Reconstructing Human Discourse after Trauma* (Budapest: CEU Press, 1999).

11 H. Dasberg, "The Unfinished Story of Trauma as a Paradigm for Psychotherapists", *Israel Journal of Psychiatry and Related Sciences* 29, 1 (1992): 48.

12 C. Taylor, *Multiculturalism. Examining the Politics of Recognition* (Princeton, New Jersey: Princeton University Press, 1994), 34.

13 S. Cisneros, quoted in R. Behar, *Translated Woman: Crossing the Border with Esperanza's Story* (Boston: Beacon Press, 1993), 270.

Glossary

Akiba (Aqiba, Akiva) ben Joseph
Famous Jewish rabbi (*c.* 50–135 CE) in ancient Palestine; a major legal scholar, who established an academy in B'nai Brak, and was also a legendary mystic and martyr. He was tortured and killed by the Romans in 135 CE.

Aktion/Aktionen (pl.) (German)
Operation involving the mass assembly, deportation, and murder of Jews by the Nazis during the *Holocaust*.

Aliya (Heb.)
"Going up". A term used in Judaism especially for immigration to the land of Israel. Aliya can also be used for "going up" to the altar (*bima*) to read from Torah.

Aliya Bet
"Illegal immigration" (Heb.). Jewish immigration into Palestine (later, Israel) without the official immigration certificate nor with British approval. This happened most often by ship. During the Third Reich, Zionist movements set up organizations to plan and implement these flights from Europe.

Aliyat Hanoar
"Youth *Aliyah*" (Heb.). Organization founded in 1932 by Henrietta Szold to rescue Jewish children and young people and give them care and education in Palestine and in the state of Israel.

AMCHA
National Israeli Center for Psychosocial Support of Survivors of the Holocaust and the Second Generation.

Am Yisrael
"Children of Israel" (Heb.).

Glossary

Aserah be'tevet
A minor fast day in Judaism which commemorates the beginning of the Babylonian siege of Jerusalem.

Bar/Bat Mitzvah
"Son (daughter)-of-the-commandment(s)" (Heb.). The phrase originally referred to a person responsible for performing the divine commandments of Judaism; it now refers to the occasion when a boy or girl reaches the age of religious majority and responsibility (thirteen years for a boy; twelve years and a day for a girl).

B'richa
The organized and illegal mass movement of Jews throughout Europe following World War II.

DP camps (Displaced Persons camps)
After World War II, several hundred thousand Jewish survivors remained in camps for displaced persons. The Allies established such camps in Allied-occupied Germany, Austria, and Italy for refugees waiting to leave Europe.

Einsatzgruppen
Mobile units of the Security Police and SS Security Service that followed the German armies to Poland in 1939 and to the Soviet Union in June 1941. Their charge was to kill all Jews as well as communist functionaries, the handicapped, institutionalized psychiatric patients, Gypsies, and others considered undesirable by the Nazi state. They were supported by units of the uniformed German Order Police and often used auxiliaries (Ukrainian, Latvian, Lithuanian, and Estonian volunteers). The victims were executed by mass shootings and buried in unmarked mass graves; later, the bodies were dug up and burned to cover evidence of what had occurred.

Eretz Yisrael/Israel
"Land of Israel" (Heb.). In Jewish thought, the special term for the area believed to have been promised to the Jewish people by God in the Tanach.

Gadna
Preparatory Israeli Army training for students in secondary schools.

Galut
"Exile" (Heb.). The term refers to the various expulsions of Jews from the ancestral homeland. Over time, it came to express the broader notion of Jewish homelessness and the state of being aliens. Thus, colloquially, "to be in galut" means to live in the diaspora and also to be in a state of physical and even spiritual alienation.

Galutiyut
"The exilic condition." In the traditional Zionist narrative this idea is not a polit-

ical concept but a description of a mental state manifesting itself mainly in the lack of self-respect *vis-à-vis* the gentile.

Gemara
"Completion" (Heb.). Popularly applied to the Jewish Talmud as a whole.

Gestapo
"Geheime Staatspolizei" "The Nazi Secret State Police" (German). The name was created from the first letter of the German name *Geheime Staats Polizei*. Established in Prussia in 1933, its power spread throughout Germany after 1936. The *Gestapo*'s chief purpose was the persecution of Jews and dissident political parties. Under Himmler's direction, the *Gestapo* was a prime force in the murder of the six million Jews.

Ha'apalah
Aliya Bet. Iillegal immigration to Israel in ships attempting to break through the British blockade around Palestine before and after World War II.

Hadracha
"Training" (Heb.).

Haganah
"Defense" (Heb.). Clandestine Jewish organization for armed self-defense in Palestine under the British Mandate, that eventually became the nucleus of the Israel Defense Forces.

Halaka(h) / Halakha / Halacha
Any normative Jewish law, custom, practice, or rite – or the entire complex. Halaka is law established or custom ratified by authoritative rabbinic jurists and teachers. Colloquially, if something is deemed *halakhic*, it is considered proper and normative behavior.

Haredim
Ultra-Orthodox Jews in Israel.

Intifada
"Shaking off" (Arabic). Palestinian civil uprising in Gaza and the West Bank, December 1987–September 1993, to protest Israeli occupation, Sept. 2000–March 2005.

The Jewish Joint Distribution Committee
Since 1914, the American Jewish Joint Distribution Committee, Inc. (JDC) has served as the overseas arm of the American Jewish community. Its mission is to serve the needs of Jews throughout the world, particularly where their lives as Jews are threatened or made more difficult.

Judenrat
Council of Jewish representatives set up in communities and ghettos under the Nazis to execute their instructions.

Kaddish
A classical Jewish prayer (mostly in Aramaic) with eschatological focus extolling God's majesty and kingdom recited at the conclusion of each major section of each liturgical service; a long version (called rabbinic kaddish) follows an act of study; also a prayer by mourners during the first year of bereavement and on the anniversary of the death of next-of-kin.

Katzetnik
"Camp inmate".

Kehilla(h)
"Community" (Heb.). Jewish sense of community, in a particular sense, within the larger people of Israel.

Kibbutz (pl. *kibbutzim*)
Communal settlement in modern Israel. Originally, kibbutzim focused, on agriculture, but many of them they are now are engaged in a variety of activities including tourism, high-tech ventures, and other industries.

Kiddush Hashem
Sanctification of the divine name; martyr.

Kinderaktion
Operation involving the mass assembly, deportation, and murder of Jewish children by the Nazis during the Holocaust.

Kinderheim
Special for homes for children. In neutral countries these homes sheltered children who were refugees and had fled Nazi occupation. They also continued to exist after the war, aiding in rehabilitation work for child survivors.

Lochomei HaGetaot
"Resistance Fighters" (Heb.). Holocaust and Jewish resistance Heritage Museum, Israel.

Magen David
"Shield of David" (Heb.). The distinctive six-pointed Jewish star, used especially since the 17th century.

Mapai
A labor party in founded in Palestine in 1930.

Matzevah
"Tombstone" and memorial stone (Heb.).

Mikvah, Miqvah, Mikveh, Mikva, Mikve
A Jewish communal bath for washing away spiritual impurity by immersion. Converts must immerse in the mikva at the end of the conversion ceremony and women use the mikvah every month the week after their period ends as part of the laws of family purity.

Mishnah
"Teaching" (Heb.). The digest of the recommended Jewish oral law as it existed at the end of the 2nd century and was collated, edited and revised by Rabbi Judah the Prince. The code is divided into six major units and sixty-three minor ones. The work is the authoritative legal tradition of the early sages and is the basis of the legal discussions of the Talmud.

Mitzvah
"Commandment, obligation" (Heb.). A ritual or ethical duty or act of obedience to God's will.

Mossad
"Organization" or institution (Heb.).

Muselmann
German term meaning "Muslim," widely used by concentration camp prisoners to refer to inmates who were on the verge of death from starvation, exhaustion, and despair. A person who had reached the Muselmann stage had little, if any, chance for survival and usually died within weeks. The origin of the term is unclear.

Oeuvre de Secours aux enfants
(Children's Aid Society), worldwide Jewish organization for children's welfare and healthcare. During World War II it established a rescue network for children in Nazi occupied France.

Oleh / Olim (pl.)
Immigrant to Israel.

Olim chadashim
New Immigrants.

Oral Law
In traditional Jewish pharisaic/rabbinic thought, God reveals instructions for living through both the written scriptures and through a parallel process of orally transmitted traditions.

Passover
(*Pesach*). The major Jewish spring holiday (with agricultural aspects) also known as the festival of unleavened bread) commemorating the Exodus or deliverance of the Hebrew people from Egypt. The festival lasts eight days, during which Jews refrain from eating all leavened foods and products. A special ritual meal called the Seder is prepared, and a traditional narrative called the *Haggadah* is recited.

Rabbi
"My master" (Heb.). An authorized teacher of the classical Jewish tradition (*see* **oral law**) after the fall of the second Temple in 70 CE. The role of the rabbi has changed considerably throughout the centuries. Traditionally, rabbis serve as the legal and spiritual guides of their congregations and communities. The title is conferred after considerable study of traditional Jewish sources. This conferral and its responsibilities is central to the chain of tradition in Judaism.

Saba
"Grandfather" (Heb.).

Sabon
"Soap" (Heb.). A mocking name given to Holocaust survivors referring to the myth that the Nazis used the bodies of murdered Jews to make soap.

Sabra(s)
"Native-born Israeli(s)" (Heb.). The word comes from the name of a cactus plant that is prickly on the outside and soft and tasty on the inside. The Israeli character is often said to resemble this fruit.

Selection (*Selektionen*)
Euphemism for the process of choosing victims for the gas chambers in the Nazi camps by separating those considered fit to work and those not.

Shaliach
Emissary, appointed agent (male pl. *sh'lichim, sh'lichei*; fem. sing. *sh'lichah*; fem. pl. *sh'lichot*).

Shmock
"Idiot" (Yid.).

Simcha
"Joy" or a refers to a joyous occasion.

Shiva
"Seven" (Heb.). Seven days of mourning after the burial of a close relative (as in, "to sit shiva").

Shloshim
"Thirty"(Heb.). An intermediate stage of 30 days of less severe mourning, including shiva.

Shoah /shoa
"catastrophe" (Heb.). Denoting the catastrophic destruction of European Jewry during World War II. The term is used in Israel.

Shoah u'Tekumah
This phrase can be translated as "Holocaust and Redemption" (Heb.). This concept became a central part of the legacy of Israeli society, the core of a commemorative view that evolved and was shaped by the experience of a nation active in absorbing and rehabilitating survivors of the Holocaust and in the foundation of the state.

Talmud
"Study" or "learning" (Heb.). Rabbinic Judaism produced two Talmuds: the one known as the "Babylonian" is the most famous in the western world, and was completed around the fifth century CE; the other, known as the "Palestinian" or "Jerusalem" Talmud, was edited perhaps in the early fourth century CE.

Torah
"Teaching, instruction" (Heb.). In general, torah refers to study of the whole gamut of Jewish tradition or to some aspect thereof. In its special sense, "the Torah" refers to the "five books of Moses" in the Hebrew scriptures.

Torah /tora
A scroll containing the five books of Moses.

Ulpan
Class or school for intensive study of Hebrew language.

United Nations Relief and Rehabilitation Administration (UNRRA)
Refugee relief agency formed by the Allies in 1943, mainly with American funds. After World War II, under the direction of the American politician Fiorello La Guardia, it aided displaced persons.

Wehrmacht
German armed forces.

Yad Vashem
Israeli authority and museum for commemorating the Holocaust in the Nazi era and Jewish resistance and heroism at that time.

Yahrzeit
"Year-time"(Yiddish). Anniversary of a death; a 24-hour candle lit to commem-

orate the death anniversary of a close relative, also lit on holy days when *Yizkor* (prayer of remembrance) is recited.

Yeshiva(h) (pl. *yeshivot*)
A Jewish rabbinic academy of higher learning.

Yishuv
The Jewish community of Palestine.

Yom Hashoah ve Hagevurah
Holocaust and Heroism Remembrance Day

Yom Kippur
The Day of Atonement.

Note:
Many of the entries in this Glossary are taken from The Jewish Virtual Library <http://www.jewishvirtuallibrary.org/index.html>.

Bibliography

Ainslie, R. C., *The Psychology of Twinship*, Lincoln and London: University of Nebraska Press, 1985.

Amery, J., *At the Mind's Limits: Contemplations by a Survivor of Auschwitz and its Realities*, Bloomington: Indiana University Press, 1980.

Apfel, R. J. and Simon, S., eds., *Minefields in Their Hearts: The Mental Health of Children in War and Communal Violence*, New Haven and London: Yale University Press, 1996.

Appelfeld, A., *Searing Light*, Tel Aviv: Kibbutz HaMeuchad, 1980. (Hebrew)

——, *Life Story*, Jerusalem: Keter, 1999. (Hebrew)

Arad, Y, Gutman, Y. and Margaliot, A., eds., *Documents of the Holocaust: Selected Sources on the Destruction of the Jews of Germany and Austria and the Soviet Union*. Jerusalem: Yad Vashem, 1981.

Aronoff, M. J., "Myths, Symbols, and Rituals of the Emerging State," in *New Perspectives on Israeli History. The Early Years of the State*, New York: New York University Press, 1991.

Bal Kadouri, K. Y., "Evidence of Witnesses, its Value and Limitations," *Yad Vashem Studies*, vol. 3 (1959): 79–90.

Ballinger, P., "The Culture of Survivors: Post Traumatic Stress Disorder and Traumatic Memory," *History and Memory*, vol. 10 (1998): 99–132.

Bar-Gil, S., Ph.D. dissertation: *Youth Aliya: Policy and Activity in the Absorption and Rehabilitation of Holocaust Survivors 1945–1953*, Hebrew University of Jerusalem, 1995. (Hebrew)

——, *Aliyat Hanoar: Policies and Activities in the rehabilitation and absorption of She'erit Hapleitah, 1945–1955*, The Hebrew University of Jerusalem, Ph.D. thesis, 1995. (Hebrew)

——, The educational absorption and rehabilitation of the children and youth of She'erit Hapletah: The Activities of Youth Aliya and the settlement movement in Europe 1945–1949, *Yalkut Moreshet* (1997) 7–27. (Hebrew)

——, "From Survivors to Pioneers", *Mifneh* (1997) 47–53. (Hebrew)

——, *Searching for a Home, Finding a Homeland. Youth Aliya: Education and Rehabilitation of She'erit Hapleitah*, Jerusalem: Yitzhak Ben Zvi, 1999. (Hebrew)

Bar-On, D. and Gilad, N., "To Rebuild Life: A Narrative Analysis of Three

Generations of an Israeli Holocaust Survivor's Family," in R. Josselson, and A. Lieblich, eds., *The Narrative Study of Lives* vol. 2, California: Thousand Oaks, Sage Publications, 1994 : 83–111.

Bar-On, D., *Fear and Hope: Three Generations of the Holocaust*, Cambridge, Mass.: Harvard University Press, 1995.

——, *The Indescribable and the Undiscussable: Reconstructing Human Discourse after Trauma*, Budapest: Central European University Press, 1999.

Barthel, D., "Getting in Touch with History: The Role of Historic Preservation in Shaping Collective Memories," *Qualitative Sociology*, vol. 19 (1996): 345–63.

Bastide, R., *The African Religions of Brazil. Towards a Sociology of the Interpenetration of Civilizations*, translated by Helen Sebba, Baltimore: Johns Hopkins University Press, 1978.

Bauer, Y., *The Jewish Emergence from Powerlessness*, Toronto: University of Toronto Press, 1979.

——, *A History of the Holocaust*, Danbury: Franklin Watts, 1982.

——, *Rethinking the Holocaust*, New Haven: Yale University Press, 2001.

Baumel, J. T., "In Everlasting Memory: Individual and Communal Holocaust Commemoration in Israel," *Israel Affairs*, vol. 1 (1995): 146–70.

——, *Kibbutz Buchenwald: Survivors and Pioneers*, New Jersey: Rutgers University Press, 1997.

Behar, R., *Translated Woman: Crossing the Border with Esperanza's Story*, Boston: Beacon Press, 1993.

Berenbaum, M., ed., *The Holocaust and History: The Known, the Unknown, the Disputed, and the Re-examined*, Bloomington: Indiana University Press, 1998.

Bergmann, M. S. and Jucovy, J. E., eds., *Generations of the Holocaust*, New York: Basic Books, 1982.

Brenner, I., "Multi-sensory Bridges in Response to Object Loss During the Holocaust," *Psychoanalytic Review*, vol. 75 (1988): 573–587.

Bruner, J., "Paradigmatic Modes of Thought." in E. Eisner, ed., *Learning and Teaching the Ways of Knowing. 84th Yearbook of The National Society for the Study of Education*, Chicago: University of Chicago Press, 1985: 97–115.

——, *Acts of Meaning* (Cambridge, Massachusetts: Harvard University Press, 1990.)

Burbury, W. M., "Effects of evacuation and of air raids on city children." *British Medical Journal*, vol. 2 (1941): 660–2.

Cahn, T., "The Diary of an Adolescent Girl in the Ghetto: A Study of Age-Specific Reactions to the Holocaust," *Psychoanalytic Review*, vol. 75 (1988): 589–617.

Caruth, C., ed., *Trauma: Explorations in Memory*, Baltimore: Johns Hopkins University Press, 1995.

——, *Unclaimed Experience: Trauma, Narrative and History*, Baltimore: Johns Hopkins University Press, 1996.

Catherall, D. R., "Differentiating Intervention Strategies for Primary and Secondary Trauma in Post-Traumatic Stress Disorder: The Example of Vietnam Veterans," *The Journal of Traumatic Stress*, vol. 2 (1989): 298–305.

Cels, J and Lansen, J. P., "Psych-Educative Groups Therapy for Jewish Child Survivors of the Holocaust and non-Jewish Child-Survivors of Japanese

Concentration Camps," *Israel Journal of Psychiatry and Related Sciences*, vol. 29 (1992): 22–32.

Chase, S. E., "Personal Vulnerability and Interpretative Authority in Narrative Research," in R. Josselson and A. Lieblich, eds., *The Narrative Study of Lives*, vol. 5, California: Thousand Oaks, Sage Publications, 1995: 45–57.

Clendinnen, I., *Reading the Holocaust*, Melbourne: Text Publishing, 1998.

Cohen, G. C., *Shtetl Finder Gazatteer*, Los Angeles: Periday, 1980.

Cohen, M. and Brom, D., "Child Survivors of the Holocaust: Symptoms and Coping after Fifty years," *Israel Journal of Psychiatry and Related Sciences*, vol. 38 (2001): 3–12.

Crapanzano, V., "Life Histories," *American Anthropologist*, vol. 86 (1984): 953–9.

Danieli, Y., "The Aging Survivor of the Holocaust: Discussion on the Achievement of Integration in Aging Survivors of the Nazi Holocaust," *Journal of Geriatric Psychiatry*, vol. 14 (1981): 191–210.

——, "Families of Survivors of the Nazi Holocaust: Some short- and long- term effects," *Stress and Anxiety*, vol. 8 (1982): 405–21.

——, "The Use of Mutual Support Approaches in the Treatment of Victims," *Grief and Bereavement in Contemporary Society III* (1988): 116–23.

Dasberg, H., "Psychological Distress of Holocaust Survivors and Offspring in Israel, Forty Years Later: A Review," *Israel Journal of Psychiatry and Related Sciences*, vol. 24 (1987): 243–256.

——, "The Unfinished Story of Trauma as a Paradigm for Psychotherapists," *Israel Journal of Psychiatry and Related Sciences*, vol. 29 (1992): 44–60.

——, "Child Survivors of the Holocaust Reach Middle Age: Psychotherapy of late grief reaction," *Journal of Social Work and Policy in Israel* 5–6 (1992): 71–83.

——, "Myths and taboos among Israeli-first and second-generation psychiatrists in regard to the Holocaust," *Echoes of the Holocaust*, vol. 6 (2000): 25–36.

——, "Adult child survivor syndrome on deprived childhoods of aging Holocaust survivors," *Israel Journal of Psychiatry and Related Sciences*, vol. 38 (2001): 13–26.

Dasberg, H., Bartura, J. and Amit, Y., "Narrative group therapy with Aging Child Survivors of the Holocaust," *Israel Journal for Psychiatry and Related Sciences*, vol. 38 (2001): 27–35.

Davidson, S., *Holding onto Humanity – The Message of Holocaust Survivors: The Shamai Davidson Papers*, ed., L. W. Charny, New York: New York University Press, 1992.

DeKoven Ezrachi, S., "See Under Memory: *Reflections on When memory Comes*," *History and Memory*, vol. 9 (1997): 364–74.

Dinur, B., "Problems Confronting 'Yad Washem' in its Work of Research," *Yad Vashem Studies*, vol. 1 (1957): 7–30.

——, "The Role of Interviewing in the Research of the Holocaust Period," *Yad Vashem Studies*, vol. 3 (1959): 77–90.

Don Yehia, E. and Liebman, C. S., *Civil Religion in Israel*, Berkley: University of California Press, 1982.

Don Yehia, E., "Memory and Political Culture: Israeli Society and the Holocaust," *Studies in Contemporary Jewry* 9 (1993): 159–61.

Dvorjetski, M., "Adjustments of Detainees to Camp and Ghetto Life and their

Subsequent Adjustment to Normal Society," *Yad Vashem Studies*, no. 5 (1963): 193–220.

Dwork, D., *Children with a Star: Jewish Youth in Nazi Europe*, New Haven and London: Yale University Press, 1991.

Dwork, D., "Recovering the Past: A Beginning," *Dimensions*, vol. 6 (1991): 18–23.

Eilati, S., *Crossing the River*, Jerusalem: Yad Vashem, 1999. (Hebrew)

Erikson, E., *Life History and the Historical Moment*, New York: W.W Norton and Company, 1975.

——, "Identity and the Life Cycle," *Psychological Issues* 1, New York: International University Press. 1959.

——, *Identity: Youth and Crisis*, New York: W.W Norton, 1968.

Felman, S. and Laub, D., *Testimony: Crises of Witnessing in Literature, Psychoanalysis, and History*, New York: Routledge, 1992.

Fogelman, E., "Group Belonging and Mourning as Factors in Resilience in Second Generation Holocaust Survivors," *Psychoanalytic Review*, vol. 85 (1988): 537–85.

Fogelman, E. and Bass-Wichelhaus, H., "The Role of Group Experiences in the Healing Process of Massive Childhood Holocaust Trauma," *Journal of Applied Psychoanalytic Studies*, vol. 4 (2002): 31–47.

Foxman, A. H., "A Broken Silence," *Dimensions*, vol. 6 (1991): 11–13.

Freud, S., "Childhood Memories and Screen Memories," *The Complete Psychological Works of Sigmund Freud*, London: Hogarth Press, 1901: 43–52.

Freud, A. and Burlingham, D. T., *War and Children*, Connecticut: Greenwood Press Publishers, 1943.

Freud, A. and Dann, S., "An experiment in group upbringing," *The Psychoanalytic Study of the Child* 3/4, Oxford, England: International University Press (1949): 127–68.

Friedlander, S., *When Memory Comes*, New York: Farrar Straus Giroux, 1979.

——, "Trauma, Transference and 'Working Through' in Writing the History of the *Shoah*," *History and Memory*, vol. 4 (1992): 39–55.

Friedman, M., "The Haredim and the Holocaust," *The Jerusalem Quarterly*, vol. 53 (1990): 86–114.

Funkenstein, A., "Collective Memory and Historical Consciousness," *History and Memory*, vol. 1 (1989): 5–26.

Furst, S. S., "The Stimulus barrier and the pathogenicity of trauma," *International Journal of Psychoanalysis*, vol. 59. (1978): 345–52.

Gampel, Y., "Facing War, Murder, Torture, and Death in Latency," *Psychoanalytic Review*, vol. 75 (1988): 499–509.

Gergen, K. J. and Gergen, M., "Narrative and the Self as Relationship," *Advances in Experimental Social Psychology*, vol. 21 (1988): 17–53.

Gilbert, M., *The Boys: Triumph over Adversity*, London: Weidenfeld and Nicholson, 1996.

Glaser, B. and Strauss, A., *The Discovery of Grounded Theory*, Chicago: Aldine, 1967.

Gottesman, M. and Wolins, M., eds., *Youth Care: An Israeli Approach, the Educational Path of Youth Aliya*, New York and London: Gordon and Breach, 1971.

Gottesman, M, ed., *Cultural Transition: The Case of Immigrant Youth*, Jerusalem: Magnes Press, 1988.

Greenspan, H., "An Immediate and Violent Impulse: Holocaust Survivor Testimony in the First Years After Liberation," in J. K. Roth and E. Maxwell, eds., *Remembering for The Future: The Holocaust in an Age of Genocide. Volume 3: Memory*, Hampshire: Palgrave, 2001.

——, *On Listening to Holocaust Survivors: Recounting and Life History*, Westport: Praeger Publishers, 1998.

——, *Who can Retell? On the Recounting of Life History by Holocaust Survivors*, Brandeis University, Ph.D. thesis. University Microfilms International, 1986.

Gutman, Y. and Saf, A., eds., *She'erit HaPletah 1944–1948 Rehabilitation and Political Struggle Proceedings of the Sixth Yad Vashem International Conference*, Jerusalem: Yad Vashem, 1990.

——, eds., *Major Changes within the Jewish People in the Wake of the Holocaust*, Jerusalem: Yad Vashem, 1996.

Haaken, J., *Pillar of Salt: Gender, Memory, and the Perils of Looking Back*. New Jersey, New Brunswick: Rutgers University Press, 1998.

Halbwachs, M., *On Collective Memory*, Chicago and London: The University of Chicago Press, 1992.

Hartman, G. H., ed., *Holocaust Remembrance: The Shapes of Memory*, Cambridge: Blackwell Publishers, 1994.

Hass, A., *The Aftermath: Living with the Holocaust*, Cambridge: Cambridge University Press, 1995.

Hassan, J., "The Missing Years: Experiences of Children Who Went Through the Holocaust", *The Journal of Holocaust Education*, vol. 4 (1995): 111–30.

Hausner, G., *Justice in Jerusalem*, New York: Schocken Books, 1966.

Hayes, P., ed., *Lessons and Legacies: the Meaning of the Holocaust in a Changing World*, Evanston, Illinois: Northwestern University Press, 1991.

Hefetz, J., *Too Young to Remember*, Detroit: Wayne State University Press, 1989.

Helmreich, W. B., *Against All Odds: Holocaust Survivors and Their Successful Lives they made in America*, New York: Simon and Schuster, 1992.

Hemmendinger, J., *Survivors: Children of the Holocaust*, New York: National Press, 1986.

——, "The Children of Buchenwald: After Liberation and Now," *Echoes of the Holocaust*, vol. 3 (1994): 40–51.

Herman, J. L., *Trauma and Recovery*, New York: Basic Books, 1992.

Hilberg, R., *Perpetrators, Victims and Bystanders: the Jewish Catastrophe 1933–1945*, New York: Harper Perennial, 1992.

Hoffman, E., *Lost in Translation: Life in a New Language*, London: Minerva, 1989.

Hogman, F., "Displaced Jewish Children During World War II: How They Coped," *Journal of Humanistic Psychology*, vol. 23 (1983): 51–66.

Hogman, F., "Role of Memories in Lives of World War II Orphans," *Journal of American Academy of Child Psychiatry*, vol. 24 (1985): 390–6.

——, "The Experience of Catholicism for Jewish Children during World War II," *Psychoanalytic Review*, vol. 75 (1988): 511–32.

——, "Trauma and Identity through Two Generations of the Holocaust," *Psychoanalytic Review*, vol. 85 (1988): 551–78.

271

Bibliography

Janoff-Bulman. R., *Shattered Assumptions: Toward a New Psychology of Trauma*, New York: The Free Press, 1992.

Horowitz, D., "After Demjanjuk: Is the Hunt for Nazis Over?" *The Jerusalem Report* IV, no. 7. (1993): 30.

Josselson, R., "Imagining the Real: Empathy, Narrative, and the Dialogic Self," in Josselson, R. and Lieblich, A., eds., *The Narrative Study of Lives*, vol. 3, California: Thousand Oaks, Sage Publications (1995): 27–44.

——, eds., "On Writing Other People's Lives," in *The Narrative Study of Lives*, vol. 3, California: Thousand Oaks, Sage Publications (1995): 60–71.

Josselson, R., *Revising Herself: The Story of Women's Identity from College to Midlife*, New York: Oxford University Press, 1996.

Kaplan, M., *Between Dignity and Despair: Jewish Life in Nazi Germany*, Oxford: Oxford University Press, 1998.

Kav Venaki, S., Nadler, A., Gershoni, H., "Sharing the Holocaust Experience: Communication Behaviors and their Consequences in Families of Ex-Partisans and Ex-Prisoners of Concentration Camps," *Family Process*, vol. 24 (1985): 273–80.

Keilson, H., *Sequential Traumatization in Children. A Clinical and Statistical follow-up study of the fate of the Jewish War Orphans in the Netherlands*, Jerusalem: The Magnes Press. 1979.

Kendall, L., *The Life and Hard Times of a Korean Shaman: Of Tales and the Telling of Tales*, Honolulu: University of Hawaii Press, 1998.

Kestenberg, J. S. and Gampel, Y., "Growing up in the Holocaust Culture," *Israel Journal of Psychiatry and Related Sciences*, vol. 20 (1983): 129–46.

——, "Child Survivors of the Holocaust – 40 years Later: Reflections and Commentary," *Journal of the American Academy of Child Psychiatry*, vol. 24 (1985): 27–50.

Kestenberg, L. S. and Brenner, I., "Children Who Survived the Holocaust: The Role of Rules and Routines in the Development of the Superego," *International Journal of Psychoanalysis*, vol. 67 (1986): 309–16.

Kestenberg, J. S., "Imagining and Remembering," *Israel Journal of Psychiatry and Related Sciences*, vol. 24 (1987): 229–41.

——, "Memories from early Childhood," *Psychoanalytic Review*, vol. 75 (1988): 561–71.

Kestenberg, M. and Kestenberg, J. S., "The Sense of Belonging and Altruism in Children who Survived the Holocaust," *Psychoanalytic Review*, vol. 75 (1988): 533–60.

Kestenberg, J. S., "Children of Survivors and Child Survivors," *Echoes of the Holocaust*, vol. 1 (1992): 27–50.

—— and Fogelman, E, eds., *Children During the Nazi Reign: Psychological Perspectives on the Interview Process*, Westport: Praeger Publishers, 1994.

——, "The Response of the Child to the Rescuer," *Echoes of the Holocaust*, vol. 4 (1995): 1–8.

—— and Brenner, I, eds., *The Last Witness: The Child Survivor of the Holocaust*, Washington D.C.: American Psychiatric Association, 1996.

—— and Kahn, C., eds., *Children Surviving Persecution: An International Study of Trauma and Healing*, Westport: Praeger Publishers, 1998.

Bibliography

Keynan, I., And the hunger was not staunched: Holocaust survivors and the emissaries from Eretz Yisrael: Germany 1945–1948, Tel Aviv: Am Oved, 1996. (Hebrew)

Kinsler, F., "A Preliminary Assessment of the Effects of Giving Testimonials, by Video Interview, upon the Mourning Process, for Child and Adult Survivors," *Grief and Bereavement in Contemporary Society* 111 (1988): 131–42.

Kirmayer, L. J, ed., "Landscapes of Memory: Trauma, Narrative and Dissociation," *Tense Past: Cultural Essays in Trauma and Memory*, London: Routledge, 1996.

Klein, H., Holocaust Survivors in Kibbutzim: "Readaptation and Reintegration," *The Israel Annals of Psychiatry and Related Disciplines*, vol. 10 (1972): 78–91.

Kogos, F., *A Dictionary of Yiddish Slang and Idioms*, New York: The Citadel Press. 1966.

Kol, M., *Youth Aliya: Past, Present and Future*, Jerusalem: Jerusalem Post Press, 1957.

Krell, R., "Therapeutic Value of Documenting Child Survivors," *Journal of the American Academy of Child Psychiatry*, vol. 24 (1985): 281–8.

——, "Child Survivors of the Holocaust: 40 Years Later," *Journal of the American Academy of Child Psychiatry*, vol. 24 (1985): 378–80.

——, ed., *Messages and Memories: Reflections on Child Survivors of the Holocaust*, Vancouver: Memory Press. 1999.

Krystal, H., ed., *Massive Psychic Trauma*, New York: International Universities Press, 1968.

——, "Integration and Self-Healing in Post-Traumatic States: A Ten Year Retrospective," *American Imago*, vol. 48 (1991): 93–118.

Kvale, S., *Inter Views: An Introduction to Qualitative Research Interviews*, Thousand Oaks, California: Sage Publications, 1996.

Langer, L., *Versions of Survival: The Holocaust and the Human Spirit*, Albany: State University of New York Press, 1982.

——, *Holocaust Testimonies: The Ruins of Memory*, New Haven: Yale University Press, 1991.

Laub, D. and Auerhahn, N. C., "Knowing and Not Knowing Massive Psychic Trauma: Forms of Traumatic Memory," *International Journal of Psycho-Analysis*, vol. 74 (1993): 283–902.

Lazare, L., *Rescue as Resistance: How Jewish Orginizations Fought the Holocaust in France*, New York: Columbia University Press, 1996.

Levi, P., *The Drowned and the Saved*, London: Abacus, 1998.

——, *Moments of Reprieve: A Memoir of Auschwitz*, New York: Penguin Books, 1995.

Lévi-Strauss, C., *Myth and Meaning*, New York: Schocken Books, 1979.

Lieblich, A., Tuval-Mashiach, R., Zilber, T., *Narrative Research: Reading, Analysis and Interpretation*, vol. 47. *Applied Social Research Methods Series*, London: Sage Publications, 1998.

Linde, C., *Life Stories: The Creation of Coherence*, New York: Oxford University Press, 1993.

Loeb, L. D., "Time, Myth and History in Judaism," *Conservative Judaism*, vol. 42 (1990): 54–66.

Lomranz, J., Shmotkin, D., Zechovoy, A., Rosenberg, E., "Time Orientation in Nazi Concentration Camp Survivors: Forty Years After," *American Journal of Orthopsychiatry*, vol. 55 (1985): 230–236.

Lomsky-Feder, E., "Social Construction of Personal Memory" (Ph.D. summary, Hebrew University of Jerusalem, 1994.)

Marcus, P., Rosenberg, A, eds., *Healing Their Wounds: Psychotherapy with Holocaust Survivors and their Families*, New York: Praeger Publishers, 1989.

Marks, J., ed., *The Hidden Children: The Secret Survivors of the Holocaust*, London: Piatkus, 1993.

Marrus, M., *The Holocaust in History*, London: Penguin Books, 1989.

Mazor, A., Gampel, Y., Enright, E. D. and Orenstein, R., "Holocaust Survivors: Coping with Post-Traumatic memories in childhood and forty years later," *Journal of Traumatic Stress*, vol. 3 (1990): 1–14.

May, R., *Cry for Myth*, New York: W.W. Norton & Company. 1991.

——, "Values, Myths and Symbols," *American Journal of Psychiatry*, vol. 132 (1975): 703–6.

Mendelsohn, Y., "Failure in Fulfilment: Psychotherapy with the Traumatized Child and Adult child Survivors," *Intervision: Child Survivors: Forms of Intervention: Amcha* 1 (1996.)

Mishne, J., "Memories of Hidden Children: Analysis of two Case Studies of Resilience," *Journal of Social Work Policy in Israel*, 9–10 (1997): 100–28.

Moskowitz, S. and Krell, R., "Child Survivors of the Holocaust: Psychological Adaptations to Survival," *Israel Journal of Psychiatry and Related Sciences*, vol. 27 (1990): 81–91.

Moskovitz, S., "Longitudinal Follow-up of Child Survivors of the Holocaust," *Journal of the American Academy of Child Psychiatry*, vol. 24 (1985): 401–7.

——, *Love Despite Hate: Child Survivors of the Holocaust and their Adult Lives*, New York: Schocken Books, 1983.

Rosenwald, G. C. and Ochberg, R. L, eds., *Storied Lives: The Cultural Politics of Self-Understanding*, New York: Yale University Press, 1992.

Ofer, D., "The Dilemma of Rescue and Redemption, Mass Immigration to Israel in the First Year of Statehood," *Yivo Annual* 20 (1990): 185–210.

——, "Linguistic Conceptualization of the Holocaust in Palestine and in Israel 1942–1953," *Journal of Contemporary History*, vol. 31 (1996): 567–95.

——, "Survivors as Immigrants: The Case of Israel and the Cyprus Detainees," *Modern Judaism*, vol. 16 (1996): 1–23.

——, "Israel and the Holocaust: The Shaping of Remembrance in the First Decade," *Legacy*, vol. 1 (1997): 4–8.

—— and Weitzman, L. J, eds., *Women in the Holocaust*, New Haven: Yale University Press, 1998.

——, "The Strength of Remembrance: Commemorating the Holocaust During the First Decade of Israel," *Jewish Social Studies*, vol. 6 (2000): 24–55.

Ortner, S. B., "On Key Symbols," *American Anthropologist*, vol. 75 (1973): 1338–46.

Bibliography

Pacy, J. S. and Wertheimer, A. P., eds., *Perspectives on the Holocaust: Essays in Honor of Raul Hilberg*, Colorado: Westview Press, 1995.

Pinchus, P., *Come From The Four Winds: The Story of Youth Aliya*, New York: Herzl Press, 1970.

Plank, K., "The Survivor's Return: Reflections on Memory and Place," *Judaism*, vol. 58 (1989): 263–77.

Rafman, S., "Children's Representations of Parental Loss due to War," *International Journal of Behavioural Development*, vol. 20 (1997): 163–77.

Rappaport, J., Bar-Sever, M and Robinson, S., "Orphaned child survivors compared to child survivors whose parents also survived the Holocaust," *Echoes of the Holocaust*, vol. 5 (1997): 55–61.

Ricoeur, P., "Narrative Time," *Critical Inquiry*, vol. 7 (1980): 169–90.

Rimmon-Keinan, S., *Discourse in Psychoanalysis and Literature*, London: Methuen, 1987.

Robinson, S., Rapaport, J., Bar-Sever, M., "The Present State of People who Survived the Holocaust as Children," *ACTA Psychiatrica Scandanavia* 89 (1994): 242–5.

Robinson, S., Adler, S., Metzer, I., "A Comparison between Elderly Holocaust Survivors and People who survived the Holocaust as Children," *Echoes of the Holocaust*, vol. 4 (1995): 22–9.

Ronai, R. C., "Multiple Reflections of Child Sex Abuse: An Argument for a Layered Account," *Journal of Contemporary Ethnography*, vol. 23. (1995): 395–426.

Rosen, A., ed., *Celebrating Elie Wiesel: Stories, Essays and Reflections*, Indiana: University of Notre Dame Press, 1998.

Rosenthal, G., "Reconstruction of Life Stories: Principles of Selection in Generating Stories for Narrative Biographical Interviews," in R. Josselson and A. Lieblich, eds., *The Narrative Study of Lives*, vol. 1, California: Thousand Oaks, Sage Publications, 1993.

Ross, B. M., *Remembering the Personal Past: Description of Autobiographical Memory*, New York: Oxford University Press, 1991.

Rotenberg, L., "A Child Survivor/Psychiatrist's Personal Adaptation," *Journal of the American Academy of Child Psychiatry*, vol. 24 (1985): 385–9.

Roth, J. K. and Maxwell, E., eds., *Remembering for The Future: The Holocaust in an Age of Genocide. Volume 3: Memory*, Hampshire: Palgrave, 2001.

Sacks, O., The Man Who Mistook his Wife for a Hat, London: Picador, 1985.

Samuel, R. and Thompson, P., *The Myths we Live By*, New York: Routledge, 1990.

Sarbin, T. R., ed., *Narrative Psychology: The Storied Nature of Human Conduct*, New York: Praeger Special Studies, 1986.

Schacter, D. L., *Searching for Memory: The Brain, The Mind, and The Past*, Basic Books, New York, 1996.

Schiff, B., *Telling Survival and the Holocaust*, University of Chicago, Ph.D. thesis. University Microfilms International, 1997.

Schwarz, B., "The Social Context of Commemoration: A Study in Collective Memory," *Social Forces* 61 (1982): 374–402.

Segev, T., *The Seventh Million: The Israelis and the Holocaust*, United States: Harper Collins, 1993.

Bibliography

Semprun, J., *Literature or Life*, New York: Penguin Books, 1998.

Shapira, A., "The Yishuv and the Survivors of the Holocaust," *Studies in Zionism*, vol. 7 (1986): 227–301.

——, "The Holocaust: Private Memories, Public Memory," *Jewish Social Studies*, vol. 4 (1998): 40–58.

——, *Land and Power: The Zionist Resort to Force: 1881–1948*, New York: Oxford University Press, 1992.

Sharon, A. and Chanoff, D., *Warrior : The Autobiography of Ariel Sharon*, New York: Simon and Schuster, 1989.

Silberstein, L. J., ed., *New Perspectives on Israeli History: The Early Years of the State*, New York: New York University Press, 1991.

Sivan, E., *Generation 1948: Myth, Profile and Memory*, Marechot: Tel Aviv, 1991. (Hebrew)

Solomon, Z., "Trauma and Society," *Journal of Traumatic Stress*, vol. 8 (1995).

——, "From Denial to Recognition: Attitudes Toward Holocaust Survivors from World War II to the Present," *Journal of Traumatic Stress*, vol. 8 (1995): 215–28.

——, "Oscillating Between Denial and Recognition of PTSD: Why Are Lessons Learned and Forgotten?" *Journal of Traumatic Stress*, vol. 8 (1995): 271–82.

Spender, S., *Learning Laughter*, London: Weidenfeld and Nicholson, 1952.

Suedfeld, P., "Thematic Content Analysis: Nomothetic Methods for Using Holocaust Narratives in Psychological Research," *Holocaust and Genocide Studies*, vol. 10 (1996): 168–80.

Suedfeld, P., ed., *Light from the Ashes: Social Science Careers of Young Holocaust Survivors*, Ann Arbor: The University of Michigan Press: 2001.

Taylor, C., *Multiculturalism. Examining the Politics of Recognition*, Princeton, New Jersey: Princeton University Press, 1994.

Toren, S. I. and Lucas, N., eds., *Israel: The First Decade of Independence*, Albany: State University Press of Albany, 1995.

Turner, C., "Holocaust Memories and History," *History of the Human Sciences*, vol. 9 (1996): 45–63.

Valent, P., *Child Survivors: Adults Living with Childhood Trauma*, Melbourne: William Heinemann, Australia, 1993.

——, "Resilience in Child Survivors of the Holocaust: Toward the Concept of Resilience," *Psychoanalytic Review*, vol. 85 (1998): 517–35.

Van der Hal, E., "And then, one day . . . whom could I tell? Children Surviving the Holocaust During their Latency," *Intervision: Child Survivors: Forms of Intervention: Amcha* 1 (1996).

Vegh, C., *I didn't say goodbye*, London: Caliban Books, 1984.

Vinitzky-Seroussi, V., *After pomp and circumstance: high school reunion as an auto-biographical occasion*, Chicago: University of Chicago Press, 1998.

Wachtel, N., "Remember and Never Forget," *History and Anthropology*, vol. 2 (1986): 307–55.

Wagenaar, W. A. and Groeneweg, J., "The Memory of Concentration Camp Survivors," *Applied Cognitive Psychology*, vol. 4 (1990): 77– 89.

Wangh, M., "On Obstacles to the Working Through of the Nazi Holocaust and on the Consequences of Failing to so," *Israel Journal of Psychiatry and Related Sciences*, vol. 20 (1983): 147–54.

Wardi, D., *Memorial Candles: Children of the Holocaust*, London: Routledge, 1992.

Weil, S., ed., Roots and Routes: Ethnicity and Migration in Global Perspective, Jerusalem: Magnes Press, 1995.

Weitz, Y., "The Political Context: The Political Dimension of Holocaust memory in the 1950s," *Iyunim b'tekumat Yisrael*, vol. 6 (1991): 271–87.

——, *Awareness and Helplessness: Mapai in face of the Shoah 1943–1945*, Jerusalem: Yad Yitzhak Ben Zvi, 1994. (Hebrew)

White, H., "The Value of Narrativity in the Representation of Reality," *Critical Inquiry*, vol. 1 (1980): 5–22.

Winter, J. and Sivan, E., eds., *War and Remembrance in the Twentieth Century*, Cambridge: Cambridge University Press, 1999.

Wistrich, R. and Ohana, D., eds., *The Shaping of Israeli Identity: Myth, Memory and Trauma*, London: Frank Cass, 1995.

Wyman, D. S., *The World Reacts to the Holocaust*, Baltimore: Johns Hopkins University Press, 1996.

Yablonka, H., "New Perspectives: The absorption of Holocaust survivors in Israel", *Iyunim b'tekumat Yisrael*, vol. 7 (1997): 285–299. (Hebrew)

——, "50 years of an encounter between Survivors and Israelis as reflected through Literature, Memory and Historiography", *Yalkut Moreshet* (1998): 83–101. (Hebrew).

——, *Survivors of the Holocaust: Israel After the War*, London: Macmillan Press, 1999.

Yehuda, R., Schneider, J., Siever, L., Brynes, J., Binder, K. and Elkin, A., "Individual Differences in Posttraumatic Stress Disorder Symptom Profiles in Holocaust Survivors in Concentration Camps or in Hiding," *Journal of Traumatic Stress*, vol. 10 (1997): 453–63.

Young, J., *The Texture of Memory: Holocaust Memorials and Meaning*, New York and London: Yale University Press, 1993.

——, "Toward a Received History of the Holocaust," *History and Memory*, vol. 9 (1997): 47–58.

Zertal, I., *From Catastrophe to Power: Holocaust Survivors and the Emergence of the Holocaust*, London: University of California Press, 1998.

Zerubavel, E., "Social Memories: Steps to a Sociology of the Past," *Qualitative Sociology*, vol. 19 (1996): 283–99.

Zerubavel, Y., *Recovered Roots: Collective Memory and the Making of Israeli National Tradition*, Chicago and London: The University of Chicago Press, 1996.

Zuccotti, S., *The Holocaust, The French and The Jews*, New York: Basic Books, 1993.

Newspapers

The Baltimore Jewish Times, 6 June, 2000.

The Baltimore Sun, 22 June, 2000.

The Washington Times, 23 June, 2000.

Index

Index

279

Index

Index

Index

Index

war experience in death camps, 51–2, 139–40, 142–6, 152–3
war experience in the ghetto, 51, 142, 143
war experience in labor camps, 51, 143
Yizkor books, 9
Yom Hashoah ve Hagevurah, 15, 17, 118–20, 129, 182, 218
Yom Kippur War, 13, 150
Youth Aliya movement *see Aliyat HaNoar*

Zionism
  creation of *sabras*, 92–3
  de-mystification of, 13
  exilic situation, 3
  and the Holocaust, 3–4
  influence of, 98
  and sovereign Jewish state, 3
  survivors' migration to Israel, 14
  Yitzchak's narrative, 147, 148, 149
Zionist-Revisionist Organization, 174
Zuccotti, Susan, 69
Zuroff, Efraim, 17